CU00724999

Ada®: Language, compilers and bibliography

Ada: Language, compilers and bibliography

Edited by
M.W. ROGERS
CEC IT Task Force, Brussels

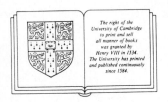

The right of the
University of Cambridge
to print and sell
all manner of books
was granted by
Henry VIII in 1534.
The University has printed
and published continuously
since 1584.

Published on behalf of
the Commission of the European Communities by
CAMBRIDGE UNIVERSITY PRESS
Cambridge
New York   New Rochelle
Melbourne   Sydney

Published by the Press Syndicate of the University of Cambridge
The Pitt Building, Trumpington Street, Cambridge CB2 1RP
32 East 57th Street, New York, NY 10022, USA
10 Stamford Road, Oakleigh, Melbourne 3166, Australia.

First published 1984

Reprinted 1988 by Redwood Burn Limited, Trowbridge, Wiltshire.

Library of Congress catalogue card number: 84-7688

British Library cataloguing in publication data

Ada. —— (Ada companion series)

  1. Ada (Computer program language)
  I. Rogers, M.W.   II. Series
  001.64'24   QA76.73.A15

  ISBN 0 521 26464 2

Document No. EUR 9245 of the
Commission of the European Communities,
Directorate-General Information Market
and Innovation, Luxembourg

LEGAL NOTICE

Contents

PART I

Reference manual for the Ada programming language

ANSI/MIL-STD-1815A-1983

ANSI/MIL-STD-1815A-1983
February 17, 1983

REFERENCE MANUAL FOR THE

Ada®

PROGRAMMING LANGUAGE

ANSI/MIL-STD-1815A-1983

United States Department of Defense

Approved February 17, 1983

American National Standards Institute, Inc.

® Ada is a registered trademark of the U.S. Government, Ada Joint Program Office.

Foreword

Ada is the result of a collective effort to design a common language for programming large scale and real-time systems.

The common high order language program began in 1974. The requirements of the United States Department of Defense were formalized in a series of documents which were extensively reviewed by the Services, industrial organizations, universities, and foreign military departments. The Ada language was designed in accordance with the final (1978) form of these requirements, embodied in the Steelman specification.

The Ada design team was led by Jean D. Ichbiah and has included Bernd Krieg-Brueckner, Brian A. Wichmann, Henry F. Ledgard, Jean-Claude Heliard, Jean-Loup Gailly, Jean-Raymond Abrial, John G.P. Barnes, Mike Woodger, Olivier Roubine, Paul N. Hilfinger, and Robert Firth.

At various stages of the project, several people closely associated with the design team made major contributions. They include J.B. Goodenough, R.F. Brender, M.W. Davis, G. Ferran, K. Lester, L. MacLaren, E. Morel, I.R. Nassi, I.C. Pyle, S.A. Schuman, and S.C. Vestal.

Two parallel efforts that were started in the second phase of this design had a deep influence on the language. One was the development of a formal definition using denotational semantics, with the participation of V. Donzeau-Gouge, G. Kahn, and B. Lang. The other was the design of a test translator with the participation of K. Ripken, P. Boullier, P. Cadiou, J. Holden, J.F. Hueras, R.G. Lange, and D.T. Cornhill. The entire effort benefitted from the dedicated assistance of Lyn Churchill and Marion Myers, and the effective technical support of B. Gravem, W.L. Heimerdinger, and P. Cleve. H.G. Schmitz served as program manager.

Over the five years spent on this project, several intense week-long design reviews were conducted, with the participation of P. Belmont, B. Brosgol, P. Cohen, R. Dewar, A. Evans, G. Fisher, H. Harte, A.L. Hisgen, P. Knueven, M. Kronental, N. Lomuto, E. Ploedereder, G. Seegmueller, V. Stenning, D. Taffs, and also F. Belz, R. Converse, K. Correll, A.N. Habermann, J. Sammet, S. Squires, J. Teller, P. Wegner, and P.R. Wetherall.

Several persons had a constructive influence with their comments, criticisms and suggestions. They include P. Brinch Hansen, G. Goos, C.A.R. Hoare, Mark Rain, W.A. Wulf, and also E. Boebert, P. Bonnard, H. Clausen, M. Cox, G. Dismukes, R. Eachus, T. Froggatt, H. Ganzinger, C. Hewitt, S. Kamin, R. Kotler, O. Lecarme, J.A.N. Lee, J.L. Mansion, F. Minel, T. Phinney, J. Roehrich, V. Schneider, A. Singer, D. Slosberg, I.C. Wand, the reviewers of Ada-Europe, AdaTEC, Afcet, those of the LMSC review team, and those of the Ada Tokyo Study Group.

These reviews and comments, the numerous evaluation reports received at the end of the first and second phase, the nine hundred language issue reports and test and evaluation reports received from fifteen different countries during the third phase of the project, the thousands of comments received during the ANSI Canvass, and the on-going work of the IFIP Working Group 2.4 on system implementation languages and that of the Purdue Europe LTPL-E committee, all had a substantial influence on the final definition of Ada.

The Military Departments and Agencies have provided a broad base of support including funding, extensive reviews, and countless individual contributions by the members of the High Order Language Working Group and other interested personnel. In particular, William A. Whitaker provided leadership for the program during the formative stages. David A. Fisher was responsible for the successful development and refinement of the language requirement documents that led to the Steelman specification.

This language definition was developed by Cii Honeywell Bull and later Alsys, and by Honeywell Systems and Research Center, under contract to the United States Department of Defense. William E. Carlson, and later Larry E. Druffel and Robert F. Mathis, served as the technical representatives of the United States Government and effectively coordinated the efforts of all participants in the Ada program.

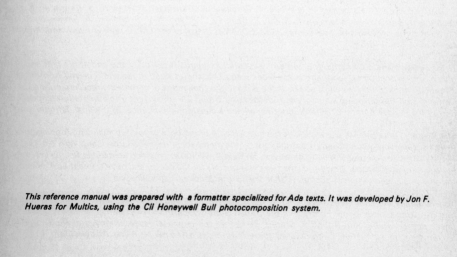

This reference manual was prepared with a formatter specialized for Ada texts. It was developed by Jon F. Hueras for Multics, using the Cii Honeywell Bull photocomposition system.

Table of Contents

Annexes

Appendices

Index

1. Introduction

Ada is a programming language designed in accordance with requirements defined by the United States Department of Defense: the so-called Steelman requirements. Overall, these requirements call for a language with considerable expressive power covering a wide application domain. As a result, the language includes facilities offered by classical languages such as Pascal as well as facilities often found only in specialized languages. Thus the language is a modern algorithmic language with the usual control structures, and with the ability to define types and subprograms. It also serves the need for modularity, whereby data, types, and subprograms can be packaged. It treats modularity in the physical sense as well, with a facility to support separate compilation.

In addition to these aspects, the language covers real-time programming, with facilities to model parallel tasks and to handle exceptions. It also covers systems programming; this requires precise control over the representation of data and access to system-dependent properties. Finally, both application-level and machine-level input-output are defined.

1.1 Scope of the Standard

This standard specifies the form and meaning of program units written in Ada. Its purpose is to promote the portability of Ada programs to a variety of data processing systems.

1.1.1 Extent of the Standard

This standard specifies:

(a) The form of a program unit written in Ada.

(b) The effect of translating and executing such a program unit.

(c) The manner in which program units may be combined to form Ada programs.

(d) The predefined program units that a conforming implementation must supply.

(e) The permissible variations within the standard, and the manner in which they must be specified.

(f) Those violations of the standard that a conforming implementation is required to detect, and the effect of attempting to translate or execute a program unit containing such violations.

(g) Those violations of the standard that a conforming implementation is not required to detect.

9   This standard does not specify:

10   (h) The means whereby a program unit written in Ada is transformed into object code executable by a processor.

11   (i) The means whereby translation or execution of program units is invoked and the executing units are controlled.

12   (j) The size or speed of the object code, or the relative execution speed of different language constructs.

13   (k) The form or contents of any listings produced by implementations; in particular, the form or contents of error or warning messages.

14   (l) The effect of executing a program unit that contains any violation that a conforming implementation is not required to detect.

15   (m) The size of a program or program unit that will exceed the capacity of a particular conforming implementation.

16   Where this standard specifies that a program unit written in Ada has an exact effect, this effect is the operational meaning of the program unit and must be produced by all conforming implementations. Where this standard specifies permissible variations in the effects of constituents of a program unit written in Ada, the operational meaning of the program unit as a whole is understood to be the range of possible effects that result from all these variations, and a conforming implementation is allowed to produce any of these possible effects. Examples of permissible variations are:

17   ● The represented values of fixed or floating numeric quantities, and the results of operations upon them.

18   ● The order of execution of statements in different parallel tasks, in the absence of explicit synchronization.

1.1.2 Conformity of an Implementation with the Standard

1   A conforming implementation is one that:

2   (a) Correctly translates and executes legal program units written in Ada, provided that they are not so large as to exceed the capacity of the implementation.

3   (b) Rejects all program units that are so large as to exceed the capacity of the implementation.

4   (c) Rejects all program units that contain errors whose detection is required by the standard.

5   (d) Supplies all predefined program units required by the standard.

6   (e) Contains no variations except where the standard permits.

7   (f) Specifies all such permitted variations in the manner prescribed by the standard.

1.2 Structure of the Standard

This reference manual contains fourteen chapters, three annexes, three appendices, and an index. 1

Each chapter is divided into sections that have a common structure. Each section introduces its 2
subject, gives any necessary syntax rules, and describes the semantics of the corresponding
language constructs. Examples and notes, and then references, may appear at the end of a section.

Examples are meant to illustrate the possible forms of the constructs described. Notes are meant 3
to emphasize consequences of the rules described in the section or elsewhere. References are
meant to attract the attention of readers to a term or phrase having a technical meaning defined in
another section.

The standard definition of the Ada programming language consists of the fourteen chapters and 4
the three annexes, subject to the following restriction: the material in each of the items listed
below is informative, and not part of the standard definition of the Ada programming language:

- Section 1.3 Design goals and sources 5

- Section 1.4 Language summary 6

- The examples, notes, and references given at the end of each section 7

- Each section whose title starts with the word "Example" or "Examples" 8

1.3 Design Goals and Sources

Ada was designed with three overriding concerns: program reliability and maintenance, program- 1
ming as a human activity, and efficiency.

The need for languages that promote reliability and simplify maintenance is well established. 2
Hence emphasis was placed on program readability over ease of writing. For example, the rules of
the language require that program variables be explicitly declared and that their type be specified.
Since the type of a variable is invariant, compilers can ensure that operations on variables are compatible with the properties intended for objects of the type. Furthermore, error-prone notations
have been avoided, and the syntax of the language avoids the use of encoded forms in favor of
more English-like constructs. Finally, the language offers support for separate compilation of
program units in a way that facilitates program development and maintenance, and which
provides the same degree of checking between units as within a unit.

Concern for the human programmer was also stressed during the design. Above all, an attempt 3
was made to keep the language as small as possible, given the ambitious nature of the application
domain. We have attempted to cover this domain with a small number of underlying concepts
integrated in a consistent and systematic way. Nevertheless we have tried to avoid the pitfalls of
excessive involution, and in the constant search for simpler designs we have tried to provide
language constructs that correspond intuitively to what the users will normally expect.

Like many other human activities, the development of programs is becoming ever more 4
decentralized and distributed. Consequently, the ability to assemble a program from independently produced software components has been a central idea in this design. The concepts of
packages, of private types, and of generic units are directly related to this idea, which has ramifica-
tions in many other aspects of the language.

Design Goals and Sources 1.3

5   No language can avoid the problem of efficiency. Languages that require over-elaborate compilers, or that lead to the inefficient use of storage or execution time, force these inefficiencies on all machines and on all programs. Every construct of the language was examined in the light of present implementation techniques. Any proposed construct whose implementation was unclear or that required excessive machine resources was rejected.

6   None of the above design goals was considered as achievable after the fact. The design goals drove the entire design process from the beginning.

7   A perpetual difficulty in language design is that one must both identify the capabilities required by the application domain and design language features that provide these capabilities. The difficulty existed in this design, although to a lesser degree than usual because of the Steelman requirements. These requirements often simplified the design process by allowing it to concentrate on the design of a given system providing a well defined set of capabilities, rather than on the definition of the capabilities themselves.

8   Another significant simplification of the design work resulted from earlier experience acquired by several successful Pascal derivatives developed with similar goals. These are the languages Euclid, Lis, Mesa, Modula, and Sue. Many of the key ideas and syntactic forms developed in these languages have counterparts in Ada. Several existing languages such as Algol 68 and Simula, and also recent research languages such as Alphard and Clu, influenced this language in several respects, although to a lesser degree than did the Pascal family.

9   Finally, the evaluation reports received on an earlier formulation (the Green language), and on alternative proposals (the Red, Blue, and Yellow languages), the language reviews that took place at different stages of this project, and the thousands of comments received from fifteen different countries during the preliminary stages of the Ada design and during the ANSI canvass, all had a significant impact on the standard definition of the language.

1.4 Language Summary

1   An Ada program is composed of one or more program units. These program units can be compiled separately. Program units may be subprograms (which define executable algorithms), package units (which define collections of entities), task units (which define parallel computations), or generic units (which define parameterized forms of packages and subprograms). Each unit normally consists of two parts: a specification, containing the information that must be visible to other units, and a body, containing the implementation details, which need not be visible to other units.

2   This distinction of the specification and body, and the ability to compile units separately, allows a program to be designed, written, and tested as a set of largely independent software components.

3   An Ada program will normally make use of a library of program units of general utility. The language provides means whereby individual organizations can construct their own libraries. The text of a separately compiled program unit must name the library units it requires.

4   *Program Units*

5   A subprogram is the basic unit for expressing an algorithm. There are two kinds of subprograms: procedures and functions. A procedure is the means of invoking a series of actions. For example, it may read data, update variables, or produce some output. It may have parameters, to provide a controlled means of passing information between the procedure and the point of call.

A function is the means of invoking the computation of a value. It is similar to a procedure, but in addition will return a result.   6

A package is the basic unit for defining a collection of logically related entities. For example, a package can be used to define a common pool of data and types, a collection of related subprograms, or a set of type declarations and associated operations. Portions of a package can be hidden from the user, thus allowing access only to the logical properties expressed by the package specification.   7

A task unit is the basic unit for defining a task whose sequence of actions may be executed in parallel with those of other tasks. Such tasks may be implemented on multicomputers, multiprocessors, or with interleaved execution on a single processor. A task unit may define either a single executing task or a task type permitting the creation of any number of similar tasks.   8

Declarations and Statements   9

The body of a program unit generally contains two parts: a declarative part, which defines the logical entities to be used in the program unit, and a sequence of statements, which defines the execution of the program unit.   10

The declarative part associates names with declared entities. For example, a name may denote a type, a constant, a variable, or an exception. A declarative part also introduces the names and parameters of other nested subprograms, packages, task units, and generic units to be used in the program unit.   11

The sequence of statements describes a sequence of actions that are to be performed. The statements are executed in succession (unless an exit, return, or goto statement, or the raising of an exception, causes execution to continue from another place).   12

An assignment statement changes the value of a variable. A procedure call invokes execution of a procedure after associating any actual parameters provided at the call with the corresponding formal parameters.   13

Case statements and if statements allow the selection of an enclosed sequence of statements based on the value of an expression or on the value of a condition.   14

The loop statement provides the basic iterative mechanism in the language. A loop statement specifies that a sequence of statements is to be executed repeatedly as directed by an iteration scheme, or until an exit statement is encountered.   15

A block statement comprises a sequence of statements preceded by the declaration of local entities used by the statements.   16

Certain statements are only applicable to tasks. A delay statement delays the execution of a task for a specified duration. An entry call statement is written as a procedure call statement; it specifies that the task issuing the call is ready for a rendezvous with another task that has this entry. The called task is ready to accept the entry call when its execution reaches a corresponding accept statement, which specifies the actions then to be performed. After completion of the rendezvous, both the calling task and the task having the entry may continue their execution in parallel. One form of the select statement allows a selective wait for one of several alternative rendezvous. Other forms of the select statement allow conditional or timed entry calls.   17

Language Summary 1.4

18 Execution of a program unit may encounter error situations in which normal program execution cannot continue. For example, an arithmetic computation may exceed the maximum allowed value of a number, or an attempt may be made to access an array component by using an incorrect index value. To deal with such error situations, the statements of a program unit can be textually followed by exception handlers that specify the actions to be taken when the error situation arises. Exceptions can be raised explicitly by a raise statement.

19 *Data Types*

20 Every object in the language has a type, which characterizes a set of values and a set of applicable operations. The main classes of types are scalar types (comprising enumeration and numeric types), composite types, access types, and private types.

21 An enumeration type defines an ordered set of distinct enumeration literals, for example a list of states or an alphabet of characters. The enumeration types BOOLEAN and CHARACTER are predefined.

22 Numeric types provide a means of performing exact or approximate numerical computations. Exact computations use integer types, which denote sets of consecutive integers. Approximate computations use either fixed point types, with absolute bounds on the error, or floating point types, with relative bounds on the error. The numeric types INTEGER , FLOAT , and DURATION are predefined.

23 Composite types allow definitions of structured objects with related components. The composite types in the language provide for arrays and records. An array is an object with indexed components of the same type. A record is an object with named components of possibly different types. The array type STRING is predefined.

24 A record may have special components called discriminants. Alternative record structures that depend on the values of discriminants can be defined within a record type.

25 Access types allow the construction of linked data structures created by the evaluation of allocators. They allow several variables of an access type to designate the same object, and components of one object to designate the same or other objects. Both the elements in such a linked data structure and their relation to other elements can be altered during program execution.

26 Private types can be defined in a package that conceals structural details that are externally irrelevant. Only the logically necessary properties (including any discriminants) are made visible to the users of such types.

27 The concept of a type is refined by the concept of a subtype, whereby a user can constrain the set of allowed values of a type. Subtypes can be used to define subranges of scalar types, arrays with a limited set of index values, and records and private types with particular discriminant values.

28 *Other Facilities*

29 Representation clauses can be used to specify the mapping between types and features of an underlying machine. For example, the user can specify that objects of a given type must be represented with a given number of bits, or that the components of a record are to be represented using a given storage layout. Other features allow the controlled use of low level, nonportable, or implementation-dependent aspects, including the direct insertion of machine code.

30 Input-output is defined in the language by means of predefined library packages. Facilities are provided for input-output of values of user-defined as well as of predefined types. Standard means of representing values in display form are also provided.

Finally, the language provides a powerful means of parameterization of program units, called   ₃₁
generic program units. The generic parameters can be types and subprograms (as well as objects)
and so allow general algorithms to be applied to all types of a given class.

1.5 Method of Description and Syntax Notation

The form of Ada program units is described by means of a context-free syntax together with   1
context-dependent requirements expressed by narrative rules.

The meaning of Ada program units is described by means of narrative rules defining both the   2
effects of each construct and the composition rules for constructs. This narrative employs
technical terms whose precise definition is given in the text (references to the section containing
the definition of a technical term appear at the end of each section that uses the term).

All other terms are in the English language and bear their natural meaning, as defined in Webster's   3
Third New International Dictionary of the English Language.

The context-free syntax of the language is described using a simple variant of Backus-Naur-Form.   4
In particular,

(a) Lower case words, some containing embedded underlines, are used to denote syntactic   5
categories, for example:

    adding_operator

Whenever the name of a syntactic category is used apart from the syntax rules themselves,   6
spaces take the place of the underlines (thus: adding operator).

(b) Boldface words are used to denote reserved words, for example: 7

    array

(c) Square brackets enclose optional items. Thus the two following rules are equivalent.   8

    return_statement ::= **return** [expression];
    return_statement ::= **return**; | **return** expression;

(d) Braces enclose a repeated item. The item may appear zero or more times; the repetitions   9
occur from left to right as with an equivalent left-recursive rule. Thus the two following rules
are equivalent.

    term ::= factor {multiplying_operator factor}
    term ::= factor | term multiplying_operator factor

10   (e)   A vertical bar separates alternative items unless it occurs immediately after an opening brace, in which case it stands for itself:

>   letter_or_digit ::= letter | digit
>   component_association ::= [choice {| choice} =>] expression

11   (f)   If the name of any syntactic category starts with an italicized part, it is equivalent to the category name without the italicized part. The italicized part is intended to convey some semantic information. For example *type*_name and *task*_name are both equivalent to name alone.

Note:

12   The syntax rules describing structured constructs are presented in a form that corresponds to the recommended paragraphing. For example, an if statement is defined as

>   if_statement ::=
>   **if** condition **then**
>   sequence_of_statements
>   {**elsif** condition **then**
>   sequence_of_statements}
>   [**else**
>   sequence_of_statements]
>   **end if;**

13   Different lines are used for parts of a syntax rule if the corresponding parts of the construct described by the rule are intended to be on different lines. Indentation in the rule is a recommendation for indentation of the corresponding part of the construct. It is recommended that all indentations be by multiples of a basic step of indentation (the number of spaces for the basic step is not defined). The preferred places for other line breaks are after semicolons. On the other hand, if a complete construct can fit on one line, this is also allowed in the recommended paragraphing.

1.6 Classification of Errors

1   The language definition classifies errors into several different categories:

2   (a)   Errors that must be detected at compilation time by every Ada compiler.

3   These errors correspond to any violation of a rule given in this reference manual, other than the violations that correspond to (b) or (c) below. In particular, violation of any rule that uses the terms *must*, *allowed*, *legal*, or *illegal* belongs to this category. Any program that contains such an error is not a legal Ada program; on the other hand, the fact that a program is legal does not mean, per se, that the program is free from other forms of error.

4   (b)   Errors that must be detected at run time by the execution of an Ada program.

5   The corresponding error situations are associated with the names of the predefined exceptions. Every Ada compiler is required to generate code that raises the corresponding exception if such an error situation arises during program execution. If an exception is certain to be raised in every execution of a program, then compilers are allowed (although not required) to report this fact at compilation time.

(c) Erroneous execution.   6

The language rules specify certain rules to be obeyed by Ada programs, although there is no   7
requirement on Ada compilers to provide either a compilation-time or a run-time detection of
the violation of such rules. The errors of this category are indicated by the use of the word
erroneous to qualify the execution of the corresponding constructs. The effect of erroneous
execution is unpredictable.

(d) Incorrect order dependences.   8

Whenever the reference manual specifies that different parts of a given construct are to be   9
executed *in some order that is not defined by the language*, this means that the implementation is allowed to execute these parts in any given order, following the rules that result from
that given order, but not in parallel. Furthermore, the construct is incorrect if execution of
these parts in a different order would have a different effect. Compilers are not required to
provide either compilation-time or run-time detection of incorrect order dependences. The
foregoing is expressed in terms of the process that is called execution; it applies equally to the
processes that are called evaluation and elaboration.

If a compiler is able to recognize at compilation time that a construct is erroneous or contains an   10
incorrect order dependence, then the compiler is allowed to generate, in place of the code
otherwise generated for the construct, code that raises the predefined exception
PROGRAM_ERROR. Similarly, compilers are allowed to generate code that checks at run time for
erroneous constructs, for incorrect order dependences, or for both. The predefined exception
PROGRAM_ERROR is raised if such a check fails.

2. Lexical Elements

The text of a program consists of the texts of one or more compilations. The text of a compilation is a sequence of lexical elements, each composed of characters; the rules of composition are given in this chapter. Pragmas, which provide certain information for the compiler, are also described in this chapter.

References: character 2.1, compilation 10.1, lexical element 2.2, pragma 2.8

2.1 Character Set

The only characters allowed in the text of a program are the graphic characters and format effectors. Each graphic character corresponds to a unique code of the *ISO* seven-bit coded character set (*ISO* standard 646), and is represented (visually) by a graphical symbol. Some graphic characters are represented by different graphical symbols in alternative national representations of the *ISO* character set. The description of the language definition in this standard reference manual uses the *ASCII* graphical symbols, the *ANSI* graphical representation of the *ISO* character set.

```
graphic_character ::= basic_graphic_character
    | lower_case_letter | other_special_character

basic_graphic_character ::=
      upper_case_letter | digit
    | special_character | space_character

basic_character ::=
      basic_graphic_character | format_effector
```

The basic character set is sufficient for writing any program. The characters included in each of the categories of basic graphic characters are defined as follows:

(a) upper case letters
     A B C D E F G H I J K L M N O P Q R S T U V W X Y Z

(b) digits
     0 1 2 3 4 5 6 7 8 9

(c) special characters
     " # & ' ( ) * + , - . / : ; < = > _ |

(d) the space character

Format effectors are the *ISO* (and *ASCII*) characters called horizontal tabulation, vertical tabulation, carriage return, line feed, and form feed.

9 The characters included in each of the remaining categories of graphic characters are defined as follows:

10 (e) lower case letters
     a b c d e f g h i j k l m n o p q r s t u v w x y z

11 (f) other special characters
     ! $ % ? @ [\ ] ^ ` { } ~

12 Allowable replacements for the special characters vertical bar (|), sharp (≠), and quotation (") are defined in section 2.10.

Notes:

13 The *ISO* character that corresponds to the sharp graphical symbol in the *ASCII* representation appears as a pound sterling symbol in the French, German, and United Kingdom standard national representations. In any case, the font design of graphical symbols (for example, whether they are in italic or bold typeface) is not part of the *ISO* standard.

14 The meanings of the acronyms used in this section are as follows: *ANSI* stands for American National Standards Institute, *ASCII* stands for American Standard Code for Information Interchange, and *ISO* stands for International Organization for Standardization.

15 The following names are used when referring to special characters and other special characters:

symbol	name	symbol	name
"	quotation	>	greater than
≠	sharp	_	underline
&	ampersand	|	vertical bar
'	apostrophe	!	exclamation mark
(	left parenthesis	$	dollar
)	right parenthesis	%	percent
*	star, multiply	?	question mark
+	plus	@	commercial at
,	comma	[	left square bracket
-	hyphen, minus	\	back-slash
.	dot, point, period	]	right square bracket
/	slash, divide	^	circumflex
:	colon	`	grave accent
;	semicolon	{	left brace
<	less than	}	right brace
=	equal	~	tilde

2.2 Lexical Elements, Separators, and Delimiters

The text of a program consists of the texts of one or more compilations. The text of each compilation is a sequence of separate lexical elements. Each lexical element is either a delimiter, an identifier (which may be a reserved word), a numeric literal, a character literal, a string literal, or a comment. The effect of a program depends only on the particular sequences of lexical elements that form its compilations, excluding the comments, if any.

In some cases an explicit *separator* is required to separate adjacent lexical elements (namely, when without separation, interpretation as a single lexical element is possible). A separator is any of a space character, a format effector, or the end of a line. A space character is a separator except within a comment, a string literal, or a space character literal. Format effectors other than horizontal tabulation are always separators. Horizontal tabulation is a separator except within a comment. [2]

The end of a line is always a separator. The language does not define what causes the end of a line. However if, for a given implementation, the end of a line is signified by one or more characters, then these characters must be format effectors other than horizontal tabulation. In any case, a sequence of one or more format effectors other than horizontal tabulation must cause at least one end of line. [3]

One or more separators are allowed between any two adjacent lexical elements, before the first of each compilation, or after the last. At least one separator is required between an identifier or a numeric literal and an adjacent identifier or numeric literal. [4]

A *delimiter* is either one of the following special characters (in the basic character set) [5]

    & ' ( ) * + , - . / : ; < = > |

or one of the following *compound delimiters* each composed of two adjacent special characters [6]

    =>   ..   **   :=   /=   >=   <=   <<   >>   <>

Each of the special characters listed for single character delimiters is a single delimiter except if this character is used as a character of a compound delimiter, or as a character of a comment, string literal, character literal, or numeric literal. [7]

The remaining forms of lexical element are described in other sections of this chapter. [8]

Notes:

Each lexical element must fit on one line, since the end of a line is a separator. The quotation, sharp, and underline characters, likewise two adjacent hyphens, are not delimiters, but may form part of other lexical elements. [9]

The following names are used when referring to compound delimiters: [10]

delimiter	name
=>	arrow
..	double dot
**	double star, exponentiate
:=	assignment (pronounced: "becomes")
/=	inequality (pronounced: "not equal")
>=	greater than or equal
<=	less than or equal
<<	left label bracket
>>	right label bracket
<>	box

References: character literal 2.5, comment 2.7, compilation 10.1, format effector 2.1, identifier 2.3, numeric literal 2.4, reserved word 2.9, space character 2.1, special character 2.1, string literal 2.6 [11]

Lexical Elements, Separators, and Delimiters 2.2

2.3 Identifiers

1   Identifiers are used as names and also as reserved words.

2   identifier ::=
      letter {[underline] letter_or_digit}

    letter_or_digit ::= letter | digit

    letter ::= upper_case_letter | lower_case_letter

3   All characters of an identifier are significant, including any underline character inserted between a letter or digit and an adjacent letter or digit. Identifiers differing only in the use of corresponding upper and lower case letters are considered as the same.

4   *Examples:*

    COUNT   X   get_symbol   Ethelyn   Marion

    SNOBOL_4   X1   PageCount   STORE_NEXT_ITEM

Note:

5   No space is allowed within an identifier since a space is a separator.

6   *References:* digit 2.1, lower case letter 2.1, name 4.1, reserved word 2.9, separator 2.2, space character 2.1, upper case letter 2.1

2.4 Numeric Literals

1   There are two classes of numeric literals: real literals and integer literals. A real literal is a numeric literal that includes a point; an integer literal is a numeric literal without a point. Real literals are the literals of the type *universal_real*. Integer literals are the literals of the type *universal_integer*.

2   numeric_literal ::= decimal_literal | based_literal

3   *References:* literal 4.2, universal_integer type 3.5.4, universal_real type 3.5.6

2.4.1 Decimal Literals

1   A decimal literal is a numeric literal expressed in the conventional decimal notation (that is, the base is implicitly ten).

2   decimal_literal ::= integer [.integer] [exponent]

    integer ::= digit {[underline] digit}

    exponent ::= E [+] integer | E - integer

An underline character inserted between adjacent digits of a decimal literal does not affect the value of this numeric literal. The letter E of the exponent, if any, can be written either in lower case or in upper case, with the same meaning. 3

An exponent indicates the power of ten by which the value of the decimal literal without the exponent is to be multiplied to obtain the value of the decimal literal with the exponent. An exponent for an integer literal must not have a minus sign. 4

Examples: 5

```
12        0       1E6      123_456     --   integer literals

12.0      0.0     0.456    3.14159_26  --   real literals

1.34E-12  1.0E+6  --   real literals with exponent
```

Notes:

Leading zeros are allowed. No space is allowed in a numeric literal, not even between constituents of the exponent, since a space is a separator. A zero exponent is allowed for an integer literal. 6

References: digit 2.1, lower case letter 2.1, numeric literal 2.4, separator 2.2, space character 2.1, upper case letter 2.1 7

2.4.2 Based Literals

A based literal is a numeric literal expressed in a form that specifies the base explicitly. The base must be at least two and at most sixteen. 1

```
based_literal ::=
    base # based_integer [.based_integer] # [exponent]

base ::= integer

based_integer ::=
    extended_digit [[underline] extended_digit]

extended_digit ::= digit | letter
```
2

An underline character inserted between adjacent digits of a based literal does not affect the value of this numeric literal. The base and the exponent, if any, are in decimal notation. The only letters allowed as extended digits are the letters A through F for the digits ten through fifteen. A letter in a based literal (either an extended digit or the letter E of an exponent) can be written either in lower case or in upper case, with the same meaning. 3

The conventional meaning of based notation is assumed; in particular the value of each extended digit of a based literal must be less than the base. An exponent indicates the power of the base by which the value of the based literal without the exponent is to be multiplied to obtain the value of the based literal with the exponent. 4

5 *Examples:*

2#1111_1111#	16#FF#	016#0FF#	--	integer literals of value 255
16#E#E1	2#1110_0000#		--	integer literals of value 224
16#F.FF#E+2	2#1.1111_1111_111#E11		--	real literals of value 4095.0

6 *References:* digit 2.1, exponent 2.4.1, letter 2.3, lower case letter 2.1, numeric literal 2.4, upper case letter 2.1

2.5 Character Literals

1 A character literal is formed by enclosing one of the 95 graphic characters (including the space) between two apostrophe characters. A character literal has a value that belongs to a character type.

2   character_literal ::= 'graphic_character'

3 *Examples:*

    'A'   '*'   '''   ' '

4 *References:* character type 3.5.2, graphic character 2.1, literal 4.2, space character 2.1

2.6 String Literals

1 A string literal is formed by a sequence of graphic characters (possibly none) enclosed between two quotation characters used as *string brackets*.

2   string_literal ::= "{graphic_character}"

3 A string literal has a value that is a sequence of character values corresponding to the graphic characters of the string literal apart from the quotation character itself. If a quotation character value is to be represented in the sequence of character values, then a pair of adjacent quotation characters must be written at the corresponding place within the string literal. (This means that a string literal that includes two adjacent quotation characters is never interpreted as two adjacent string literals.)

4 The *length* of a string literal is the number of character values in the sequence represented. (Each doubled quotation character is counted as a single character.)

5 *Examples:*

    "Message of the day:"

    ""   -- an empty string literal
    " "   "A"   """"   -- three string literals of length 1

    "Characters such as $, %, and } are allowed in string literals"

Note:

A string literal must fit on one line since it is a lexical element (see 2.2). Longer sequences of 6
graphic character values can be obtained by catenation of string literals. Similarly catenation of
constants declared in the package ASCII can be used to obtain sequences of character values that
include nongraphic character values (the so-called control characters). Examples of such uses of
catenation are given below:

```
"FIRST PART OF A SEQUENCE OF CHARACTERS " &
"THAT CONTINUES ON THE NEXT LINE"
```

```
"sequence that includes the" & ASCII.ACK & "control character"
```

References: ascii predefined package C, catenation operation 4.5.3, character value 3.5.2, constant 3.2.1, 7
declaration 3.1, end of a line 2.2, graphic character 2.1, lexical element 2.2

2.7 Comments

A comment starts with two adjacent hyphens and extends up to the end of the line. A comment 1
can appear on any line of a program. The presence or absence of comments has no influence on
whether a program is legal or illegal. Furthermore, comments do not influence the effect of a
program; their sole purpose is the enlightenment of the human reader.

Examples: 2

```
--   the last sentence above echoes the Algol 68 report

end;   --   processing of LINE is complete

--   a long comment may be split onto
--   two or more consecutive lines

----------------   the first two hyphens start the comment
```

Note:

Horizontal tabulation can be used in comments, after the double hyphen, and is equivalent to one 3
or more spaces (see 2.2).

References: end of a line 2.2, illegal 1.6, legal 1.6, space character 2.1 4

2.8 Pragmas

A pragma is used to convey information to the compiler. A pragma starts with the reserved word 1
pragma followed by an identifier that is the name of the pragma.

```
pragma ::=                                                              2
    pragma identifier [(argument_association {, argument_association})];

argument_association ::=
    [argument_identifier =>] name
  | [argument_identifier =>] expression
```

3   Pragmas are only allowed at the following places in a program:

4   ● After a semicolon delimiter, but not within a formal part or discriminant part.

5   ● At any place where the syntax rules allow a construct defined by a syntactic category whose name ends with "declaration", "statement", "clause", or "alternative", or one of the syntactic categories variant and exception handler; but not in place of such a construct. Also at any place where a compilation unit would be allowed.

6   Additional restrictions exist for the placement of specific pragmas.

7   Some pragmas have arguments. Argument associations can be either positional or named as for parameter associations of subprogram calls (see 6.4). Named associations are, however, only possible if the argument identifiers are defined. A name given in an argument must be either a name visible at the place of the pragma or an identifier specific to the pragma.

8   The pragmas defined by the language are described in Annex B: they must be supported by every implementation. In addition, an implementation may provide implementation-defined pragmas, which must then be described in Appendix F. An implementation is not allowed to define pragmas whose presence or absence influences the legality of the text outside such pragmas. Consequently, the legality of a program does not depend on the presence or absence of implementation-defined pragmas.

9   A pragma that is not language-defined has no effect if its identifier is not recognized by the (current) implementation. Furthermore, a pragma (whether language-defined or implementation-defined) has no effect if its placement or its arguments do not correspond to what is allowed for the pragma. The region of text over which a pragma has an effect depends on the pragma.

10   *Examples:*

```
pragma LIST(OFF);
pragma OPTIMIZE(TIME);
pragma INLINE(SETMASK);
pragma SUPPRESS(RANGE_CHECK, ON => INDEX);
```

Note:

11   It is recommended (but not required) that implementations issue warnings for pragmas that are not recognized and therefore ignored.

12   *References:* compilation unit 10.1, delimiter 2.2, discriminant part 3.7.1, exception handler 11.2, expression 4.4, formal part 6.1, identifier 2.3, implementation-defined pragma F, language-defined pragma B, legal 1.6, name 4.1, reserved word 2.9, statement 5, static expression 4.9, variant 3.7.3, visibility 8.3

13   *Categories ending with "declaration" comprise:* basic declaration 3.1, component declaration 3.7, entry declaration 9.5, generic parameter declaration 12.1

14   *Categories ending with "clause" comprise:* alignment clause 13.4, component clause 13.4, context clause 10.1.1, representation clause 13.1, use clause 8.4, with clause 10.1.1

15   *Categories ending with "alternative" comprise:* accept alternative 9.7.1, case statement alternative 5.4, delay alternative 9.7.1, select alternative 9.7.1, selective wait alternative 9.7.1, terminate alternative 9.7.1

2.9 Reserved Words

The identifiers listed below are called *reserved words* and are reserved for special significance in the language. For readability of this manual, the reserved words appear in lower case boldface.

abort	declare	generic	of	select
abs	delay	goto	or	separate
accept	delta		others	subtype
access	digits	if	out	
all	do	in		task
and		is	package	terminate
array			pragma	then
at	else		private	type
	elsif	limited	procedure	
	end	loop		
begin	entry		raise	use
body	exception		range	
	exit	mod	record	when
			rem	while
		new	renames	with
case	for	not	return	
constant	function	null	reverse	xor

A reserved word must not be used as a declared identifier.

Notes:

Reserved words differing only in the use of corresponding upper and lower case letters are considered as the same (see 2.3). In some attributes the identifier that appears after the apostrophe is identical to some reserved word.

References: attribute 4.1.4, declaration 3.1, identifier 2.3, lower case letter 2.1, upper case letter 2.1

2.10 Allowable Replacements of Characters

The following replacements are allowed for the vertical bar, sharp, and quotation basic characters:

- A vertical bar character (|) can be replaced by an exclamation mark (!) where used as a delimiter.

- The sharp characters (#) of a based literal can be replaced by colons (:) provided that the replacement is done for both occurrences.

- The quotation characters (") used as string brackets at both ends of a string literal can be replaced by percent characters (%) provided that the enclosed sequence of characters contains no quotation character, and provided that both string brackets are replaced. Any percent character within the sequence of characters must then be doubled and each such doubled percent character is interpreted as a single percent character value.

5   These replacements do not change the meaning of the program.

Notes:

6   It is recommended that use of the replacements for the vertical bar, sharp, and quotation
characters be restricted to cases where the corresponding graphical symbols are not available.
Note that the vertical bar appears as a broken bar on some equipment; replacement is not recommended in this case.

7   The rules given for identifiers and numeric literals are such that lower case and upper case letters
can be used indifferently; these lexical elements can thus be written using only characters of the
basic character set. If a string literal of the predefined type STRING contains characters that are
not in the basic character set, the same sequence of character values can be obtained by
catenating string literals that contain only characters of the basic character set with suitable
character constants declared in the predefined package ASCII. Thus the string literal "AB $CD"
could be replaced by "AB" & ASCII.DOLLAR & "CD". Similarly, the string literal "ABcd" with lower
case letters could be replaced by "AB" & ASCII.LC_C & ASCII.LC_D.

8   *References:* ascii predefined package C, based literal 2.4.2, basic character 2.1, catenation operation 4.5.3, character
value 3.5.2, delimiter 2.2, graphic character 2.1, graphical symbol 2.1, identifier 2.3, lexical element 2.2, lower case
letter 2.1, numeric literal 2.4, string bracket 2.6, string literal 2.6, upper case letter 2.1

3. Declarations and Types

This chapter describes the types in the language and the rules for declaring constants, variables, and named numbers. 〔1〕

3.1 Declarations

The language defines several kinds of entities that are declared, either explicitly or implicitly, by declarations. Such an entity can be a numeric literal, an object, a discriminant, a record component, a loop parameter, an exception, a type, a subtype, a subprogram, a package, a task unit, a generic unit, a single entry, an entry family, a formal parameter (of a subprogram, entry, or generic subprogram), a generic formal parameter, a named block or loop, a labeled statement, or an operation (in particular, an attribute or an enumeration literal; see 3.3.3). 〔1〕

There are several forms of declaration. A basic declaration is a form of declaration defined as follows. 〔2〕

```
basic_declaration ::=
      object_declaration          | number_declaration
    | type_declaration            | subtype_declaration
    | subprogram_declaration      | package_declaration
    | task_declaration            | generic_declaration
    | exception_declaration       | generic_instantiation
    | renaming_declaration        | deferred_constant_declaration
```
〔3〕

Certain forms of declaration always occur (explicitly) as part of a basic declaration; these forms are discriminant specifications, component declarations, entry declarations, parameter specifications, generic parameter declarations, and enumeration literal specifications. A loop parameter specification is a form of declaration that occurs only in certain forms of loop statement. 〔4〕

The remaining forms of declaration are implicit: the name of a block, the name of a loop, and a statement label are implicitly declared. Certain operations are implicitly declared (see 3.3.3). 〔5〕

For each form of declaration the language rules define a certain region of text called the *scope* of the declaration (see 8.2). Several forms of declaration associate an identifier with a declared entity. Within its scope, and only there, there are places where it is possible to use the identifier to refer to the associated declared entity; these places are defined by the visibility rules (see 8.3). At such places the identifier is said to be a *name* of the entity (its simple name); the name is said to *denote* the associated entity. 〔6〕

Certain forms of enumeration literal specification associate a character literal with the corresponding declared entity. Certain forms of declaration associate an operator symbol or some other notation with an explicitly or implicitly declared operation. 〔7〕

The process by which a declaration achieves its effect is called the *elaboration* of the declaration; this process happens during program execution. 〔8〕

9   After its elaboration, a declaration is said to be *elaborated*. Prior to the completion of its elaboration (including before the elaboration), the declaration is not yet elaborated. The elaboration of any declaration has always at least the effect of achieving this change of state (from not yet elaborated to elaborated). The phrase *"the elaboration has no other effect"* is used in this manual whenever this change of state is the only effect of elaboration for some form of declaration. An elaboration process is also defined for declarative parts, declarative items, and compilation units (see 3.9 and 10.5).

10   Object, number, type, and subtype declarations are described here. The remaining basic declarations are described in later chapters.

Note:

11   The syntax rules use the term *identifier* for the first occurrence of an identifier in some form of declaration; the term *simple name* is used for any occurrence of an identifier that already denotes some declared entity.

12   *References:* attribute 4.1.4, block name 5.6, block statement 5.6, character literal 2.5, component declaration 3.7, declarative item 3.9, declarative part 3.9, deferred constant declaration 7.4, discriminant specification 3.7.1, elaboration 3.9, entry declaration 9.5, enumeration literal specification 3.5.1, exception declaration 11.1, generic declaration 12.1, generic instantiation 12.3, generic parameter declaration 12.1, identifier 2.3, label 5.1, loop name 5.5, loop parameter specification 5.5, loop statement 5.5, name 4.1, number declaration 3.2.2, numeric literal 2.4, object declaration 3.2.1, operation 3.3, operator symbol 6.1, package declaration 7.1, parameter specification 6.1, record component 3.7, renaming declaration 8.5, representation clause 13.1, scope 8.2, simple name 4.1, subprogram body 6.3, subprogram declaration 6.1, subtype declaration 3.3.2, task declaration 9.1, type declaration 3.3.1, visibility 8.3

3.2 Objects and Named Numbers

1   An *object* is an entity that contains (has) a value of a given type. An object is one of the following:

2   ● an object declared by an object declaration or by a single task declaration,

3   ● a formal parameter of a subprogram, entry, or generic subprogram,

4   ● a generic formal object,

5   ● a loop parameter,

6   ● an object designated by a value of an access type,

7   ● a component or a slice of another object.

8   A number declaration is a special form of object declaration that associates an identifier with a value of type *universal_integer* or *universal_real*.

9
```
object_declaration ::=
    identifier_list : [constant] subtype_indication [:= expression];
  | identifier_list : [constant] constrained_array_definition  [:= expression];

number_declaration ::=
    identifier_list : constant := universal_static_expression;

identifier_list ::=  identifier {, identifier}
```

An object declaration is called a *single object declaration* if its identifier list has a single identifier; it is called a *multiple object declaration* if the identifier list has two or more identifiers. A multiple object declaration is equivalent to a sequence of the corresponding number of single object declarations. For each identifier of the list, the equivalent sequence has a single object declaration formed by this identifier, followed by a colon and by whatever appears at the right of the colon in the multiple object declaration; the equivalent sequence is in the same order as the identifier list.

A similar equivalence applies also for the identifier lists of number declarations, component declarations, discriminant specifications, parameter specifications, generic parameter declarations, exception declarations, and deferred constant declarations.

In the remainder of this reference manual, explanations are given for declarations with a single identifier; the corresponding explanations for declarations with several identifiers follow from the equivalence stated above.

Example:

```
-- the multiple object declaration

JOHN, PAUL : PERSON_NAME := new PERSON(SEX => M);  --  see 3.8.1

-- is equivalent to the two single object declarations in the order given

JOHN  : PERSON_NAME := new PERSON(SEX => M);
PAUL  : PERSON_NAME := new PERSON(SEX => M);
```

References: access type 3.8, constrained array definition 3.6, component 3.3, declaration 3.1, deferred constant declaration 7.4, designate 3.8, discriminant specification 3.7.1, entry 9.5, exception declaration 11.1, expression 4.4, formal parameter 6.1, generic formal object 12.1.1, generic parameter declaration 12.1, generic unit 12, generic subprogram 12.1, identifier 2.3, loop parameter 5.5, numeric type 3.5, parameter specification 6.1, scope 8.2, simple name 4.1, single task declaration 9.1, slice 4.1.2, static expression 4.9, subprogram 6, subtype indication 3.3.2, type 3.3, universal_integer type 3.5.4, universal_real type 3.5.6

3.2.1 Object Declarations

An object declaration declares an object wh se type is given either by a subtype indication or by a constrained array definition. If the object declaration includes the assignment compound delimiter followed by an expression, the expression specifies an initial value for the declared object; the type of the expression must be that of the object.

The declared object is a *constant* if the reserved word **constant** appears in the object declaration; the declaration must then include an explicit initialization. The value of a constant cannot be modified after initialization. Formal parameters of mode **in** of subprograms and entries, and generic formal parameters of mode **in**, are also constants; a loop parameter is a constant within the corresponding loop; a subcomponent or slice of a constant is a constant.

An object that is not a constant is called a *variable* (in particular, the object declared by an object declaration that does not include the reserved word **constant** is a variable). The only ways to change the value of a variable are either directly by an assignment, or indirectly when the variable is updated (see 6.2) by a procedure or entry call statement (this action can be performed either on the variable itself, on a subcomponent of the variable, or on another variable that has the given variable as subcomponent).

4   The elaboration of an object declaration proceeds as follows:

5   (a) The subtype indication or the constrained array definition is first elaborated. This establishes the subtype of the object.

6   (b) If the object declaration includes an explicit initialization, the initial value   is obtained by evaluating the corresponding expression. Otherwise any implicit initial values for the object or for its subcomponents are evaluated.

7   (c) The object is created.

8   (d) Any initial value (whether explicit or implicit) is assigned to the object or to the corresponding subcomponent.

9   implicit initial values are defined for objects declared by object declarations, and for components of such objects, in the following cases:

10   ● If the type of an object is an access type, the implicit initial value is the null value of the access type.

11   ● If the type of an object is a task type, the implicit initial (and only) value designates a corresponding task.

12   ● If the type of an object is a type with discriminants and the subtype of the object is constrained, the implicit initial (and only) value of each discriminant is defined by the subtype of the object.

13   ● If the type of an object is a composite type, the implicit initial value of each component that has a default expression is obtained by evaluation of this expression, unless the component is a discriminant of a constrained object (the previous case).

14   In the case of a component that is itself a composite object and whose value is defined neither by an explicit initialization nor by a default expression, any implicit initial values for components of the composite object are defined by the same rules as for a declared object.

15   The steps (a) to (d) are performed in the order indicated. For step (b), if the default expression for a discriminant is evaluated, then this evaluation is performed before that of default expressions for subcomponents that depend on discriminants, and also before that of default expressions that include the name of the discriminant. Apart from the previous rule, the evaluation of default expressions is performed in some order that is not defined by the language.

16   The initialization of an object (the declared object or one of its subcomponents) checks that the initial value belongs to the subtype of the object; for an array object declared by an object declaration, an implicit subtype conversion is first applied as for an assignment statement, unless the object is a constant whose subtype is an unconstrained array type. The exception CONSTRAINT_ERROR is raised if this check fails.

17   The value of a scalar variable is undefined after elaboration of the corresponding object declaration unless an initial value is assigned to the variable by an initialization (explicitly or implicitly).

18   If the operand of a type conversion or qualified expression is a variable that has scalar subcomponents with undefined values, then the values of the corresponding subcomponents of the result are undefined. The execution of a program is erroneous if it attempts to evaluate a scalar variable with an undefined value. Similarly, the execution of a program is erroneous if it attempts to apply a predefined operator to a variable that has a scalar subcomponent with an undefined value.

Examples of variable declarations: [19]

```
COUNT, SUM    : INTEGER;
SIZE          : INTEGER range 0 .. 10_000 := 0;
SORTED        : BOOLEAN := FALSE;
COLOR_TABLE   : array(1 .. N) of COLOR;
OPTION        : BIT_VECTOR(1 .. 10) := (others => TRUE);
```

Examples of constant declarations: [20]

```
LIMIT       : constant INTEGER := 10_000;
LOW_LIMIT   : constant INTEGER := LIMIT/10;
TOLERANCE   : constant REAL := DISPERSION(1.15);
```

Note:

The expression initializing a constant object need not be a static expression (see 4.9). In the above   [21]
examples, LIMIT and LOW_LIMIT are initialized with static expressions, but TOLERANCE is not if
DISPERSION is a user-defined function.

References: access type 3.8, assignment 5.2, assignment compound delimiter 5.2, component 3.3, composite type   [22]
3.3, constrained array definition 3.6, constrained subtype 3.3, constraint_error exception 11.1, conversion 4.6,
declaration 3.1, default expression for a discriminant 3.7, default initial value for an access type 3.8, depend on a discriminant 3.7.1, designate 3.8, discriminant 3.3, elaboration 3.9, entry 9.5, evaluation 4.5, expression 4.4, formal
parameter 6.1, generic formal parameter 12.1 12.3, generic unit 12, in some order 1.6, limited type 7.4.4, mode in
6.1, package 7, predefined operator 4.5, primary 4.4, private type 7.4, qualified expression 4.7, reserved word 2.9,
scalar type 3.5, slice 4.1.2, subcomponent 3.3, subprogram 6, subtype 3.3, subtype indication 3.3.2, task 9, task type
9.2, type 3.3, visible part 7.2

3.2.2 Number Declarations

A number declaration is a special form of constant declaration. The type of the static expression   [1]
given for the initialization of a number declaration must be either the type *universal_integer* or the
type *universal_real*. The constant declared by a number declaration is called a *named number* and
has the type of the static expression.

Note:

The rules concerning expressions of a universal type are explained in section 4.10. It is a conse-   [2]
quence of these rules that if every primary contained in the expression is of the type *univer-
sal_integer*, then the named number is also of this type. Similarly, if every primary is of the type
universal_real, then the named number is also of this type.

Examples of number declarations: [3]

```
PI                : constant := 3.14159_26536;   -- a real number
TWO_PI            : constant := 2.0*PI;          -- a real number
MAX               : constant := 500;             -- an integer number
POWER_16          : constant := 2**16;           -- the integer 65_536
ONE, UN, EINS     : constant := 1;               -- three different names for 1
```

References: identifier 2.3, primary 4.4, static expression 4.9, type 3.3, universal_integer type 3.5.4, universal_real   [4]
type 3.5.6, universal type 4.10

3.3 Types and Subtypes

1   A type is characterized by a set of values and a set of operations.

2   There exist several *classes* of types. *Scalar* types are integer types, real types, and types defined by enumeration of their values; values of these types have no components. *Array* and *record* types are composite; a value of a composite type consists of *component* values. An *access* type is a type whose values provide access to objects. *Private* types are types for which the set of possible values is well defined, but not directly available to the users of such types. Finally, there are *task* types. (Private types are described in chapter 7, task types are described in chapter 9, the other classes of types are described in this chapter.)

3   Certain record and private types have special components called *discriminants* whose values distinguish alternative forms of values of one of these types. If a private type has discriminants, they are known to users of the type. Hence a private type is only known by its name, its discriminants if any, and by the corresponding set of operations.

4   The set of possible values for an object of a given type can be subjected to a condition that is called a *constraint* (the case where the constraint imposes no restriction is also included); a value is said to *satisfy* a constraint if it satisfies the corresponding condition. A *subtype* is a type together with a constraint; a value is said to *belong to a subtype* of a given type if it belongs to the type and satisfies the constraint; the given type is called the *base type* of the subtype. A type is a subtype of itself; such a subtype is said to be *unconstrained*: it corresponds to a condition that imposes no restriction. The base type of a type is the type itself.

5   The set of operations defined for a subtype of a given type includes the operations that are defined for the type; however the assignment operation to a variable having a given subtype only assigns values that belong to the subtype. Additional operations, such as qualification (in a qualified expression), are implicitly defined by a subtype declaration.

6   Certain types have *default initial values* defined for objects of the type; certain other types have *default expressions* defined for some or all of their components. Certain operations of types and subtypes are called *attributes*; these operations are denoted by the form of name described in section 4.1.4.

7   The term *subcomponent* is used in this manual in place of the term component to indicate either a component, or a component of another component or subcomponent. Where other subcomponents are excluded, the term component is used instead.

8   A given type must not have a subcomponent whose type is the given type itself.

9   The name of a class of types is used in this manual as a qualifier for objects and values that have a type of the class considered. For example, the term "array object" is used for an object whose type is an array type; similarly, the term "access value" is used for a value of an access type.

Note:

10   The set of values of a subtype is a subset of the values of the base type. This subset need not be a proper subset; it can be an empty subset.

11   *References:* access type 3.8, array type 3.6, assignment 5.2, attribute 4.1.4, component of an array 3.6, component of a record 3.7, discriminant constraint 3.7.2, enumeration type 3.5.1, integer type 3.5.4, object 3.2.1, private type 7.4, qualified expression 4.7, real type 3.5.6, record type 3.7, subtype declaration 3.3.2, task type 9.1, type declaration 3.3.1

3.3.1 Type Declarations

A type declaration declares a type.

```
type_declaration  ::=  full_type_declaration
   |  incomplete_type_declaration | private_type_declaration

full_type_declaration ::=
      type identifier [discriminant_part] is type_definition;

type_definition ::=
      enumeration_type_definition  |  integer_type_definition
   |  real_type_definition         |  array_type_definition
   |  record_type_definition       |  access_type_definition
`  |  derived_type_definition
```

The elaboration of a full type declaration consists of the elaboration of the discriminant part, if any (except in the case of the full type declaration for an incomplete or private type declaration), and of the elaboration of the type definition.

The types created by the elaboration of distinct type definitions are distinct types. Moreover, the elaboration of the type definition for a numeric or derived type creates both a base type and a sub-type of the base type; the same holds for a constrained array definition (one of the two forms of array type definition).

The simple name declared by a full type declaration denotes the declared type, unless the type declaration declares both a base type and a subtype of the base type, in which case the simple name denotes the subtype, and the base type is anonymous. A type is said to be *anonymous* if it has no simple name. For explanatory purposes, this reference manual sometimes refers to an anonymous type by a pseudo-name, written in italics, and uses such pseudo-names at places where the syntax normally requires an identifier.

Examples of type definitions:

```
(WHITE, RED, YELLOW, GREEN, BLUE, BROWN, BLACK)
range 1 .. 72
array(1 .. 10) of INTEGER
```

Examples of type declarations:

```
type COLOR    is (WHITE, RED, YELLOW, GREEN, BLUE, BROWN, BLACK);
type COLUMN   is range 1 .. 72;
type TABLE    is array(1 .. 10) of INTEGER;
```

Notes:

Two type definitions always define two distinct types, even if they are textually identical. Thus, the array type definitions given in the declarations of A and B below define distinct types.

```
A : array(1 .. 10) of BOOLEAN;
B : array(1 .. 10) of BOOLEAN;
```

If A and B are declared by a multiple object declaration as below, their types are nevertheless different, since the multiple object declaration is equivalent to the above two single object declarations.

```
A, B : array(1 .. 10) of BOOLEAN;
```

10   Incomplete type declarations are used for the definition of recursive and mutually dependent types (see 3.8.1). Private type declarations are used in package specifications and in generic parameter declarations (see 7.4 and 12.1).

11   *References:* access type definition 3.8, array type definition 3.6, base type 3.3, constrained array definition 3.6, constrained subtype 3.3, declaration 3.1, derived type 3.4, derived type definition 3.4, discriminant part 3.7.1, elaboration 3.9, enumeration type definition 3.5.1, identifier 2.3, incomplete type declaration 3.8.1, integer type definition 3.5.4, multiple object declaration 3.2, numeric type 3.5, private type declaration 7.4, real type definition 3.5.6, reserved word 2.9, type 3.3

3.3.2 Subtype Declarations

1   A subtype declaration declares a subtype.

2
```
subtype_declaration ::=
    subtype identifier is subtype_indication;

subtype_indication ::=  type_mark [constraint]

type_mark ::= type_name | subtype_name

constraint ::=
      range_constraint  | floating_point_constraint | fixed_point_constraint
    | index_constraint  | discriminant_constraint
```

3   A type mark denotes a type or a subtype. If a type mark is the name of a type, the type mark denotes this type and also the corresponding unconstrained subtype. The *base type of a type mark* is, by definition, the base type of the type or subtype denoted by the type mark.

4   A subtype indication defines a subtype of the base type of the type mark.

5   If an index constraint appears after a type mark in a subtype indication, the type mark must not already impose an index constraint. Likewise for a discriminant constraint, the type mark must not already impose a discriminant constraint.

6   The elaboration of a subtype declaration consists of the elaboration of the subtype indication. The elaboration of a subtype indication creates a subtype. If the subtype indication does not include a constraint, the subtype is the same as that denoted by the type mark. The elaboration of a subtype indication that includes a constraint proceeds as follows:

7   (a) The constraint is first elaborated.

8   (b) A check is then made that the constraint is *compatible* with the type or subtype denoted by the type mark.

9   The condition imposed by a constraint is the condition obtained after elaboration of the constraint. (The rules of constraint elaboration are such that the expressions and ranges of constraints are evaluated by the elaboration of these constraints.) The rules defining compatibility are given for each form of constraint in the appropriate section. These rules are such that if a constraint is compatible with a subtype, then the condition imposed by the constraint cannot contradict any condition already imposed by the subtype on its values. The exception CONSTRAINT_ERROR is raised if any check of compatibility fails.

Examples of subtype declarations: 10

```
subtype RAINBOW    is COLOR range RED .. BLUE;      -- see 3.3.1
subtype RED_BLUE   is RAINBOW;
subtype INT        is INTEGER;
subtype SMALL_INT  is INTEGER range -10 .. 10;
subtype UP_TO_K    is COLUMN range 1 .. K;          -- see 3.3.1
subtype SQUARE     is MATRIX(1 .. 10, 1 .. 10);     -- see 3.6
subtype MALE       is PERSON(SEX => M);             -- see 3.8
```

Note:

A subtype declaration does not define a new type. 11

References: base type 3.3, compatibility of discriminant constraints 3.7.2, compatibility of fixed point constraints 12
3.5.9, compatibility of floating point constraints 3.5.7, compatibility of index constraints 3.6.1, compatibility of range
constraints 3.5, constraint_error exception 11.1, declaration 3.1, discriminant 3.3, discriminant constraint 3.7.2,
elaboration 3.9, evaluation 4.5, expression 4.4, floating point constraint 3.5.7, fixed point constraint 3.5.9, index constraint 3.6.1, range constraint 3.5, reserved word 2.9, subtype 3.3, type 3.3, type name 3.3.1, unconstrained subtype
3.3

3.3.3 Classification of Operations

The set of operations of a type includes the explicitly declared subprograms that have a parameter 1
or result of the type; such subprograms are necessarily declared after the type declaration.

The remaining operations are each implicitly declared for a given type declaration, immediately 2
after the type definition. These implicitly declared operations comprise the *basic* operations, the
predefined operators (see 4.5), and enumeration literals. In the case of a derived type declaration,
the implicitly declared operations include any derived subprograms. The operations implicitly
declared for a given type declaration occur after the type declaration and before the next explicit
declaration, if any. The implicit declarations of derived subprograms occur last.

A basic operation is an operation that is inherent in one of the following: 3

- An assignment (in assignment statements and initializations), an allocator, a membership test, 4
  or a short-circuit control form.

- A selected component, an indexed component, or a slice. 5

- A qualification (in qualified expressions), an explicit type conversion, or an implicit type con- 6
  version of a value of type *universal_integer* or *universal_real* to the corresponding value of
  another numeric type.

- A numeric literal (for a universal type), the literal **null** (for an access type), a string literal, an 7
  aggregate, or an attribute.

For every type or subtype T, the following attribute is defined: 8

T'BASE   The base type of T. This attribute is allowed only as the prefix of the name of 9
             another attribute: for example, T'BASE'FIRST.

Note:

10   Each literal is an operation whose evaluation yields the corresponding value (see 4.2). Likewise, an aggregate is an operation whose evaluation yields a value of a composite type (see 4.3). Some operations of a type *operate on* values of the type, for example, predefined operators and certain subprograms and attributes. The evaluation of some operations of a type *returns* a value of the type, for example, literals and certain functions, attributes, and predefined operators. Assignment is an operation that operates on an object and a value. The evaluation of the operation corresponding to a selected component, an indexed component, or a slice, yields the object or value denoted by this form of name.

11   *References:* aggregate 4.3, allocator 4.8, assignment 5.2, attribute 4.1.4, character literal 2.5, composite type 3.3, conversion 4.6, derived subprogram 3.4, enumeration literal 3.5.1, formal parameter 6.1, function 6.5, indexed component 4.1.1, initial value 3.2.1, literal 4.2, membership test 4.5 4.5.2, null literal 3.8, numeric literal 2.4, numeric type 3.5, object 3.2.1, 6.1, predefined operator 4.5, qualified expression 4.7, selected component 4.1.3, short-circuit control form 4.5 4.5.1, slice 4.1.2, string literal 2.6, subprogram 6, subtype 3.3, type 3.3, type declaration 3.3.1, universal_integer type 3.5.4, universal_real type 3.5.6, universal type 4.10

3.4 Derived Types

1   A derived type definition defines a new (base) type whose characteristics are derived from those of a *parent type;* the new type is called a *derived type.* A derived type definition further defines a *derived subtype,* which is a subtype of the derived type.

2   derived_type_definition ::= **new** subtype_indication

3   The subtype indication that occurs after the reserved word **new** defines the *parent subtype.* The parent type is the base type of the parent subtype. If a constraint exists for the parent subtype, a similar constraint exists for the derived subtype; the only difference is that for a range constraint, and likewise for a floating or fixed point constraint that includes a range constraint, the value of each bound is replaced by the corresponding value of the derived type. The characteristics of the derived type are defined as follows:

4   • The derived type belongs to the same class of types as the parent type. The set of possible values for the derived type is a copy of the set of possible values for the parent type. If the parent type is composite, then the same components exist for the derived type, and the subtype of corresponding components is the same.

5   • For each basic operation of the parent type, there is a corresponding basic operation of the derived type. Explicit type conversion of a value of the parent type into the corresponding value of the derived type is allowed and vice versa as explained in section 4.6.

6   • For each enumeration literal or predefined operator of the parent type there is a corresponding operation for the derived type.

7   • If the parent type is a task type, then for each entry of the parent type there is a corresponding entry for the derived type.

8   • If a default expression exists for a component of an object having the parent type, then the same default expression is used for the corresponding component of an object having the derived type.

- If the parent type is an access type, then the parent and the derived type share the same collection; there is a null access value for the derived type and it is the default initial value of that type. 9

- If an explicit representation clause exists for the parent type and if this clause appears before the derived type definition, then there is a corresponding representation clause (an implicit one) for the derived type. 10

- Certain subprograms that are operations of the parent type are said to be *derivable*. For each derivable subprogram of the parent type, there is a corresponding derived subprogram for the derived type. Two kinds of derivable subprograms exist. First, if the parent type is declared immediately within the visible part of a package, then a subprogram that is itself explicitly declared immediately within the visible part becomes derivable after the end of the visible part, if it is an operation of the parent type. (The explicit declaration is by a subprogram declaration, a renaming declaration, or a generic instantiation.) Second, if the parent type is itself a derived type, then any subprogram that has been derived by this parent type is further derivable, unless the parent type is declared in the visible part of a package and the derived subprogram is hidden by a derivable subprogram of the first kind. 11

Each operation of the derived type is implicitly declared at the place of the derived type declaration. The implicit declarations of any derived subprograms occur last. 12

The specification of a derived subprogram is obtained implicitly by systematic replacement of the parent type by the derived type in the specification of the derivable subprogram. Any subtype of the parent type is likewise replaced by a subtype of the derived type with a similar constraint (as for the transformation of a constraint of the parent subtype into the corresponding constraint of the derived subtype). Finally, any expression of the parent type is made to be the operand of a type conversion that yields a result of the derived type. 13

Calling a derived subprogram is equivalent to calling the corresponding subprogram of the parent type, in which each actual parameter that is of the derived type is replaced by a type conversion of this actual parameter to the parent type (this means that a conversion to the parent type happens before the call for the modes **in** and **in out**; a reverse conversion to the derived type happens after the call for the modes **in out** and **out**, see 6.4.1). In addition, if the result of a called function is of the parent type, this result is converted to the derived type. 14

If a derived or private type is declared immediately within the visible part of a package, then, within this visible part, this type must not be used as the parent type of a derived type definition. (For private types, see also section 7.4.1.) 15

For the elaboration of a derived type definition, the subtype indication is first elaborated, the derived type is then created, and finally, the derived subtype is created. 16

Examples: 17

```
type LOCAL_COORDINATE is new COORDINATE;      -- two different types
type MIDWEEK is new DAY range TUE .. THU;      -- see 3.5.1
type COUNTER is new POSITIVE;                  -- same range as POSITIVE

type SPECIAL_KEY is new KEY_MANAGER.KEY;       -- see 7.4.2
-- the derived subprograms have the following specifications:

-- procedure GET_KEY(K : out SPECIAL_KEY);
-- function "<"(X,Y : SPECIAL_KEY) return BOOLEAN;
```

Notes:

18   The rules of derivation of basic operations and enumeration literals imply that the notation for any literal or aggregate of the derived type is the same as for the parent type; such literals and aggregates are said to be *overloaded*. Similarly, it follows that the notation for denoting a component, a discriminant, an entry, a slice, or an attribute is the same for the derived type as for the parent type.

19   Hiding of a derived subprogram is allowed even within the same declarative region (see 8.3). A derived subprogram hides a predefined operator that has the same parameter and result type profile (see 6.6).

20   A generic subprogram declaration is not derivable since it declares a generic unit rather than a subprogram. On the other hand, an instantiation of a generic subprogram is a (nongeneric) subprogram, which is derivable if it satisfies the requirements for derivability of subprograms.

21   If the parent type is a boolean type, the predefined relational operators of the derived type deliver a result of the predefined type BOOLEAN (see 4.5.2).

22   If a representation clause is given for the parent type but appears after the derived type declaration, then no corresponding representation clause applies to the derived type; hence an explicit representation clause for such a derived type is allowed.

23   For a derived subprogram, if a parameter belongs to the derived type, the subtype of this parameter need not have any value in common with the derived subtype.

24   *References:* access value 3.8, actual parameter 6.4.1, aggregate 4.3, attribute 4.1.4, base type 3.3, basic operation 3.3.3, boolean type 3.5.3, bound of a range 3.5, class of type 3.3, collection 3.8, component 3.3, composite type 3.3, constraint 3.3, conversion 4.6, declaration 3.1, declarative region 8.1, default expression 3.2.1, default initial value for an access type 3.8, discriminant 3.3, elaboration 3.9, entry 9.5, enumeration literal 3.5.1, floating point constraint 3.5.7, fixed point constraint 3.5.9, formal parameter 6.1, function call 6.4, generic declaration 12.1, immediately within 8.1, implicit declaration 3.1, literal 4.2, mode 6.1, overloading 6.6 8.7, package 7, package specification 7.1, parameter association 6.4, predefined operator 4.5, private type 7.4, procedure 6, procedure call statement 6.4, range constraint 3.5, representation clause 13.1, reserved word 2.9, slice 4.1.2, subprogram 6, subprogram specification 6.1, subtype indication 3.3.2, subtype 3.3, type 3.3, type definition 3.3.1, visible part 7.2

3.5 Scalar Types

1   Scalar types comprise enumeration types, integer types, and real types. Enumeration types and integer types are called *discrete* types; each value of a discrete type has a position number which is an integer value. Integer types and real types are called *numeric* types. All scalar types are ordered, that is, all relational operators are predefined for their values.

2   range_constraint ::= **range** range

        range ::= *range*_attribute
          | simple_expression .. simple_expression

A range specifies a subset of values of a scalar type. The range L .. R specifies the values from L to R inclusive if the relation L <= R is true. The values L and R are called the *lower bound* and *upper bound* of the range, respectively. A value V is said to *satisfy* a range constraint if it belongs to the range; the value V is said to *belong* to the range if the relations L <= V and V <= R are both TRUE. A *null* range is a range for which the relation R < L is TRUE; no value belongs to a null range. The operators <= and < in the above definitions are the predefined operators of the scalar type. ₃

If a range constraint is used in a subtype indication, either directly or as part of a floating or fixed point constraint, the type of the simple expressions (likewise, of the bounds of a range attribute) must be the same as the base type of the type mark of the subtype indication. A range constraint is *compatible* with a subtype if each bound of the range belongs to the subtype, or if the range constraint defines a null range; otherwise the range constraint is not compatible with the subtype. ₄

The elaboration of a range constraint consists of the evaluation of the range. The evaluation of a range defines its lower bound and its upper bound. If simple expressions are given to specify the bounds, the evaluation of the range evaluates these simple expressions in some order that is not defined by the language. ₅

Attributes ₆

For any scalar type T or for any subtype T of a scalar type, the following attributes are defined: ₇

T'FIRST   Yields the lower bound of T. The value of this attribute has the same type as T. ₈

T'LAST   Yields the upper bound of T. The value of this attribute has the same type as T. ₉

Note:

Indexing and iteration rules use values of discrete types. ₁₀

References: attribute 4.1.4, constraint 3.3, enumeration type 3.5.1, erroneous 1.6, evaluation 4.5, fixed point ₁₁
constraint 3.5.9, floating point constraint 3.5.7, index 3.6, integer type 3.5.4, loop statement 5.5, range attribute
3.6.2, real type 3.5.6, relational operator 4.5 4.5.2, satisfy a constraint 3.3, simple expression 4.4, subtype indication
3.3.2, type mark 3.3.2

3.5.1 Enumeration Types

An enumeration type definition defines an enumeration type. ₁

```
enumeration_type_definition ::=
    (enumeration_literal_specification {, enumeration_literal_specification})

enumeration_literal_specification ::=  enumeration_literal

enumeration_literal ::=  identifier | character_literal
```
  ₂

The identifiers and character literals listed by an enumeration type definition must be distinct. Each enumeration literal specification is the declaration of the corresponding enumeration literal: this declaration is equivalent to the declaration of a parameterless function, the designator being the enumeration literal, and the result type being the enumeration type. The elaboration of an enumeration type definition creates an enumeration type; this elaboration includes that of every enumeration literal specification. ₃

Enumeration Types 3.5.1

4   Each enumeration literal yields a different enumeration value. The predefined order relations between enumeration values follow the order of corresponding position numbers. The position number of the value of the first listed enumeration literal is zero; the position number for each other enumeration literal is one more than for its predecessor in the list.

5   If the same identifier or character literal is specified in more than one enumeration type definition, the corresponding literals are said to be *overloaded*. At any place where an overloaded enumeration literal occurs in the text of a program, the type of the enumeration literal must be determinable from the context (see 8.7).

6   *Examples:*

```
type DAY     is (MON, TUE, WED, THU, FRI, SAT, SUN);
type SUIT    is (CLUBS, DIAMONDS, HEARTS, SPADES);
type GENDER  is (M, F);
type LEVEL   is (LOW, MEDIUM, URGENT);
type COLOR   is (WHITE, RED, YELLOW, GREEN, BLUE, BROWN, BLACK);
type LIGHT   is (RED, AMBER, GREEN); -- RED and GREEN are overloaded

type HEXA    is ('A', 'B', 'C', 'D', 'E', 'F');
type MIXED   is ('A', 'B', '*', B, NONE, '?', '%');

subtype WEEKDAY is DAY    range MON .. FRI;
subtype MAJOR   is SUIT   range HEARTS .. SPADES;
subtype RAINBOW is COLOR  range RED .. BLUE;  -- the color RED, not the light
```

Note:

7   If an enumeration literal occurs in a context that does not otherwise suffice to determine the type of the literal, then qualification by the name of the enumeration type is one way to resolve the ambiguity (see 8.7).

8   *References:* character literal 2.5, declaration 3.1, designator 6.1, elaboration 3.9, 6.1, function 6.5, identifier 2.3, name 4.1, overloading 6.6 8.7, position number 3.5, qualified expression 4.7, relational operator 4.5 4.5.2, type 3.3, type definition 3.3.1

3.5.2 Character Types

1   An enumeration type is said to be a character type if at least one of its enumeration literals is a character literal. The predefined type CHARACTER is a character type whose values are the 128 characters of the *ASCII* character set. Each of the 95 graphic characters of this character set is denoted by the corresponding character literal.

2   *Example:*

```
type ROMAN_DIGIT is ('I', 'V', 'X', 'L', 'C', 'D', 'M');
```

Notes:

3   The predefined package ASCII includes the declaration of constants denoting control characters and of constants denoting graphic characters that are not in the basic character set.

A conventional character set such as *EBCDIC* can be declared as a character type; the internal codes of the characters can be specified by an enumeration representation clause as explained in section 13.3. ₄

References: ascii predefined package C, basic character 2.1, character literal 2.5, constant 3.2.1, declaration 3.1, enumeration type 3.5.1, graphic character 2.1, identifier 2.3, literal 4.2, predefined type C, type 3.3 ₅

3.5.3 Boolean Types

There is a predefined enumeration type named BOOLEAN. It contains the two literals FALSE and TRUE ordered with the relation FALSE < TRUE. A boolean type is either the type BOOLEAN or a type that is derived, directly or indirectly, from a boolean type. ₁

References: derived type 3.4, enumeration literal 3.5.1, enumeration type 3.5.1, relational operator 4.5 4.5.2, type 3.3 ₂

3.5.4 Integer Types

An integer type definition defines an integer type whose set of values includes at least those of the specified range. ₁

    integer_type_definition ::=   range_constraint ₂

If a range constraint is used as an integer type definition, each bound of the range must be defined by a static expression of some integer type, but the two bounds need not have the same integer type. (Negative bounds are allowed.) ₃

A type declaration of the form: ₄

    type T is range L .. R;

is, by definition, equivalent to the following declarations: ₅

    type *integer_type* is new predefined_integer_type;
    subtype T is *integer_type* range *integer_type*(L) .. *integer_type*(R);

where *integer_type* is an anonymous type, and where the predefined integer type is implicitly selected by the implementation, so as to contain the values L to R inclusive. The integer type declaration is illegal if none of the predefined integer types satisfies this requirement, excepting *universal_integer*. The elaboration of the declaration of an integer type consists of the elaboration of the equivalent type and subtype declarations. ₆

The predefined integer types include the type INTEGER. An implementation may also have predefined types such as SHORT_INTEGER and LONG_INTEGER, which have (substantially) shorter and longer ranges, respectively, than INTEGER. The range of each of these types must be symmetric about zero, excepting an extra negative value which may exist in some implementations. The base type of each of these types is the type itself. ₇

8   Integer literals are the literals of an anonymous predefined integer type that is called *universal_integer* in this reference manual. Other integer types have no literals. However, for each integer type there exists an implicit conversion that converts a *universal_integer* value into the corresponding value (if any) of the integer type. The circumstances under which these implicit conversions are invoked are described in section 4.6.

9   The position number of an integer value is the corresponding value of the type *universal_integer*.

10   The same arithmetic operators are predefined for all integer types (see 4.5). The exception NUMERIC_ERROR is raised by the execution of an operation (in particular an implicit conversion) that cannot deliver the correct result (that is, if the value corresponding to the mathematical result is not a value of the integer type). However, an implementation is not required to raise the exception NUMERIC_ERROR if the operation is part of a larger expression whose result can be computed correctly, as described in section 11.6.

11   *Examples:*

```
type PAGE_NUM    is range 1 .. 2_000;
type LINE_SIZE   is range 1 .. MAX_LINE_SIZE;

subtype SMALL_INT    is INTEGER    range -10 .. 10;
subtype COLUMN_PTR   is LINE_SIZE  range 1 .. 10;
subtype BUFFER_SIZE  is INTEGER    range 0 .. MAX;
```

Notes:

12   The name declared by an integer type declaration is a subtype name. On the other hand, the predefined operators of an integer type deliver results whose range is defined by the parent predefined type; such a result need not belong to the declared subtype, in which case an attempt to assign the result to a variable of the integer subtype raises the exception CONSTRAINT_ERROR .

13   The smallest (most negative) value supported by the predefined integer types of an implementation is the named number SYSTEM.MIN_INT and the largest (most positive) value is SYSTEM.MAX_INT (see 13.7).

14   *References:* anonymous type 3.3.1, belong to a subtype 3.3, bound of a range 3.5, constraint_error exception 11.1, conversion 4.6, identifier 2.3, integer literal 2.4, literal 4.2, numeric_error exception 11.1, parent type 3.4, predefined operator 4.5, range constraint 3.5, static expression 4.9, subtype declaration 3.3.2, system predefined package 13.7, type 3.3, type declaration 3.3.1, type definition 3.3.1, universal type 4.10

3.5.5 Operations of Discrete Types

1   The basic operations of a discrete type include the operations involved in assignment, the membership tests, and qualification; for a boolean type they include the short-circuit control forms; for an integer type they include the explicit conversion of values of other numeric types to the integer type, and the implicit conversion of values of the type *universal_integer* to the type.

2   Finally, for every discrete type or subtype T, the basic operations include the attributes listed below. In this presentation, T is referred to as being a subtype (the subtype T) for any property that depends on constraints imposed by T; other properties are stated in terms of the base type of T.

The first group of attributes yield characteristics of the subtype T. This group includes the attribute   3
BASE (see 3.3.2), the attributes FIRST and LAST (see 3.5), the representation attribute SIZE (see
13.7.2), and the attribute WIDTH defined as follows:

T'WIDTH Yields the maximum image length over all values of the subtype T (the *image* is the   4
sequence of characters returned by the attribute IMAGE, see below). Yields zero
for a null range. The value of this attribute is of the type *universal_integer*.

All attributes of the second group are functions with a single parameter. The corresponding actual   5
parameter is indicated below by X.

T'POS This attribute is a function. The parameter X must be a value of the base type of T.   6
The result type is the type *universal_integer*. The result is the position number of
the value of the parameter.

T'VAL This attribute is a special function with a single parameter which can be of any   7
integer type. The result type is the base type of T. The result is the value whose
position number is the *universal_integer* value corresponding to X. The exception
CONSTRAINT_ERROR is raised if the *universal_integer* value corresponding to X is
not in the range T'POS(T'BASE'FIRST) .. T'POS(T'BASE'LAST).

T'SUCC This attribute is a function. The parameter X must be a value of the base type of T.   8
The result type is the base type of T. The result is the value whose position number
is one greater than that of X. The exception CONSTRAINT_ERROR is raised if X
equals T'BASE'LAST.

T'PRED This attribute is a function. The parameter X must be a value of the base type of T.   9
The result type is the base type of T. The result is the value whose position number
is one less than that of X. The exception CONSTRAINT_ERROR is raised if X equals
T'BASE'FIRST.

T'IMAGE This attribute is a function. The parameter X must be a value of the base type of T.   10
The result type is the predefined type STRING. The result is the *image* of the value
of X, that is, a sequence of characters representing the value in display form. The
image of an integer value is the corresponding decimal literal; without underlines,
leading zeros, exponent, or trailing spaces; but with a single leading character that
is either a minus sign or a space. The lower bound of the image is one.

  The image of an enumeration value is either the corresponding identifier in upper   11
case or the corresponding character literal (including the two apostrophes);
neither leading nor trailing spaces are included. The image of a character C, other
than a graphic character, is implementation-defined; the only requirement is that
the image must be such that C equals CHARACTER'VALUE (CHARACTER'IMAGE (C)).

T'VALUE This attribute is a function. The parameter X must be a value of the predefined type   12
STRING. The result type is the base type of T. Any leading and any trailing spaces
of the sequence of characters that corresponds to the parameter are ignored.

  For an enumeration type, if the sequence of characters has the syntax of an   13
enumeration literal and if this literal exists for the base type of T, the result is the
corresponding enumeration value. For an integer type, if the sequence of
characters has the syntax of an integer literal, with an optional single leading
character that is a plus or minus sign, and if there is a corresponding value in the
base type of T, the result is this value. In any other case, the exception
CONSTRAINT_ERROR is raised.

14   In addition, the attributes A'SIZE and A'ADDRESS are defined for an object A of a discrete type (see 13.7.2).

15   Besides the basic operations, the operations of a discrete type include the predefined relational operators. For enumeration types, operations include enumeration literals. For boolean types, operations include the predefined unary logical negation operator **not**, and the predefined logical operators. For integer types, operations include the predefined *arithmetic* operators: these are the binary and unary adding operators - and +, all multiplying operators, the unary operator **abs**, and the exponentiating operator.

16   The operations of a subtype are the corresponding operations of its base type except for the following: assignment, membership tests, qualification, explicit type conversions, and the attributes of the first group; the effect of each of these operations depends on the subtype (assignments, membership tests, qualifications, and conversions involve a subtype check; attributes of the first group yield a characteristic of the subtype).

Notes:

17   For a subtype of a discrete type, the results delivered by the attributes SUCC, PRED, VAL, and VALUE need not belong to the subtype; similarly, the actual parameters of the attributes POS, SUCC, PRED, and IMAGE need not belong to the subtype. The following relations are satisfied (in the absence of an exception) by these attributes:

```
T'POS(T'SUCC(X))  =  T'POS(X) +  1
T'POS(T'PRED(X))  =  T'POS(X) -  1

T'VAL(T'POS(X))   =  X
T'POS(T'VAL(N))   =  N
```

18   *Examples:*

```
--  For the types and subtypes declared in section 3.5.1 we have:

--  COLOR'FIRST     = WHITE,     COLOR'LAST     = BLACK
--  RAINBOW'FIRST   = RED,       RAINBOW'LAST   = BLUE

--  COLOR'SUCC(BLUE)   = RAINBOW'SUCC(BLUE)   = BROWN
--  COLOR'POS(BLUE)    = RAINBOW'POS(BLUE)    = 4
--  COLOR'VAL(0)       = RAINBOW'VAL(0)       = WHITE
```

19   *References:* abs operator 4.5 4.5.6, assignment 5.2, attribute 4.1.4, base type 3.3, basic operation 3.3.3, binary adding operator 4.5 4.5.3, boolean type 3.5.3, bound of a range 3.5, character literal 2.5, constraint 3.3, constraint_error exception 11.1, conversion 4.6, discrete type 3.5, enumeration literal 3.5.1, exponentiating operator 4.5 4.5.6, function 6.5, graphic character 2.1, identifier 2.3, integer type 3.5.4, logical operator 4.5 4.5.1, membership test 4.5 4.5.2, multiplying operator 4.5 4.5.5, not operator 4.5 4.5.6, numeric literal 2.4, numeric type 3.5, object 3.2, operation 3.3, position number 3.5, predefined operator 4.5, predefined type C, qualified expression 4.7, relational operator 4.5 4.5.2, short-circuit control form 4.5 4.5.1, string type 3.6.3, subtype 3.3, type 3.3, unary adding operator 4.5 4.5.4, universal_integer type 3.5.4, universal type 4.10

3.5.5 Operations of Discrete Types

3.5.6 Real Types

Real types provide approximations to the real numbers, with relative bounds on errors for floating point types, and with absolute bounds for fixed point types.

    real_type_definition ::=
        floating_point_constraint | fixed_point_constraint

A set of numbers called *model numbers* is associated with each real type. Error bounds on the predefined operations are given in terms of the model numbers. An implementation of the type must include at least these model numbers and represent them exactly.

An implementation-dependent set of numbers, called the *safe numbers*, is also associated with each real type. The set of safe numbers of a real type must include at least the set of model numbers of the type. The range of safe numbers is allowed to be larger than the range of model numbers, but error bounds on the predefined operations for safe numbers are given by the same rules as for model numbers. Safe numbers therefore provide guaranteed error bounds for operations on an implementation-dependent range of numbers; in contrast, the range of model numbers depends only on the real type definition and is therefore independent of the implementation.

Real literals are the literals of an anonymous predefined real type that is called *universal_real* in this reference manual. Other real types have no literals. However, for each real type, there exists an implicit conversion that converts a *universal_real* value into a value of the real type. The conditions under which these implicit conversions are invoked are described in section 4.6. If the *universal_real* value is a safe number, the implicit conversion delivers the corresponding value; if it belongs to the range of safe numbers but is not a safe number, then the converted value can be any value within the range defined by the safe numbers next above and below the *universal_real* value.

The execution of an operation that yields a value of a real type may raise the exception NUMERIC_ERROR, as explained in section 4.5.7, if it cannot deliver a correct result (that is, if the value corresponding to one of the possible mathematical results does not belong to the range of safe numbers); in particular, this exception can be raised by an implicit conversion. However, an implementation is not required to raise the exception NUMERIC_ERROR if the operation is part of a larger expression whose result can be computed correctly (see 11.6).

The elaboration of a real type definition includes the elaboration of the floating or fixed point constraint and creates a real type.

Note:

An algorithm written to rely only upon the minimum numerical properties guaranteed by the type definition for model numbers will be portable without further precautions.

References: conversion 4.6, elaboration 3.9, fixed point constraint 3.5.9, floating point constraint 3.5.7, literal 4.2, numeric_error exception 11.1, predefined operation 3.3.3, real literal 2.4, type 3.3, type definition 3.3.1, universal type 4.10

3.5.7 Floating Point Types

1   For floating point types, the error bound is specified as a relative precision by giving the required minimum number of significant decimal digits.

2   floating_point_constraint ::=
        floating_accuracy_definition [range_constraint]

    floating_accuracy_definition ::= **digits** *static*_simple_expression

3   The minimum number of significant decimal digits is specified by the value of the static simple expression of the floating accuracy definition. This value must belong to some integer type and must be positive (nonzero); it is denoted by D in the remainder of this section. If the floating point constraint is used as a real type definition and includes a range constraint, then each bound of the range must be defined by a static expression of some real type, but the two bounds need not have the same real type.

4   For a given *radix*, the following canonical form is defined for any floating point model number other than zero:

    sign $*$ *mantissa* $*$ (*radix* $**$ *exponent*)

5   In this form: *sign* is either +1 or -1; *mantissa* is expressed in a number base given by *radix*; and *exponent* is an integer number (possibly negative) such that the integer part of mantissa is zero and the first digit of its fractional part is not a zero.

6   The specified number D is the minimum number of decimal digits required after the point in the decimal mantissa (that is, if *radix* is ten). The value of D in turn determines a corresponding number B that is the minimum number of binary digits required after the point in the binary mantissa (that is, if *radix* is two). The number B associated with D is the smallest value such that the relative precision of the binary form is no less than that specified for the decimal form. (The number B is the integer next above (D$*$log(10)/log(2)) + 1.)

7   The model numbers defined by a floating accuracy definition comprise zero and all numbers whose binary canonical form has exactly B digits after the point in the mantissa and an exponent in the range -4$*$B .. +4$*$B. The guaranteed minimum accuracy of operations of a floating point type is defined in terms of the model numbers of the floating point constraint that forms the corresponding real type definition (see 4.5.7).

8   The predefined floating point types include the type FLOAT. An implementation may also have predefined types such as SHORT_FLOAT and LONG_FLOAT, which have (substantially) less and more accuracy, respectively, than FLOAT. The base type of each predefined floating point type is the type itself. The model numbers of each predefined floating point type are defined in terms of the number D of decimal digits returned by the attribute DIGITS (see 3.5.8).

9   For each predefined floating point type (consequently also for each type derived therefrom), a set of safe numbers is defined as follows. The safe numbers have the same number B of mantissa digits as the model numbers of the type and have an exponent in the range -E .. +E where E is implementation-defined and at least equal to the 4$*$B of model numbers. (Consequently, the safe numbers include the model numbers.) The rules defining the accuracy of operations with model and safe numbers are given in section 4.5.7. The safe numbers of a subtype are those of its base type.

A floating point type declaration of one of the two forms (that is, with or without the optional range constraint indicated by the square brackets): 10

    type T is digits D [range L .. R];

is, by definition, equivalent to the following declarations: 11

    type *floating_point_type* is new predefined_floating_point_type;
    subtype T is *floating_point_type* digits D
    [range *floating_point_type*(L) .. *floating_point_type*(R)];

where *floating_point_type* is an anonymous type, and where the predefined floating point type is 12
implicitly selected by the implementation so that its model numbers include the model numbers
defined by D; furthermore, if a range L .. R is supplied, then both L and R must belong to the range
of safe numbers. The floating point declaration is illegal if none of the predefined floating point
types satisfies these requirements, excepting *universal_real*. The maximum number of digits that
can be specified in a floating accuracy definition is given by the system-dependent named number
SYSTEM.MAX_DIGITS (see 13.7.1).

The elaboration of a floating point type declaration consists of the elaboration of the equivalent 13
type and subtype declarations.

If a floating point constraint follows a type mark in a subtype indication, the type mark must 14
denote a floating point type or subtype. The floating point constraint is *compatible* with the type
mark only if the number D specified in the floating accuracy definition is not greater than the corresponding number D for the type or subtype denoted by the type mark. Furthermore, if the
floating point constraint includes a range constraint, the floating point constraint is compatible
with the type mark only if the range constraint is, itself, compatible with the type mark.

The elaboration of such a subtype indication includes the elaboration of the range constraint, if 15
there is one; it creates a floating point subtype whose model numbers are defined by the corresponding floating accuracy definition. A value of a floating point type belongs to a floating point
subtype if and only if it belongs to the range defined by the subtype.

The same arithmetic operators are predefined for all floating point types (see 4.5). 16

Notes:

A range constraint is allowed in a floating point subtype indication, either directly after the type 17
mark, or as part of a floating point constraint. In either case the bounds of the range must belong
to the base type of the type mark (see 3.5). The imposition of a floating point constraint on a type
mark in a subtype indication cannot reduce the allowed range of values unless it includes a range
constraint (the range of model numbers that correspond to the specified number of digits can be
smaller than the range of numbers of the type mark). A value that belongs to a floating point subtype need not be a model number of the subtype.

Examples: 18

    type COEFFICIENT is digits 10 range -1.0 .. 1.0;

    type REAL   is digits 8;
    type MASS is digits 7 range 0.0 .. 1.0E35;

    subtype SHORT_COEFF is COEFFICIENT digits 5;   -- a subtype with less accuracy
    subtype PROBABILITY is REAL range 0.0 .. 1.0;   -- a subtype with a smaller range

Notes on the examples:

19   The implemented accuracy for COEFFICIENT is that of a predefined type having at least 10 digits of precision. Consequently the specification of 5 digits of precision for the subtype SHORT_COEFF is allowed. The largest model number for the type MASS is approximately 1.27E30 and hence less than the specified upper bound (1.0E35). Consequently the declaration of this type is legal only if this upper bound is in the range of the safe numbers of a predefined floating point type having at least 7 digits of precision.

20   *References:* anonymous type 3.3.1, arithmetic operator 3.5.5 4.5, based literal 2.4.2, belong to a subtype 3.3, bound of a range 3.5, compatible 3.3.2, derived type 3.4, digit 2.1, elaboration 3.1 3.9, error bound 3.5.6, exponent 2.4.1 integer type 3.5.4, model number 3.5.6, operation 3.3, predefined operator 4.5, predefined type C, range constraint 3.5, real type 3.5.6, real type definition 3.5.6, safe number 3.5.6, simple expression 4.4, static expression 4.9, subtype declaration 3.3.2, subtype indication 3.3.2, subtype 3.3, type 3.3, type declaration 3.3.1, type mark 3.3.2

3.5.8 Operations of Floating Point Types

1   The basic operations of a floating point type include the operations involved in assignment, membership tests, qualification, the explicit conversion of values of other numeric types to the floating point type, and the implicit conversion of values of the type *universal_real* to the type.

2   In addition, for every floating point type or subtype T, the basic operations include the attributes listed below. In this presentation, T is referred to as being a subtype (the subtype T) for any property that depends on constraints imposed by T; other properties are stated in terms of the base type of T.

3   The first group of attributes yield characteristics of the subtype T. The attributes of this group are the attribute BASE (see 3.3.2), the attributes FIRST and LAST (see 3.5), the representation attribute SIZE (see 13.7.2), and the following attributes:

4   T'DIGITS   Yields the number of decimal digits in the decimal mantissa of model numbers of the subtype T. (This attribute yields the number D of section 3.5.7.) The value of this attribute is of the type *universal_integer*.

5   T'MANTISSA   Yields the number of binary digits in the binary mantissa of model numbers of the subtype T. (This attribute yields the number B of section 3.5.7.) The value of this attribute is of the type *universal_integer*.

6   T'EPSILON   Yields the absolute value of the difference between the model number 1.0 and the next model number above, for the subtype T. The value of this attribute is of the type *universal_real*.

7   T'EMAX   Yields the largest exponent value in the binary canonical form of model numbers of the subtype T. (This attribute yields the product 4∗B of section 3.5.7.) The value of this attribute is of the type *universal_integer*.

8   T'SMALL   Yields the smallest positive (nonzero) model number of the subtype T. The value of this attribute is of the type *universal_real*.

9   T'LARGE   Yields the largest positive model number of the subtype T. The value of this attribute is of the type *universal_real*.

The attributes of the second group include the following attributes which yield characteristics of the safe numbers: [10]

T'SAFE_EMAX   Yields the largest exponent value in the binary canonical form of safe numbers of the base type of T. (This attribute yields the number E of section 3.5.7.) The value of this attribute is of the type *universal_integer*. [11]

T'SAFE_SMALL   Yields the smallest positive (nonzero) safe number of the base type of T. The value of this attribute is of the type *universal_real*. [12]

T'SAFE_LARGE   Yields the largest positive safe number of the base type of T. The value of this attribute is of the type *universal_real*. [13]

In addition, the attributes A'SIZE and A'ADDRESS are defined for an object A of a floating point type (see 13.7.2). Finally, for each floating point type there are machine-dependent attributes that are not related to model numbers and safe numbers. They correspond to the attribute designators MACHINE_RADIX, MACHINE_MANTISSA, MACHINE_EMAX, MACHINE_EMIN, MACHINE_ROUNDS, and MACHINE_OVERFLOWS (see 13.7.3). [14]

Besides the basic operations, the operations of a floating point type include the relational operators, and the following predefined arithmetic operators: the binary and unary adding operators - and +, the multiplying operators * and /, the unary operator **abs**, and the exponentiating operator. [15]

The operations of a subtype are the corresponding operations of the type except for the following: assignment, membership tests, qualification, explicit conversion, and the attributes of the first group; the effects of these operations are redefined in terms of the subtype. [16]

Notes:

The attributes EMAX, SMALL, LARGE, and EPSILON are provided for convenience. They are all related to MANTISSA by the following formulas: [17]

```
T'EMAX      = 4*T'MANTISSA
T'EPSILON   = 2.0**(1 - T'MANTISSA)
T'SMALL     = 2.0**(-T'EMAX - 1)
T'LARGE     = 2.0**T'EMAX * (1.0 - 2.0**(-T'MANTISSA))
```

The attribute MANTISSA, giving the number of binary digits in the mantissa, is itself related to DIGITS. The following relations hold between the characteristics of the model numbers and those of the safe numbers: [18]

```
T'BASE'EMAX    <= T'SAFE_EMAX
T'BASE'SMALL   >= T'SAFE_SMALL
T'BASE'LARGE   <= T'SAFE_LARGE
```

The attributes T'FIRST and T'LAST need not yield model or safe numbers. If a certain number of digits is specified in the declaration of a type or subtype T, the attribute T'DIGITS yields this number. [19]

References: abs operator 4.5 4.5.6, arithmetic operator 3.5.5 4.5, assignment 5.2, attribute 4.1.4, base type 3.3, basic operation 3.3.3, binary adding operator 4.5 4.5.3, bound of a range 3.5, constraint 3.3, conversion 4.6, digit 2.1, exponentiating operator 4.5 4.5.6, floating point type 3.5.7, membership test 4.5 4.5.2, model number 3.5.6, multiplying operator 4.5 4.5.5, numeric type 3.5, object 3.2, operation 3.3, predefined operator 4.5, qualified expression 4.7, relational operator 4.5 4.5.2, safe number 3.5.6, subtype 3.3, type 3.3, unary adding operator 4.5 4.5.4, universal type 4.10, universal_integer type 3.5.4, universal_real type 3.5.6 [20]

                                Operations of Floating Point Types 3.5.8

3.5.9 Fixed Point Types

1 For fixed point types, the error bound is specified as an absolute value, called the *delta* of the fixed point type.

2
```
fixed_point_constraint ::=
    fixed_accuracy_definition [range_constraint]

fixed_accuracy_definition ::= delta static_simple_expression
```

3 The delta is specified by the value of the static simple expression of the fixed accuracy definition. This value must belong to some real type and must be positive (nonzero). If the fixed point constraint is used as a real type definition, then it must include a range constraint; each bound of the specified range must be defined by a static expression of some real type but the two bounds need not have the same real type. If the fixed point constraint is used in a subtype indication, the range constraint is optional.

4 A canonical form is defined for any fixed point model number other than zero. In this form: *sign* is either +1 or -1; *mantissa* is a positive (nonzero) integer; and any model number is a multiple of a certain positive real number called *small*, as follows:

> *sign* ∗ *mantissa* ∗ *small*

5 For the model numbers defined by a fixed point constraint, the number *small* is chosen as the largest power of two that is not greater than the delta of the fixed accuracy definition. Alternatively, it is possible to specify the value of *small* by a length clause (see 13.2), in which case model numbers are multiples of the specified value. The guaranteed minimum accuracy of operations of a fixed point type is defined in terms of the model numbers of the fixed point constraint that forms the corresponding real type definition (see 4.5.7).

6 For a fixed point constraint that includes a range constraint, the model numbers comprise zero and all multiples of *small* whose *mantissa* can be expressed using exactly B binary digits, where the value of B is chosen as the smallest integer number for which each bound of the specified range is either a model number or lies at most *small* distant from a model number. For a fixed point constraint that does not include a range constraint (this is only allowed after a type mark, in a subtype indication), the model numbers are defined by the delta of the fixed accuracy definition and by the range of the subtype denoted by the type mark.

7 An implementation must have at least one anonymous predefined fixed point type. The base type of each such fixed point type is the type itself. The model numbers of each predefined fixed point type comprise zero and all numbers for which *mantissa* (in the canonical form) has the number of binary digits returned by the attribute MANTISSA, and for which the number *small* has the value returned by the attribute SMALL.

8 A fixed point type declaration of the form:

```
type T is delta D range L .. R;
```

9 is, by definition, equivalent to the following declarations:

```
type fixed_point_type is new predefined_fixed_point_type;
subtype T is fixed_point_type
    range fixed_point_type(L) .. fixed_point_type(R);
```

In these declarations, *fixed_point_type* is an anonymous type, and the predefined fixed point type is implicitly selected by the implementation so that its model numbers include the model numbers defined by the fixed point constraint (that is, by D, L, and R, and possibly by a length clause specifying *small*).

10

The fixed point declaration is illegal if no predefined type satisfies these requirements. The safe numbers of a fixed point type are the model numbers of its base type.

11

The elaboration of a fixed point type declaration consists of the elaboration of the equivalent type and subtype declarations.

12

If the fixed point constraint follows a type mark in a subtype indication, the type mark must denote a fixed point type or subtype. The fixed point constraint is *compatible* with the type mark only if the delta specified by the fixed accuracy definition is not smaller than the delta for the type or subtype denoted by the type mark. Furthermore, if the fixed point constraint includes a range constraint, the fixed point constraint is compatible with the type mark only if the range constraint is, itself, compatible with the type mark.

13

The elaboration of such a subtype indication includes the elaboration of the range constraint, if there is one; it creates a fixed point subtype whose model numbers are defined by the corresponding fixed point constraint and also by the length clause specifying small, if there is one. A value of a fixed point type belongs to a fixed point subtype if and only if it belongs to the range defined by the subtype.

14

The same arithmetic operators are predefined for all fixed point types (see 4.5). Multiplication and division of fixed point values deliver results of an anonymous predefined fixed point type that is called *universal_fixed* in this reference manual; the accuracy of this type is arbitrarily fine. The values of this type must be converted explicitly to some numeric type.

15

Notes:

If S is a subtype of a fixed point type or subtype T, then the set of model numbers of S is a subset of those of T. If a length clause has been given for T, then both S and T have the same value for *small*. Otherwise, since *small* is a power of two, the *small* of S is equal to the *small* of T multiplied by a nonnegative power of two.

16

A range constraint is allowed in a fixed point subtype indication, either directly after the type mark, or as part of a fixed point constraint. In either case the bounds of the range must belong to the base type of the type mark (see 3.5).

17

Examples:

18

```
type VOLT is delta 0.125 range 0.0 .. 255.0;
subtype ROUGH_VOLTAGE is VOLT delta 1.0;  --  same range as VOLT

--  A pure fraction which requires all the available space in a word
--  on a two's complement machine can be declared as the type FRACTION:

DEL : constant := 1.0/2**(WORD_LENGTH - 1);
type FRACTION is delta DEL range -1.0 .. 1.0 - DEL;
```

References: anonymous type 3.3.1, arithmetic operator 3.5.5 4.5, base type 3.3, belong to a subtype 3.3, bound of a range 3.5, compatible 3.3.2, conversion 4.6, elaboration 3.9, error bound 3.5.6, length clause 13.2, model number 3.5.6, numeric type 3.5, operation 3.3, predefined operator 4.5, range constraint 3.5, real type 3.5.6, real type definition 3.5.6, safe number 3.5.6, simple expression 4.4, static expression 4.9, subtype 3.3, subtype declaration 3.3.2, subtype indication 3.3.2, type 3.3, type declaration 3.3.1, type mark 3.3.2

19

3.5.10 Operations of Fixed Point Types

1   The basic operations of a fixed point type include the operations involved in assignment, membership tests, qualification, the explicit conversion of values of other numeric types to the fixed point type, and the implicit conversion of values of the type *universal_real* to the type.

2   In addition, for every fixed point type or subtype T the basic operations include the attributes listed below. In this presentation T is referred to as being a subtype (the subtype T) for any property that depends on constraints imposed by T; other properties are stated in terms of the base type of T.

3   The first group of attributes yield characteristics of the subtype T. The attributes of this group are the attributes BASE (see 3.3.2), the attributes FIRST and LAST (see 3.5), the representation attribute SIZE (see 13.7.2) and the following attributes:

4   T'DELTA   Yields the value of the delta specified in the fixed accuracy definition for the subtype T. The value of this attribute is of the type *universal_real*.

5   T'MANTISSA   Yields the number of binary digits in the mantissa of model numbers of the subtype T. (This attribute yields the number B of section 3.5.9.) The value of this attribute is of the type *universal_integer*.

6   T'SMALL   Yields the smallest positive (nonzero) model number of the subtype T. The value of this attribute is of the type *universal_real*.

7   T'LARGE   Yields the largest positive model number of the subtype T. The value of this attribute is of the type *universal_real*.

8   T'FORE   Yields the minimum number of characters needed for the integer part of the decimal representation of any value of the subtype T, assuming that the representation does not include an exponent, but includes a one-character prefix that is either a minus sign or a space. (This minimum number does not include superfluous zeros or underlines, and is at least two.) The value of this attribute is of the type *universal_integer*.

9   T'AFT   Yields the number of decimal digits needed after the point to accommodate the precision of the subtype T, unless the delta of the subtype T is greater than 0.1, in which case the attribute yields the value one. (T'AFT is the smallest positive integer N for which (10**N)*T'DELTA is greater than or equal to one.) The value of this attribute is of the type *universal_integer*.

10   The attributes of the second group include the following attributes which yield characteristics of the safe numbers:

11   T'SAFE_SMALL   Yields the smallest positive (nonzero) safe number of the base type of T. The value of this attribute is of the type *universal_real*.

12   T'SAFE_LARGE   Yields the largest positive safe number of the base type of T. The value of this attribute is of the type *universal_real*.

13   In addition, the attributes A'SIZE and A'ADDRESS are defined for an object A of a fixed point type (see 13.7.2). Finally, for each fixed point type or subtype T, there are the machine-dependent attributes T'MACHINE_ROUNDS and T'MACHINE_OVERFLOWS (see 13.7.3).

Besides the basic operations, the operations of a fixed point type include the relational operators, and the following predefined arithmetic operators: the binary and unary adding operators - and +, the multiplying operators * and /, and the operator **abs**. 14

The operations of a subtype are the corresponding operations of the type except for the following: assignment, membership tests, qualification, explicit conversion, and the attributes of the first group; the effects of these operations are redefined in terms of the subtype. 15

Notes:

The value of the attribute T'FORE depends only on the range of the subtype T. The value of the attribute T'AFT depends only on the value of T'DELTA. The following relations exist between attributes of a fixed point type: 16

```
T'LARGE        = (2**T'MANTISSA - 1) * T'SMALL
T'SAFE_LARGE   = T'BASE'LARGE
T'SAFE_SMALL   = T'BASE'SMALL
```

References: abs operator 4.5 4.5.6, arithmetic operator 3.5.5 4.5, assignment 5.2, base type 3.3, basic operation 3.3.3, binary adding operator 4.5 4.5.3, bound of a range 3.5, conversion 4.6, delta 3.5.9, fixed point type 3.5.9, membership test 4.5 4.5.2, model number 3.5.6, multiplying operator 4.5 4.5.5, numeric type 3.5, object 3.2, operation 3.3, qualified expression 4.7, relational operator 4.5 4.5.2, safe number 3.5.6, subtype 3.3, unary adding operator 4.5 4.5.4, universal_integer type 3.5.4, universal_real type 3.5.6 17

3.6 Array Types

An array object is a composite object consisting of components that have the same subtype. The name for a component of an array uses one or more index values belonging to specified discrete types. The value of an array object is a composite value consisting of the values of its components. 1

```
array_type_definition ::=                                              2
    unconstrained_array_definition | constrained_array_definition

unconstrained_array_definition ::=
    array(index_subtype_definition {, index_subtype_definition}) of
        component_subtype_indication

constrained_array_definition ::=
    array index_constraint of component_subtype_indication

index_subtype_definition ::= type_mark range <>

index_constraint ::=  (discrete_range {, discrete_range})

discrete_range ::= discrete_subtype_indication | range
```

An array object is characterized by the number of indices (the *dimensionality* of the array), the type and position of each index, the lower and upper bounds for each index, and the type and possible constraint of the components. The order of the indices is significant. 3

4　　A one-dimensional array has a distinct component for each possible index value. A multidimensional array has a distinct component for each possible sequence of index values that can be formed by selecting one value for each index position (in the given order). The possible values for a given index are all the values between the lower and upper bounds, inclusive; this range of values is called the *index range*.

5　　An unconstrained array definition defines an array type. For each object that has the array type, the number of indices, the type and position of each index, and the subtype of the components are as in the type definition; the values of the lower and upper bounds for each index belong to the corresponding index subtype, except for null arrays as explained in section 3.6.1. The *index subtype* for a given index position is, by definition, the subtype denoted by the type mark of the corresponding index subtype definition. The compound delimiter <> (called a *box*) of an index subtype definition stands for an undefined range (different objects of the type need not have the same bounds). The elaboration of an unconstrained array definition creates an array type; this elaboration includes that of the component subtype indication.

6　　A constrained array definition defines both an array type and a subtype of this type:

7　　● The array type is an implicitly declared anonymous type; this type is defined by an (implicit) unconstrained array definition, in which the component subtype indication is that of the constrained array definition, and in which the type mark of each index subtype definition denotes the subtype defined by the corresponding discrete range.

8　　● The array subtype is the subtype obtained by imposition of the index constraint on the array type.

9　　If a constrained array definition is given for a type declaration, the simple name declared by this declaration denotes the array subtype.

10　　The elaboration of a constrained array definition creates the corresponding array type and array subtype. For this elaboration, the index constraint and the component subtype indication are elaborated. The evaluation of each discrete range of the index constraint and the elaboration of the component subtype indication are performed in some order that is not defined by the language.

11　　*Examples of type declarations with unconstrained array definitions:*

```
type VECTOR     is array(INTEGER   range <>) of REAL;
type MATRIX     is array(INTEGER   range <>, INTEGER range <>) of REAL;
type BIT_VECTOR is array(INTEGER   range <>) of BOOLEAN;
type ROMAN      is array(POSITIVE  range <>) of ROMAN_DIGIT;
```

12　　*Examples of type declarations with constrained array definitions:*

```
type TABLE    is array(1 .. 10) of INTEGER;
type SCHEDULE is array(DAY) of BOOLEAN;
type LINE     is array(1 .. MAX_LINE_SIZE) of CHARACTER;
```

13　　*Examples of object declarations with constrained array definitions:*

```
GRID : array(1 .. 80, 1 .. 100) of BOOLEAN;
MIX  : array(COLOR range RED .. GREEN) of BOOLEAN;
PAGE : array(1 .. 50) of LINE; --  an array of arrays
```

Note:

For a one-dimensional array, the rule given means that a type declaration with a constrained array definition such as   14

    type T **is array**(POSITIVE **range** MIN .. MAX) **of** COMPONENT;

is equivalent (in the absence of an incorrect order dependence) to the succession of declarations   15

    subtype *index_subtype* **is** POSITIVE **range** MIN .. MAX;
    type *array_type* **is array**(*index_subtype* **range** <>) **of** COMPONENT;
    subtype T **is** *array_type*(*index_subtype*);

where *index_subtype* and *array_type* are both anonymous. Consequently, T is the name of a sub-   16
type and all objects declared with this type mark are arrays that have the same bounds. Similar
transformations apply to multidimensional arrays.

A similar transformation applies to an object whose declaration includes a constrained array defini-   17
tion. A consequence of this is that no two such objects have the same type.

References: anonymous type 3.3.1, bound of a range 3.5, component 3.3, constraint 3.3, discrete type 3.5,   18
elaboration 3.1 3.9, in some order 1.6, name 4.1, object 3.2, range 3.5, subtype 3.3, subtype indication 3.3.2, type
3.3, type declaration 3.3.1, type definition 3.3.1, type mark 3.3.2

3.6.1 Index Constraints and Discrete Ranges

An index constraint determines the range of possible values for every index of an array type, and   1
thereby the corresponding array bounds.

For a discrete range used in a constrained array definition and defined by a range, an implicit con-   2
version to the predefined type INTEGER is assumed if each bound is either a numeric literal, a
named number, or an attribute, and the type of both bounds (prior to the implicit conversion) is the
type *universal_integer*. Otherwise, both bounds must be of the same discrete type, other than
universal_integer; this type must be determinable independently of the context, but using the fact
that the type must be discrete and that both bounds must have the same type. These rules apply
also to a discrete range used in an iteration rule (see 5.5) or in the declaration of a family of entries
(see 9.5).

If an index constraint follows a type mark in a subtype indication, then the type or subtype denoted   3
by the type mark must not already impose an index constraint. The type mark must denote either
an unconstrained array type or an access type whose designated type is such an array type. In
either case, the index constraint must provide a discrete range for each index of the array type and
the type of each discrete range must be the same as that of the corresponding index.

An index constraint is *compatible* with the type denoted by the type mark if and only if the con-   4
straint defined by each discrete range is compatible with the corresponding index subtype. If any of
the discrete ranges defines a null range, any array thus constrained is a *null array*, having no components. An array value *satisfies* an index constraint if at each index position the array value and
the index constraint have the same index bounds. (Note, however, that assignment and certain
other operations on arrays involve an implicit subtype conversion.)

5   The bounds of each array object are determined as follows:

6   ● For a variable declared by an object declaration, the subtype indication of the corresponding object declaration must define a constrained array subtype (and, thereby, the bounds). The same requirement exists for the subtype indication of a component declaration, if the type of the record component is an array type; and for the component subtype indication of an array type definition, if the type of the array components is itself an array type.

7   ● For a constant declared by an object declaration, the bounds of the constant are defined by the initial value if the subtype of the constant is unconstrained; they are otherwise defined by this subtype (in the latter case, the initial value is the result of an implicit subtype conversion). The same rule applies to a generic formal parameter of mode **in**.

8   ● For an array object designated by an access value, the bounds must be defined by the allocator that creates the array object. (The allocated object is constrained with the corresponding values of the bounds.)

9   ● For a formal parameter of a subprogram or entry, the bounds are obtained from the corresponding actual parameter. (The formal parameter is constrained with the corresponding values of the bounds.)

10 ● For a renaming declaration and for a generic formal parameter of mode **in out**, the bounds are those of the renamed object or of the corresponding generic actual parameter.

11 For the elaboration of an index constraint, the discrete ranges are evaluated in some order that is not defined by the language.

12 *Examples of array declarations including an index constraint:*

```
BOARD       : MATRIX(1 .. 8,   1 .. 8);  --  see 3.6
RECTANGLE   : MATRIX(1 .. 20,  1 .. 30);
INVERSE     : MATRIX(1 .. N,   1 .. N);  --  N need not be static

FILTER      : BIT_VECTOR(0 .. 31);
```

13 *Example of array declaration with a constrained array subtype:*

```
MY_SCHEDULE : SCHEDULE;  --  all arrays of type SCHEDULE have the same bounds
```

14 *Example of record type with a component that is an array:*

```
type VAR_LINE(LENGTH : INTEGER) is
   record
      IMAGE : STRING(1 .. LENGTH);
   end record;

NULL_LINE : VAR_LINE(0);  --  NULL_LINE.IMAGE is a null array
```

Notes:

15 The elaboration of a subtype indication consisting of a type mark followed by an index constraint checks the compatibility of the index constraint with the type mark (see 3.3.2).

16 All components of an array have the same subtype. In particular, for an array of components that are one-dimensional arrays, this means that all components have the same bounds and hence the same length.

References: access type 3.8, access type definition 3.8, access value 3.8, actual parameter 6.4.1, allocator 4.8, array bound 3.6, array component 3.6, array type 3.6, array type definition 3.6, bound of a range 3.5, compatible 3.3.2, component declaration 3.7, constant 3.2.1, constrained array definition 3.6, constrained array subtype 3.6, conversion 4.6, designate 3.8, designated type 3.8, discrete range 3.6, entry 9.5, entry family declaration 9.5, expression 4.4, formal parameter 6.1, function 6.5, generic actual parameter 12.3, generic formal parameter 12.1 12.3, generic parameter 12.1, index 3.6, index constraint 3.6.1, index subtype 3.6, initial value 3.2.1, integer literal 2.4, integer type 3.5.4, iteration rule 5.5, mode 12.1.1, name 4.1, null range 3.5, object 3.2, object declaration 3.2.1, predefined type C, range 3.5, record component 3.7, renaming declaration 8.5, result subtype 6.1, satisfy 3.3, subprogram 6, subtype conversion 4.6, subtype indication 3.3.2, type mark 3.3.2, unconstrained array type 3.6, unconstrained subtype 3.3, universal type 4.10, universal_integer type 3.5.4, variable 3.2.1

17

3.6.2 Operations of Array Types

The basic operations of an array type include the operations involved in assignment and aggregates (unless the array type is limited), membership tests, indexed components, qualification, and explicit conversion; for one-dimensional arrays the basic operations also include the operations involved in slices, and also string literals if the component type is a character type.

1

If A is an array object, an array value, or a constrained array subtype, the basic operations also include the attributes listed below. These attributes are not allowed for an unconstrained array type. The argument N used in the attribute designators for the N-th dimension of an array must be a static expression of type *universal_integer*. The value of N must be positive (nonzero) and no greater than the dimensionality of the array.

2

A'FIRST   Yields the lower bound of the first index range. The value of this attribute has the same type as this lower bound.

3

A'FIRST(N)   Yields the lower bound of the N-th index range. The value of this attribute has the same type as this lower bound.

4

A'LAST   Yields the upper bound of the first index range. The value of this attribute has the same type as this upper bound.

5

A'LAST(N)   Yields the upper bound of the N-th index range. The value of this attribute has the same type as this upper bound.

6

A'RANGE   Yields the first index range, that is, the range A'FIRST .. A'LAST.

7

A'RANGE(N)   Yields the N-th index range, that is, the range A'FIRST(N) .. A'LAST(N).

8

A'LENGTH   Yields the number of values of the first index range (zero for a null range). The value of this attribute is of the type *universal_integer*.

9

A'LENGTH(N)   Yields the number of values of the N-th index range (zero for a null range). The value of this attribute is of the type *universal_integer*.

10

In addition, the attribute T'BASE is defined for an array type or subtype T (see 3.3.3); the attribute T'SIZE is defined for an array type or subtype T, and the attributes A'SIZE and A'ADDRESS are defined for an array object A (see 13.7.2).

11

12   Besides the basic operations, the operations of an array type include the predefined comparison for
      equality and inequality, unless the array type is limited. For one-dimensional arrays, the operations
      include catenation, unless the array type is limited; if the component type is a discrete type, the
      operations also include all predefined relational operators; if the component type is a boolean
      type, then the operations also include the unary logical negation operator **not**, and the logical
      operators.

13   *Examples (using arrays declared in the examples of section 3.6.1):*

      ```
      --   FILTER'FIRST       =    0    FILTER'LAST      =    31    FILTER'LENGTH   =    32
      --   RECTANGLE'LAST(1)  =    20   RECTANGLE'LAST(2) =   30
      ```

      Notes:

14   The attributes A'FIRST and A'FIRST(1) yield the same value. A similar relation exists for the
      attributes A'LAST, A'RANGE, and A'LENGTH. The following relations are satisfied (except for a null
      array) by the above attributes if the index type is an integer type:

      ```
      A'LENGTH     = A'LAST    - A'FIRST    + 1
      A'LENGTH(N)  = A'LAST(N) - A'FIRST(N) + 1
      ```

15   An array type is limited if its component type is limited (see 7.4.4).

16   *References:* aggregate 4.3, array type 3.6, assignment 5.2, attribute 4.1.4, basic operation 3.3.3, bound of a range
      3.5, catenation operator 4.5 4.5.3, character type 3.5.2, constrained array subtype 3.6, conversion 4.6, designator
      6.1, dimension 3.6, index 3.6, indexed component 4.1.1, limited type 7.4.4, logical operator 4.5 4.5.1, membership
      test 4.5 4.5.2, not operator 4.5 4.5.6, null range 3.5, object 3.2, operation 3.3, predefined operator 4.5, qualified
      expression 4.7, relational operator 4.5 4.5.2, slice 4.1.2, static expression 4.9, string literal 2.6, subcomponent 3.3,
      type 3.3, unconstrained array type 3.6, universal type 4.10, universal_integer type 3.5.4

3.6.3 The Type String

1   The values of the predefined type STRING are one-dimensional arrays of the predefined type
     CHARACTER, indexed by values of the predefined subtype POSITIVE :

     ```
     subtype POSITIVE is INTEGER range 1 .. INTEGER'LAST;
     type STRING is array(POSITIVE range <>) of CHARACTER;
     ```

2   *Examples:*

     ```
     STARS        : STRING(1 .. 120)  := (1 .. 120 => '*' );
     QUESTION     : constant STRING   := "HOW MANY CHARACTERS?";
     --  QUESTION'FIRST = 1, QUESTION'LAST = 20 (the number of characters)

     ASK_TWICE    : constant STRING   := QUESTION & QUESTION;
     NINETY_SIX   : constant ROMAN    := "XCVI";        -- see 3.6
     ```

     Notes:

3   String literals (see 2.6 and 4.2) are basic operations applicable to the type STRING and to any
     other one-dimensional array type whose component type is a character type. The catenation
     operator is a predefined operator for the type STRING and for one-dimensional array types; it is
     represented as &. The relational operators <, <=, >, and >= are defined for values of these types,
     and correspond to lexicographic order (see 4.5.2).

References: aggregate 4.3, array 3.6, catenation operator 4.5 4.5.3, character type 3.5.2, component type (of an **4** array) 3.6, dimension 3.6, index 3.6, lexicographic order 4.5.2, positional aggregate 4.3, predefined operator 4.5, predefined type C, relational operator 4.5 4.5.2, string literal 2.6, subtype 3.3, type 3.3

3.7 Record Types

A record object is a composite object consisting of named components. The value of a record **1** object is a composite value consisting of the values of its components.

```
record_type_definition  ::=                                              2
   record
      component_list
   end  record

component_list  ::=
      component_declaration {component_declaration}
   | {component_declaration} variant_part
   |  null;

component_declaration  ::=
      identifier_list : component_subtype_definition [:= expression];

component_subtype_definition  ::=  subtype_indication
```

Each component declaration declares a component of the record type. Besides components **3** declared by component declarations, the components of a record type include any components declared by discriminant specifications of the record type declaration. The identifiers of all components of a record type must be distinct. The use of a name that denotes a record component other than a discriminant is not allowed within the record type definition that declares the component.

A component declaration with several identifiers is equivalent to a sequence of single component **4** declarations, as explained in section 3.2. Each single component declaration declares a record component whose subtype is specified by the component subtype definition.

If a component declaration includes the assignment compound delimiter followed by an expres- **5** sion, the expression is the default expression of the record component; the default expression must be of the type of the component. Default expressions are not allowed for components that are of a limited type.

If a record type does not have a discriminant part, the same components are present in all values **6** of the type. If the component list of a record type is defined by the reserved word **null** and there is no discriminant part, then the record type has no components and all records of the type are *null* records.

The elaboration of a record type definition creates a record type; it consists of the elaboration of **7** any corresponding (single) component declarations, in the order in which they appear, including any component declaration in a variant part. The elaboration of a component declaration consists of the elaboration of the component subtype definition.

For the elaboration of a component subtype definition, if the constraint does not depend on a dis- **8** criminant (see 3.7.1), then the subtype indication is elaborated. If, on the other hand, the constraint depends on a discriminant, then the elaboration consists of the evaluation of any included expression that is not a discriminant.

9   *Examples of record type declarations:*

```
type DATE is
  record
     DAY     : INTEGER range 1 .. 31;
     MONTH : MONTH_NAME;
     YEAR    : INTEGER range 0 .. 4000;
  end record;

type COMPLEX is
  record
     RE   : REAL := 0.0;
     IM   : REAL := 0.0;
  end record;
```

10   *Examples of record variables:*

```
TOMORROW, YESTERDAY : DATE;
A, B, C : COMPLEX;

-- both components of A, B, and C are implicitly initialized to zero
```

Notes:

11   The default expression of a record component is implicitly evaluated by the elaboration of the declaration of a record object, in the absence of an explicit initialization (see 3.2.1). If a component declaration has several identifiers, the expression is evaluated once for each such component of the object (since the declaration is equivalent to a sequence of single component declarations).

12   Unlike the components of an array, the components of a record need not be of the same type.

13   *References:* assignment compound delimiter 2.2, component 3.3, composite value 3.3, constraint 3.3, declaration 3.1, depend on a discriminant 3.7.1, discriminant 3.3, discriminant part 3.7 3.7.1, elaboration 3.9, expression 4.4, identifier 2.3, identifier list 3.2, limited type 7.4.4, name 4.1, object 3.2, subtype 3.3, type 3.3, type mark 3.3.2, variant part 3.7.3

3.7.1 Discriminants

1   A discriminant part specifies the discriminants of a type. A discriminant of a record is a component of the record. The type of a discriminant must be discrete.

2
```
discriminant_part ::=
    (discriminant_specification {; discriminant_specification})

discriminant_specification ::=
    identifier_list : type_mark [:= expression]
```

3   A discriminant part is only allowed in the type declaration for a record type, in a private type declaration or an incomplete type declaration (the corresponding full declaration must then declare a record type), and in the generic parameter declaration for a formal private type.

A discriminant specification with several identifiers is equivalent to a sequence of single discriminant specifications, as explained in section 3.2. Each single discriminant specification declares a discriminant. If a discriminant specification includes the assignment compound delimiter followed by an expression, the expression is the default expression of the discriminant; the default expression must be of the type of the discriminant. Default expressions must be provided either for all or for none of the discriminants of a discriminant part.

The use of the name of a discriminant is not allowed in default expressions of a discriminant part if the specification of the discriminant is itself given in the discriminant part.

Within a record type definition the only allowed uses of the name of a discriminant of the record type are: in the default expressions for record components; in a variant part as the discriminant name; and in a component subtype definition, either as a bound in an index constraint, or to specify a discriminant value in a discriminant constraint. A discriminant name used in these component subtype definitions must appear by itself, not as part of a larger expression. Such component subtype definitions and such constraints are said to *depend on a discriminant*.

A component is said to *depend on a discriminant* if it is a record component declared in a variant part, or a record component whose component subtype definition depends on a discriminant, or finally, one of the subcomponents of a component that itself depends on a discriminant.

Each record value includes a value for each discriminant specified for the record type; it also includes a value for each record component that does not depend on a discriminant. The values of the discriminants determine which other component values are in the record value.

Direct assignment to a discriminant of an object is not allowed; furthermore a discriminant is not allowed as an actual parameter of mode **in out** or **out**, or as a generic actual parameter of mode **in out**. The only allowed way to change the value of a discriminant of a variable is to assign a (complete) value to the variable itself. Similarly, an assignment to the variable itself is the only allowed way to change the constraint of one of its components, if the component subtype definition depends on a discriminant of the variable.

The elaboration of a discriminant part has no other effect.

Examples:

```
type BUFFER(SIZE : BUFFER_SIZE := 100) is          -- see 3.5.4
   record
      POS    : BUFFER_SIZE := 0;
      VALUE  : STRING(1 .. SIZE);
   end record;

type SQUARE(SIDE : INTEGER) is
   record
      MAT : MATRIX(1 .. SIDE, 1 .. SIDE);           -- see 3.6
   end record;

type DOUBLE_SQUARE(NUMBER : INTEGER) is
   record
      LEFT  : SQUARE (NUMBER);
      RIGHT : SQUARE (NUMBER);
   end record;
```

```
type ITEM(NUMBER : POSITIVE) is
   record
      CONTENT : INTEGER;
      -- no component depends on the discriminant
   end record;
```

12   *References:* assignment 5.2, assignment compound delimiter 2.2, bound of a range 3.5, component 3.3, component declaration 3.7, component of a record 3.7, declaration 3.1, discrete type 3.5, discriminant 3.3, discriminant constraint 3.7.2, elaboration 3.9, expression 4.4, generic formal type 12.1, generic parameter declaration 12.1, identifier 2.3, identifier list 3.2, incomplete type declaration 3.8.1, index constraint 3.6.1, name 4.1, object 3.2, private type 7.4, private type declaration 7.4, record type 3.7, scope 8.2, simple name 4.1, subcomponent 3.3, subtype indication 3.3.2, type declaration 3.3.1, type mark 3.3.2, variant part 3.7.3

3.7.2 Discriminant Constraints

1   A discriminant constraint is only allowed in a subtype indication, after a type mark. This type mark must denote either a type with discriminants, or an access type whose designated type is a type with discriminants. A discriminant constraint specifies the values of these discriminants.

2
```
discriminant_constraint ::=
   (discriminant_association {, discriminant_association})

discriminant_association ::=
   [discriminant_simple_name {| discriminant_simple_name} =>] expression
```

3   Each discriminant association associates an expression with one or more discriminants. A discriminant association is said to be *named* if the discriminants are specified explicitly by their names; it is otherwise said to be *positional*. For a positional association, the (single) discriminant is implicitly specified by position, in textual order. Named associations can be given in any order, but if both positional and named associations are used in the same discriminant constraint, then positional associations must occur first, at their normal position. Hence once a named association is used, the rest of the discriminant constraint must use only named associations.

4   For a named discriminant association, the discriminant names must denote discriminants of the type for which the discriminant constraint is given. A discriminant association with more than one discriminant name is only allowed if the named discriminants are all of the same type. Furthermore, for each discriminant association (whether named or positional), the expression and the associated discriminants must have the same type. A discriminant constraint must provide exactly one value for each discriminant of the type.

5   A discriminant constraint is compatible with the type denoted by a type mark, if and only if each discriminant value belongs to the subtype of the corresponding discriminant. In addition, for each subcomponent whose component subtype specification depends on a discriminant, the discriminant value is substituted for the discriminant in this component subtype specification and the compatibility of the resulting subtype indication is checked.

6   A composite value satisfies a discriminant constraint if and only if each discriminant of the composite value has the value imposed by the discriminant constraint.

The initial values of the discriminants of an object of a type with discriminants are determined as   7
follows:

- For a variable declared by an object declaration, the subtype indication of the corresponding   8
  object declaration must impose a discriminant constraint unless default expressions exist for
  the discriminants; the discriminant values are defined either by the constraint or, in its
  absence, by the default expressions. The same requirement exists for the subtype indication of
  a component declaration, if the type of the record component has discriminants; and for the
  component subtype indication of an array type, if the type of the array components is a type
  with discriminants.

- For a constant declared by an object declaration, the values of the discriminants are those of   9
  the initial value if the subtype of the constant is unconstrained; they are otherwise defined by
  this subtype (in the latter case, an exception is raised if the initial value does not belong to this
  subtype). The same rule applies to a generic parameter of mode **in**.

- For an object designated by an access value, the discriminant values must be defined by the   10
  allocator that creates the object. (The allocated object is constrained with the corresponding
  discriminant values.)

- For a formal parameter of a subprogram or entry, the discriminants of the formal parameter   11
  are initialized with those of the corresponding actual parameter. (The formal parameter is
  constrained if the corresponding actual parameter is constrained, and in any case if the mode
  is **in** or if the subtype of the formal parameter is constrained.)

- For a renaming declaration and for a generic formal parameter of mode **in out**, the discrimi-   12
  nants are those of the renamed object or of the corresponding generic actual parameter.

For the elaboration of a discriminant constraint, the expressions given in the discriminant associa-   13
tions are evaluated in some order that is not defined by the language; the expression of a named
association is evaluated once for each named discriminant.

Examples (using types declared in the previous section):   14

```
LARGE    : BUFFER(200);   --   constrained, always 200 characters (explicit discriminant value)
MESSAGE  : BUFFER;        --   unconstrained, initially 100 characters (default discriminant value)

BASIS    : SQUARE(5);     --   constrained, always 5 by 5
ILLEGAL  : SQUARE;        --   illegal, a SQUARE must be constrained
```

Note:

The above rules and the rules defining the elaboration of an object declaration (see 3.2) ensure   15
that discriminants always have a value. In particular, if a discriminant constraint is imposed on an
object declaration, each discriminant is initialized with the value specified by the constraint.
Similarly, if the subtype of a component has a discriminant constraint, the discriminants of the
component are correspondingly initialized.

References: access type 3.8, access type definition 3.8, access value 3.8, actual parameter 6.4.1, allocator 4.8, array   16
type definition 3.6, bound of a range 3.5, compatible 3.3.2, component 3.3, component declaration 3.7, component
subtype indication 3.7, composite value 3.3, constant 3.2.1, constrained subtype 3.3, constraint 3.3, declaration 3.1,
default expression for a discriminant 3.7, depend on a discriminant 3.7.1, designate 3.8, designated type 3.8, discriminant 3.3, elaboration 3.9, entry 9.5, evaluation 4.5, expression 4.4, formal parameter 6.1, generic actual parameter
12.3, generic formal parameter 12.1 12.3, mode in 6.1, mode in out 6.1, name 4.1, object 3.2, object declaration
3.2.1, renaming declaration 8.5, reserved word 2.9, satisfy 3.3, simple name 4.1, subcomponent 3.3, subprogram 6,
subtype 3.3, subtype indication 3.3.2, type 3.3, type mark 3.3.2, variable 3.2.1

3.7.3 Variant Parts

1   A record type with a variant part specifies alternative lists of components. Each variant defines the components for the corresponding value or values of the discriminant.

2
```
variant_part ::=
   case discriminant_simple_name is
       variant
       {variant}
   end case;

variant ::=
   when choice {| choice} =>
       component_list

choice ::= simple_expression
   | discrete_range | others | component_simple_name
```

3   Each variant starts with a list of choices which must be of the same type as the discriminant of the variant part. The type of the discriminant of a variant part must not be a generic formal type. If the subtype of the discriminant is static, then each value of this subtype must be represented once and only once in the set of choices of the variant part, and no other value is allowed. Otherwise, each value of the (base) type of the discriminant must be represented once and only once in the set of choices.

4   The simple expressions and discrete ranges given as choices in a variant part must be static. A choice defined by a discrete range stands for all values in the corresponding range (none if a null range). The choice **others** is only allowed for the last variant and as its only choice; it stands for all values (possibly none) not given in the choices of previous variants. A component simple name is not allowed as a choice of a variant (although it is part of the syntax of choice).

5   A record value contains the values of the components of a given variant if and only if the discriminant value is equal to one of the values specified by the choices of the variant. This rule applies in turn to any further variant that is, itself, included in the component list of the given variant. If the component list of a variant is specified by **null**, the variant has no components.

6   *Example of record type with a variant part:*

```
type DEVICE is (PRINTER, DISK, DRUM);
type STATE  is (OPEN, CLOSED);

type PERIPHERAL(UNIT : DEVICE := DISK) is
  record
    STATUS : STATE;
    case UNIT is
      when PRINTER =>
        LINE_COUNT : INTEGER range 1 .. PAGE_SIZE;
      when others =>
        CYLINDER    : CYLINDER_INDEX;
        TRACK       : TRACK_NUMBER;
    end case;
  end record;
```

Examples of record subtypes:

```
subtype DRUM_UNIT  is PERIPHERAL(DRUM);
subtype DISK_UNIT  is PERIPHERAL(DISK);
```

Examples of constrained record variables: 8

```
WRITER  : PERIPHERAL(UNIT => PRINTER);
ARCHIVE : DISK_UNIT;
```

Note:

Choices with discrete values are also used in case statements and in array aggregates. Choices   9
with component simple names are used in record aggregates.

References: array aggregate 4.3.2, base type 3.3, component 3.3, component list 3.7, discrete range 3.6,   10
discriminant 3.3, generic formal type 12.1.2, null range 3.5, record aggregate 4.3.1, range 3.5, record type 3.7, simple
expression 4.4, simple name 4.1, static discrete range 4.9, static expression 4.9, static subtype 4.9, subtype 3.3

3.7.4 Operations of Record Types

The basic operations of a record type include the operations involved in assignment and   1
aggregates (unless the type is limited), membership tests, selection of record components,
qualification, and type conversion (for derived types).

For any object A of a type with discriminants, the basic operations also include the following   2
attribute:

A'CONSTRAINED   Yields the value TRUE if a discriminant constraint applies to the object A,   3
or if the object is a constant (including a formal parameter or generic for-
mal parameter of mode in); yields the value FALSE otherwise. If A is a
generic formal parameter of mode in out, or if A is a formal parameter of
mode in out or out and the type mark given in the corresponding
parameter specification denotes an unconstrained type with discriminants, then the value of this attribute is obtained from that of the corresponding actual parameter. The value of this attribute is of the
predefined type BOOLEAN.

In addition, the attributes T'BASE and T'SIZE are defined for a record type or subtype T (see 3.3.3);   4
the attributes A'SIZE and A'ADDRESS are defined for a record object A (see 13.7.2).

Besides the basic operations, the operations of a record type include the predefined comparison   5
for equality and inequality, unless the type is limited.

Note:

A record type is limited if the type of any of its components is limited (see 7.4.4).   6

References: actual parameter 6.4.1, aggregate 4.3, assignment 5.2, attribute 4.1.4, basic operation 3.3.3, boolean   7
type 3.5.3, constant 3.2.1, conversion 4.6, derived type 3.4, discriminant 3.3, discriminant constraint 3.7.2, formal
parameter 6.1, generic actual parameter 12.3, generic formal parameter 12.1 12.3, limited type 7.4.4, membership
test 4.5 4.5.2, mode 6.1, object 3.2.1, operation 3.3, predefined operator 4.5, predefined type C, qualified expression
4.7, record type 3.7, relational operator 4.5 4.5.2, selected component 4.1.3, subcomponent 3.3, subtype 3.3, type
3.3

3.8 Access Types

1 An object declared by an object declaration is created by the elaboration of the object declaration and is denoted by a simple name or by some other form of name. In contrast, there are objects that are created by the evaluation of *allocators* (see 4.8) and that have no simple name. Access to such an object is achieved by an *access value* returned by an allocator; the access value is said to *designate* the object.

2   access_type_definition ::= **access** subtype_indication

3 For each access type, there is a literal **null** which has a null access value designating no object at all. The null value of an access type is the default initial value of the type. Other values of an access type are obtained by evaluation of a special operation of the type, called an allocator. Each such access value designates an object of the subtype defined by the subtype indication of the access type definition; this subtype is called the *designated subtype*; the base type of this subtype is called the *designated type*. The objects designated by the values of an access type form a *collection* implicitly associated with the type.

4 The elaboration of an access type definition consists of the elaboration of the subtype indication and creates an access type.

5 If an access object is constant, the contained access value cannot be changed and always designates the same object. On the other hand, the value of the designated object need not remain the same (assignment to the designated object is allowed unless the designated type is limited).

6 The only forms of constraint that are allowed after the name of an access type in a subtype indication are index constraints and discriminant constraints. (See sections 3.6.1 and 3.7.2 for the rules applicable to these subtype indications.) An access value *belongs* to a corresponding subtype of an access type either if the access value is the null value or if the value of the designated object satisfies the constraint.

7 *Examples:*

    type FRAME **is access** MATRIX;   --   see 3.6

    type BUFFER_NAME **is access** BUFFER;   --   see 3.7.1

Notes:

8 An access value delivered by an allocator can be assigned to several access objects. Hence it is possible for an object created by an allocator to be designated by more than one variable or constant of the access type. An access value can only designate an object created by an allocator; in particular, it cannot designate an object declared by an object declaration.

9 If the type of the objects designated by the access values is an array type or a type with discriminants, these objects are constrained with either the array bounds or the discriminant values supplied implicitly or explicitly for the corresponding allocators (see 4.8).

10 Access values are called *pointers* or *references* in some other languages.

11 *References:* allocator 4.8, array type 3.6, assignment 5.2, belong to a subtype 3.3, constant 3.2.1, constraint 3.3, discriminant constraint 3.7.2, elaboration 3.9, index constraint 3.6.1, index specification 3.6, limited type 7.4.4, literal 4.2, name 4.1, object 3.2.1, object declaration 3.2.1, reserved word 2.9, satisfy 3.3, simple name 4.1, subcomponent 3.3, subtype 3.3, subtype indication 3.3.2, type 3.3, variable 3.2.1

3.8.1 Incomplete Type Declarations

There are no particular limitations on the designated type of an access type. In particular, the type [1] of a component of the designated type can be another access type, or even the same access type. This permits mutually dependent and recursive access types. Their declarations require a prior incomplete (or private) type declaration for one or more types.

> incomplete_type_declaration ::= **type** identifier [discriminant_part]; [2]

For each incomplete type declaration, there must be a corresponding declaration of a type with the [3] same identifier. The corresponding declaration must be either a full type declaration or the declaration of a task type. In the rest of this section, explanations are given in terms of full type declarations; the same rules apply also to declarations of task types. If the incomplete type declaration occurs immediately within either a declarative part or the visible part of a package specification, then the full type declaration must occur later and immediately within this declarative part or visible part. If the incomplete type declaration occurs immediately within the private part of a package, then the full type declaration must occur later and immediately within either the private part itself, or the declarative part of the corresponding package body.

A discriminant part must be given in the full type declaration if and only if one is given in the [4] incomplete type declaration; if discriminant parts are given, then they must conform (see 6.3.1 for the conformance rules). Prior to the end of the full type declaration, the only allowed use of a name that denotes a type declared by an incomplete type declaration is as the type mark in the subtype indication of an access type definition; the only form of constraint allowed in this subtype indication is a discriminant constraint.

The elaboration of an incomplete type declaration creates a type. If the incomplete type declaration [5] tion has a discriminant part, this elaboration includes that of the discriminant part: in such a case, the discriminant part of the full type declaration is not elaborated.

Example of a recursive type: [6]

```
type CELL;  --  incomplete type declaration
type LINK is access CELL;

type CELL is
   record
      VALUE  : INTEGER;
      SUCC   : LINK;
      PRED   : LINK;
   end record;

HEAD  : LINK := new CELL'(0, null, null);
NEXT  : LINK := HEAD.SUCC;
```

Examples of mutually dependent access types:

```
type PERSON(SEX : GENDER);    --  incomplete type declaration
type CAR;                     --  incomplete type declaration

type PERSON_NAME is access PERSON;
type CAR_NAME    is access CAR;

type CAR is
   record
      NUMBER  : INTEGER;
      OWNER   : PERSON_NAME;
   end record;
```

```
type PERSON(SEX : GENDER) is
  record
    NAME     : STRING(1 .. 20);
    BIRTH    : DATE;
    AGE      : INTEGER range 0 .. 130;
    VEHICLE  : CAR_NAME;
    case SEX is
      when M  => WIFE     : PERSON_NAME(SEX => F);
      when F  => HUSBAND  : PERSON_NAME(SEX => M);
    end case;
  end record;

  MY_CAR, YOUR_CAR, NEXT_CAR : CAR_NAME;  --  implicitly initialized with null value
```

8   *References:* access type 3.8, access type definition 3.8, component 3.3, conform 6.3.1, constraint 3.3, declaration 3.1, declarative item 3.9, designate 3.8, discriminant constraint 3.7.2, discriminant part 3.7.1, elaboration 3.9, identifier 2.3, name 4.1, subtype indication 3.3.2, type 3.3, type mark 3.3.2

3.8.2 Operations of Access Types

1   The basic operations of an access type include the operations involved in assignment, allocators for the access type, membership tests, qualification, explicit conversion, and the literal **null**. If the designated type is a type with discriminants, the basic operations include the selection of the corresponding discriminants; if the designated type is a record type, they include the selection of the corresponding components; if the designated type is an array type, they include the formation of indexed components and slices; if the designated type is a task type, they include selection of entries and entry families. Furthermore, the basic operations include the formation of a selected component with the reserved word **all** (see 4.1.3).

2   It the designated type is an array type, the basic operations include the attributes that have the attribute designators FIRST, LAST, RANGE, and LENGTH (likewise, the attribute designators of the N-th dimension). The prefix of each of these attributes must be a value of the access type. These attributes yield the corresponding characteristics of the designated object (see 3.6.2).

3   If the designated type is a task type, the basic operations include the attributes that have the attribute designators TERMINATED and CALLABLE (see 9.9). The prefix of each of these attributes must be a value of the access type. These attributes yield the corresponding characteristics of the designated task objects.

4   In addition, the attribute T'BASE (see 3.3.3) and the representation attributes T'SIZE and T'STORAGE_SIZE (see 13.7.2) are defined for an access type or subtype T; the attributes A'SIZE and A'ADDRESS are defined for an access object A (see 13.7.2).

5   Besides the basic operations, the operations of an access type include the predefined comparison for equality and inequality.

6   *References:* access type 3.8, allocator 4.8, array type 3.6, assignment 5.2, attribute 4.1.4, attribute designator 4.1.4, base type 3.3, basic operation 3.3.3, collection 3.8, constrained array subtype 3.6, conversion 4.6, designate 3.8, designated subtype 3.8, designated type 3.8, discriminant 3.3, indexed component 4.1.1, literal 4.2, membership test 4.5 4.5.2, object 3.2.1, operation 3.3, private type 7.4, qualified expression 4.7, record type 3.7, selected component 4.1.3, slice 4.1.2, subtype 3.3, task type 9.1, type 3.3

3.9 Declarative Parts

A declarative part contains declarative items (possibly none).   1

    declarative_part ::=   2
        {basic_declarative_item} {later_declarative_item}

    basic_declarative_item ::= basic_declaration
        | representation_clause | use_clause

    later_declarative_item ::= body
        | subprogram_declaration | package_declaration
        | task_declaration | generic_declaration
        | use_clause | generic_instantiation

    body ::= proper_body | body_stub

    proper_body ::= subprogram_body | package_body | task_body

The elaboration of a declarative part consists of the elaboration of the declarative items, if any, in   3
the order in which they are given in the declarative part. After its elaboration, a declarative item is
said to be *elaborated*. Prior to the completion of its elaboration (including before the elaboration),
the declarative item is not yet elaborated.

For several forms of declarative item, the language rules (in particular scope and visibility rules) are   4
such that it is either impossible or illegal to use an entity before the elaboration of the declarative
item that declares this entity. For example, it is not possible to use the name of a type for an object
declaration if the corresponding type declaration is not yet elaborated. In the case of bodies, the
following checks are performed:

- For a subprogram call, a check is made that the body of the subprogram is already elaborated.   5

- For the activation of a task, a check is made that the body of the corresponding task unit is   6
  already elaborated.

- For the instantiation of a generic unit that has a body, a check is made that this body is   7
  already elaborated.

The exception PROGRAM_ERROR is raised if any of these checks fails.   8

If a subprogram declaration, a package declaration, a task declaration, or a generic declaration is a   9
declarative item of a given declarative part, then the body (if there is one) of the program unit
declared by the declarative item must itself be a declarative item of this declarative part (and must
appear later). If the body is a body stub, then a separately compiled subunit containing the corresponding proper body is required for the program unit (see 10.2).

References: activation 9.3, instantiation 12.3, program_error exception 11.1, scope 8.2, subprogram call 6.4, type   10
3.3, visibility 8.3

Elaboration of declarations: 3.1, component declaration 3.7, deferred constant declaration 7.4.3, discriminant   11
specification 3.7.1, entry declaration 9.5, enumeration literal specification 3.5.1, generic declaration 12.1, generic
instantiation 12.3, incomplete type declaration 3.8.1, loop parameter specification 5.5, number declaration 3.2.2,
object declaration 3.2.1, package declaration 7.2, parameter specification 6.1, private type declaration 7.4.1, renaming declaration 8.5, subprogram declaration 6.1, subtype declaration 3.3.2, task declaration 9.1, type declaration 3.3. 1

12   *Elaboration of type definitions:*   3.3.1, access type definition 3.8, array type definition 3.6, derived type definition 3.4, enumeration type definition 3.5.1, integer type definition 3.5.4, real type definition 3.5.6, record type definition 3.7

13   *Elaboration of other constructs:*   context clause 10.1, body stub 10.2, compilation unit 10.1, discriminant part 3.7.1, generic body 12.2, generic formal parameter 12.1 12.3, library unit 10.5, package body 7.1, representation clause 13.1, subprogram body 6.3, subunit 10.2, task body 9.1, task object 9.2, task specification 9.1, use clause 8.4, with clause 10.1.1

4. Names and Expressions

The rules applicable to the different forms of name and expression, and to their evaluation, are given in this chapter.

4.1 Names

Names can denote declared entities, whether declared explicitly or implicitly (see 3.1). Names can also denote objects designated by access values; subcomponents and slices of objects and values; single entries, entry families, and entries in families of entries. Finally, names can denote attributes of any of the foregoing.

```
name ::= simple_name
    | character_literal      | operator_symbol
    | indexed_component      | slice
    | selected_component     | attribute

simple_name ::= identifier

prefix ::= name | function_call
```

A simple name for an entity is either the identifier associated with the entity by its declaration, or another identifier associated with the entity by a renaming declaration.

Certain forms of name (indexed and selected components, slices, and attributes) include a *prefix* that is either a name or a function call. If the type of a prefix is an access type, then the prefix must not be a name that denotes a formal parameter of mode **out** or a subcomponent thereof.

If the prefix of a name is a function call, then the name denotes a component, a slice, an attribute, an entry, or an entry family, either of the result of the function call, or (if the result is an access value) of the object designated by the result.

A prefix is said to be *appropriate for a type* in either of the following cases:

- The type of the prefix is the type considered.

- The type of the prefix is an access type whose designated type is the type considered.

The evaluation of a name determines the entity denoted by the name. This evaluation has no other effect for a name that is a simple name, a character literal, or an operator symbol.

The evaluation of a name that has a prefix includes the evaluation of the prefix, that is, of the corresponding name or function call. If the type of the prefix is an access type, the evaluation of the prefix includes the determination of the object designated by the corresponding access value; the exception CONSTRAINT_ERROR is raised if the value of the prefix is a null access value, except in the case of the prefix of a representation attribute (see 13.7.2).

11   *Examples of simple names:*

```
PI        --  the simple name of a number              (see 3.2.2)
LIMIT     --  the simple name of a constant            (see 3.2.1)
COUNT     --  the simple name of a scalar variable     (see 3.2.1)
BOARD     --  the simple name of an array variable     (see 3.6.1)
MATRIX    --  the simple name of a type                (see 3.6)
RANDOM    --  the simple name of a function            (see 6.1)
ERROR     --  the simple name of an exception          (see 11.1)
```

12   *References:* access type 3.8, access value 3.8, attribute 4.1.4, belong to a type 3.3, character literal 2.5, component 3.3, constraint_error exception 11.1, declaration 3.1, designate 3.8, designated type 3.8, entity 3.1, entry 9.5, entry family 9.5, evaluation 4.5, formal parameter 6.1, function call 6.4, identifier 2.3, indexed component 4.1.1, mode 6.1, null access value 3.8, object 3.2.1, operator symbol 6.1, raising of exceptions 11, renaming declarations 8.5, selected component 4.1.3, slice 4.1.2, subcomponent 3.3, type 3.3

4.1.1 Indexed Components

1   An indexed component denotes either a component of an array or an entry in a family of entries.

2   indexed_component ::= prefix(expression {, expression})

3   In the case of a component of an array, the prefix must be appropriate for an array type. The expressions specify the index values for the component; there must be one such expression for each index position of the array type. In the case of an entry in a family of entries, the prefix must be a name that denotes an entry family of a task object, and the expression (there must be exactly one) specifies the index value for the individual entry.

4   Each expression must be of the type of the corresponding index. For the evaluation of an indexed component, the prefix and the expressions are evaluated in some order that is not defined by the language. The exception CONSTRAINT_ERROR is raised if an index value does not belong to the range of the corresponding index of the prefixing array or entry family.

5   *Examples of indexed components:*

```
MY_SCHEDULE(SAT)     --  a component of a one-dimensional array   (see 3.6.1)
PAGE(10)             --  a component of a one-dimensional array   (see 3.6)
BOARD(M, J + 1)      --  a component of a two-dimensional array   (see 3.6.1)
PAGE(10)(20)         --  a component of a component               (see 3.6)
REQUEST(MEDIUM)      --  an entry in a family of entries          (see 9.5)
NEXT_FRAME(L)(M, N)  --  a component of a function call           (see 6.1)
```

Notes on the examples:

6   Distinct notations are used for components of multidimensional arrays (such as BOARD) and arrays of arrays (such as PAGE). The components of an array of arrays are arrays and can therefore be indexed. Thus PAGE(10)(20) denotes the 20th component of PAGE(10). In the last example NEXT_FRAME(L) is a function call returning an access value which designates a two-dimensional array.

7   *References:* appropriate for a type 4.1, array type 3.6, component 3.3, component of an array 3.6, constraint_error exception 11.1, dimension 3.6, entry 9.5, entry family 9.5, evaluation 4.5, expression 4.4, function call 6.4, in some order 1.6, index 3.6, name 4.1, prefix 4.1, raising of exceptions 11, returned value 5.8 6.5, task object 9.2

4.1.2 Slices

A slice denotes a one-dimensional array formed by a sequence of consecutive components of a one-dimensional array. A slice of a variable is a variable; a slice of a constant is a constant; a slice of a value is a value.   1

    slice ::= prefix(discrete_range)   2

The prefix of a slice must be appropriate for a one-dimensional array type. The type of the slice is the base type of this array type. The bounds of the discrete range define those of the slice and must be of the type of the index; the slice is a *null slice* denoting a null array if the discrete range is a null range.   3

For the evaluation of a name that is a slice, the prefix and the discrete range are evaluated in some order that is not defined by the language. The exception CONSTRAINT_ERROR is raised by the evaluation of a slice, other than a null slice, if any of the bounds of the discrete range does not belong to the index range of the prefixing array. (The bounds of a null slice need not belong to the subtype of the index.)   4

Examples of slices: 5

```
STARS(1 .. 15)            -- a slice of 15 characters          (see 3.6.3)
PAGE(10 .. 10 + SIZE)     -- a slice of 1 + SIZE components    (see 3.6 and 3.2.1)
PAGE(L)(A .. B)           -- a slice of the array PAGE(L)      (see 3.6)
STARS(1 .. 0)             -- a null slice                      (see 3.6.3)
MY_SCHEDULE(WEEKDAY)      -- bounds given by subtype           (see 3.6 and 3.5.1)
STARS(5 .. 15)(K)         -- same as STARS(K)                  (see 3.6.3)
                          -- provided that K is in 5 .. 15
```

Notes:

For a one-dimensional array A, the name A(N .. N) is a slice of one component; its type is the base type of A. On the other hand, A(N) is a component of the array A and has the corresponding component type.   6

References: appropriate for a type 4.1, array 3.6, array type 3.6, array value 3.8, base type 3.3, belong to a subtype 3.3, bound of a discrete range 3.6.1, component 3.3, component type 3.3, constant 3.2.1, constraint 3.3, constraint_error exception 11.1, dimension 3.6, discrete range 3.6, evaluation 4.5, index 3.6, index range 3.6, name 4.1, null array 3.6.1, null range 3.5, prefix 4.1, raising of exceptions 11, type 3.3, variable 3.2.1   7

4.1.3 Selected Components

Selected components are used to denote record components, entries, entry families, and objects designated by access values; they are also used as *expanded names* as described below.   1

    selected_component ::= prefix.selector   2

    selector ::= simple_name
      | character_literal | operator_symbol | all

3   The following four forms of selected components are used to denote a discriminant, a record component, an entry, or an object designated by an access value:

4   (a) A discriminant:

5   The selector must be a simple name denoting a discriminant of an object or value. The prefix must be appropriate for the type of this object or value.

6   (b) A component of a record:

7   The selector must be a simple name denoting a component of a record object or value. The prefix must be appropriate for the type of this object or value.

8   For a component of a variant, a check is made that the values of the discriminants are such that the record has this component. The exception CONSTRAINT_ERROR is raised if this check fails.

9   (c) A single entry or an entry family of a task:

10   The selector must be a simple name denoting a single entry or an entry family of a task. The prefix must be appropriate for the type of this task.

11 (d) An object designated by an access value:

12   The selector must be the reserved word **all**. The value of the prefix must belong to an access type.

13 A selected component of one of the remaining two forms is called an *expanded name*. In each case the selector must be either a simple name, a character literal, or an operator symbol. A function call is not allowed as the prefix of an expanded name. An expanded name can denote:

14 (e) An entity declared in the visible part of a package:

15   The prefix must denote the package. The selector must be the simple name, character literal, or operator symbol of the entity.

16 (f) An entity whose declaration occurs immediately within a named construct:

17   The prefix must denote a construct that is either a program unit, a block statement, a loop statement, or an accept statement. In the case of an accept statement, the prefix must be either the simple name of the entry or entry family, or an expanded name ending with such a simple name (that is, no index is allowed). The selector must be the simple name, character literal, or operator symbol of an entity whose declaration occurs immediately within the construct.

18   This form of expanded name is only allowed within the construct itself (including the body and any subunits, in the case of a program unit). A name declared by a renaming declaration is not allowed as the prefix. If the prefix is the name of a subprogram or accept statement and if there is more than one visible enclosing subprogram or accept statement of this name, the expanded name is ambiguous, independently of the selector.

19 If, according to the visibility rules, there is at least one possible interpretation of the prefix of a selected component as the name of an enclosing subprogram or accept statement, then the only interpretations considered are those of rule (f), as expanded names (no interpretations of the prefix as a function call are then considered).

The evaluation of a name that is a selected component includes the evaluation of the prefix.   20

Examples of selected components: 21

TOMORROW.MONTH	--	a record component	(see 3.7)
NEXT_CAR.OWNER	--	a record component	(see 3.8.1)
NEXT_CAR.OWNER.AGE	--	a record component	(see 3.8.1)
WRITER.UNIT	--	a record component (a discriminant)	(see 3.7.3)
MIN_CELL(H).VALUE	--	a record component of the result	(see 6.1 and 3.8.1)
	--	of the function call MIN_CELL(H)	
CONTROL.SEIZE	--	an entry of the task CONTROL	(see 9.1 and 9.2)
POOL(K).WRITE	--	an entry of the task POOL(K)	(see 9.1 and 9.2)
NEXT_CAR.all	--	the object designated by	
	--	the access variable NEXT_CAR	(see 3.8.1)

Examples of expanded names: 22

TABLE_MANAGER.INSERT	--	a procedure of the visible part of a package	(see 7.5)
KEY_MANAGER."<"	--	an operator of the visible part of a package	(see 7.4.2)
DOT_PRODUCT.SUM	--	a variable declared in a procedure body	(see 6.5)
BUFFER.POOL	--	a variable declared in a task unit	(see 9.12)
BUFFER.READ	--	an entry of a task unit	(see 9.12)
SWAP.TEMP	--	a variable declared in a block statement	(see 5.6)
STANDARD.BOOLEAN	--	the name of a predefined type	(see 8.6 and C)

Note:

For a record with components that are other records, the above rules imply that the simple name   23
must be given at each level for the name of a subcomponent. For example, the name
NEXT_CAR.OWNER.BIRTH.MONTH cannot be shortened (NEXT_CAR.OWNER.MONTH is not
allowed).

References: accept statement 9.5, access type 3.8, access value 3.8, appropriate for a type 4.1, block statement 5.6,   24
body of a program unit 3.9, character literal 2.5, component of a record 3.7, constraint_error exception 11.1, declaration 3.1, designate 3.8, discriminant 3.3, entity 3.1, entry 9.5, entry family 9.5, function call 6.4, index 3.6, loop statement 5.5, object 3.2.1, occur immediately within 8.1, operator 4.5, operator symbol 6.1, overloading 8.3, package 7,
predefined type C, prefix 4.1, procedure body 6.3, program unit 6, raising of exceptions 11, record 3.7, record component 3.7, renaming declaration 8.5, reserved word 2.9, simple name 4.1, subprogram 6, subunit 10.2, task 9, task
object 9.2, task unit 9, variable 3.7.3, variant 3.7.3, visibility 8.3, visible part 3.7.3

4.1.4 Attributes

An attribute denotes a basic operation of an entity given by a prefix.   1

    attribute ::= prefix'attribute_designator   2

    attribute_designator ::= simple_name [(*universal_static*_expression)]

The applicable attribute designators depend on the prefix. An attribute can be a basic operation   3
delivering a value; alternatively it can be a function, a type, or a range. The meaning of the prefix of
an attribute must be determinable independently of the attribute designator and independently of
the fact that it is the prefix of an attribute.

4   The attributes defined by the language are summarized in Annex A. In addition, an implementation may provide implementation-defined attributes; their description must be given in Appendix F. The attribute designator of any implementation-defined attribute must not be the same as that of any language-defined attribute.

5   The evaluation of a name that is an attribute consists of the evaluation of the prefix.

Notes:

6   The attribute designators DIGITS, DELTA, and RANGE have the same identifier as a reserved word. However, no confusion is possible since an attribute designator is always preceded by an apostrophe. The only predefined attribute designators that have a universal expression are those for certain operations of array types (see 3.6.2).

7   *Examples of attributes:*

```
COLOR'FIRST            -- minimum value of the enumeration type COLOR   (see 3.3.1  3.5)
RAINBOW'BASE'FIRST     -- same as COLOR'FIRST                           (see 3.3.2  3.3.3)
REAL'DIGITS            -- precision of the type REAL                    (see 3.5.7  3.5.8)
BOARD'LAST(2)          -- upper bound of the second dimension of BOARD  (see 3.6.1  3.6.2)
BOARD'RANGE(1)         -- index range of the first dimension of BOARD   (see 3.6.1  3.6.2)
POOL(K)'TERMINATED     -- TRUE if task POOL(K) is terminated            (see 9.2    9.9)
DATE'SIZE              -- number of bits for records of type DATE       (see 3.7    13.7.2)
MESSAGE'ADDRESS        -- address of the record variable MESSAGE        (see 3.7.2  13.7.2)
```

8   *References:* appropriate for a type 4.1, basic operation 3.3.3, declared entity 3.1, name 4.1, prefix 4.1, reserved word 2.9, simple name 4.1, static expression 4.9, type 3.3, universal expression 4.10

4.2 Literals

1   A literal is either a numeric literal, an enumeration literal, the literal **null**, or a string literal. The evaluation of a literal yields the corresponding value.

2   Numeric literals are the literals of the types *universal_integer* and *universal_real*. Enumeration literals include character literals and yield values of the corresponding enumeration types. The literal **null** yields a null access value which designates no objects at all.

3   A string literal is a basic operation that combines a sequence of characters into a value of a one-dimensional array of a character type; the bounds of this array are determined according to the rules for positional array aggregates (see 4.3.2). For a null string literal, the upper bound is the predecessor, as given by the PRED attribute, of the lower bound. The evaluation of a null string literal raises the exception CONSTRAINT_ERROR if the lower bound does not have a predecessor (see 3.5.5).

4   The type of a string literal and likewise the type of the literal **null** must be determinable solely from the context in which this literal appears, excluding the literal itself, but using the fact that the literal **null** is a value of an access type, and similarly that a string literal is a value of a one-dimensional array type whose component type is a character type.

5   The character literals corresponding to the graphic characters contained within a string literal must be visible at the place of the string literal (although these characters themselves are not used to determine the type of the string literal).

Examples: 6

```
3.14159_26536    --   a real literal
1_345            --   an integer literal
CLUBS            --   an enumeration literal
'A'              --   a character literal
"SOME TEXT"      --   a string literal
```

References: access type 3.8, aggregate 4.3, array 3.6, array bound 3.6, array type 3.6, character literal 2.5, character   7
type 3.5.2, component type 3.3, constraint_error exception 11.1, designate 3.8, dimension 3.6, enumeration literal
3.5.1, graphic character 2.1, integer literal 2.4, null access value 3.8, null literal 3.8, numeric literal 2.4, object 3.2.1,
real literal 2.4, string literal 2.6, type 3.3, universal_integer type 3.5.4, universal_real type 3.5.6, visibility 8.3

4.3 Aggregates

An aggregate is a basic operation that combines component values into a composite value of a   1
record or array type.

```
aggregate ::=                                                                            2
   (component_association  {, component_association})

component_association ::=
   [choice {| choice} => ] expression
```

Each component association associates an expression with components (possibly none). A compo-   3
nent association is said to be *named* if the components are specified explicitly by choices; it is
otherwise said to be *positional*. For a positional association, the (single) component is implicitly
specified by position, in the order of the corresponding component declarations for record components, in index order for array components.

Named associations can be given in any order (except for the choice **others**), but if both positional   4
and named associations are used in the same aggregate, then positional associations must occur
first, at their normal position. Hence once a named association is used, the rest of the aggregate
must use only named associations. Aggregates containing a single component association must
always be given in named notation. Specific rules concerning component associations exist for
record aggregates and array aggregates.

Choices in component associations have the same syntax as in variant parts (see 3.7.3). A choice   5
that is a component simple name is only allowed in a record aggregate. For a component association, a choice that is a simple expression or a discrete range is only allowed in an array aggregate;
a choice that is a simple expression specifies the component at the corresponding index value;
similarly a discrete range specifies the components at the index values in the range. The choice
others is only allowed in a component association if the association appears last and has this
single choice; it specifies all remaining components, if any.

Each component of the value defined by an aggregate must be represented once and only once in   6
the aggregate. Hence each aggregate must be complete and a given component is not allowed to
be specified by more than one choice.

The type of an aggregate must be determinable solely from the context in which the aggregate   7
appears, excluding the aggregate itself, but using the fact that this type must be composite and not
limited. The type of an aggregate in turn determines the required type for each of its components.

Notes:

8 The above rule implies that the determination of the type of an aggregate cannot use any information from within the aggregate. In particular, this determination cannot use the type of the expression of a component association, or the form or the type of a choice. An aggregate can always be distinguished from an expression enclosed by parentheses: this is a consequence of the fact that named notation is required for an aggregate with a single component.

9 *References:* array aggregate 4.3.2, array type 3.6, basic operation 3.3.3, choice 3.7.3, component 3.3, composite type 3.3, composite value 3.3, discrete range 3.6, expression 4.4, index 3.6, limited type 7.4.4, primary 4.4, record aggregate 4.3.1, record type 3.7, simple expression 4.4, simple name 4.1, type 3.3, variant part 3.7.3

4.3.1 Record Aggregates

1 If the type of an aggregate is a record type, the component names given as choices must denote components (including discriminants) of the record type. If the choice **others** is given as a choice of a record aggregate, it must represent at least one component. A component association with the choice **others** or with more than one choice is only allowed if the represented components are all of the same type. The expression of a component association must have the type of the associated record components.

2 The value specified for a discriminant that governs a variant part must be given by a static expression (note that this value determines which dependent components must appear in the record value).

3 For the evaluation of a record aggregate, the expressions given in the component associations are evaluated in some order that is not defined by the language. The expression of a named association is evaluated once for each associated component. A check is made that the value of each subcomponent of the aggregate belongs to the subtype of this subcomponent. The exception CONSTRAINT_ERROR is raised if this check fails.

4 *Example of a record aggregate with positional associations:*

        (4, JULY, 1776)   -- see 3.7

5 *Examples of record aggregates with named associations:*

        (DAY => 4, MONTH => JULY, YEAR => 1776)
        (MONTH => JULY, DAY => 4, YEAR => 1776)

        (DISK, CLOSED, TRACK => 5, CYLINDER => 12)   -- see 3.7.3
        (UNIT => DISK, STATUS => CLOSED, CYLINDER => 9, TRACK => 1)

6 *Example of component association with several choices:*

        (VALUE => 0, SUCC|PRED => new CELL'(0, null, null))   -- see 3.8.1
        -- The allocator is evaluated twice: SUCC and PRED designate different cells

Note:

7 For an aggregate with positional associations, discriminant values appear first since the discriminant part is given first in the record type declaration; they must be in the same order as in the discriminant part.

References: aggregate 4.3, allocator 4.8, choice 3.7.3, component association 4.3, component name 3.7, constraint 3.3, constraint_error exception 11.1, depend on a discriminant 3.7.1, discriminant 3.3, discriminant part 3.7.1, evaluate 4.5, expression 4.4, in some order 1.6, program 10, raising of exceptions 11, record component 3.7, record type 3.7, satisfy 3.3, static expression 4.9, subcomponent 3.3, subtype 3.3.2, type 3.3, variant part 3.7.3

8

4.3.2 Array Aggregates

If the type of an aggregate is a one-dimensional array type, then each choice must specify values of the index type, and the expression of each component association must be of the component type.

1

If the type of an aggregate is a multidimensional array type, an n-dimensional aggregate is written as a one-dimensional aggregate, in which the expression specified for each component association is itself written as an (n-1)-dimensional aggregate which is called a *subaggregate*; the index subtype of the one-dimensional aggregate is given by the first index position of the array type. The same rule is used to write a subaggregate if it is again multidimensional, using successive index positions. A string literal is allowed in a multidimensional aggregate at the place of a one-dimensional array of a character type. In what follows, the rules concerning array aggregates are formulated in terms of one-dimensional aggregates.

2

Apart from a final component association with the single choice **others**, the rest (if any) of the component associations of an array aggregate must be either all positional or all named. A named association of an array aggregate is only allowed to have a choice that is not static, or likewise a choice that is a null range, if the aggregate includes a single component association and this component association has a single choice. An **others** choice is static if the applicable index constraint is static.

3

The bounds of an array aggregate that has an **others** choice are determined by the applicable index constraint. An **others** choice is only allowed if the aggregate appears in one of the following contexts (which defines the applicable index constraint):

4

(a) The aggregate is an actual parameter, a generic actual parameter, the result expression of a function, or the expression that follows an assignment compound delimiter. Moreover, the subtype of the corresponding formal parameter, generic formal parameter, function result, or object is a constrained array subtype.

5

For an aggregate that appears in such a context and contains an association with an **others** choice, named associations are allowed for other associations only in the case of a (nongeneric) actual parameter or function result. If the aggregate is a multidimensional array, this restriction also applies to each of its subaggregates.

6

(b) The aggregate is the operand of a qualified expression whose type mark denotes a constrained array subtype.

7

(c) The aggregate is the expression of the component association of an enclosing (array or record) aggregate. Moreover, if this enclosing aggregate is a multidimensional array aggregate then it is itself in one of these three contexts.

8

The bounds of an array aggregate that does not have an **others** choice are determined as follows. For an aggregate that has named associations, the bounds are determined by the smallest and largest choices given. For a positional aggregate, the lower bound is determined by the applicable index constraint if the aggregate appears in one of the contexts (a) through (c); otherwise, the lower bound is given by S'FIRST where S is the index subtype; in either case, the upper bound is determined by the number of components.

9

10 The evaluation of an array aggregate that is not a subaggregate proceeds in two steps. First, the choices of this aggregate and of its subaggregates, if any, are evaluated in some order that is not defined by the language. Second, the expressions of the component associations of the array aggregate are evaluated in some order that is not defined by the language; the expression of a named association is evaluated once for each associated component. The evaluation of a subaggregate consists of this second step (the first step is omitted since the choices have already been evaluated).

11 For the evaluation of an aggregate that is not a null array, a check is made that the index values defined by choices belong to the corresponding index subtypes, and also that the value of each subcomponent of the aggregate belongs to the subtype of this subcomponent. For an n-dimensional multidimensional aggregate, a check is made that all (n-1)-dimensional subaggregates have the same bounds. The exception CONSTRAINT_ERROR is raised if any of these checks fails.

Note:

12 The allowed contexts for an array aggregate including an **others** choice are such that the bounds of such an aggregate are always known from the context.

13 *Examples of array aggregates with positional associations:*

```
(7, 9, 5, 1, 3, 2, 4, 8, 6, 0)
TABLE'(5, 8, 4, 1, others => 0)  --  see 3.6
```

14 *Examples of array aggregates with named associations:*

```
(1 .. 5 => (1 .. 8 => 0.0))       -- two-dimensional
(1 .. N => new CELL)              -- N new cells, in particular for N = 0

TABLE'(2 | 4 | 10 =>  1, others   => 0)
SCHEDULE'(MON .. FRI => TRUE,  others => FALSE)  -- see 3.6
SCHEDULE'(WED | SUN => FALSE,  others => TRUE )
```

15 *Examples of two-dimensional array aggregates:*

```
-- Three aggregates for the same value of type MATRIX (see 3.6):

((1.1, 1.2, 1.3), (2.1, 2.2, 2.3))
(1 => (1.1, 1.2, 1.3), 2 => (2.1, 2.2, 2.3))
(1 => (1 => 1.1, 2 => 1.2, 3 => 1.3), 2 => (1 => 2.1, 2 => 2.2, 3 => 2.3))
```

16 *Examples of aggregates as initial values:*

```
A : TABLE := (7, 9, 5, 1, 3, 2, 4, 8, 6, 0);        -- A(1)=7, A(10)=0
B : TABLE := TABLE'(2 | 4 | 10 => 1, others => 0);  -- B(1)=0, B(10)=1
C : constant MATRIX := (1 .. 5 => (1 .. 8 => 0.0)); -- C'FIRST(1)=1, C'LAST(2)=8

D : BIT_VECTOR(M .. N) := (M .. N => TRUE);  -- see 3.6
E : BIT_VECTOR(M .. N) := (others   => TRUE);
F : STRING(1 .. 1) := (1 => 'F');  -- a one component aggregate: same as "F"
```

17 *References:* actual parameter 6.4.1, aggregate 4.3, array type 3.6, assignment compound delimiter 5.2, choice 3.7.3, component 3.3, component association 4.3, component type 3.3, constrained array subtype 3.6, constraint 3.3, constraint_error exception 11.1, dimension 3.6, evaluate 4.5, expression 4.4, formal parameter 6.1, function 6.5, in some order 1.6, index constraint 3.6.1, index range 3.6, index subtype 3.6, index type 3.6, named component association 4.3, null array 3.6.1, object 3.2, positional component association 4.3, qualified expression 4.7, raising of exceptions 11, static expression 4.9, subcomponent 3.3, type 3.3

4.3.2 Array Aggregates   **4-10**

4.4 Expressions

An expression is a formula that defines the computation of a value.

```
expression ::=
      relation {and relation}   |  relation {and then relation}
    | relation {or relation}    |  relation {or else relation}
    | relation {xor relation}
```

```
relation ::=
      simple_expression [relational_operator simple_expression]
    | simple_expression [not] in range
    | simple_expression [not] in type_mark
```

```
simple_expression ::= [unary_adding_operator] term {binary_adding_ operator term}
```

```
term ::= factor {multiplying_operator factor}
```

```
factor ::= primary [** primary] | abs primary | not primary
```

```
primary ::=
      numeric_literal | null | aggregate | string_literal | name | allocator
    | function_call | type_conversion | qualified_expression | (expression)
```

Each primary has a value and a type. The only names allowed as primaries are named numbers; attributes that yield values; and names denoting objects (the value of such a primary is the value of the object) or denoting values. Names that denote formal parameters of mode **out** are not allowed as primaries; names of their subcomponents are only allowed in the case of discriminants.

The type of an expression depends only on the type of its constituents and on the operators applied; for an overloaded constituent or operator, the determination of the constituent type, or the identification of the appropriate operator, depends on the context. For each predefined operator, the operand and result types are given in section 4.5.

Examples of primaries:

```
4.0                  --  real literal
PI                   --  named number
(1 .. 10 => 0)       --  array aggregate
SUM                  --  variable
INTEGER'LAST         --  attribute
SINE(X)              --  function call
COLOR'(BLUE)         --  qualified expression
REAL(M*N)            --  conversion
(LINE_COUNT + 10)    --  parenthesized expression
```

Examples of expressions:.

```
VOLUME                        --  primary
not DESTROYED                 --  factor
2*LINE_COUNT                  --  term
-4.0                          --  simple expression
-4.0 + A                      --  simple expression
B**2 - 4.0*A*C                --  simple expression
PASSWORD(1 .. 3) = "BWV"      --  relation
COUNT in SMALL_INT            --  relation
COUNT not in SMALL_INT        --  relation
INDEX = 0 or ITEM_HIT         --  expression
(COLD and SUNNY) or WARM      --  expression (parentheses are required)
A**(B**C)                     --  expression (parentheses are required)
```

7 *References:* aggregate 4.3, allocator 4.8, array aggregate 4.3.2, attribute 4.1.4, binary adding operator 4.5 4.5.3, context of overload resolution 8.7, exponentiating operator 4.5 4.5.6, function call 6.4, multiplying operator 4.5 4.5.5, name 4.1, named number 3.2, null literal 3.8, numeric literal 2.4, object 3.2, operator 4.5, overloading 8.3, overloading an operator 6.7, qualified expression 4.7, range 3.5, real literal 2.4, relation 4.5.1, relational operator 4.5 4.5.2, result type 6.1, string literal 2.6, type 3.3, type conversion 4.6, type mark 3.3.2, unary adding operator 4.5 4.5.4, variable 3.2.1

4.5 Operators and Expression Evaluation

1 The language defines the following six classes of operators. The corresponding operator symbols (except /=), and only those, can be used as designators in declarations of functions for user-defined operators. They are given in the order of increasing precedence.

2

logical_operator	::=	**and** | **or** | **xor**
relational_operator	::=	= | /= | < | <= | > | >=
binary_adding_operator	::=	+ | - | &
unary_adding_operator	::=	+ | -
multiplying_operator	::=	* | / | **mod** | **rem**
highest_precedence_operator	::=	** | **abs** | **not**

3 The short-circuit control forms **and then** and **or else** have the same precedence as logical operators. The membership tests **in** and **not in** have the same precedence as relational operators.

4 For a term, simple expression, relation, or expression, operators of higher precedence are associated with their operands before operators of lower precedence. In this case, for a sequence of operators of the same precedence level, the operators are associated in textual order from left to right; parentheses can be used to impose specific associations.

5 The operands of a factor, of a term, of a simple expression, or of a relation, and the operands of an expression that does not contain a short-circuit control form, are evaluated in some order that is not defined by the language (but before application of the corresponding operator). The right operand of a short-circuit control form is evaluated if and only if the left operand has a certain value (see 4.5.1).

6 For each form of type declaration, certain of the above operators are *predefined*, that is, they are implicitly declared by the type declaration. For each such implicit operator declaration, the names of the parameters are LEFT and RIGHT for binary operators; the single parameter is called RIGHT for unary adding operators and for the unary operators **abs** and **not**. The effect of the predefined operators is explained in subsections 4.5.1 through 4.5.7.

7 The predefined operations on integer types either yield the mathematically correct result or raise the exception NUMERIC_ERROR. A predefined operation that delivers a result of an integer type (other than *universal_integer*) can only raise the exception NUMERIC_ERROR if the mathematical result is not a value of the type. The predefined operations on real types yield results whose accuracy is defined in section 4.5.7. A predefined operation that delivers a result of a real type (other than *universal_real*) can only raise the exception NUMERIC_ERROR if the result is not within the range of the safe numbers of the type, as explained in section 4.5.7.

Examples of precedence:

```
not SUNNY or WARM      --   same as (not SUNNY) or WARM
X > 4.0 and Y > 0.0    -- ` same as (X > 4.0) and (Y > 0.0)

-4.0*A**2              --   same as -(4.0 * (A**2))
abs(1 + A) + B         --   same as (abs (1 + A)) + B
Y**(-3)                --   parentheses are necessary
A / B * C              --   same as (A/B)*C
A + (B + C)            --   evaluate B + C before adding it to A
```

References: designator 6.1, expression 4.4, factor 4.4, implicit declaration 3.1, in some order 1.6, integer type 3.5.4, membership test 4.5.2, name 4.1, numeric_error exception 11.1, overloading 6.6 8.7, raising of an exception 11, range 3.5, real type 3.5.6, relation 4.4, safe number 3.5.6, short-circuit control form 4.5 4.5.1, simple expression 4.4, term 4.4, type 3.3, type declaration 3.3.1, universal_integer type 3.5.4, universal_real type 3.5.6

4.5.1 Logical Operators and Short-circuit Control Forms

The following logical operators are predefined for any boolean type and any one-dimensional array type whose components are of a boolean type; in either case the two operands have the same type.

Operator	Operation	Operand type	Result type
and	conjunction	any boolean type array of boolean components	same boolean type same array type
or	inclusive disjunction	any boolean type array of boolean components	same boolean type same array type
xor	exclusive disjunction	any boolean type array of boolean components	same boolean type same array type

The operations on arrays are performed on a component-by-component basis on matching components, if any (as for equality, see 4.5.2). The bounds of the resulting array are those of the left operand. A check is made that for each component of the left operand there is a matching component of the right operand, and vice versa. The exception CONSTRAINT_ERROR is raised if this check fails.

The short-circuit control forms **and then** and **or else** are defined for two operands of a boolean type and deliver a result of the same type. The left operand of a short-circuit control form is always evaluated first. If the left operand of an expression with the control form **and then** evaluates to FALSE, the right operand is not evaluated and the value of the expression is FALSE. If the left operand of an expression with the control form **or else** evaluates to TRUE, the right operand is not evaluated and the value of the expression is TRUE. If both operands are evaluated, **and then** delivers the same result as **and**, and **or else** delivers the same result as **or**.

Note: The conventional meaning of the logical operators is given by the following truth table:

A	B	A **and** B	A **or** B	A **xor** B
TRUE	TRUE	TRUE	TRUE	FALSE
TRUE	FALSE	FALSE	TRUE	TRUE
FALSE	TRUE	FALSE	TRUE	TRUE
FALSE	FALSE	FALSE	FALSE	FALSE

7 *Examples of logical operators:*

```
SUNNY or WARM
FILTER(1 .. 10) and FILTER(15 .. 24)    --    see 3.6.1
```

8 *Examples of short-circuit control forms:*

```
NEXT_CAR.OWNER /= null and then NEXT_CAR.OWNER.AGE > 25    --    see 3.8.1
N = 0 or else A(N) = HIT_VALUE
```

9 *References:* array type 3.6, boolean type 3.5.3, bound of an index range 3.6.1, component of an array 3.6, constraint_error exception 11.1, dimension 3.6, false boolean value 3.5.3, index subtype 3.6, matching components of arrays 4.5.2, null array 3.6.1, operation 3.3, operator 4.5, predefined operator 4.5, raising of exceptions 11, true boolean value 3.5.3, type 3.3

4.5.2 Relational Operators and Membership Tests

1 The equality and inequality operators are predefined for any type that is not limited. The other relational operators are the ordering operators < (less than), <= (less than or equal), > (greater than), and >= (greater than or equal). The ordering operators are predefined for any scalar type, and for any discrete array type, that is, a one-dimensional array type whose components are of a discrete type. The operands of each predefined relational operator have the same type. The result type is the predefined type BOOLEAN.

2 The relational operators have their conventional meaning: the result is equal to TRUE if the corresponding relation is satisfied; the result is FALSE otherwise. The inequality operator gives the complementary result to the equality operator: FALSE if equal, TRUE if not equal.

3
Operator	Operation	Operand type	Result type
= /=	equality and inequality	any type	BOOLEAN
< <= > >=	test for ordering	any scalar type	BOOLEAN
		discrete array type	BOOLEAN

4 Equality for the discrete types is equality of the values. For real operands whose values are *nearly* equal, the results of the predefined relational operators are given in section 4.5.7. Two access values are equal either if they designate the same object, or if both are equal to the null value of the access type.

5 For two array values or two record values of the same type, the left operand is equal to the right operand if and only if for each component of the left operand there is a *matching component* of the right operand and vice versa; and the values of matching components are equal, as given by the predefined equality operator for the component type. In particular, two null arrays of the same type are always equal; two null records of the same type are always equal.

6 For comparing two records of the same type, *matching components* are those which have the same component identifier.

7 For comparing two one-dimensional arrays of the same type, *matching components* are those (if any) whose index values match in the following sense: the lower bounds of the index ranges are defined to match, and the successors of matching indices are defined to match. For comparing two multidimensional arrays, matching components are those whose index values match in successive index positions.

If equality is explicitly defined for a limited type, it does not extend to composite types having sub-components of the limited type (explicit definition of equality is allowed for such composite types). **8**

The ordering operators $<$, $<=$, $>$, and $>=$ that are defined for discrete array types correspond to *lexicographic* order using the predefined order relation of the component type. A null array is lexicographically less than any array having at least one component. In the case of nonnull arrays, the left operand is lexicographically less than the right operand if the first component of the left operand is less than that of the right; otherwise the left operand is lexicographically less than the right operand only if their first components are equal and the tail of the left operand is lexicographically less than that of the right (the tail consists of the remaining components beyond the first and can be null). **9**

The membership tests **in** and **not in** are predefined for all types. The result type is the predefined type BOOLEAN. For a membership test with a range, the simple expression and the bounds of the range must be of the same scalar type; for a membership test with a type mark, the type of the simple expression must be the base type of the type mark. The evaluation of the membership test **in** yields the result TRUE if the value of the simple expression is within the given range, or if this value belongs to the subtype denoted by the given type mark; otherwise this evaluation yields the result FALSE (for a value of a real type, see 4.5.7). The membership test **not in** gives the complementary result to the membership test **in**. **10**

Examples: **11**

```
X /= Y

""  <  "A"  and  "A"  <  "AA"      --  TRUE
"AA"  <  "B"  and  "A"  <  "A  "    --  TRUE

MY_CAR = null              -- true if MY_CAR has been set to null (see 3.8.1)
MY_CAR = YOUR_CAR          -- true if we both share the same car
MY_CAR.all = YOUR_CAR.all  -- true if the two cars are identical

N not in 1 .. 10       -- range membership test
TODAY in MON .. FRI    -- range membership test
TODAY in WEEKDAY       -- subtype membership test  (see 3.5.1)
ARCHIVE in DISK_UNIT   -- subtype membership test  (see 3.7.3)
```

Notes:

No exception is ever raised by a predefined relational operator or by a membership test, but an exception can be raised by the evaluation of the operands. **12**

If a record type has components that depend on discriminants, two values of this type have matching components if and only if their discriminants are equal. Two nonnull arrays have matching components if and only if the value of the attribute LENGTH(N) for each index position N is the same for both. **13**

References: access value 3.8, array type 3.6, base type 3.3, belong to a subtype 3.3, boolean predefined type 3.5.3, bound of a range 3.5, component 3.3, component identifier 3.7, component type 3.3, composite type 3.3, designate 3.8, dimension 3.6, discrete type 3.5, evaluation 4.5, exception 11, index 3.6, index range 3.6, limited type 7.4.4, null access value 3.8, null array 3.6.1, null record 3.7, object 3.2.1, operation 3.3, operator 4.5, predefined operator 4.5, raising of exceptions 11, range 3.5, record type 3.7, scalar type 3.5, simple expression 4.4, subcomponent 3.3, successor 3.5.5, type 3.3, type mark 3.3.2 **14**

4.5.3 Binary Adding Operators

1   The binary adding operators + and - are predefined for any numeric type and have their conventional meaning. The catenation operators & are predefined for any one-dimensional array type that is not limited.

2

Operator	Operation	Left operand type	Right operand type	Result type
+	addition	any numeric type	same numeric type	same numeric type
-	subtraction	any numeric type	same numeric type	same numeric type
&	catenation	any array type	same array type	same array type
		any array type	the component type	same array type
		the component type	any array type	same array type
		the component type	the component type	any array type

3   For real types, the accuracy of the result is determined by the operand type (see 4.5.7).

4   If both operands are one-dimensional arrays, the result of the catenation is a one-dimensional array whose length is the sum of the lengths of its operands, and whose components comprise the components of the left operand followed by the components of the right operand. The lower bound of this result is the lower bound of the left operand, unless the left operand is a null array, in which case the result of the catenation is the right operand.

5   If either operand is of the component type of an array type, the result of the catenation is given by the above rules, using in place of this operand an array having this operand as its only component and having the lower bound of the index subtype of the array type as its lower bound.

6   The exception CONSTRAINT_ERROR is raised by catenation if the upper bound of the result exceeds the range of the index subtype, unless the result is a null array. This exception is also raised if any operand is of the component type but has a value that does not belong to the component subtype.

7   *Examples:*

```
Z + 0.1        --  Z must be of a real type

"A" & "BCD"    --  catenation of two string literals
'A' & "BCD"    --  catenation of a character literal and a string literal
'A' & 'A'      --  catenation of two character literals
```

8   *References:* array type 3.6, character literal 2.5, component type 3.3, constraint_error exception 11.1, dimension 3.6, index subtype 3.6, length of an array 3.6.2, limited type 7.4.4, null array 3.6.1, numeric type 3.5, operation 3.3, operator 4.5, predefined operator 4.5, raising of exceptions 11, range of an index subtype 3.6.1, real type 3.5.6, string literal 2.6, type 3.3

4.5.4 Unary Adding Operators

1   The unary adding operators + and - are predefined for any numeric type and have their conventional meaning. For each of these operators, the operand and the result have the same type.

Operator	Operation	Operand type	Result type	
+	identity	any numeric type	same numeric type	2
-	negation	any numeric type	same numeric type	

References: numeric type 3.5, operation 3.3, operator 4.5, predefined operator 4.5, type 3.3   3

4.5.5 Multiplying Operators

The operators ∗ and / are predefined for any integer and any floating point type and have their con-   1
ventional meaning; the operators **mod** and **rem** are predefined for any integer type. For each of
these operators, the operands and the result have the same base type. For floating point types, the
accuracy of the result is determined by the operand type (see 4.5.7).

Operator	Operation	Operand type	Result type	
∗	multiplication	any integer type any floating point type	same integer type same floating point type	2
/	integer division floating division	any integer type any floating point type	same integer type same floating point type	
mod	modulus	any integer type	same integer type	
rem	remainder	any integer type	same integer type	

Integer division and remainder are defined by the relation   3

$$A = (A/B) * B + (A \text{ rem } B)$$

where (A **rem** B) has the sign of A and an absolute value less than the absolute value of B. Integer   4
division satisfies the identity

$$(-A)/B = -(A/B) = A/(-B)$$

The result of the modulus operation is such that (A **mod** B) has the sign of B and an absolute value   5
less than the absolute value of B; in addition, for some integer value N, this result must satisfy the
relation

$$A = B * N + (A \text{ mod } B)$$

For each fixed point type, the following multiplication and division operators, with an operand of   6
the predefined type INTEGER , are predefined.

Operator	Operation	Left operand type	Right operand type	Result type	
∗	multiplication	any fixed point type INTEGER	INTEGER any fixed point type	same as left same as right	7
/	division	any fixed point type	INTEGER	same as left	

8   Integer multiplication of fixed point values is equivalent to repeated addition. Division of a fixed point value by an integer does not involve a change in type but is approximate (see 4.5.7).

9   Finally, the following multiplication and division operators are declared in the predefined package STANDARD. These two special operators apply to operands of all fixed point types (it is a consequence of other rules that they cannot be renamed or given as generic actual parameters).

10

Operator	Operation	Left operand type	Right operand type	Result type
*	multiplication	any fixed point type	any fixed point type	*universal_fixed*
/	division	any fixed point type	any fixed point type	*universal_fixed*

11   Multiplication of operands of the same or of different fixed point types is exact and delivers a result of the anonymous predefined fixed point type *universal_fixed* whose delta is arbitrarily small. The result of any such multiplication must always be explicitly converted to some numeric type. This ensures explicit control of the accuracy of the computation. The same considerations apply to division of a fixed point value by another fixed point value. No other operators are defined for the type *universal_fixed*.

12   The exception NUMERIC_ERROR is raised by integer division, **rem**, and **mod** if the right operand is zero.

13   *Examples:*

```
I  : INTEGER := 1;
J  : INTEGER := 2;
K  : INTEGER := 3;

X  : REAL digits 6 := 1.0;          --    see 3.5.7
Y  : REAL digits 6 := 2.0;

F  : FRACTION delta 0.0001 := 0.1;  --    see 3.5.9
G  : FRACTION delta 0.0001 := 0.1;
```

Expression	Value	Result Type
I*J	2	same as I and J, that is, INTEGER
K/J	1	same as K and J, that is, INTEGER
K **mod** J	1	same as K and J, that is, INTEGER
X/Y	0.5	same as X and Y, that is, REAL
F/2	0.05	same as F, that is, FRACTION
3*F	0.3	same as F, that is, FRACTION
F*G	0.01	*universal_fixed*, conversion needed
FRACTION(F*G)	0.01	FRACTION, as stated by the conversion
REAL(J)*Y	4.0	REAL, the type of both operands after conversion of J

Notes:

For positive A and B, A/B is the quotient and A **rem** B is the remainder when A is divided by B. The
following relations are satisfied by the **rem** operator:

```
A   rem  (-B)  =    A rem  B
(-A)  rem   B   =   -(A rem  B)
```

For any integer K, the following identity holds:

```
A mod B      =   (A + K*B) mod  B
```

The relations between integer division, remainder, and modulus are illustrated by the following
table:

A	B	A/B	A rem B	A mod B	A	B	A/B	A rem B	A mod B
10	5	2	0	0	-10	5	-2	0	0
11	5	2	1	1	-11	5	-2	-1	4
12	5	2	2	2	-12	5	-2	-2	3
13	5	2	3	3	-13	5	-2	-3	2
14	5	2	4	4	-14	5	-2	-4	1
10	-5	-2	0	0	-10	-5	2	0	0
11	-5	-2	1	-4	-11	-5	2	-1	-1
12	-5	-2	2	-3	-12	-5	2	-2	-2
13	-5	-2	3	-2	-13	-5	2	-3	-3
14	-5	-2	4	-1	-14	-5	2	-4	-4

References: actual parameter 6.4.1, base type 3.3, declaration 3.1, delta of a fixed point type 3.5.9, fixed point type
3.5.9, floating point type 3.5.7, generic formal subprogram 12.1, integer type 3.5.4, numeric type 3.5, numeric_error
exception 11.1, predefined operator 4.5, raising of exceptions 11, renaming declaration 8.5, standard predefined
package 8.6, type conversion 4.6

4.5.6 Highest Precedence Operators

The highest precedence unary operator **abs** is predefined for any numeric type. The highest
precedence unary operator **not** is predefined for any boolean type and any one-dimensional array
type whose components have a boolean type.

Operator	Operation	Operand type	Result type
abs	absolute value	any numeric type	same numeric type
not	logical negation	any boolean type array of boolean components	same boolean type same array type

The operator **not** that applies to a one-dimensional array of boolean components yields a one-
dimensional boolean array with the same bounds; each component of the result is obtained by
logical negation of the corresponding component of the operand (that is, the component that has
the same index value).

4 The highest precedence *exponentiating* operator ∗∗ is predefined for each integer type and for each floating point type. In either case the right operand, called the exponent, is of the predefined type INTEGER.

5
Operator	Operation	Left operand type	Right operand type	Result type
∗∗	exponentiation	any integer type	INTEGER	same as left
		any floating point type	INTEGER	same as left

6 Exponentiation with a positive exponent is equivalent to repeated multiplication of the left operand by itself, as indicated by the exponent and from left to right. For an operand of a floating point type, the exponent can be negative, in which case the value is the reciprocal of the value with the positive exponent. Exponentiation by a zero exponent delivers the value one. Exponentiation of a value of a floating point type is approximate (see 4.5.7). Exponentiation of an integer raises the exception CONSTRAINT_ERROR for a negative exponent.

7 *References:* array type 3.6, boolean type 3.5.3, bound of an array 3.6.1, component of an array 3.6, constraint_error exception 11.1, dimensionality 3.6, floating point type 3.5.9, index 3.6, integer type 3.5.4, multiplication operation 4.5.5, predefined operator 4.5, raising of exceptions 11

4.5.7 Accuracy of Operations with Real Operands

1 A real subtype specifies a set of model numbers. Both the accuracy required from any basic or predefined operation giving a real result, and the result of any predefined relation between real operands are defined in terms of these model numbers.

2 A *model interval* of a subtype is any interval whose bounds are model numbers of the subtype. The model interval associated with a value that belongs to a real subtype is the smallest model interval (of the subtype) that includes the value. (The model interval associated with a model number of a subtype consists of that number only.)

3 For any basic operation or predefined operator that yields a result of a real subtype, the required bounds on the result are given by a model interval defined as follows:

4 ● The result model interval is the smallest model interval (of the result subtype) that includes the minimum and the maximum of all the values obtained by applying the (exact) mathematical operation, when each operand is given any value of the model interval (of the operand subtype) defined for the operand.

5 ● The model interval of an operand that is itself the result of an operation, other than an implicit conversion, is the result model interval of this operation.

6 ● The model interval of an operand whose value is obtained by implicit conversion of a universal expression is the model interval associated with this value within the operand subtype.

7 The result model interval is undefined if the absolute value of one of the above mathematical results exceeds the largest safe number of the result type. Whenever the result model interval is undefined, it is highly desirable that the exception NUMERIC_ERROR be raised if the implementation cannot produce an actual result that is in the range of safe numbers. This is, however, not required by the language rules, in recognition of the fact that certain target machines do not permit easy detection of overflow situations. The value of the attribute MACHINE_OVERFLOWS indicates whether the target machine raises the exception NUMERIC_ERROR in overflow situations (see 13.7.3).

The safe numbers of a real type are defined (see 3.5.6) as a superset of the model numbers, for **8** which error bounds follow the same rules as for model numbers. Any definition given in this section in terms of model intervals can therefore be extended to safe intervals of safe numbers. A consequence of this extension is that an implementation is not allowed to raise the exception NUMERIC_ERROR when the result interval is a safe interval.

For the result of exponentiation, the model interval defining the bounds on the result is obtained by **9** applying the above rules to the sequence of multiplications defined by the exponent, and to the final division in the case of a negative exponent.

For the result of a relation between two real operands, consider for each operand the model interval (of the operand subtype) defined for the operand; the result can be any value obtained by **10** applying the mathematical comparison to values arbitrarily chosen in the corresponding operand model intervals. If either or both of the operand model intervals is undefined (and if neither of the operand evaluations raises an exception) then the result of the comparison is allowed to be any possible value (that is, either TRUE or FALSE).

The result of a membership test is defined in terms of comparisons of the operand value with the **11** lower and upper bounds of the given range or type mark (the usual rules apply to these comparisons).

Note:

For a floating point type the numbers 15.0, 3.0, and 5.0 are always model numbers. Hence X/Y **12** where X equals 15.0 and Y equals 3.0 yields exactly 5.0 according to the above rules. In the general case, division does not yield model numbers and in consequence one cannot assume that $(1.0/X)*X = 1.0$.

References: attribute 4.1.4, basic operation 3.3.3, bound of a range 3.5, error bound 3.5.6, exponentiation operation **13** 4.5.6, false boolean value 3.5.3, floating point type 3.5.9, machine_overflows attribute 13.7.1, membership test 4.5.2, model number 3.5.6, multiplication operation 4.5.5, numeric_error exception 11.1, predefined operation 3.3.3, raising of exceptions 11, range 3.5, real type 3.5.6, relation 4.4, relational operator 4.5.2 4.5, safe number 3.5.6, subtype 3.3, true boolean value 3.5.3, type conversion 4.6, type mark 3.3.2, universal expression 4.10

4.6 Type Conversions

The evaluation of an explicit type conversion evaluates the expression given as the operand, and **1** converts the resulting value to a specified *target* type. Explicit type conversions are allowed between closely related types as defined below.

    type_conversion ::= type_mark(expression)   **2**

The target type of a type conversion is the base type of the type mark. The type of the operand of a **3** type conversion must be determinable independently of the context (in particular, independently of the target type). Furthermore, the operand of a type conversion is not allowed to be a literal null, an allocator, an aggregate, or a string literal; an expression enclosed by parentheses is allowed as the operand of a type conversion only if the expression alone is allowed.

A conversion to a subtype consists of a conversion to the target type followed by a check that the **4** result of the conversion belongs to the subtype. A conversion of an operand of a given type to the type itself is allowed.

5   The other allowed explicit type conversions correspond to the following three cases:

6   (a) Numeric types

7   The operand can be of any numeric type; the value of the operand is converted to the target
         type which must also be a numeric type. For conversions involving real types, the result is
         within the accuracy of the specified subtype (see 4.5.7). The conversion of a real value to an
         integer type rounds to the nearest integer; if the operand is halfway between two integers
         (within the accuracy of the real subtype) rounding may be either up or down.

8   (b) Derived types

9   The conversion is allowed if one of the target type and the operand type is derived from the
         other, directly or indirectly, or if there exists a third type from which both types are derived,
         directly or indirectly.

10   (c) Array types

11   The conversion is allowed if the operand type and the target type are array types that satisfy
         the following conditions: both types must have the same dimensionality; for each index posi-
         tion the index types must either be the same or be convertible to each other; the component
         types must be the same; finally, if the component type is a type with discriminants or an
         access type, the component subtypes must be either both constrained or both unconstrained.
         If the type mark denotes an unconstrained array type, then, for each index position, the
         bounds of the result are obtained by converting the bounds of the operand to the cor-
         responding index type of the target type. If the type mark denotes a constrained array sub-
         type, then the bounds of the result are those imposed by the type mark. In either case, the
         value of each component of the result is that of the matching component of the operand (see
         4.5.2).

12   In the case of conversions of numeric types and derived types, the exception CONSTRAINT_ERROR
     is raised by the evaluation of a type conversion if the result of the conversion fails to satisfy a con-
     straint imposed by the type mark.

13   In the case of array types, a check is made that any constraint on the component subtype is the
     same for the operand array type as for the target array type. If the type mark denotes an
     unconstrained array type and if the operand is not a null array, then, for each index position, a
     check is made that the bounds of the result belong to the corresponding index subtype of the
     target type. If the type mark denotes a constrained array subtype, a check is made that for each
     component of the operand there is a matching component of the target subtype, and vice versa.
     The exception CONSTRAINT_ERROR is raised if any of these checks fails.

14   If a conversion is allowed from one type to another, the reverse conversion is also allowed. This
     reverse conversion is used where an actual parameter of mode **in out** or **out** has the form of a type
     conversion of a (variable) name as explained in section 6.4.1.

15   Apart from the explicit type conversions, the only allowed form of type conversion is the implicit
     conversion of a value of the type *universal_integer* or *universal_real* into another numeric type. An
     implicit conversion of an operand of type *universal_integer* to another integer type, or of an
     operand of type *universal_real* to another real type, can only be applied if the operand is either a
     numeric literal, a named number, or an attribute; such an operand is called a *convertible* universal
     operand in this section. An implicit conversion of a convertible universal operand is applied if and
     only if the innermost complete context (see 8.7) determines a unique (numeric) target type for the
     implicit conversion, and there is no legal interpretation of this context without this conversion.

Notes:

The rules for implicit conversions imply that no implicit conversion is ever applied to the operand of an explicit type conversion. Similarly, implicit conversions are not applied if both operands of a predefined relational operator are convertible universal operands.   15

The language allows implicit subtype conversions in the case of array types (see 5.2.1). An explicit type conversion can have the effect of a change of representation (in particular see 13.6). Explicit conversions are also used for actual parameters (see 6.4).   16

Examples of numeric type conversion: 17

```
REAL(2*J)      -- value is converted to floating point
INTEGER(1.6)   -- value is 2
INTEGER(-0.4)  -- value is 0
```

Example of conversion between derived types: 18

```
type A_FORM is new B_FORM;

X : A_FORM;
Y : B_FORM;

X := A_FORM(Y);
Y := B_FORM(X); -- the reverse conversion
```

Examples of conversions between array types: 19

```
type SEQUENCE is array (INTEGER range <>) of INTEGER;
subtype DOZEN is SEQUENCE(1 .. 12);
LEDGER : array(1 .. 100) of INTEGER;

SEQUENCE(LEDGER)             -- bounds are those of LEDGER
SEQUENCE(LEDGER(31 .. 42))   -- bounds are 31 and 42
DOZEN(LEDGER(31 .. 42))      -- bounds are those of DOZEN
```

Examples of implicit conversions: 20

```
X : INTEGER := 2;

X + 1 + 2          -- implicit conversion of each integer literal
1 + 2 + X          -- implicit conversion of each integer literal
X + (1 + 2)        -- implicit conversion of each integer literal

2 = (1 + 1)        -- no implicit conversion: the type is universal_integer
A'LENGTH = B'LENGTH  -- no implicit conversion: the type is universal_integer
C : constant := 3 + 2;  -- no implicit conversion: the type is universal_integer

X = 3 and 1 = 2    -- implicit conversion of 3, but not of 1 and 2
```

References: actual parameter 6.4.1, array type 3.6, attribute 4.1.4, base type 3.3, belong to a subtype 3.3, component 3.3, constrained array subtype 3.6, constraint_error exception 11.1, derived type 3.4, dimension 3.6, expression 4.4, floating point type 3.5.7, index 3.6, index subtype 3.6, index type 3.6, integer type 3.5.4, matching component 4.5.2, mode 6.1, name 4.1, named number 3.2, null array 3.6.1, numeric literal 2.4, numeric type 3.5, raising of exceptions 11, real type 3.5.6, representation 13.1, statement 5, subtype 3.3, type 3.3, type mark 3.3.2, unconstrained array type 3.6, universal_integer type 3.5.4, universal_real type 3.5.6, variable 3.2.1   21

4.7 Qualified Expressions

1 A qualified expression is used to state explicitly the type, and possibly the subtype, of an operand that is the given expression or aggregate.

2   qualified_expression ::=
          type_mark'(expression) | type_mark'aggregate

3 The operand must have the same type as the base type of the type mark. The value of a qualified expression is the value of the operand. The evaluation of a qualified expression evaluates the operand and checks that its value belongs to the subtype denoted by the type mark. The exception CONSTRAINT_ERROR is raised if this check fails.

4 *Examples:*

```
type MASK is (FIX, DEC, EXP, SIGNIF);
type CODE is (FIX, CLA, DEC, TNZ, SUB);

PRINT (MASK'(DEC));    --  DEC is of type MASK
PRINT (CODE'(DEC));    --  DEC is of type CODE

for J in CODE'(FIX) .. CODE'(DEC) loop ...  -- qualification needed for either FIX or DEC
for J in CODE range FIX .. DEC loop ...     -- qualification unnecessary
for J in CODE'(FIX) .. DEC loop ...         -- qualification unnecessary for DEC

DOZEN'(1 | 3 | 5 | 7 => 2, others => 0) -- see 4.6
```

Notes:

5 Whenever the type of an enumeration literal or aggregate is not known from the context, a qualified expression can be used to state the type explicitly. For example, an overloaded enumeration literal must be qualified in the following cases: when given as a parameter in a subprogram call to an overloaded subprogram that cannot otherwise be identified on the basis of remaining parameter or result types, in a relational expression where both operands are overloaded enumeration literals, or in an array or loop parameter range where both bounds are overloaded enumeration literals. Explicit qualification is also used to specify which one of a set of overloaded parameterless functions is meant, or to constrain a value to a given subtype.

6 *References:* aggregate 4.3, array 3.6, base type 3.3, bound of a range 3.5, constraint_error exception 11.1, context of overload resolution 8.7, enumeration literal 3.5.1, expression 4.4, function 6.5, loop parameter 5.5, overloading 8.5, raising of exceptions 11, range 3.3, relation 4.4, subprogram 6, subprogram call 6.4, subtype 3.3, type 3.3, type mark 3.3.2

4.8 Allocators

1 The evaluation of an allocator creates an object and yields an access value that designates the object.

2   allocator ::=
          new subtype_indication | new qualified_expression

The type of the object created by an allocator is the base type of the type mark given in either the   3
subtype indication or the qualified expression. For an allocator with a qualified expression, this
expression defines the initial value of the created object. The type of the access value returned by
an allocator must be determinable solely from the context, but using the fact that the value
returned is of an access type having the named designated type.

The only allowed forms of constraint in the subtype indication of an allocator are index and dis-   4
criminant constraints. If an allocator includes a subtype indication and if the type of the object
created is an array type or a type with discriminants that do not have default expressions, then the
subtype indication must either denote a constrained subtype, or include an explicit index or discriminant constraint.

If the type of the created object is an array type or a type with discriminants, then the created   5
object is always constrained. If the allocator includes a subtype indication, the created object is
constrained either by the subtype or by the default discriminant values. If the allocator includes a
qualified expression, the created object is constrained by the bounds or discriminants of the initial
value. For other types, the subtype of the created object is the subtype defined by the subtype
indication of the access type definition.

For the evaluation of an allocator, the elaboration of the subtype indication or the evaluation of the   6
qualified expression is performed first. The new object is then created. Initializations are then performed as for a declared object (see 3.2.1); the initialization is considered explicit in the case of a
qualified expression; any initializations are implicit in the case of a subtype indication. Finally, an
access value that designates the created object is returned.

An implementation must guarantee that any object created by the evaluation of an allocator   7
remains allocated for as long as this object or one of its subcomponents is accessible directly or
indirectly, that is, as long as it can be denoted by some name. Moreover, if an object or one of its
subcomponents belongs to a task type, it is considered to be accessible as long as the task is not
terminated. An implementation may (but need not) reclaim the storage occupied by an object
created by an allocator, once this object has become inaccessible.

When an application needs closer control over storage allocation for objects designated by values   8
of an access type, such control may be achieved by one or more of the following means:

(a) The total amount of storage available for the collection of objects of an access type can be set   9
     by means of a length clause (see 13.2).

(b) The pragma CONTROLLED informs the implementation that automatic storage reclamation   10
     must not be performed for objects designated by values of the access type, except upon leav-
     ing the innermost block statement, subprogram body, or task body that encloses the access
     type declaration, or after leaving the main program.

     pragma CONTROLLED (*access_type_*simple_name);

     A pragma CONTROLLED for a given access type is allowed at the same places as a   11
     representation clause for the type (see 13.1). This pragma is not allowed for a derived type.

(c) The explicit deallocation of the object designated by an access value can be achieved by call-   12
     ing a procedure obtained by instantiation of the predefined generic library procedure
     UNCHECKED_DEALLOCATION (see 13.10.1).

The exception STORAGE_ERROR is raised by an allocator if there is not enough storage. Note also   13
that the exception CONSTRAINT_ERROR can be raised by the evaluation of the qualified
expression, by the elaboration of the subtype indication, or by the initialization.

Allocators 4.8

14 *Examples (for access types declared in section 3.8):*

```
new CELL'(0, null, null)                                 -- initialized explicitly
new CELL'(VALUE => 0, SUCC => null, PRED => null)        -- initialized explicitly
new CELL                                                 -- not initialized

new MATRIX(1 .. 10, 1 .. 20)                             -- the bounds only are given
new MATRIX'(1 .. 10 => (1 .. 20 => 0.0))                 -- initialized explicitly

new BUFFER(100)                                          -- the discriminant only is given

new BUFFER'(SIZE => 80, POS => 0, VALUE => (1 .. 80 => 'A'))  -- initialized explicitly
```

15   *References:* access type 3.8, access type definition 3.8, access value 3.8, array type 3.6, block statement 5.6, bound of an array 3.6.1, collection 3.8, constrained subtype 3.3, constraint 3.3, constraint_error exception 11.1, context of overload resolution 8.7, derived type 3.4, designate 3.8, discriminant 3.3, discriminant constraint 3.7.2, elaboration 3.9, evaluation of a qualified expression 4.7, generic procedure 12.1, index constraint 3.6.1, initial value 3.2.1, initialization 3.2.1, instantiation 12.3, length clause 13.2, library unit 10.1, main program 10.1, name 4.1, object 3.2.1, object declaration 3.2.1, pragma 2.8, procedure 6, qualified expression 4.7, raising of exceptions 11, representation clause 13.1, simple name 4.1, storage_error exception 11.1, subcomponent 3.3, subprogram body 6.3, subtype 3.3, subtype indication 3.3.2, task body 9.1, task type 9.2, terminated task 9.4, type 3.3, type declaration 3.3.1, type mark 3.3.2 type with discriminants 3.3

4.9 Static Expressions and Static Subtypes

1   Certain expressions of a scalar type are said to be *static*. Similarly, certain discrete ranges are said to be static, and the type marks of certain scalar subtypes are said to denote static subtypes.

2   An expression of a scalar type is said to be static if and only if every primary is one of those listed in (a) through (h) below, every operator denotes a predefined operator, and the evaluation of the expression delivers a value (that is, it does not raise an exception):

3   (a) An enumeration literal (including a character literal).

4   (b) A numeric literal.

5   (c) A named number.

6   (d) A constant explicitly declared by a constant declaration with a static subtype, and initialized with a static expression.

7   (e) A function call whose function name is an operator symbol that denotes a predefined operator, including a function name that is an expanded name; each actual parameter must also be a static expression.

8   (f) A language-defined attribute of a static subtype; for an attribute that is a function, the actual parameter must also be a static expression.

(g)   A qualified expression whose type mark denotes a static subtype and whose operand is a   9
static expression.

(h)   A static expression enclosed in parentheses.   10

A static range is a range whose bounds are static expressions. A static range constraint is a range   11
constraint whose range is static. A static subtype is either a scalar base type, other than a generic
formal type; or a scalar subtype formed by imposing on a static subtype either a static range constraint, or a floating or fixed point constraint whose range constraint, if any, is static. A static discrete range is either a static subtype or a static range. A static index constraint is an index constraint for which each index subtype of the corresponding array type is static, and in which each
discrete range is static. A static discriminant constraint is a discriminant constraint for which the
subtype of each discriminant is static, and in which each expression is static.

Notes:

The accuracy of the evaluation of a static expression having a real type is defined by the rules given   12
in section 4.5.7. If the result is not a model number (or a safe number) of the type, the value
obtained by this evaluation at compilation time need not be the same as the value that would be
obtained by an evaluation at run time.

Array attributes are not static: in particular, the RANGE attribute is not static.   13

References: actual parameter 6.4.1, attribute 4.1.4, base type 3.3, bound of a range 3.5, character literal 2.5,   14
constant 3.2.1, constant declaration 3.2.1, discrete range 3.6, discrete type 3.5, enumeration literal 3.5.1, exception
11, expression 4.4, function 6.5, generic actual parameter 12.3, generic formal type 12.1.2, implicit declaration 3.1,
initialize 3.2.1, model number 3.5.6, named number 3.2, numeric literal 2.4, predefined operator 4.5, qualified expression 4.7, raising of exceptions 11, range constraint 3.5, safe number 3.5.6, scalar type 3.5, subtype 3.3, type mark
3.3.2

4.10   Universal Expressions

A *universal_expression* is either an expression that delivers a result of type *universal_integer* or   1
one that delivers a result of type *universal_real*.

The same operations are predefined for the type *universal_integer* as for any integer type. The   2
same operations are predefined for the type *universal_real* as for any floating point type. In addition, these operations include the following multiplication and division operators:

| Operator | Operation | Left operand type | Right operand type | Result type | 3
|---|---|---|---|---|
| * | multiplication | universal_real | universal_integer | universal_real |
| | | universal_integer | universal_real | universal_real |
| / | division | universal_real | universal_integer | universal_real |

The accuracy of the evaluation of a universal expression of type *universal_real* is at least as good   4
as that of the most accurate predefined floating point type supported by the implementation, apart
from *universal_real* itself. Furthermore, if a universal expression is a static expression, then the
evaluation must be exact.

5   For the evaluation of an operation of a nonstatic universal expression, an implementation is allowed to raise the exception NUMERIC_ERROR only if the result of the operation is a real value whose absolute value exceeds the largest safe number of the most accurate predefined floating point type (excluding *universal_real*), or an integer value greater than SYSTEM.MAX_INT or less than SYSTEM.MIN_INT.

Note:

6   It is a consequence of the above rules that the type of a universal expression is *universal_integer* if every primary contained in the expression is of this type (excluding actual parameters of attributes that are functions, and excluding right operands of exponentiation operators) and that otherwise the type is *universal_real*.

7   *Examples:*

```
1 + 1      -- 2
abs(-10)*3  -- 30

KILO : constant := 1000;
MEGA : constant := KILO*KILO;    -- 1_000_000
LONG : constant := FLOAT'DIGITS*2;

HALF_PI     : constant := PI/2;              -- see 3.2.2
DEG_TO_RAD  : constant := HALF_PI/90;
RAD_TO_DEG  : constant := 1.0/DEG_TO_RAD; -- equivalent to 1.0/((3.14159_26536/2)/90)
```

8   *References:* actual parameter 6.4.1, attribute 4.1.4, evaluation of an expression 4.5, floating point type 3.5.9, function 6.5, integer type 3.5.4, multiplying operator 4.5 4.5.5, predefined operation 3.3.3, primary 4.4, real type 3.5.6, safe number 3.5.6, system.max_int 13.7, system.min_int 13.7, type 3.3, universal_integer type 3.5.4, universal_real type 3.5.6

5. Statements

A *statement* defines an action to be performed; the process by which a statement achieves its   1
action is called *execution* of the statement.

This chapter describes the general rules applicable to all statements. Some specific statements are   2
discussed in later chapters. Procedure call statements are described in Chapter 6 on subprograms.
Entry call, delay, accept, select, and abort statements are described in Chapter 9 on tasks. Raise
statements are described in Chapter 11 on exceptions, and code statements in Chapter 13. The
remaining 'forms of statements are presented in this chapter.

References: abort statement 9.10, accept statement 9.5, code statement 13.8, delay statement 9.6, entry call   3
statement 9.5, procedure call statement 6.4, raise statement 11.3, select statement 9.7

5.1 Simple and Compound Statements - Sequences of Statements

A statement is either simple or compound. A simple statement encloses no other statement. A   1
compound statement can enclose simple statements and other compound statements.

    sequence_of_statements ::= statement {statement}   2

    statement ::=
       {label} simple_statement | {label} compound_statement

    simple_statement ::= null_statement
       | assignment_statement | procedure_call_statement
       | exit_statement | return_statement
       | goto_statement | entry_call_statement
       | delay_statement | abort_statement
       | raise_statement | code_statement

    compound_statement ::=
          if_statement | case_statement
       | loop_statement | block_statement
       | accept_statement | select_statement

    label ::= <<*label*_simple_name>>

    null_statement ::= **null**;

A statement is said to be *labeled* by the label name of any label of the statement. A label name,   3
and similarly a loop or block name, is implicitly declared at the end of the declarative part of the
innermost block statement, subprogram body, package body, task body, or generic body that
encloses the labeled statement, the named loop statement, or the named block statement, as the
case may be. For a block statement without a declarative part, an implicit declarative part (and
preceding **declare**) is assumed.

4   The implicit declarations for different label names, loop names, and block names occur in the same order as the beginnings of the corresponding labeled statements, loop statements, and block statements. Distinct identifiers must be used for all label, loop, and block names that are implicitly declared within the body of a program unit, including within block statements enclosed by this body, but excluding within other enclosed program units (a program unit is either a subprogram, a package, a task unit, or a generic unit).

5   Execution of a null statement has no other effect than to pass to the next action.

6   The execution of a sequence of statements consists of the execution of the individual statements in succession until the sequence is completed, or a transfer of control takes place. A transfer of control is caused either by the execution of an exit, return, or goto statement; by the selection of a terminate alternative; by the raising of an exception; or (indirectly) by the execution of an abort statement.

7   *Examples of labeled statements:*

        <<HERE>> <<ICI>> <<AQUI>> <<HIER>> **null**;

        <<AFTER>> X := 1;

    Note:

8   The scope of a declaration starts at the place of the declaration itself (see 8.2). In the case of a label, loop, or block name, it follows from this rule that the scope of the *implicit* declaration starts before the first *explicit* occurrence of the corresponding name, since this occurrence is either in a statement label, a loop statement, a block statement, or a goto statement. An implicit declaration in a block statement may hide a declaration given in an outer program unit or block statement (according to the usual rules of hiding explained in section 8.3).

9   *References:* abort statement 9.10, accept statement 9.5, assignment statement 5.2, block name 5.6, block statement 5.6, case statement 5.4, code statement 13.8, declaration 3.1, declarative part 3.9, delay statement 9.6, entry call statement 9.5, exception 11, exit statement 5.7, generic body 12.1, generic unit 12, goto statement 5.9, hiding 8.3, identifier 2.3, if statement 5.3, implicit declaration 3.1, loop name 5.5, loop statement 5.5, package 7, package body 7.1, procedure call statement 6.4, program unit 6, raise statement 11.3, raising of exceptions 11, return statement 5.8, scope 8.2, select statement 9.7, simple name 4.1, subprogram 6, subprogram body 6.3, task 9, task body 9.1, task unit 9.1, terminate alternative 9.7.1, terminated task 9.4

5.2 Assignment Statement

1   An assignment statement replaces the current value of a variable with a new value specified by an expression. The named variable and the right-hand side expression must be of the same type; this type must not be a limited type.

2   assignment_statement ::=
            *variable*_name := expression;

3   For the execution of an assignment statement, the variable name and the expression are first evaluated, in some order that is not defined by the language. A check is then made that the value of the expression belongs to the subtype of the variable, except in the case of a variable that is an array (the assignment then involves a subtype conversion as described in section 5.2.1). Finally, the value of the expression becomes the new value of the variable.

The exception CONSTRAINT_ERROR is raised if the above-mentioned subtype check fails; in such a   4
case the current value of the variable is left unchanged. If the variable is a subcomponent that
depends on discriminants of an unconstrained record variable, then the execution of the assignment is erroneous if the value of any of these discriminants is changed by this execution.

Examples: 5

```
VALUE  := MAX_VALUE - 1;
SHADE  := BLUE;

NEXT_FRAME(F)(M, N) := 2.5;      -- see 4.1.1
U := DOT_PRODUCT(V, W);          -- see 6.5

WRITER := (STATUS => OPEN, UNIT => PRINTER, LINE_COUNT => 60);  -- see 3.7.3
NEXT_CAR.all := (72074, null);   -- see 3.8.1
```

Examples of constraint checks: 6

```
I, J : INTEGER range 1 .. 10;
K    : INTEGER range 1 .. 20;
   ...

I := J;   -- identical ranges
K := J;   -- compatible ranges
J := K;   -- will raise the exception CONSTRAINT_ERROR if K > 10
```

Notes:

The values of the discriminants of an object designated by an access value cannot be changed (not   7
even by assigning a complete value to the object itself) since such objects, created by allocators,
are always constrained (see 4.8); however, subcomponents of such objects may be unconstrained.

If the right-hand side expression is either a numeric literal or named number, or an attribute that   8
yields a result of type *universal_integer* or *universal_real*, then an implicit type conversion is performed, as described in section 4.6.

The determination of the type of the variable of an assignment statement may require considera-   9
tion of the expression if the variable name can be interpreted as the name of a variable designated
by the access value returned by a function call, and similarly, as a component or slice of such a
variable (see section 8.7 for the context of overload resolution).

References: access type 3.8, allocator 4.8, array 3.6, array assignment 5.2.1, component 3.6 3.7, constraint_error   10
exception 11.1, designate 3.8, discriminant 3.7.1, erroneous 1.6, evaluation 4.5, expression 4.4, function call 6.4,
implicit type conversion 4.6, name 4.1, numeric literal 2.4, object 3.2, overloading 6.6 8.7, slice 4.1.2, subcomponent
3.3, subtype 3.3, subtype conversion 4.6, type 3.3, universal_integer type 3.5.4, universal_real type 3.5.6, variable
3.2.1

5.2.1 Array Assignments

If the variable of an assignment statement is an array variable (including a slice variable), the value   1
of the expression is implicitly converted to the subtype of the array variable; the result of this subtype conversion becomes the new value of the array variable.

2   This means that the new value of each component of the array variable is specified by the matching component in the array value obtained by evaluation of the expression (see 4.5.2 for the definition of matching components). The subtype conversion checks that for each component of the array variable there is a matching component in the array value, and vice versa. The exception CONSTRAINT_ERROR is raised if this check fails; in such a case the value of each component of the array variable is left unchanged.

3   *Examples:*

```
A   : STRING(1 .. 31);
B   : STRING(3 .. 33);
  ...

A   := B;    --   same number of components

A(1 .. 9)   := "tar sauce";
A(4 .. 12) := A(1 .. 9);   --   A(1 .. 12)  =  "tartar sauce"
```

Notes:

4   Array assignment is defined even in the case of overlapping slices, because the expression on the right-hand side is evaluated before performing any component assignment. In the above example, an implementation yielding A(1 .. 12) = "tartartartar" would be incorrect.

5   The implicit subtype conversion described above for assignment to an array variable is performed only for the value of the right-hand side expression as a whole; it is not performed for subcomponents that are array values.

6   *References:* array 3.6, assignment 5.2, constraint_error exception 11.1, matching array components 4.5.2, slice 4.1.2, subtype conversion 4.6, type 3.3, variable 3.2.1

5.3 If Statements

1   An if statement selects for execution one or none of the enclosed sequences of statements, depending on the (truth) value of one or more corresponding conditions.

2
```
if_statement ::=
    if condition then
      sequence_of_statements
    { elsif condition then
      sequence_of_statements}
    [ else
      sequence_of_statements]
    end if;

condition ::= boolean_expression
```

3   An expression specifying a condition must be of a boolean type.

4   For the execution of an if statement, the condition specified after **if**, and any conditions specified after **elsif**, are evaluated in succession (treating a final **else** as **elsif** TRUE **then**), until one evaluates to TRUE or all conditions are evaluated and yield FALSE. If one condition evaluates to TRUE, then the corresponding sequence of statements is executed; otherwise none of the sequences of statements is executed.

Examples: 5

```
if MONTH = DECEMBER and DAY = 31 then
    MONTH := JANUARY;
    DAY    := 1;
    YEAR   := YEAR + 1;
end if;

if LINE_TOO_SHORT then
    raise LAYOUT_ERROR;
elsif LINE_FULL then
    NEW_LINE;
    PUT(ITEM);
else
    PUT(ITEM);
end if;

if MY_CAR.OWNER.VEHICLE /= MY_CAR then          -- see 3.8
    REPORT ("Incorrect data");
end if;
```

References: boolean type 3.5.3, evaluation 4.5, expression 4.4, sequence of statements 5.1   6

5.4 Case Statements

A case statement selects for execution one of a number of alternative sequences of statements;   1
the chosen alternative is defined by the value of an expression.

```
case_statement ::=                                                             2
    case expression is
        case_statement_alternative
      { case_statement_alternative}
    end case;

case_statement_alternative ::=
    when choice {| choice } =>
        sequence_of_statements
```

The expression must be of a discrete type which must be determinable independently of the con-   3
text in which the expression occurs, but using the fact that the expression must be of a discrete
type. Moreover, the type of this expression must not be a generic formal type. Each choice in a
case statement alternative must be of the same type as the expression; the list of choices specifies
for which values of the expression the alternative is chosen.

If the expression is the name of an object whose subtype is static, then each value of this subtype   4
must be represented once and only once in the set of choices of the case statement, and no other
value is allowed; this rule is likewise applied if the expression is a qualified expression or type conversion whose type mark denotes a static subtype. Otherwise, for other forms of expression, each
value of the (base) type of the expression must be represented once and only once in the set of
choices, and no other value is allowed.

5 The simple expressions and discrete ranges given as choices in a case statement must be static. A choice defined by a discrete range stands for all values in the corresponding range (none if a null range). The choice **others** is only allowed for the last alternative and as its only choice; it stands for all values (possibly none) not given in the choices of previous alternatives. A component simple name is not allowed as a choice of a case statement alternative.

6 The execution of a case statement consists of the evaluation of the expression followed by the execution of the chosen sequence of statements.

7 *Examples:*

```
case SENSOR is
    when ELEVATION    => RECORD_ELEVATION (SENSOR_VALUE);
    when AZIMUTH      => RECORD_AZIMUTH  (SENSOR_VALUE);
    when DISTANCE     => RECORD_DISTANCE (SENSOR_VALUE);
    when others       => null;
end case;

case TODAY is
    when MON          => COMPUTE_INITIAL_BALANCE;
    when FRI          => COMPUTE_CLOSING_BALANCE;
    when TUE .. THU   => GENERATE_REPORT(TODAY);
    when SAT .. SUN   => null;
end case;

case BIN_NUMBER(COUNT) is
    when 1            => UPDATE_BIN(1);
    when 2            => UPDATE_BIN(2);
    when 3 | 4 =>
        EMPTY_BIN(1);
        EMPTY_BIN(2);
    when others => raise ERROR;
end case;
```

Notes:

8 The execution of a case statement chooses one and only one alternative, since the choices are exhaustive and mutually exclusive. Qualification of the expression of a case statement by a static subtype can often be used to limit the number of choices that need be given explicitly.

9 An **others** choice is required in a case statement if the type of the expression is the type *universal_integer* (for example, if the expression is an integer literal), since this is the only way to cover all values of the type *universal_integer*.

10 *References:* base type 3.3, choice 3.7.3, context of overload resolution 8.7, discrete type 3.5, expression 4.4, function call 6.4, generic formal type 12.1, conversion 4.6, discrete type 3.5, enumeration literal 3.5.1, expression 4.4, name 4.1, object 3.2.1, overloading 6.6 8.7, qualified expression 4.7, sequence of statements 5.1, static discrete range 4.9, static subtype 4.9, subtype 3.3, type 3.3, type conversion 4.6, type mark 3.3.2

5.5 Loop Statements

A loop statement includes a sequence of statements that is to be executed repeatedly, zero or more times.

```
loop_statement ::=
    [loop_simple_name:]
     [ iteration_scheme] loop
         sequence_of_statements
       end loop [loop_simple_name];

iteration_scheme ::= while condition
   |  for loop_parameter_specification

loop_parameter_specification ::=
     identifier in [reverse] discrete_range
```

If a loop statement has a loop simple name, this simple name must be given both at the beginning and at the end.

A loop statement without an iteration scheme specifies repeated execution of the sequence of statements. Execution of the loop statement is complete when the loop is left as a consequence of the execution of an exit statement, or as a consequence of some other transfer of control (see 5.1).

For a loop statement with a **while** iteration scheme, the condition is evaluated before each execution of the sequence of statements; if the value of the condition is TRUE, the sequence of statements is executed, if FALSE the execution of the loop statement is complete.

For a loop statement with a **for** iteration scheme, the loop parameter specification is the declaration of the *loop parameter* with the given identifier. The loop parameter is an object whose type is the base type of the discrete range (see 3.6.1). Within the sequence of statements, the loop parameter is a constant. Hence a loop parameter is not allowed as the (left-hand side) variable of an assignment statement. Similarly the loop parameter must not be given as an **out** or **in out** parameter of a procedure or entry call statement, or as an **in out** parameter of a generic instantiation.

For the execution of a loop statement with a **for** iteration scheme, the loop parameter specification is first elaborated. This elaboration creates the loop parameter and evaluates the discrete range.

If the discrete range is a null range, the execution of the loop statement is complete. Otherwise, the sequence of statements is executed once for each value of the discrete range (subject to the loop not being left as a consequence of the execution of an exit statement or as a consequence of some other transfer of control). Prior to each such iteration, the corresponding value of the discrete range is assigned to the loop parameter. These values are assigned in increasing order unless the reserved word **reverse** is present, in which case the values are assigned in decreasing order.

Example of a loop statement without an iteration scheme:

```
loop
   GET(CURRENT_CHARACTER);
   exit when CURRENT_CHARACTER  =  '*';
end loop;
```

10 *Example of a loop statement with a while iteration scheme:*

```
while BID(N).PRICE < CUT_OFF.PRICE loop
   RECORD_BID(BID(N).PRICE);
   N := N + 1;
end loop;
```

11 *Example of a loop statement with a for iteration scheme:*

```
for J in BUFFER'RANGE loop      -- legal even with a null range
   if BUFFER(J) /= SPACE then
      PUT(BUFFER(J));
   end if;
end loop;
```

12 *Example of a loop statement with a loop simple name:*

```
SUMMATION:
   while NEXT /= HEAD loop      -- see 3.8
      SUM  := SUM + NEXT.VALUE;
      NEXT := NEXT.SUCC;
   end loop SUMMATION;
```

Notes:

13 The scope of a loop parameter extends from the loop parameter specification to the end of the loop statement, and the visibility rules are such that a loop parameter is only visible within the sequence of statements of the loop.

14 The discrete range of a for loop is evaluated just once. Use of the reserved word **reverse** does not alter the discrete range, so that the following iteration schemes are not equivalent; the first has a null range.

```
for J in reverse 1 .. 0
for J in 0 .. 1
```

15 Loop names are also used in exit statements, and in expanded names (in a prefix of the loop parameter).

16 *References:* actual parameter 6.4.1, assignment statement 5.2, base type 3.3, bound of a range 3.5, condition 5.3, constant 3.2.1, context of overload resolution 8.7, conversion 4.6, declaration 3.1, discrete range 3.6.1, elaboration 3.1, entry call statement 9.5, evaluation 4.5, exit statement 5.7, expanded name 4.1.3, false boolean value 3.5.3, generic actual parameter 12.3, generic instantiation 12.3, goto statement 5.9, identifier 2.3, integer type 3.5.4, null range 3.5, object 3.2.1, prefix 4.1, procedure call 6.4, raising of exceptions 11, reserved word 2.9, return statement 5.8, scope 8.2, sequence of statements 5.1, simple name 4.1, terminate alternative 9.7.1, true boolean value 3.5.3 3.5.4, visibility 8.3

5.6 Block Statements

A block statement encloses a sequence of statements optionally preceded by a declarative part   1
and optionally followed by exception handlers.

```
block_statement ::=                                                       2
    [block_simple_name:]
        [ declare
            declarative_part]
        begin
            sequence_of_statements
        [ exception
            exception_handler
            { exception_handler}]
        end [block_simple_name];
```

If a block statement has a block simple name, this simple name must be given both at the beginn-   3
ing and at the end.

The execution of a block statement consists of the elaboration of its declarative part (if any) fol-   4
lowed by the execution of the sequence of statements. If the block statement has exception
handlers, these service corresponding exceptions that are raised during the execution of the
sequence of statements (see 11.2).

Example: 5

```
SWAP:
    declare
        TEMP : INTEGER;
    begin
        TEMP := V; V := U; U := TEMP;
    end SWAP;
```

Notes:

If task objects are declared within a block statement whose execution is completed, the block   6
statement is not left until all its dependent tasks are terminated (see 9.4). This rule applies also to
a completion caused by an exit, return, or goto statement; or by the raising of an exception.

Within a block statement, the block name can be used in expanded names denoting local entities   7
such as SWAP.TEMP in the above example (see 4.1.3 (f)).

References: declarative part 3.9, dependent task 9.4, exception handler 11.2, exit statement 5.7, expanded name   8
4.1.3, goto statement 5.9, raising of exceptions 11, return statement 5.8, sequence of statements 5.1, simple name
4.1, task object 9.2

5.7   Exit Statements

1   An exit statement is used to complete the execution of an enclosing loop statement (called the loop in what follows); the completion is conditional if the exit statement includes a condition.

2
```
exit_statement ::=
    exit [loop_name] [when condition];
```

3   An exit statement with a loop name is only allowed within the named loop, and applies to that loop; an exit statement without a loop name is only allowed within a loop, and applies to the innermost enclosing loop (whether named or not). Furthermore, an exit statement that applies to a given loop must not appear within a subprogram body, package body, task body, generic body, or accept statement, if this construct is itself enclosed by the given loop.

4   For the execution of an exit statement, the condition, if present, is first evaluated. Exit from the loop then takes place if the value is TRUE or if there is no condition.

5   *Examples:*

```
for N in 1 .. MAX_NUM_ITEMS loop
    GET_NEW_ITEM(NEW_ITEM);
    MERGE_ITEM(NEW_ITEM, STORAGE_FILE);
    exit when NEW_ITEM = TERMINAL_ITEM;
end loop;

MAIN_CYCLE:
    loop
        --   initial statements
        exit MAIN_CYCLE when FOUND;
        --   final statements
    end loop MAIN_CYCLE;
```

Note:

6   Several nested loops can be exited by an exit statement that names the outer loop.

7   *References:* accept statement 9.5, condition 5.3, evaluation 4.5, generic body 12.1, loop name 5.5, loop statement 5.5, package body 7.1, subprogram body 6.3, true boolean value 3.5.3

5.8   Return Statements

1   A return statement is used to complete the execution of the innermost enclosing function, procedure, or accept statement.

2
```
return_statement ::= return [expression];
```

3   A return statement is only allowed within the body of a subprogram or generic subprogram, or within an accept statement, and applies to the innermost (enclosing) such construct; a return statement is not allowed within the body of a task unit, package, or generic package enclosed by this construct (on the other hand, it is allowed within a compound statement enclosed by this construct and, in particular, in a block statement).

A return statement for an accept statement or for the body of a procedure or generic procedure   4
must not include an expression. A return statement for the body of a function or generic function
must include an expression.

The value of the expression defines the result returned by the function. The type of this expression   5
must be the base type of the type mark given after the reserved word **return** in the specification of
the function or generic function (this type mark defines the result subtype).

For the execution of a return statement, the expression (if any) is first evaluated and a check is   6
made that the value belongs to the result subtype. The execution of the return statement is thereby
completed if the check succeeds; so also is the execution of the subprogram or of the accept
statement. The exception CONSTRAINT_ERROR is raised at the place of the return statement if the
check fails.

Examples: 7

```
return;                          -- in a procedure
return KEY_VALUE(LAST_INDEX);    -- in a function
```

Note:

If the expression is either a numeric literal or named number, or an attribute that yields a result of   8
type *universal_integer* or *universal_real*, then an implicit conversion of the result is performed as
described in section 4.6.

References: accept statement 9.5, attribute A, block statement 5.6, constraint_error exception 11.1, expression 4.4,   9
function body 6.3, function call 6.4, generic body 12.1, implicit type conversion 4.6, named number 3.2, numeric
literal 2.4, package body 7.1, procedure body 6.3, reserved word 2.9, result subtype 6.1, subprogram body 6.3, subprogram specification 6.1, subtype 3.3, task body 9.1, type mark 3.3.2, universal_integer type 3.5.4, universal_real
type 3.5.6

5.9 Goto Statements

A goto statement specifies an explicit transfer of control from this statement to a *target* statement   1
named by a label.

```
goto_statement ::= goto label_name;
```
    2

The innermost sequence of statements that encloses the target statement must also enclose the   3
goto statement (note that the goto statement can be a statement of an inner sequence). Furthermore, if a goto statement is enclosed by an accept statement or the body of a program unit, then
the target statement must not be outside this enclosing construct; conversely, it follows from the
previous rule that if the target statement is enclosed by such a construct, then the goto statement
cannot be outside.

The execution of a goto statement transfers control to the named target statement.   4

Note:

5   The above rules allow transfer of control to a statement of an enclosing sequence of statements but not the reverse. Similarly, they prohibit transfers of control such as between alternatives of a case statement, if statement, or select statement; between exception handlers; or from an exception handler of a frame back to the sequence of statements of this frame.

6   *Example:*

```
<<COMPARE>>
   if A(I) < ELEMENT then
      if LEFT(I) /= 0 then
         I := LEFT(I);
         goto COMPARE;
      end if;
      -- some statements
   end if;
```

7   *References:* accept statement 9.5, block statement 5.6, case statement 5.4, compound statement 5.1, exception handler 11.2, frame 11.2, generic body 12.1, if statement 5.3, label 5.1, package body 7.1, program unit 6, select statement 9.7, sequence of statements 5.1, statement 5.1, subprogram body 6.3, task body 9.1, transfer of control 5.1

6. Subprograms

Subprograms are one of the four forms of *program unit*, of which programs can be composed. The other forms are packages, task units, and generic units.

A subprogram is a program unit whose execution is invoked by a subprogram call. There are two forms of subprogram: procedures and functions. A procedure call is a statement; a function call is an expression and returns a value. The definition of a subprogram can be given in two parts: a subprogram declaration defining its calling conventions, and a subprogram body defining its execution.

References: function 6.5, function call 6.4, generic unit 12, package 7, procedure 6.1, procedure call 6.4, subprogram body 6.3, subprogram call 6.4, subprogram declaration 6.1, task unit 9

6.1 Subprogram Declarations

A subprogram declaration declares a procedure or a function, as indicated by the initial reserved word.

```
subprogram_declaration ::= subprogram_specification;

subprogram_specification ::=
      procedure identifier [formal_part]
    | function designator [formal_part] return type_mark

designator ::= identifier | operator_symbol

operator_symbol ::= string_literal

formal_part ::=
    (parameter_specification {; parameter_specification})

parameter_specification ::=
    identifier_list : mode type_mark [:= expression]

mode ::= [in] | in out | out
```

The specification of a procedure specifies its identifier and its *formal parameters* (if any). The specification of a function specifies its designator, its formal parameters (if any) and the subtype of the returned value (the *result subtype*). A designator that is an operator symbol is used for the overloading of an operator. The sequence of characters represented by an operator symbol must be an operator belonging to one of the six classes of overloadable operators defined in section 4.5 (extra spaces are not allowed and the case of letters is not significant).

4   A parameter specification with several identifiers is equivalent to a sequence of single parameter specifications, as explained in section 3.2. Each single parameter specification declares a formal parameter. If no mode is explicitly given, the mode **in** is assumed. If a parameter specification ends with an expression, the expression is the *default expression* of the formal parameter. A default expression is only allowed in a parameter specification if the mode is **in** (whether this mode is indicated explicitly or implicitly). The type of a default expression must be that of the corresponding formal parameter.

5   The use of a name that denotes a formal parameter is not allowed in default expressions of a formal part if the specification of the parameter is itself given in this formal part.

6   The elaboration of a subprogram declaration elaborates the corresponding formal part. The elaboration of a formal part has no other effect.

7   *Examples of subprogram declarations:*

```
procedure TRAVERSE_TREE;
procedure INCREMENT(X : in out INTEGER);
procedure RIGHT_INDENT(MARGIN : out LINE_SIZE);      -- see 3.5.4
procedure SWITCH(FROM, TO : in out LINK);            -- see 3.8.1

function RANDOM return PROBABILITY;                  -- see 3.5.7

function MIN_CELL(X : LINK) return CELL;             -- see 3.8.1
function NEXT_FRAME(K : POSITIVE) return FRAME;      -- see 3.8
function DOT_PRODUCT(LEFT,RIGHT: VECTOR) return REAL; -- see 3.6

function "*"(LEFT,RIGHT : MATRIX) return MATRIX;     -- see 3.6
```

8   *Examples of in parameters with default expressions:*

```
procedure PRINT_HEADER(PAGES   : in NATURAL;
                       HEADER  : in LINE    := (1 .. LINE'LAST => ' ');  -- see 3.6
                       CENTER  : in BOOLEAN := TRUE);
```

Notes:

9   The evaluation of default expressions is caused by certain subprogram calls, as described in section 6.4.2 (default expressions are not evaluated during the elaboration of the subprogram declaration).

10 All subprograms can be called recursively and are reentrant.

11 *References:* declaration 3.1, elaboration 3.9, evaluation 4.5, expression 4.4, formal parameter 6.2, function 6.5, identifier 2.3, identifier list 3.2, mode 6.2, name 4.1, elaboration has no other effect 3.9, operator 4.5, overloading 6.6 8.7, procedure 6, string literal 2.6, subprogram call 6.4, type mark 3.3.2

6.2 Formal Parameter Modes

The value of an object is said to be *read* when this value is evaluated; it is also said to be read   1
when one of its subcomponents is read. The value of a variable is said to be *updated* when an
assignment is performed to the variable, and also (indirectly) when the variable is used as actual
parameter of a subprogram call or entry call statement that updates its value; it is also said to be
updated when one of its subcomponents is updated.

A formal parameter of a subprogram has one of the three following modes: 2

in   The formal parameter is a constant and permits only reading of the value of the   3
        associated actual parameter.

in out The formal parameter is a variable and permits both reading and updating of the value of the   4
        associated actual parameter.

out   The formal parameter is a variable and permits updating of the value of the associated actual   5
        parameter.

        The value of a scalar parameter that is not updated by the call is undefined upon return; the
        same holds for the value of a scalar subcomponent, other than a discriminant. Reading
        the bounds and discriminants of the formal parameter and of its subcomponents is allowed,
        but no other reading.

For a scalar parameter, the above effects are achieved by copy: at the start of each call, if the mode   6
is **in** or **in out**, the value of the actual parameter is copied into the associated formal parameter;
then after normal completion of the subprogram body, if the mode is **in out** or **out**, the value of the
formal parameter is copied back into the associated actual parameter. For a parameter whose
type is an access type, copy-in is used for all three modes, and copy-back for the modes **in out** and
out.

For a parameter whose type is an array, record, or task type, an implementation may likewise   7
achieve the above effects by copy, as for scalar types. In addition, if copy is used for a parameter of
mode **out**, then copy-in is required at least for the bounds and discriminants of the actual
parameter and of its subcomponents, and also for each subcomponent whose type is an access
type. Alternatively, an implementation may achieve these effects by reference, that is, by arranging
that every use of the formal parameter (to read or to update its value) be treated as a use of the
associated actual parameter, throughout the execution of the subprogram call. The language does
not define which of these two mechanisms is to be adopted for parameter passing, nor whether
different calls to the same subprogram are to use the same mechanism. The execution of a
program is erroneous if its effect depends on which mechanism is selected by the implementation.

For a parameter whose type is a private type, the above effects are achieved according to the rule   8
that applies to the corresponding full type declaration.

Within the body of a subprogram, a formal parameter is subject to any constraint resulting from   9
the type mark given in its parameter specification. For a formal parameter of an unconstrained
array type, the bounds are obtained from the actual parameter, and the formal parameter is constrained by these bounds (see 3.6.1). For a formal parameter whose declaration specifies an
unconstrained (private or record) type with discriminants, the discriminants of the formal
parameter are initialized with the values of the corresponding discriminants of the actual
parameter; the formal parameter is unconstrained if and only if the mode is **in out** or **out** and the
variable name given for the actual parameter denotes an unconstrained variable (see 3.7.1 and
6.4.1).

If the actual parameter of a subprogram call is a subcomponent that depends on discriminants of   10
an unconstrained record variable, then the execution of the call is erroneous if the value of any of
the discriminants of the variable is changed by this execution; this rule does not apply if the mode
is **in** and the type of the subcomponent is a scalar type or an access type.

Notes:

11   For parameters of array and record types, the parameter passing rules have these consequences:

12   ● If the execution of a subprogram is abandoned as a result of an exception, the final value of an actual parameter of such a type can be either its value before the call or a value assigned to the formal parameter during the execution of the subprogram.

13   ● If no actual parameter of such a type is accessible by more than one path, then the effect of a subprogram call (unless abandoned) is the same whether or not the implementation uses copying for parameter passing. If, however, there are multiple access paths to such a parameter (for example, if a global variable, or another formal parameter, refers to the same actual parameter), then the value of the formal is undefined after updating the actual other than by updating the formal. A program using such an undefined value is erroneous.

14   The same parameter modes are defined for formal parameters of entries (see 9.5) with the same meaning as for subprograms.   Different parameter modes are defined for generic formal parameters (see 12.1.1).

15   For all modes, if an actual parameter designates a task, the associated formal parameter designates the same task; the same holds for a subcomponent of an actual parameter and the corresponding subcomponent of the associated formal parameter.

16   *References:* access type 3.8, actual parameter 6.4.1, array type 3.6, assignment 5.2, bound of an array 3.6.1, constraint 3.3, depend on a discriminant 3.7.1, discriminant 3.7.1, entry call statement 9.5, erroneous 1.6, evaluation 4.5, exception 11, expression 4.4, formal parameter 6.1, generic formal parameter 12.1, global 8.1, mode 6.1, null access value 3.8, object 3.2, parameter specification 6.1, private type 7.4, record type 3.7, scalar type 3.5, subcomponent 3.3, subprogram body 6.3, subprogram call statement 6.4, task 9, task type 9.2, type mark 3.3.2, unconstrained array type 3.6, unconstrained type with discriminants 3.7.1, unconstrained variable 3.2.1, variable 3.2.1

6.3 Subprogram Bodies

1   A subprogram body specifies the execution of a subprogram.

2
```
subprogram_body ::=
    subprogram_specification is
        [ declarative_part]
    begin
        sequence_of_statements
    [ exception
        exception_handler
        { exception_handler}]
    end [designator];
```

3   The declaration of a subprogram is optional. In the absence of such a declaration, the subprogram specification of the subprogram body (or body stub) acts as the declaration. For each subprogram declaration, there must be a corresponding body (except for a subprogram written in another language, as explained in section 13.9). If both a declaration and a body are given, the subprogram specification of the body must conform to the subprogram specification of the declaration (see section 6.3.1 for conformance rules).

If a designator appears at the end of a subprogram body, it must repeat the designator of the sub- 4
program specification.

The elaboration of a subprogram body has no other effect than to establish that the body can from 5
then on be used for the execution of calls of the subprogram.

The execution of a subprogram body is invoked by a subprogram call (see 6.4). For this execution, 6
after establishing the association between formal parameters and actual parameters, the
declarative part of the body is elaborated, and the sequence of statements of the body is then
executed. Upon completion of the body, return is made to the caller (and any necessary copying
back of formal to actual parameters occurs (see 6.2)). The optional exception handlers at the end
of a subprogram body handle exceptions raised during the execution of the sequence of statements of the subprogram body (see 11.4).

Note:

It follows from the visibility rules that if a subprogram declared in a package is to be visible outside 7
the package, a subprogram specification must be given in the visible part of the package. The same
rules dictate that a subprogram declaration must be given if a call of the subprogram occurs textually before the subprogram body (the declaration must then occur earlier than the call in the
program text). The rules given in sections 3.9 and 7.1 imply that a subprogram declaration and the
corresponding body must both occur immediately within the same declarative region.

Example of subprogram body: 8

```
procedure PUSH(E : in ELEMENT_TYPE; S : in out STACK) is
begin
   if S.INDEX = S.SIZE then
      raise STACK_OVERFLOW;
   else
      S.INDEX := S.INDEX + 1;
      S.SPACE(S.INDEX) := E;
   end if;
end PUSH;
```

References: actual parameter 6.4.1, body stub 10.2, conform 6.3.1, declaration 3.1, declarative part 3.9, declarative
region 8.1, designator 6.1, elaboration 3.9, elaboration has no other effect 3.1, exception 11, exception handler 11.2,
formal parameter 6.1, occur immediately within 8.1, package 7, sequence of statements 5.1, subprogram 6, sub- 9
program call 6.4, subprogram declaration 6.1, subprogram specification 6.1, visibility 8.3, visible part 7.2

6.3.1 Conformance Rules

Whenever the language rules require or allow the specification of a given subprogram to be 1
provided in more than one place, the following variations are allowed at each place:

- A numeric literal can be replaced by a different numeric literal if and only if both have the 2
  same value.

- A simple name can be replaced by an expanded name in which this simple name is the selec- 3
  tor, if and only if at both places the meaning of the simple name is given by the same declaration.

- A string literal given as an operator symbol can be replaced by a different string literal if and 4
  only if both represent the same operator.

5   Two subprogram specifications are said to *conform* if, apart from comments and the above allowed variations, both specifications are formed by the same sequence of lexical elements, and corresponding lexical elements are given the same meaning by the visibility and overloading rules.

6   Conformance is likewise defined for formal parts, discriminant parts, and type marks (for deferred constants and for actual parameters that have the form of a type conversion (see 6.4.1)).

Notes:

7   A simple name can be replaced by an expanded name even if the simple name is itself the prefix of a selected component. For example, Q.R can be replaced by P.Q.R if Q is declared immediately within P.

8   The following specifications do not conform since they are not formed by the same sequence of lexical elements:

        procedure P(X,Y : INTEGER)
        procedure P(X : INTEGER; Y : INTEGER)
        procedure P(X,Y : **in** INTEGER)

9   *References:* actual parameter 6.4 6.4.1, allow 1.6, comment 2.7, declaration 3.1, deferred constant 7.4.3, direct visibility 8.3, discriminant part 3.7.1, expanded name 4.1.3, formal part 6.1, lexical element 2, name 4.1, numeric literal 2.4, operator symbol 6.1, overloading 6.6 8.7, prefix 4.1, selected component 4.1.3, selector 4.1.3, simple name 4.1, subprogram specification 6.1, type conversion 4.6, visibility 8.3

6.3.2 Inline Expansion of Subprograms

1   The pragma INLINE is used to indicate that inline expansion of the subprogram body is desired for every call of each of the named subprograms. The form of this pragma is as follows:

2   **pragma** INLINE (name {, name});

Each name is either the name of a subprogram or the name of a generic subprogram. The pragma INLINE is only allowed at the place of a declarative item in a declarative part or package specification, or after a library unit in a compilation, but before any subsequent compilation unit.

3   If the pragma appears at the place of a declarative item, each name must denote a subprogram or a generic subprogram declared by an earlier declarative item of the same declarative part or package specification. If several (overloaded) subprograms satisfy this requirement, the pragma applies to all of them. If the pragma appears after a given library unit, the only name allowed is the name of this unit. If the name of a generic subprogram is mentioned in the pragma, this indicates that inline expansion is desired for calls of all subprograms obtained by instantiation of the named generic unit.

4   The meaning of a subprogram is not changed by the pragma INLINE. For each call of the named subprograms, an implementation is free to follow or to ignore the recommendation expressed by the pragma. (Note, in particular, that the recommendation cannot generally be followed for a recursive subprogram.)

5   *References:* allow 1.6, compilation 10.1, compilation unit 10.1, declarative item 3.9, declarative part 3.9, generic subprogram 12.1, generic unit 12 12.1, instantiation 12.3, library unit 10.1, name 4.1, overloading 6.6 8.7, package specification 7.1, pragma 2.8, subprogram 6, subprogram body 6.3, subprogram call 6.4

6.4 Subprogram Calls

A subprogram call is either a procedure call statement or a function call; it invokes the execution   1
of the corresponding subprogram body. The call specifies the association of the actual parameters,
if any, with formal parameters of the subprogram.

procedure_call_statement ::=   2
    *procedure*_name [actual_parameter_part];

function_call ::=
    *function*_name [actual_parameter_part]

actual_parameter_part ::=
    (parameter_association {, parameter_association})

parameter_association ::=
    [formal_parameter =>] actual_parameter

formal_parameter ::= *parameter*_simple_name

actual_parameter ::=
    expression | *variable*_name | type_mark(*variable*_name)

Each parameter association associates an actual parameter with a corresponding formal   3
parameter. A parameter association is said to be *named* if the formal parameter is named explicitly; it is otherwise said to be *positional*. For a positional association, the actual parameter corresponds to the formal parameter with the same position in the formal part.

Named associations can be given in any order, but if both positional and named associations are   4
used in the same call, positional associations must occur first, at their normal position. Hence
once a named association is used, the rest of the call must use only named associations.

For each formal parameter of a subprogram, a subprogram call must specify exactly one cor-   5
responding actual parameter. This actual parameter is specified either explicitly, by a parameter
association, or, in the absence of such an association, by a default expression (see 6.4.2).

The parameter associations of a subprogram call are evaluated in some order that is not defined by   6
the language. Similarly, the language rules do not define in which order the values of **in out** or **out**
parameters are copied back into the corresponding actual parameters (when this is done).

Examples of procedure calls: 7

```
TRAVERSE_TREE;                                          --  see 6.1
TABLE_MANAGER.INSERT(E);                                --  see 7.5
PRINT_HEADER(128, TITLE, TRUE);                         --  see 6.1

SWITCH(FROM => X, TO => NEXT);                          --  see 6.1
PRINT_HEADER(128, HEADER => TITLE, CENTER => TRUE);     --  see 6.1
PRINT_HEADER(HEADER => TITLE, CENTER => TRUE, PAGES => 128);   --  see 6.1
```

Examples of function calls: 8

```
DOT_PRODUCT(U, V)    --  see 6.1 and 6.5
CLOCK                --  see 9.6
```

9   *References:* default expression for a formal parameter 6.1, erroneous 1.6, expression 4.4, formal parameter 6.1, formal part 6.1, name 4.1, simple name 4.1, subprogram 6, type mark 3.3.2, variable 3.2.1

6.4.1 Parameter Associations

1   Each actual parameter must have the same type as the corresponding formal parameter.

2   An actual parameter associated with a formal parameter of mode **in** must be an expression; it is evaluated before the call.

3   An actual parameter associated with a formal parameter of mode **in out** or **out** must be either the name of a variable, or of the form of a type conversion whose argument is the name of a variable. In either case, for the mode **in out**, the variable must not be a formal parameter of mode **out** or a subcomponent thereof. For an actual parameter that has the form of a type conversion, the type mark must conform (see 6.3.1) to the type mark of the formal parameter; the allowed operand and target types are the same as for type conversions (see 4.6).

4   The variable name given for an actual parameter of mode **in out** or **out** is evaluated before the call. If the actual parameter has the form of a type conversion, then before the call, for a parameter of mode **in out**, the variable is converted to the specified type; after (normal) completion of the sub-program body, for a parameter of mode **in out** or **out**, the formal parameter is converted back to the type of the variable. (The type specified in the conversion must be that of the formal parameter.)

5   The following constraint checks are performed for parameters of scalar and access types:

6   • Before the call: for a parameter of mode **in** or **in out**, it is checked that the value of the actual parameter belongs to the subtype of the formal parameter.

7   • After (normal) completion of the subprogram body: for a parameter of mode **in out** or **out**, it is checked that the value of the formal parameter belongs to the subtype of the actual variable. In the case of a type conversion, the value of the formal parameter is converted back and the check applies to the result of the conversion.

8   In each of the above cases, the execution of the program is erroneous if the checked value is undefined.

9   For other types, for all modes, a check is made before the call as for scalar and access types; no check is made upon return.

10   The exception CONSTRAINT_ERROR is raised at the place of the subprogram call if either of these checks fails.

Note:

11   For array types and for types with discriminants, the check before the call is sufficient (a check upon return would be redundant) if the type mark of the formal parameter denotes a constrained subtype, since neither array bounds nor discriminants can then vary.

If this type mark denotes an unconstrained array type, the formal parameter is constrained with the bounds of the corresponding actual parameter and no check (neither before the call nor upon return) is needed (see 3.6.1). Similarly, no check is needed if the type mark denotes an unconstrained type with discriminants, since the formal parameter is then constrained exactly as the corresponding actual parameter (see 3.7.1).

References: actual parameter 6.4, array bound 3.6, array type 3.6, call of a subprogram 6.4, conform 6.3.1, constrained subtype 3.3, constraint 3.3, constraint_error exception 11.1, discriminant 3.7.1, erroneous 1.6, evaluation 4.5, evaluation of a name 4.1, expression 4.4, formal parameter 6.1, mode 6.1, name 4.1, parameter association 6.4, subtype 3.3, type 3.3, type conversion 4.6, type mark 3.3.2, unconstrained array type 3.6, unconstrained type with discriminants 3.7.1, undefined value 3.2.1, variable 3.2.1

6.4.2 Default Parameters

If a parameter specification includes a default expression for a parameter of mode **in**, then corresponding subprogram calls need not include a parameter association for the parameter. If a parameter association is thus omitted from a call, then the rest of the call, following any initial positional associations, must use only named associations.

For any omitted parameter association, the default expression is evaluated before the call and the resulting value is used as an implicit actual parameter.

Examples of procedures with default values:

```
procedure ACTIVATE( PROCESS   : in PROCESS_NAME;
                    AFTER     : in PROCESS_NAME := NO_PROCESS;
                    WAIT      : in DURATION := 0.0;
                    PRIOR     : in BOOLEAN := FALSE);

procedure PAIR(LEFT, RIGHT : PERSON_NAME := new PERSON);
```

Examples of their calls:

```
ACTIVATE(X);
ACTIVATE(X, AFTER => Y);
ACTIVATE(X, WAIT => 60.0, PRIOR => TRUE);
ACTIVATE(X, Y, 10.0, FALSE);

PAIR;
PAIR(LEFT => new PERSON, RIGHT => new PERSON);
```

Note:

If a default expression is used for two or more parameters in a multiple parameter specification, the default expression is evaluated once for each omitted parameter. Hence in the above examples, the two calls of PAIR are equivalent.

References: actual parameter 6.4.1, default expression for a formal parameter 6.1, evaluation 4.5, formal parameter 6.1, mode 6.1, named parameter association 6.4, parameter association 6.4, parameter specification 6.1, positional parameter association 6.4, subprogram call 6.4

6.5 Function Subprograms

1 A function is a subprogram that returns a value (the result of the function call). The specification of a function starts with the reserved word **function**, and the parameters, if any, must have the mode **in** (whether this mode is specified explicitly or implicitly). The statements of the function body (excluding statements of program units that are inner to the function body) must include one or more return statements specifying the returned value.

2 The exception PROGRAM_ERROR is raised if a function body is left otherwise than by a return statement. This does not apply if the execution of the function is abandoned as a result of an exception.

3 *Example:*

```
function DOT_PRODUCT(LEFT, RIGHT : VECTOR) return REAL is
   SUM : REAL := 0.0;
begin
   CHECK(LEFT'FIRST = RIGHT'FIRST and LEFT'LAST = RIGHT'LAST);
   for J in LEFT'RANGE loop
      SUM := SUM + LEFT(J)*RIGHT(J);
   end loop;
   return SUM;
end DOT_PRODUCT;
```

4 *References:* exception 11, formal parameter 6.1, function 6.1, function body 6.3, function call 6.4, function specification 6.1, mode 6.1, program_error exception 11.1, raising of exceptions 11, return statement 5.8, statement 5

6.6 Parameter and Result Type Profile - Overloading of Subprograms

1 Two formal parts are said to have the same *parameter type profile* if and only if they have the same number of parameters, and at each parameter position corresponding parameters have the same base type. A subprogram or entry has the same *parameter and result type profile* as another subprogram or entry if and only if both have the same parameter type profile, and either both are functions with the same result base type, or neither of the two is a function.

2 The same subprogram identifier or operator symbol can be used in several subprogram specifications. The identifier or operator symbol is then said to be *overloaded*; the subprograms that have this identifier or operator symbol are also said to be overloaded and to overload each other. As explained in section 8.3, if two subprograms overload each other, one of them can hide the other only if both subprograms have the same parameter and result type profile (see section 8.3 for the other requirements that must be met for hiding).

3 A call to an overloaded subprogram is ambiguous (and therefore illegal) if the name of the subprogram, the number of parameter associations, the types and the order of the actual parameters, the names of the formal parameters (if named associations are used), and the result type (for functions) are not sufficient to determine exactly one (overloaded) subprogram specification.

Examples of overloaded subprograms: 4

    procedure PUT(X : INTEGER);
    procedure PUT(X : STRING);

    procedure SET(TINT   : COLOR);
    procedure SET(SIGNAL : LIGHT);

Examples of calls: 5

    PUT(28);
    PUT("no possible ambiguity here");

    SET(TINT   => RED);
    SET(SIGNAL => RED);
    SET(COLOR'(RED));

    -- SET(RED) would be ambiguous since RED may
    -- denote a value either of type COLOR or of type LIGHT

Notes:

The notion of parameter and result type profile does not include parameter names, parameter   6
modes, parameter subtypes, default expressions and their presence or absence.

Ambiguities may (but need not) arise when actual parameters of the call of an overloaded sub-   7
program are themselves overloaded function calls, literals, or aggregates. Ambiguities may also
(but need not) arise when several overloaded subprograms belonging to different packages are
visible. These ambiguities can usually be resolved in several ways: qualified expressions can be
used for some or all actual parameters, and for the result, if any; the name of the subprogram can
be expressed more explicitly as an expanded name; finally, the subprogram can be renamed.

References: actual parameter 6.4.1, aggregate 4.3, base type 3.3, default expression for a formal parameter 6.1,   8
entry 9.5, formal parameter 6.1, function 6.5, function call 6.4, hiding 8.3, identifier 2.3, illegal 1.6, literal 4.2, mode
6.1, named parameter association 6.4, operator symbol 6.1, overloading 8.7, package 7, parameter of a subprogram
6.2, qualified expression 4.7, renaming declaration 8.5, result subtype 6.1, subprogram 6, subprogram specification
6.1, subtype 3.3, type 3.3

6.7 Overloading of Operators

The declaration of a function whose designator is an operator symbol is used to overload an   1
operator. The sequence of characters of the operator symbol must be either a logical, a relational, a
binary adding, a unary adding, a multiplying, or a highest precedence operator (see 4.5). Neither
membership tests nor the short-circuit control forms are allowed as function designators.

The subprogram specification of a unary operator must have a single parameter. The subprogram   2
specification of a binary operator must have two parameters; for each use of this operator, the first
parameter takes the left operand as actual parameter, the second parameter takes the right
operand. Similarly, a generic function instantiation whose designator is an operator symbol is only
allowed if the specification of the generic function has the corresponding number of parameters.
Default expressions are not allowed for the parameters of an operator (whether the operator is
declared with an explicit subprogram specification or by a generic instantiation).

3 For each of the operators "+" and "-", overloading is allowed both as a unary and as a binary operator.

4 The explicit declaration of a function that overloads the equality operator "=", other than by a renaming declaration, is only allowed if both parameters are of the same limited type. An overloading of equality must deliver a result of the predefined type BOOLEAN; it also implicitly overloads the inequality operator "/=" so that this still gives the complementary result to the equality operator. Explicit overloading of the inequality operator is not allowed.

5 A renaming declaration whose designator is the equality operator is only allowed to rename another equality operator. (For example, such a renaming declaration can be used when equality is visible by selection but not directly visible.)

Note:

6 Overloading of relational operators does not affect basic comparisons such as testing for membership in a range or the choices in a case statement.

7 *Examples:*

```
function "+" (LEFT, RIGHT : MATRIX)  return MATRIX;
function "+" (LEFT, RIGHT : VECTOR)  return VECTOR;

--   assuming that A, B, and C are of the type VECTOR
--   the three following assignments are equivalent

A := B + C;

A := "+"(B, C);
A := "+"(LEFT => B, RIGHT => C);
```

8 *References:* allow 1.6, actual parameter 6.4.1, binary adding operator 4.5 4.5.3, boolean predefined type 3.5.3, character 2.1, complementary result 4.5.2, declaration 3.1, default expression for a formal parameter 6.1, designator 6.1, directly visible 8.3, equality operator 4.5, formal parameter 6.1, function declaration 6.1, highest precedence operator 4.5 4.5.6, implicit declaration 3.1, inequality operator 4.5.2, limited type 7.4.4, logical operator 4.5 4.5.1, membership test 4.5 4.5.2, multiplying operator 4.5 4.5.5, operator 4.5, operator symbol 6.1, overloading 6.6 8.7, relational operator 4.5 4.5.2, short-circuit control form 4.5 4.5.1, type definition 3.3.1, unary adding operator 4.5 4.5.4, visible by selection 8.3

7. Packages

Packages are one of the four forms of program unit, of which programs can be composed. The other forms are subprograms, task units, and generic units.

Packages allow the specification of groups of logically related entities. In their simplest form packages specify pools of common object and type declarations. More generally, packages can be used to specify groups of related entities including also subprograms that can be called from outside the package, while their inner workings remain concealed and protected from outside users.

References: generic unit 12, program unit 6, subprogram 6, task unit 9, type declaration 3.3.1

7.1 Package Structure

A package is generally provided in two parts: a package specification and a package body. Every package has a package specification, but not all packages have a package body.

```
package_declaration ::= package_specification;

package_specification ::=
    package identifier is
        {basic_declarative_item}
    [ private
        {basic_declarative_item}]
    end [package_simple_name]

package_body ::=
    package body package_simple_name is
        [ declarative_part]
    [ begin
        sequence_of_statements
    [ exception
        exception_handler
        { exception_handler}]]
    end [package_simple_name];
```

The simple name at the start of a package body must repeat the package identifier. Similarly if a simple name appears at the end of the package specification or body, it must repeat the package identifier.

If a subprogram declaration, a package declaration, a task declaration, or a generic declaration is a declarative item of a given package specification, then the body (if there is one) of the program unit declared by the declarative item must itself be a declarative item of the declarative part of the body of the given package.

Notes:

5   A simple form of package, specifying a pool of objects and types, does not require a package body. One of the possible uses of the sequence of statements of a package body is to initialize such objects. For each subprogram declaration there must be a corresponding body (except for a subprogram written in another language, as explained in section 13.9). If the body of a program unit is a body stub, then a separately compiled subunit containing the corresponding proper body is required for the program unit (see 10.2). A body is not a basic declarative item and so cannot appear in a package specification.

6   A package declaration is either a library package (see 10.2) or a declarative item declared within another program unit.

7   *References:* basic declarative item 3.9, body stub 10.2, declarative item 3.9, declarative part 3.9, exception handler 11.2, generic body 12.2, generic declaration 12.1, identifier 2.3, library unit 10.1, object 3.2, package body 7.3, program unit 6, proper body 3.9, sequence of statements 5.1, simple name 4.1, subprogram body 6.3, subprogram declaration 6.1, subunit 10.2, task body 9.1, task declaration 9.1, type 3.3

7.2 Package Specifications and Declarations

1   The first list of declarative items of a package specification is called the *visible part* of the package. The optional list of declarative items after the reserved word **private** is called the *private part* of the package.

2   An entity declared in the private part of a package is not visible outside the package itself (a name denoting such an entity is only possible within the package). In contrast, expanded names denoting entities declared in the visible part can be used even outside the package; furthermore, direct visibility of such entities can be achieved by means of use clauses (see 4.1.3 and 8.4).

3   The elaboration of a package declaration consists of the elaboration of its basic declarative items in the given order.

Notes:

4   The visible part of a package contains all the information that another program unit is able to know about the package. A package consisting of only a package specification (that is, without a package body) can be used to represent a group of common constants or variables, or a common pool of objects and types, as in the examples below.

5   *Example of a package describing a group of common variables:*

```
package PLOTTING_DATA is
   PEN_UP : BOOLEAN;

   CONVERSION_FACTOR,
   X_OFFSET, Y_OFFSET,
   X_MIN,    Y_MIN,
   X_MAX,    Y_MAX:   REAL;      -- see 3.5.7

   X_VALUE : array (1 .. 500) of REAL;
   Y_VALUE : array (1 .. 500) of REAL;
end PLOTTING_DATA;
```

Example of a package describing a common pool of objects and types: 6

```
package WORK_DATA is
   type DAY is (MON, TUE, WED, THU, FRI, SAT, SUN);
   type HOURS_SPENT is delta 0.25 range 0.0 .. 24.0;
   type TIME_TABLE    is array (DAY) of HOURS_SPENT:

   WORK_HOURS    : TIME_TABLE;
   NORMAL_HOURS  : constant TIME_TABLE :=
                      (MON .. THU => 8.25, FRI => 7.0, SAT | SUN => 0.0);
end WORK_DATA;
```

References: basic declarative item 3.9, constant 3.2.1, declarative item 3.9, direct visibility 8.3, elaboration 3.9,   7
expanded name 4.1.3, name 4.1, number declaration 3.2.2, object declaration 3.2.1, package 7, package declaration
7.1, package identifier 7.1, package specification 7.1, scope 8.2, simple name 4.1, type declaration 3.3.1, use clause
8.4, variable 3.2.1

7.3 Package Bodies

In contrast to the entities declared in the visible part of a package specification, the entities decla-   1
red in the package body are only visible within the package body itself. As a consequence, a package with a package body can be used for the construction of a group of related subprograms (a *package* in the usual sense), in which the logical operations available to the users are clearly isolated
from the internal entities.

For the elaboration of a package body, its declarative part is first elaborated, and its sequence of   2
statements (if any) is then executed. The optional exception handlers at the end of a package body
service exceptions raised during the execution of the sequence of statements of the package body.

Notes:

A variable declared in the body of a package is only visible within this body and, consequently, its   3
value can only be changed within the package body. In the absence of local tasks, the value of
such a variable remains unchanged between calls issued from outside the package to subprograms
declared in the visible part. The properties of such a variable are similar to those of an "own"
variable of Algol 60.

The elaboration of the body of a subprogram declared in the visible part of a package is caused by   4
the elaboration of the body of the package. Hence a call of such a subprogram by an outside program unit raises the exception PROGRAM_ERROR if the call takes place before the elaboration of
the package body (see 3.9).

5   *Example of a package:*

```
package RATIONAL_NUMBERS is

    type RATIONAL is
      record
        NUMERATOR    : INTEGER;
        DENOMINATOR  : POSITIVE;
      end record;

    function EQUAL (X,Y : RATIONAL) return BOOLEAN;

    function "/"    (X,Y : INTEGER)  return RATIONAL;  --  to construct a rational number

    function "+"    (X,Y : RATIONAL) return RATIONAL;
    function "-"    (X,Y : RATIONAL) return RATIONAL;
    function "*"    (X,Y : RATIONAL) return RATIONAL;
    function "/"    (X,Y : RATIONAL) return RATIONAL;
end;

package body RATIONAL_NUMBERS is

    procedure SAME_DENOMINATOR (X,Y : in out RATIONAL) is
    begin
      --  reduces X and Y to the same denominator:
      ...
    end;

    function EQUAL(X,Y : RATIONAL) return BOOLEAN is
      U,V : RATIONAL;
    begin
      U := X;
      V := Y;
      SAME_DENOMINATOR (U,V);
      return U.NUMERATOR = V.NUMERATOR;
    end EQUAL;

    function "/" (X,Y : INTEGER) return RATIONAL is
    begin
      if Y > 0 then
        return (NUMERATOR => X,   DENOMINATOR => Y);
      else
        return (NUMERATOR => -X,  DENOMINATOR => -Y);
      end if;
    end "/";

    function "+"  (X,Y : RATIONAL) return RATIONAL is ...  end "+";
    function "-"  (X,Y : RATIONAL) return RATIONAL is ...  end "-";
    function "*"  (X,Y : RATIONAL) return RATIONAL is ...  end "*";
    function "/"  (X,Y : RATIONAL) return RATIONAL is ...  end "/";

end RATIONAL_NUMBERS;
```

6   *References:* declaration 3.1, declarative part 3.9, elaboration 3.1 3.9, exception 11, exception handler 11.2, name 4.1, package specification 7.1, program unit 6, program_error exception 11.1, sequence of statements 5.1, subprogram 6, variable 3.2.1, visible part 7.2

7.4 Private Type and Deferred Constant Declarations

The declaration of a type as a private type in the visible part of a package serves to separate the characteristics that can be used directly by outside program units (that is, the logical properties) from other characteristics whose direct use is confined to the package (the details of the definition of the type itself). Deferred constant declarations declare constants of private types.

```
private_type_declaration ::=
    type identifier [discriminant_part] is [limited] private;

deferred_constant_declaration ::=
    identifier_list : constant type_mark;
```

A private type declaration is only allowed as a declarative item of the visible part of a package, or as the generic parameter declaration for a generic formal type in a generic formal part.

The type mark of a deferred constant declaration must denote a private type or a subtype of a private type; a deferred constant declaration and the declaration of the corresponding private type must both be declarative items of the visible part of the same package. A deferred constant declaration with several identifiers is equivalent to a sequence of single deferred constant declarations as explained in section 3.2.

Examples of private type declarations:

```
type KEY is private;
type FILE_NAME is limited private;
```

Example of deferred constant declaration:

```
NULL_KEY : constant KEY;
```

References: constant 3.2.1, declaration 3.1, declarative item 3.9, deferred constant 7.4.3, discriminant part 3.7.1, generic formal part 12.1, generic formal type 12.1, generic parameter declaration 12.1, identifier 2.3, identifier list 3.2, limited type 7.4.4, package 7, private type 7.4.1, program unit 6, subtype 3.3, type 3.3, type mark 3.3.2, visible part 7.2

7.4.1 Private Types

If a private type declaration is given in the visible part of a package, then a corresponding declaration of a type with the same identifier must appear as a declarative item of the private part of the package. The corresponding declaration must be either a full type declaration or the declaration of a task type. In the rest of this section explanations are given in terms of full type declarations; the same rules apply also to declarations of task types.

2 A private type declaration and the corresponding full type declaration define a single type. The private type declaration, together with the visible part, define the operations that are available to outside program units (see section 7.4.2 on the operations that are available for private types). On the other hand, the full type declaration defines other operations whose direct use is only possible within the package itself.

3 If the private type declaration includes a discriminant part, the full declaration must include a discriminant part that conforms (see 6.3.1 for the conformance rules) and its type definition must be a record type definition. Conversely, if the private type declaration does not include a discriminant part, the type declared by the full type declaration (the *full type*) must not be an unconstrained type with discriminants. The full type must not be an unconstrained array type. A limited type (in particular a task type) is allowed for the full type only if the reserved word **limited** appears in the private type declaration (see 7.4.4).

4 Within the specification of the package that declares a private type and before the end of the corresponding full type declaration, a restriction applies to the use of a name that denotes the private type or a subtype of the private type and, likewise, to the use of a name that denotes any type or subtype that has a subcomponent of the private type. The only allowed occurrences of such a name are in a deferred constant declaration, a type or subtype declaration, a subprogram specification, or an entry declaration; moreover, occurrences within derived type definitions or within simple expressions are not allowed.

5 The elaboration of a private type declaration creates a private type. If the private type declaration has a discriminant part, this elaboration includes that of the discriminant part. The elaboration of the full type declaration consists of the elaboration of the type definition; the discriminant part, if any, is not elaborated (since the conforming discriminant part of the private type declaration has already been elaborated).

Notes:

6 It follows from the given rules that neither the declaration of a variable of a private type, nor the creation by an allocator of an object of the private type are allowed before the full declaration of the type. Similarly before the full declaration, the name of the private type cannot be used in a generic instantiation or in a representation clause.

7 *References:* allocator 4.8, array type 3.6, conform 6.3.1, declarative item 3.9, deferred constant declaration 7.4.3, derived type 3.4, discriminant part 3.7.1, elaboration 3.9, entry declaration 9.5, expression 4.4, full type declaration 3.3.1, generic instantiation 12.3, identifier 2.3, incomplete type declaration 3.8.1, limited type 7.4.4, name 4.1, operation 3.3, package 7, package specification 7.1, private part 7.2, private type 7.4, private type declaration 7.4, record type definition 3.7, representation clause 13.1, reserved word 2.9, subcomponent 3.3, subprogram specification 6.1, subtype 3.3, subtype declaration 3.3.2, type 3.3, type declaration 3.3.1, type definition 3.3.1, unconstrained array type 3.6, variable 3.2.1, visible part 7.2

7.4.2 Operations of a Private Type

1 The operations that are implicitly declared by a private type declaration include basic operations. These are the operations involved in assignment (unless the reserved word **limited** appears in the declaration), membership tests, selected components for the selection of any discriminant, qualification, and explicit conversions.

For a private type T, the basic operations also include the attributes T'BASE (see 3.3.3) and T'SIZE   2
(see 13.7.2). For an object A of a private type, the basic operations include the attribute
A'CONSTRAINED if the private type has discriminants (see 3.7.4), and in any case, the attributes
A'SIZE and A'ADDRESS (see 13.7.2).

Finally, the operations implicitly declared by a private type declaration include the predefined com-   3
parison for equality and inequality unless the reserved word **limited** appears in the private type
declaration.

The above operations, together with subprograms that have a parameter or result of the private   4
type and that are declared in the visible part of the package, are the only operations from the
package that are available outside the package for the private type.

Within the package that declares the private type, the additional operations implicitly declared by   5
the full type declaration are also available. However, the redefinition of these implicitly declared
operations is allowed within the same declarative region, including between the private type
declaration and the corresponding full declaration. An explicitly declared subprogram hides an
implicitly declared operation that has the same parameter and result type profile (this is only possible if the implicitly declared operation is a derived subprogram or a predefined operator).

If a composite type has subcomponents of a private type and is declared outside the package that   6
declares the private type, then the operations that are implicitly declared by the declaration of the
composite type include all operations that only depend on the characteristics that result from the
private type declaration alone. (For example the operator $<$ is not included for a one-dimensional
array type.)

If the composite type is itself declared within the package that declares the private type (including   7
within an inner package or generic package), then additional operations that depend on the
characteristics of the full type are implicitly declared, as required by the rules applicable to the
composite type (for example the operator $<$ is declared for a one-dimensional array type if the full
type is discrete). These additional operations are implicitly declared at the earliest place within the
immediate scope of the composite type and after the full type declaration.

The same rules apply to the operations that are implicitly declared for an access type whose   8
designated type is a private type or a type declared by an incomplete type declaration.

For every private type or subtype T the following attribute is defined: 9

T'CONSTRAINED Yields the value FALSE if T denotes an unconstrained nonformal private type   10
with discriminants; also yields the value FALSE if T denotes a generic formal
private type, and the associated actual subtype is either an unconstrained type
with discriminants or an unconstrained array type; yields the value TRUE
otherwise. The value of this attribute is of the predefined type BOOLEAN.

Note:

A private type declaration and the corresponding full type declaration define two different views of   11
one and the same type. Outside of the defining package the characteristics of the type are those
defined by the visible part. Within these outside program units the type is just a private type and
any language rule that applies only to another class of types does not apply. The fact that the full
declaration might *implement* the private type with a type of a particular class (for example, as an
array type) is only relevant within the package itself.

12 The consequences of this actual implementation are, however, valid everywhere. For example: any default initialization of components takes place; the attribute SIZE provides the size of the full type; task dependence rules still apply to components that are task objects.

13 *Example:*

```
package KEY_MANAGER is
   type KEY is private;
   NULL_KEY : constant KEY;
   procedure GET_KEY(K : out KEY);
   function "<" (X, Y : KEY) return BOOLEAN;
private
   type KEY is new NATURAL;
   NULL_KEY : constant KEY := 0;
end;

package body KEY_MANAGER is
   LAST_KEY : KEY := 0;
   procedure GET_KEY(K : out KEY) is
   begin
      LAST_KEY := LAST_KEY + 1;
      K := LAST_KEY;
   end GET_KEY;

   function "<" (X, Y : KEY) return BOOLEAN is
   begin
      return INTEGER(X) < INTEGER(Y);
   end "<";
end KEY_MANAGER;
```

Notes on the example:

14 Outside of the package KEY_MANAGER, the operations available for objects of type KEY include assignment, the comparison for equality or inequality, the procedure GET_KEY and the operator "<"; they do not include other relational operators such as ">=", or arithmetic operators.

15 The explicitly declared operator "<" hides the predefined operator "<" implicitly declared by the full type declaration. Within the body of the function, an explicit conversion of X and Y to the type INTEGER is necessary to invoke the "<" operator of this type. Alternatively, the result of the function could be written as **not** (X >= Y), since the operator ">=" is not redefined.

16 The value of the variable LAST_KEY, declared in the package body, remains unchanged between calls of the procedure GET_KEY. (See also the Notes of section 7.3.)

17 *References:* assignment 5.2, attribute 4.1.4, basic operation 3.3.3, component 3.3, composite type 3.3, conversion 4.6, declaration 3.1, declarative region 8.1, derived subprogram 3.4, derived type 3.4, dimension 3.6, discriminant 3.3, equality 4.5.2, full type 7.4.1, full type declaration 3.3.1, hiding 8.3, immediate scope 8.2, implicit declaration 3.1, incomplete type declaration 3.8.1, membership test 4.5, operation 3.3, package 7, parameter of a subprogram 6.2, predefined function 8.6, predefined operator 4.5, private type 7.4, private type declaration 7.4, program unit 6, qualification 4.7, relational operator 4.5, selected component 4.1.3, subprogram 6, task dependence 9.4, visible part 7.2

7.4.3 Deferred Constants

If a deferred constant declaration is given in the visible part of a package then a constant declaration (that is, an object declaration declaring a constant object, with an explicit initialization) with the same identifier must appear as a declarative item of the private part of the package. This object declaration is called the *full* declaration of the deferred constant. The type mark given in the full declaration must conform to that given in the deferred constant declaration (see 6.3.1). Multiple or single declarations are allowed for the deferred and the full declarations, provided that the equivalent single declarations conform.

Within the specification of the package that declares a deferred constant and before the end of the corresponding full declaration, the use of a name that denotes the deferred constant is only allowed in the default expression for a record component or for a formal parameter (not for a generic formal parameter).

The elaboration of a deferred constant declaration has no other effect.

The execution of a program is erroneous if it attempts to use the value of a deferred constant before the elaboration of the corresponding full declaration.

Note:

The full declaration for a deferred constant that has a given private type must not appear before the corresponding full type declaration. This is a consequence of the rules defining the allowed uses of a name that denotes a private type (see 7.4.1).

References: conform 6.3.1, constant declaration 3.2.1, declarative item 3.9, default expression for a discriminant 3.7.1, deferred constant 7.4, deferred constant declaration 7.4, elaboration has no other effect 3.1, formal parameter 6.1, generic formal parameter 12.1 12.3, identifier 2.3, object declaration 3.2.1, package 7, package specification 7.1, private part 7.2, record component 3.7, type mark 3.3.2, visible part 7.2

7.4.4 Limited Types

A limited type is a type for which neither assignment nor the predefined comparison for equality and inequality is *implicitly* declared.

A private type declaration that includes the reserved word **limited** declares a limited type. A task type is a limited type. A type derived from a limited type is itself a limited type. Finally, a composite type is limited if the type of any of its subcomponents is limited.

The operations available for a private type that is limited are as given in section 7.4.2 for private types except for the absence of assignment and of a predefined comparison for equality and inequality.

For a formal parameter whose type is limited and whose declaration occurs in an explicit subprogram declaration, the mode **out** is only allowed if this type is private and the subprogram declaration occurs within the visible part of the package that declares the private type. The same holds for formal parameters of entry declarations and of generic procedure declarations. The corresponding full type must not be limited if the mode **out** is used for any such formal parameter. Otherwise, the corresponding full type is allowed (but not required) to be a limited type (in particular, it is allowed to be a task type). If the full type corresponding to a limited private type is not itself limited, then assignment for the type is available within the package, but not outside.

5   The following are consequences of the rules for limited types:

6   ● An explicit initialization is not allowed in an object declaration if the type of the object is limited.

7   ● A default expression is not allowed in a component declaration if the type of the record component is limited.

8   ● An explicit initial value is not allowed in an allocator if the designated type is limited.

9   ● A generic formal parameter of mode in must not be of a limited type.

Notes:

10   The above rules do not exclude a default expression for a formal parameter of a limited type; they do not exclude a deferred constant of a limited type if the full type is not limited. An explicit declaration of an equality operator is allowed for a limited type (see 6.7).

11   Aggregates are not available for a limited composite type (see 3.6.2 and 3.7.4). Catenation is not available for a limited array type (see 3.6.2).

12   *Example:*

```
package I_O_PACKAGE is
   type FILE_NAME is limited private;

   procedure OPEN  (F  : in out FILE_NAME);
   procedure CLOSE (F  : in out FILE_NAME);
   procedure READ  (F  : in FILE_NAME; ITEM : out INTEGER);
   procedure WRITE (F  : in FILE_NAME; ITEM : in  INTEGER);
private
   type FILE_NAME is
      record
         INTERNAL_NAME : INTEGER := 0;
      end record;
end I_O_PACKAGE;

package body I_O_PACKAGE is
   LIMIT : constant := 200;
   type FILE_DESCRIPTOR is record  ...  end record;
   DIRECTORY : array (1 .. LIMIT) of FILE_DESCRIPTOR;
   ...
   procedure OPEN  (F : in out FILE_NAME) is  ...  end;
   procedure CLOSE (F : in out FILE_NAME) is  ...  end;
   procedure READ  (F : in FILE_NAME; ITEM : out INTEGER) is ... end;
   procedure WRITE (F : in FILE_NAME; ITEM : in  INTEGER) is ... end;
begin
   ...
end I_O_PACKAGE;
```

Notes on the example:

13   In the example above, an outside subprogram making use of I_O_PACKAGE may obtain a file name by calling OPEN and later use it in calls to READ and WRITE. Thus, outside the package, a file name obtained from OPEN acts as a kind of password; its internal properties (such as containing a numeric value) are not known and no other operations (such as addition or comparison of internal names) can be performed on a file name.

This example is characteristic of any case where complete control over the operations of a type is desired. Such packages serve a dual purpose. They prevent a user from making use of the internal structure of the type. They also implement the notion of an *encapsulated* data type where the only operations on the type are those given in the package specification. 14

References: aggregate 4.3, allocator 4.8, assignment 5.2, catenation operator 4.5, component declaration 3.7, component type 3.3, composite type 3.3, default expression for a discriminant 3.7, deferred constant 7.4.3, derived type 3.4, designate 3.8, discriminant specification 3.7.1, equality 4.5.2, formal parameter 6.1, full type 7.4.1, full type declaration 3.3.1, generic formal parameter 12.1 12.3, implicit declaration 3.1, initial value 3.2.1, mode 12.1.1, object 3.2, operation 3.3, package 7, predefined operator 4.5, private type 7.4, private type declaration 7.4, record component 3.7, record type 3.7, relational operator 4.5, subcomponent 3.3, subprogram 6, task type 9.1 9.2, type 3.3 15

7.5 Example of a Table Management Package

The following example illustrates the use of packages in providing high level procedures with a simple interface to the user. 1

The problem is to define a table management package for inserting and retrieving items. The items are inserted into the table as they are supplied. Each inserted item has an order number. The items are retrieved according to their order number, where the item with the lowest order number is retrieved first. 2

From the user's point of view, the package is quite simple. There is a type called ITEM designating table items, a procedure INSERT for inserting items, and a procedure RETRIEVE for obtaining the item with the lowest order number. There is a special item NULL_ITEM that is returned when the table is empty, and an exception TABLE_FULL which is raised by INSERT if the table is already full. 3

A sketch of such a package is given below. Only the specification of the package is exposed to the user. 4

```
package TABLE_MANAGER is

    type ITEM is
      record
          ORDER_NUM   : INTEGER;
          ITEM_CODE   : INTEGER;
          QUANTITY    : INTEGER;
          ITEM_TYPE   : CHARACTER;
      end record;

    NULL_ITEM : constant ITEM :=
        (ORDER_NUM | ITEM_CODE | QUANTITY => 0, ITEM_TYPE => ' ');

    procedure INSERT   (NEW_ITEM   : in   ITEM);
    procedure RETRIEVE (FIRST_ITEM : out  ITEM);

    TABLE_FULL : exception;  --  raised by INSERT when table full
end;
```
5

6   The details of implementing such packages can be quite complex; in this case they involve a two-way linked table of internal items. A local housekeeping procedure EXCHANGE is used to move an internal item between the busy and the free lists. The initial table linkages are established by the initialization part. The package body need not be shown to the users of the package.

7
```
package body TABLE_MANAGER is
    SIZE : constant := 2000;
    subtype INDEX is INTEGER range 0 .. SIZE;

    type INTERNAL_ITEM is
        record
            CONTENT  : ITEM;
            SUCC     : INDEX;
            PRED     : INDEX;
        end record;

    TABLE : array (INDEX) of INTERNAL_ITEM;
    FIRST_BUSY_ITEM  : INDEX := 0;
    FIRST_FREE_ITEM  : INDEX := 1;

    function FREE_LIST_EMPTY  return BOOLEAN is ... end;
    function BUSY_LIST_EMPTY  return BOOLEAN is ... end;
    procedure EXCHANGE (FROM : in INDEX; TO : in INDEX) is ... end;

    procedure INSERT (NEW_ITEM : in ITEM) is
    begin
        if FREE_LIST_EMPTY then
            raise TABLE_FULL;
        end if;
        --   remaining code for INSERT
    end INSERT;

    procedure RETRIEVE (FIRST_ITEM : out ITEM) is ... end;

begin
    --   initialization of the table linkages
end TABLE_MANAGER;
```

7.6 Example of a Text Handling Package

1   This example illustrates a simple text handling package. The users only have access to the visible part; the implementation is hidden from them in the private part and the package body (not shown).

2   From a user's point of view, a TEXT is a variable-length string. Each text object has a maximum length, which must be given when the object is declared, and a current value, which is a string of some length between zero and the maximum. The maximum possible length of a text object is an implementation-defined constant.

3   The package defines first the necessary types, then functions that return some characteristics of objects of the type, then the conversion functions between texts and the predefined CHARACTER and STRING types, and finally some of the standard operations on varying strings. Most operations are overloaded on strings and characters as well as on the type TEXT, in order to minimize the number of explicit conversions the user has to write.

```
package TEXT_HANDLER is
   MAXIMUM : constant := SOME_VALUE;    --  implementation-defined      4
   subtype INDEX is INTEGER range 0 .. MAXIMUM;

   type TEXT(MAXIMUM_LENGTH : INDEX) is limited private;

   function LENGTH  (T : TEXT)  return INDEX;
   function VALUE   (T : TEXT)  return STRING;
   function EMPTY   (T : TEXT)  return BOOLEAN;

   function TO_TEXT (S : STRING;      MAX : INDEX) return TEXT;    --  maximum length MAX
   function TO_TEXT (C : CHARACTER; MAX : INDEX) return TEXT;
   function TO_TEXT (S : STRING)      return TEXT;   --  maximum length S'LENGTH
   function TO_TEXT (C : CHARACTER)  return TEXT;

   function "&" (LEFT : TEXT;      RIGHT : TEXT)      return TEXT;
   function "&" (LEFT : TEXT;      RIGHT : STRING)     return TEXT;
   function "&" (LEFT : STRING;    RIGHT : TEXT)      return TEXT;
   function "&" (LEFT : TEXT;      RIGHT : CHARACTER) return TEXT;
   function "&" (LEFT : CHARACTER; RIGHT : TEXT)      return TEXT;

   function "="  (LEFT : TEXT; RIGHT : TEXT) return BOOLEAN;
   function "<"  (LEFT : TEXT; RIGHT : TEXT) return BOOLEAN;
   function "<=" (LEFT : TEXT; RIGHT : TEXT) return BOOLEAN;
   function ">"  (LEFT : TEXT; RIGHT : TEXT) return BOOLEAN;
   function ">=" (LEFT : TEXT; RIGHT : TEXT) return BOOLEAN;

   procedure SET (OBJECT : in out TEXT; VALUE : in TEXT);
   procedure SET (OBJECT : in out TEXT; VALUE : in STRING);
   procedure SET (OBJECT : in out TEXT; VALUE : in CHARACTER);

   procedure APPEND (TAIL : in TEXT;      TO : in out TEXT);
   procedure APPEND (TAIL : in STRING;     TO : in out TEXT);
   procedure APPEND (TAIL : in CHARACTER;  TO : in out TEXT);

   procedure AMEND (OBJECT : in out TEXT;  BY : in TEXT;      POSITION : in INDEX);
   procedure AMEND (OBJECT : in out TEXT;  BY : in STRING;    POSITION : in INDEX);
   procedure AMEND (OBJECT : in out TEXT;  BY : in CHARACTER; POSITION : in INDEX);

   --  amend replaces part of the object by the given text, string, or character
   --  starting at the given position in the object

   function LOCATE (FRAGMENT : TEXT;      WITHIN : TEXT) return INDEX;
   function LOCATE (FRAGMENT : STRING;     WITHIN : TEXT) return INDEX;
   function LOCATE (FRAGMENT : CHARACTER;  WITHIN : TEXT) return INDEX;

   --  all return 0 if the fragment is not located

private
   type TEXT(MAXIMUM_LENGTH : INDEX) is
      record
         POS    : INDEX := 0;
         VALUE  : STRING(1 .. MAXIMUM_LENGTH);
      end record;
end TEXT_HANDLER;
```

5   *Example of use of the text handling package:*

6   A program opens an output file, whose name is supplied by the string NAME. This string has the
     form

         [DEVICE :] [FILENAME [.EXTENSION]]

7   There are standard defaults for device, filename, and extension. The user-supplied name is passed
     to EXPAND_FILE_NAME as a parameter, and the result is the expanded version, with any necessary
     defaults added.

8   ```
     function EXPAND_FILE_NAME (NAME : STRING) return STRING is
        use TEXT_HANDLER;

        DEFAULT_DEVICE   : constant STRING := "SY:";
        DEFAULT_FILE_NAME : constant STRING := "RESULTS";
        DEFAULT_EXTENSION : constant STRING := ".DAT";

        MAXIMUM_FILE_NAME_LENGTH : constant INDEX := SOME_APPROPRIATE_VALUE;
        FILE_NAME : TEXT(MAXIMUM_FILE_NAME_LENGTH);

     begin

        SET(FILE_NAME, NAME);

        if EMPTY(FILE_NAME) then
           SET(FILE_NAME, DEFAULT_FILE_NAME);
        end if;

        if LOCATE(':', FILE_NAME) = 0 then
           SET(FILE_NAME, DEFAULT_DEVICE & FILE_NAME);
        end if;

        if LOCATE('.', FILE_NAME) = 0 then
           APPEND(DEFAULT_EXTENSION, TO => FILE_NAME);
        end if;

        return VALUE(FILE_NAME);

     end EXPAND_FILE_NAME;
     ```
     ```

8. Visibility Rules

The rules defining the scope of declarations and the rules defining which identifiers are visible at various points in the text of the program are described in this chapter. The formulation of these rules uses the notion of a declarative region.

References: declaration 3.1, declarative region 8.1, identifier 2.3, scope 8.2, visibility 8.3

8.1 Declarative Region

A declarative region is a portion of the program text. A single declarative region is formed by the text of each of the following:

- A subprogram declaration, a package declaration, a task declaration, or a generic declaration, together with the corresponding body, if any. If the body is a body stub, the declarative region also includes the corresponding subunit. If the program unit has subunits, they are also included.

- An entry declaration together with the corresponding accept statements.

- A record type declaration, together with a corresponding private or incomplete type declaration if any, and together with a corresponding record representation clause if any.

- A renaming declaration that includes a formal part, or a generic parameter declaration that includes either a formal part or a discriminant part.

- A block statement or a loop statement.

In each of the above cases, the declarative region is said to be *associated* with the corresponding declaration or statement. A declaration is said to *occur immediately within* a declarative region if this region is the innermost region that encloses the declaration, not counting the declarative region (if any) associated with the declaration itself.

A declaration that occurs immediately within a declarative region is said to be *local* to the region. Declarations in outer (enclosing) regions are said to be *global* to an inner (enclosed) declarative region. A local entity is one declared by a local declaration; a global entity is one declared by a global declaration.

Some of the above forms of declarative region include several disjoint parts (for example, other declarative items can be between the declaration of a package and its body). Each declarative region is nevertheless considered as a (logically) continuous portion of the program text. Hence if any rule defines a portion of text as the text that *extends* from some specific point of a declarative region to the end of this region, then this portion is the corresponding subset of the declarative region (for example it does not include intermediate declarative items between the two parts of a package).

Notes:

10   As defined in section 3.1, the term declaration includes basic declarations, implicit declarations, and those declarations that are part of basic declarations, for example, discriminant and parameter specifications. It follows from the definition of a declarative region that a discriminant specification occurs immediately within the region associated with the enclosing record type declaration. Similarly, a parameter specification occurs immediately within the region associated with the enclosing subprogram body or accept statement.

11   The package STANDARD forms a declarative region which encloses all library units: the implicit declaration of each library unit is assumed to occur immediately within this package (see sections 8.6 and 10.1.1).

12   Declarative regions can be nested within other declarative regions. For example, subprograms, packages, task units, generic units, and block statements can be nested within each other, and can contain record type declarations, loop statements, and accept statements.

13   *References:* accept statement 9.5, basic declaration 3.1, block statement 5.6, body stub 10.2, declaration 3.1, discriminant part 3.7.1, discriminant specification 3.7.1, entry declaration 9.5, formal part 6.1, generic body 12.2, generic declaration 12.1, generic parameter declaration 12.1, implicit declaration 3.1, incomplete type declaration 3.8.1, library unit 10.1, loop statement 5.5, package 7, package body 7.1, package declaration 7.1, parameter specification 6.1, private type declaration 7.4, record representation clause 13.4, record type 3.7, renaming declaration 8.5, standard package 8.6, subprogram body 6.3, subprogram declaration 6.1, subunit 10.2, task body 9.1, task declaration 9.1, task unit 9

8.2 Scope of Declarations

1   For each form of declaration, the language rules define a certain portion of the program text called the *scope* of the declaration. The scope of a declaration is also called the scope of any entity declared by the declaration. Furthermore, if the declaration associates some notation with a declared entity, this portion of the text is also called the scope of this notation (either an identifier, a character literal, an operator symbol, or the notation for a basic operation). Within the scope of an entity, and only there, there are places where it is legal to use the associated notation in order to refer to the declared entity. These places are defined by the rules of visibility and overloading.

2   The scope of a declaration that occurs immediately within a declarative region extends from the beginning of the declaration to the end of the declarative region; this part of the scope of a declaration is called the *immediate scope*. Furthermore, for any of the declarations listed below, the scope of the declaration extends beyond the immediate scope:

3   (a) A declaration that occurs immediately within the visible part of a package declaration.

4   (b) An entry declaration.

5   (c) A component declaration.

6   (d) A discriminant specification.

7   (e) A parameter specification.

8   (f) A generic parameter declaration.

In each of these cases, the given declaration occurs immediately within some enclosing declaration, and the scope of the given declaration extends to the end of the scope of the enclosing declaration. 9

In the absence of a subprogram declaration, the subprogram specification given in the subprogram body or in the body stub acts as the declaration and rule (e) applies also in such a case. 10

Note:

The above scope rules apply to all forms of declaration defined by section 3.1; in particular, they apply also to implicit declarations. Rule (a) applies to a package declaration and thus not to the package specification of a generic declaration. For nested declarations, the rules (a) through (f) apply at each level. For example, if a task unit is declared in the visible part of a package, the scope of an entry of the task unit extends to the end of the scope of the task unit, that is, to the end of the scope of the enclosing package. The scope of a use clause is defined in section 8.4. 11

References: basic operation 3.3.3, body stub 10.2, character literal 2.5, component declaration 3.7, declaration 3.1, declarative region 8.1, discriminant specification 3.7.1, entry declaration 9.5, extends 8.1, generic declaration 12.1, generic parameter declaration 12.1, identifier 2.3, implicit declaration 3.1, occur immediately within 8.1, operator symbol 6.1, overloading 6.6 8.7, package declaration 7.1, package specification 7.1, parameter specification 6.1, record type 3.7, renaming declaration 8.5, subprogram body 6.3, subprogram declaration 6.1, task declaration 9.1, task unit 9, type declaration 3.3.1, use clause 8.4, visibility 8.3, visible part 7.2 12

8.3 Visibility

The meaning of the occurrence of an identifier at a given place in the text is defined by the visibility rules and also, in the case of overloaded declarations, by the overloading rules. The identifiers considered in this chapter include any identifier other than a reserved word, an attribute designator, a pragma identifier, the identifier of a pragma argument, or an identifier given as a pragma argument. The places considered in this chapter are those where a lexical element (such as an identifier) occurs. The overloaded declarations considered in this chapter are those for subprograms, enumeration literals, and single entries. 1

For each identifier and at each place in the text, the visibility rules determine a set of declarations (with this identifier) that define possible meanings of an occurrence of the identifier. A declaration is said to be *visible* at a given place in the text when, according to the visibility rules, the declaration defines a possible meaning of this occurrence. Two cases arise. 2

- The visibility rules determine *at most one* possible meaning. In such a case the visibility rules are sufficient to determine the declaration defining the meaning of the occurrence of the identifier, or in the absence of such a declaration, to determine that the occurrence is not legal at the given point. 3

- The visibility rules determine *more than one* possible meaning. In such a case the occurrence of the identifier is legal at this point if and only if *exactly one* visible declaration is acceptable for the overloading rules in the given context (see section 6.6 for the rules of overloading and section 8.7 for the context used for overload resolution). 4

5 A declaration is only visible within a certain part of its scope; this part starts at the end of the declaration except in a package specification, in which case it starts at the reserved word **is** given after the identifier of the package specification. (This rule applies, in particular, for implicit declarations.)

6 Visibility is either by selection or direct. A declaration is visible *by selection* at places that are defined as follows.

7 (a) For a declaration given in the visible part of a package declaration: at the place of the selector after the dot of an expanded name whose prefix denotes the package.

8 (b) For an entry declaration of a given task type: at the place of the selector after the dot of a selected component whose prefix is appropriate for the task type.

9 (c) For a component declaration of a given record type declaration: at the place of the selector after the dot of a selected component whose prefix is appropriate for the type; also at the place of a component simple name (before the compound delimiter =>) in a named component association of an aggregate of the type.

10 (d) For a discriminant specification of a given type declaration: at the same places as for a component declaration; also at the place of a discriminant simple name (before the compound delimiter =>) in a named discriminant association of a discriminant constraint for the type.

11 (e) For a parameter specification of a given subprogram specification or entry declaration: at the place of the formal parameter (before the compound delimiter =>) in a named parameter association of a corresponding subprogram or entry call.

12 (f) For a generic parameter declaration of a given generic unit: at the place of the generic formal parameter (before the compound delimiter =>) in a named generic association of a corresponding generic instantiation.

13 Finally, within the declarative region associated with a construct other than a record type declaration, any declaration that occurs immediately within the region is visible by selection at the place of the selector after the dot of an expanded name whose prefix denotes the construct.

14 Where it is not visible by selection, a visible declaration is said to be *directly visible*. A declaration is directly visible within a certain part of its immediate scope; this part extends to the end of the immediate scope of the declaration, but excludes places where the declaration is hidden as explained below. In addition, a declaration occurring immediately within the visible part of a package can be made directly visible by means of a use clause according to the rules described in section 8.4. (See also section 8.6 for the visibility of library units.)

15 A declaration is said to be *hidden* within (part of) an inner declarative region if the inner region contains a homograph of this declaration; the outer declaration is then hidden within the immediate scope of the inner homograph. Each of two declarations is said to be a *homograph* of the other if both declarations have the same identifier and overloading is allowed for at most one of the two. If overloading is allowed for both declarations, then each of the two is a homograph of the other if they have the same identifier, operator symbol, or character literal, as well as the same parameter and result type profile (see 6.6).

16 Within the specification of a subprogram, every declaration with the same designator as the subprogram is hidden; the same holds within a generic instantiation that declares a subprogram, and within an entry declaration or the formal part of an accept statement; where hidden in this manner, a declaration is visible neither by selection nor directly.

Two declarations that occur immediately within the same declarative region must not be 17
homographs, unless either or both of the following requirements are met: (a) exactly one of them
is the implicit declaration of a predefined operation; (b) exactly one of them is the implicit declaration of a derived subprogram. In such cases, a predefined operation is always hidden by the other
homograph; a derived subprogram hides a predefined operation, but is hidden by any other
homograph. Where hidden in this manner, an implicit declaration is hidden within the entire scope
of the other declaration (regardless of which declaration occurs first); the implicit declaration is
visible neither by selection nor directly.

Whenever a declaration with a certain identifier is visible from a given point, the identifier and the 18
declared entity (if any) are also said to be visible from that point. Direct visibility and visibility by
selection are likewise defined for character literals and operator symbols. An operator is directly
visible if and only if the corresponding operator declaration is directly visible. Finally, the notation
associated with a basic operation is directly visible within the entire scope of this operation.

Example: 19

```
procedure  P  is
   A,  B  :  BOOLEAN;

   procedure  Q  is
      C   :  BOOLEAN;
      B   :  BOOLEAN;   --   an inner homograph of B
   begin
      ...
      B   :=  A;    --    means Q.B  :=  P.A;
      C   :=  P.B;  --    means Q.C  :=  P.B;
   end;
begin
   ...
   A  :=  B;   --   means P.A  :=  P.B;
end;
```

Note on the visibility of library units:

The visibility of library units is determined by with clauses (see 10.1.1) and by the fact that library 20
units are implicitly declared in the package STANDARD (see 8.6).

Note on homographs:

The same identifier may occur in different declarations and may thus be associated with different 21
entities, even if the scopes of these declarations overlap. Overlap of the scopes of declarations
with the same identifier can result from overloading of subprograms and of enumeration literals.
Such overlaps can also occur for entities declared in package visible parts and for entries, record
components, and parameters, where there is overlap of the scopes of the enclosing package
declarations, task declarations, record type declarations, subprogram declarations, renaming
declarations, or generic declarations. Finally overlapping scopes can result from nesting.

Note on immediate scope, hiding, and visibility:

The rules defining immediate scope, hiding, and visibility imply that a reference to an identifier 22
within its own declaration is illegal (except for packages and generic packages). The identifier
hides outer homographs within its immediate scope, that is, from the start of the declaration; on
the other hand, the identifier is visible only after the end of the declaration. For this reason, all but
the last of the following declarations are illegal:

```
K : INTEGER := K * K;                -- illegal
T : T;                               -- illegal
procedure P(X : P);                  -- illegal
procedure Q(X : REAL := Q);          -- illegal, even if there is a function named Q
procedure R(R : REAL);   --  an inner declaration is legal (although confusing)
```

23 *References:* accept statement 9.5, aggregate 4.3, appropriate for a type 4.1, argument 2.8, basic operation 3.3.3, character literal 2.5, component association 4.3, component declaration 3.7, compound delimiter 2.2, declaration 3.1, declarative region 8.1, designate 3.8, discriminant constraint 3.7.2, discriminant specification 3.7.1, entry call 9.5, entry declaration 9.5, entry family 9.5, enumeration literal specification 3.5.1, expanded name 4.1.3, extends 8.1, formal parameter 6.1, generic association 12.3, generic formal parameter 12.1, generic instantiation 12.3, generic package 12.1, generic parameter declaration 12.1, generic unit 12, identifier 2.3, immediate scope 8.2, implicit declaration 3.1, lexical element 2.2, library unit 10.1, object 3.2, occur immediately within 8.1, operator 4.5, operator symbol 6.1, overloading 6.6 8.7, package 7, parameter 6.2, parameter association 6.4, parameter specification 6.1, pragma 2.8, program unit 6, record type 3.7, reserved word 2.9, scope 8.2, selected component 4.1.3, selector 4.1.3, simple name 4.1, subprogram 6, subprogram call 6.4, subprogram declaration 6.1, subprogram specification 6.1, task type 9.1, task unit 9, type 3.3, type declaration 3.3.1, use clause 8.4, visible part 7.2

8.4 Use Clauses

1 A use clause achieves direct visibility of declarations that appear in the visible parts of named packages.

2   use_clause ::= **use** *package*_name {, *package*_name};

3 For each use clause, there is a certain region of text called the *scope* of the use clause. This region starts immediately after the use clause. If a use clause is a declarative item of some declarative region, the scope of the clause extends to the end of the declarative region. If a use clause occurs within a context clause of a compilation unit, the scope of the use clause extends to the end of the declarative region associated with the compilation unit.

4 In order to define which declarations are made directly visible at a given place by use clauses, consider the set of packages named by all use clauses whose scopes enclose this place, omitting from this set any packages that enclose this place. A declaration that can be made directly visible by a use clause (a potentially visible declaration) is any declaration that occurs immediately within the visible part of a package of the set. A potentially visible declaration is actually made directly visible except in the following two cases:

5 ● A potentially visible declaration is not made directly visible if the place considered is within the immediate scope of a homograph of the declaration.

6 ● Potentially visible declarations that have the same identifier are not made directly visible unless each of them is either an enumeration literal specification or the declaration of a subprogram (by a subprogram declaration, a renaming declaration, a generic instantiation, or an implicit declaration).

7 The elaboration of a use clause has no other effect.

Note:

8 The above rules guarantee that a declaration that is made directly visible by a use clause cannot hide an otherwise directly visible declaration. The above rules are formulated in terms of the set of packages named by use clauses.

Consequently, the following lines of text all have the same effect (assuming only one package P).   9

```
use P;
use P; use P, P;
```

Example of conflicting names in two packages: 10

```
procedure R is
  package TRAFFIC is
    type COLOR is (RED, AMBER, GREEN);
    ...
  end TRAFFIC;

  package WATER_COLORS is
    type COLOR is (WHITE, RED, YELLOW, GREEN, BLUE, BROWN, BLACK);
    ...
  end WATER_COLORS;

  use TRAFFIC;          -- COLOR, RED, AMBER, and GREEN are directly visible
  use WATER_COLORS;   -- two homographs of GREEN are directly visible
                        -- but COLOR is no longer directly visible

  subtype LIGHT  is TRAFFIC.COLOR;        -- Subtypes are used to resolve
  subtype SHADE  is WATER_COLORS.COLOR;  -- the conflicting type name COLOR

  SIGNAL : LIGHT;
  PAINT  : SHADE;
begin
  SIGNAL := GREEN;   --   that of TRAFFIC
  PAINT  := GREEN;   --   that of WATER_COLORS
end R;
```

Example of name identification with a use clause: 11

```
package D is
  T, U, V : BOOLEAN;
end D;

procedure P is
  package E is
    B, W, V : INTEGER;
  end E;

  procedure Q is
    T, X : REAL;
    use D, E;
  begin
    --   the name T   means Q.T, not D.T
    --   the name U   means D.U
    --   the name B   means E.B
    --   the name W   means E.W
    --   the name X   means Q.X
    --   the name V   is illegal : either D.V or E.V must be used
    ...
  end Q;
begin
  ...
end P;
```

Use Clauses 8.4

12   *References:* compilation unit 10.1, context clause 10.1, declaration 3.1, declarative item 3.9, declarative region 8.1, direct visibility 8.3, elaboration 3.1 3.9, elaboration has no other effect 3.1, enumeration literal specification 3.5.1, extends 8.1, hiding 8.3, homograph 8.3, identifier 2.3, immediate scope 8.2, name 4.1, occur immediately within 8.1, package 7, scope 8.2, subprogram declaration 6.1, visible part 7.2

8.5   Renaming Declarations

1   A renaming declaration declares another name for an entity.

2
```
renaming_declaration ::=
     identifier : type_mark      renames object_name;
   | identifier : exception      renames exception_name;
   | package identifier          renames package_name;
   | subprogram_specification    renames subprogram_or_entry_name;
```

3   The elaboration of a renaming declaration evaluates the name that follows the reserved word **renames** and thereby determines the entity denoted by this name (the renamed entity). At any point where a renaming declaration is visible, the identifier, or operator symbol of this declaration denotes the renamed entity.

4   The first form of renaming declaration is used for the renaming of objects. The renamed entity must be an object of the base type of the type mark. The properties of the renamed object are not affected by the renaming declaration. In particular, its value and whether or not it is a constant are unaffected; similarly, the constraints that apply to an object are not affected by renaming (any constraint implied by the type mark of the renaming declaration is ignored). The renaming declaration is legal only if exactly one object has this type and can be denoted by the object name.

5   The following restrictions apply to the renaming of a subcomponent that depends on discriminants of a variable. The renaming is not allowed if the subtype of the variable, as defined in a corresponding object declaration, component declaration, or component subtype indication, is an unconstrained type; or if the variable is a generic formal object (of mode **in out**). Similarly if the variable is a formal parameter, the renaming is not allowed if the type mark given in the parameter specification denotes an unconstrained type whose discriminants have default expressions.

6   The second form of renaming declaration is used for the renaming of exceptions; the third form, for the renaming of packages.

7   The last form of renaming declaration is used for the renaming of subprograms and entries. The renamed subprogram or entry and the subprogram specification given in the renaming declaration must have the same parameter and result type profile (see 6.6). The renaming declaration is legal only if exactly one visible subprogram or entry satisfies the above requirements and can be denoted by the given subprogram or entry name. In addition, parameter modes must be identical for formal parameters that are at the same parameter position.

8   The subtypes of the parameters and result (if any) of a renamed subprogram or entry are not affected by renaming. These subtypes are those given in the original subprogram declaration, generic instantiation, or entry declaration (not those of the renaming declaration); even for calls that use the new name. On the other hand, a renaming declaration can introduce parameter names and default expressions that differ from those of the renamed subprogram; named associations of calls with the new subprogram name must use the new parameter name; calls with the old subprogram name must use the old parameter names.

A procedure can only be renamed as a procedure. Either of a function or operator can be renamed as either of a function or operator; for renaming as an operator, the subprogram specification given in the renaming declaration is subject to the rules given in section 6.7 for operator declarations. Enumeration literals can be renamed as functions; similarly, attributes defined as functions (such as SUCC and PRED) can be renamed as functions. An entry can only be renamed as a procedure; the new name is only allowed to appear in contexts that allow a procedure name. An entry of a family can be renamed, but an entry family cannot be renamed as a whole. 9

Examples: 10

```
declare
  L : PERSON renames LEFTMOST_PERSON;  -- see 3.8.1
begin
  L.AGE := L.AGE + 1;
end;

FULL : exception renames TABLE_MANAGER.TABLE_FULL; -- see 7.5

package TM renames TABLE_MANAGER;

function REAL_PLUS(LEFT, RIGHT : REAL    ) return REAL    renames "+";
function INT_PLUS (LEFT, RIGHT : INTEGER) return INTEGER renames "+";

function ROUGE  return COLOR renames RED; --   see 3.5.1
function ROT    return COLOR renames RED;
function ROSSO  return COLOR renames ROUGE;

function NEXT(X : COLOR) return COLOR renames COLOR'SUCC; -- see 3.5.5
```

Example of a renaming declaration with new parameter names: 11

```
function "*" (X,Y : VECTOR) return REAL renames DOT_PRODUCT; -- see 6.1
```

Example of a renaming declaration with a new default expression: 12

```
function MINIMUM(L : LINK := HEAD) return CELL renames MIN_CELL; -- see 6.1
```

Notes:

Renaming may be used to resolve name conflicts and to act as a shorthand. Renaming with a different identifier or operator symbol does not hide the old name; the new name and the old name need not be visible at the same points. The attributes POS and VAL cannot be renamed since the corresponding specifications cannot be written; the same holds for the predefined multiplying operators with a *universal_fixed* result. 13

Calls with the new name of a renamed entry are procedure call statements and are not allowed at places where the syntax requires an entry call statement in conditional and timed entry calls; similarly, the COUNT attribute is not available for the new name. 14

A task object that is declared by an object declaration can be renamed as an object. However, a single task cannot be renamed since the corresponding task type is anonymous. For similar reasons, an object of an anonymous array type cannot be renamed. No syntactic form exists for renaming a generic unit. 15

A subtype can be used to achieve the effect of renaming a type (including a task type) as in 16

```
subtype MODE is TEXT_IO.FILE_MODE ;
```

17   *References:* allow 1.6, attribute 4.1.4, base type 3.3, conditional entry call 9.7.2, constant 3.2.1, constrained subtype 3.3, constraint 3.3, declaration 3.1, default expression 6.1, depend on a discriminant 3.7.1, discriminant 3.7.1, elaboration 3.1 3.9, entry 9.5, entry call 9.5, entry call statement 9.5, entry declaration 9.5, entry family 9.5, enumeration literal 3.5.1, evaluation of a name 4.1, exception 11, formal parameter 6.1, function 6.5, identifier 2.3, legal 1.6, mode 6.1, name 4.1, object 3.2, object declaration 3.2, operator 6.7, operator declaration 6.7, operator symbol 6.1, package 7, parameter 6.2, parameter specification 6.1, procedure 6.1, procedure call statement 6.4, reserved word 2.9, subcomponent 3.3, subprogram 6, subprogram call 6.4, subprogram declaration 6.1, subprogram specification 6.1, subtype 3.3.2, task object 9.2, timed entry call 9.7.3, type 3.3, type mark 3.3.2, variable 3.2.1, visibility 8.3

8.6 The Package Standard

1   The predefined types (for example the types BOOLEAN, CHARACTER and INTEGER) are the types that are declared in a predefined package called STANDARD; this package also includes the declarations of their predefined operations. The package STANDARD is described in Annex C. Apart from the predefined numeric types, the specification of the package STANDARD must be the same for all implementations of the language.

2   The package STANDARD forms a declarative region which encloses every library unit and consequently the main program; the declaration of every library unit is assumed to occur immediately within this package. The implicit declarations of library units are assumed to be ordered in such a way that the scope of a given library unit includes any compilation unit that mentions the given library unit in a with clause. However, the only library units that are visible within a given compilation unit are as follows: they include the library units named by all with clauses that apply to the given unit, and moreover, if the given unit is a secondary unit of some library unit, they include this library unit.

Notes:

3   If all block statements of a program are named, then the name of each program unit can always be written as an expanded name starting with STANDARD (unless this package is itself hidden).

4   If a type is declared in the visible part of a library package, then it is a consequence of the visibility rules that a basic operation (such as assignment) for this type is directly visible at places where the type itself is not visible (whether by selection or directly). However this operation can only be applied to operands that are visible and the declaration of these operands requires the visibility of either the type or one of its subtypes.

5   *References:* applicable with clause 10.1.1, block name 5.6, block statement 5.6, declaration 3.1, declarative region 8.1, expanded name 4.1.3, hiding 8.3, identifier 2.3, implicit declaration 3.1, library unit 10.1, loop statement 5.5, main program 10.1, must 1.6, name 4.1, occur immediately within 8.1, operator 6.7, package 7, program unit 6, secondary unit 10.1, subtype 3.3, type 3.3, visibility 8.3, with clause 10.1.1

8.7 The Context of Overload Resolution

1   Overloading is defined for subprograms, enumeration literals, operators, and single entries, and also for the operations that are inherent in several basic operations such as assignment, membership tests, allocators, the literal **null**, aggregates, and string literals.

For overloaded entities, overload resolution determines the actual meaning that an occurrence of an identifier has, whenever the visibility rules have determined that more than one meaning is acceptable at the place of this occurrence; overload resolution likewise determines the actual meaning of an occurrence of an operator or some basic operation.   2

At such a place all visible declarations are considered. The occurrence is only legal if there is exactly one interpretation of each constituent of the innermost complete context; a *complete context* is one of the following: 3

- A declaration.   4

- A statement.   5

- A representation clause.   6

When considering possible interpretations of a complete context, the only rules considered are the syntax rules, the scope and visibility rules, and the rules of the form described below.   7

(a)   Any rule that requires a name or expression to have a certain type, or to have the same type as another name or expression.   8

(b)   Any rule that requires the type of a name or expression to be a type of a certain class; similarly, any rule that requires a certain type to be a discrete, integer, real, universal, character, boolean, or nonlimited type.   9

(c)   Any rule that requires a prefix to be appropriate for a certain type.   10

(d)   Any rule that specifies a certain type as the result type of a basic operation, and any rule that specifies that this type is of a certain class.   11

(e)   The rules that require the type of an aggregate or string literal to be determinable solely from the enclosing complete context (see 4.3 and 4.2). Similarly, the rules that require the type of the prefix of an attribute, the type of the expression of a case statement, or the type of the operand of a type conversion, to be determinable independently of the context (see 4.1.4, 5.4, 4.6, and 6.4.1).   12

(f)   The rules given in section 6.6, for the resolution of overloaded subprogram calls; in section 4.6, for the implicit conversions of universal expressions; in section 3.6.1, for the interpretation of discrete ranges with bounds having a universal type; and in section 4.1.3, for the interpretation of an expanded name whose prefix denotes a subprogram or an accept statement.   13

Subprogram names used as pragma arguments follow a different rule: the pragma can apply to several overloaded subprograms, as explained in section 6.3.2 for the pragma INLINE, in section 11.7 for the pragma SUPPRESS, and in section 13.9 for the pragma INTERFACE.   14

Similarly, the simple names given in context clauses (see 10.1.1) and in address clauses (see 13.5) follow different rules.   15

The Context of Overload Resolution 8.7

Notes:

16   If there is only one possible interpretation, the identifier denotes the corresponding entity. However, this does not mean that the occurrence is necessarily legal since other requirements exist which are not considered for overload resolution; for example, the fact that an expression is static, the parameter modes, whether an object is constant, conformance rules, forcing occurrences for a representation clause, order of elaboration, and so on.

17   Similarly, subtypes are not considered for overload resolution (the violation of a constraint does not make a program illegal but raises an exception during program execution).

18   A loop parameter specification is a declaration, and hence a complete context.

19   Rules that require certain constructs to have the same parameter and result type profile fall under the category (a); the same holds for rules that require conformance of two constructs since conformance requires that corresponding names be given the same meaning by the visibility and overloading rules.

20   *References:* aggregate 4.3, allocator 4.8, assignment 5.2, basic operation 3.3.3, case statement 5.4, class of type 3.3, declaration 3.1, entry 9.5, enumeration literal 3.5.1, exception 11, expression 4.4, formal part 6.1, identifier 2.3, legal 1.6, literal 4.2, loop parameter specification 5.5, membership test 4.5.2, name 4.1, null literal 3.8, operation 3.3.3, operator 4.5, overloading 6.6, pragma 2.8, representation clause 13.1, statement 5, static expression 4.9, static subtype 4.9, subprogram 6, subtype 3.3, type conversion 4.6, visibility 8.3

21   *Rules of the form (a):* address clause 13.5, assignment 5.2, choice 3.7.3 4.3.2 5.4, component association 4.3.1 4.3.2, conformance rules 9.5, default expression 3.7 3.7.1 6.1 12.1.1, delay statement 9.6, discrete range 3.6.1 5.5 9.5, discriminant constraint 3.7.2, enumeration representation clause 13.3, generic parameter association 12.3.1, index constraint 3.6.1, index expression 4.1.1 4.1.2 9.5, initial value 3.2.1, membership test 4.5.2, parameter association 6.4.1, parameter and result type profile 8.5 12.3.6, qualified expression 4.7, range constraint 3.5, renaming of an object 8.5, result expression 5.8

22   *Rules of the form (b):* abort statement 9.10, assignment 5.2, case expression 5.4, condition 5.3 5.5 5.7 9.7.1, discrete range 3.6.1 5.5 9.5, fixed point type declaration 3.5.9, floating point type declaration 3.5.7, integer type declaration 3.5.4, length clause 13.2, membership test 4.4, number declaration 3.2.2, record representation clause 13.4, selected component 4.1.3, short-circuit control form 4.4, val attribute 3.5.5

23   *Rules of the form (c):* indexed component 4.1.1, selected component 4.1.3, slice 4.1.2

24   *Rules of the form (d):* aggregate 4.3, allocator 4.8, membership test 4.4, null literal 4.2, numeric literal 2.4, short-circuit control form 4.4, string literal 4.2

9. Tasks

The execution of a program that does not contain a task is defined in terms of a sequential execution of its actions, according to the rules described in other chapters of this manual. These actions can be considered to be executed by a single *logical processor*.

Tasks are entities whose executions proceed *in parallel* in the following sense. Each task can be considered to be executed by a logical processor of its own. Different tasks (different logical processors) proceed independently, except at points where they synchronize.

Some tasks have *entries*. An entry of a task can be *called* by other tasks. A task *accepts* a call of one of its entries by executing an accept statement for the entry. Synchronization is achieved by *rendezvous* between a task issuing an entry call and a task accepting the call. Some entries have parameters; entry calls and accept statements for such entries are the principal means of communicating values between tasks.

The properties of each task are defined by a corresponding *task unit* which consists of a *task specification* and a *task body*. Task units are one of the four forms of program unit of which programs can be composed. The other forms are subprograms, packages and generic units. The properties of task units, tasks, and entries, and the statements that affect the interaction between tasks (that is, entry call statements, accept statements, delay statements, select statements, and abort statements) are described in this chapter.

Note:

Parallel tasks (parallel logical processors) may be implemented on multicomputers, multiprocessors, or with interleaved execution on a single *physical processor*. On the other hand, whenever an implementation can detect that the same effect can be guaranteed if parts of the actions of a given task are executed by different physical processors acting in parallel, it may choose to execute them in this way; in such a case, several physical processors implement a single logical processor.

References: abort statement 9.10, accept statement 9.5, delay statement 9.6, entry 9.5, entry call statement 9.5, generic unit 12, package 7, parameter in an entry call 9.5, program unit 6, rendezvous 9.5, select statement 9.7, subprogram 6, task body 9.1, task specification 9.1

9.1 Task Specifications and Task Bodies

A task unit consists of a task specification and a task body. A task specification that starts with the reserved words **task type** declares a task type. The value of an object of a task type designates a task having the entries, if any, that are declared in the task specification; these entries are also called entries of this object. The execution of the task is defined by the corresponding task body.

2   A task specification without the reserved word **type** defines a *single task*. A task declaration with this form of specification is equivalent to the declaration of an anonymous task type immediately followed by the declaration of an object of the task type, and the task unit identifier names the object. In the remainder of this chapter, explanations are given in terms of task type declarations; the corresponding explanations for single task declarations follow from the stated equivalence.

3   task_declaration ::= task_specification;

    task_specification ::=
      task [**type**] identifier [**is**
        {entry_declaration}
        {representation_clause}
      end [*task*_simple_name]]

    task_body ::=
      task body *task*_simple_name **is**
        [declarative_part]
      begin
        sequence_of_statements
      [**exception**
        exception_handler
        { exception_handler}]
      end [*task*_simple_name];

4   The simple name at the start of a task body must repeat the task unit identifier. Similarly if a simple name appears at the end of the task specification or body, it must repeat the task unit identifier. Within a task body, the name of the corresponding task unit can also be used to refer to the task object that designates the task currently executing the body; furthermore, the use of this name as a type mark is not allowed within the task unit itself.

5   For the elaboration of a task specification, entry declarations and representation clauses, if any, are elaborated in the order given. Such representation clauses only apply to the entries declared in the task specification (see 13.5).

6   The elaboration of a task body has no other effect than to establish that the body can from then on be used for the execution of tasks designated by objects of the corresponding task type.

7   The execution of a task body is invoked by the activation of a task object of the corresponding type (see 9.3). The optional exception handlers at the end of a task body handle exceptions raised during the execution of the sequence of statements of the task body (see 11.4).

8   *Examples of specifications of task types:*

    task type RESOURCE **is**
      entry SEIZE;
      entry RELEASE;
    end RESOURCE;

    task type KEYBOARD_DRIVER **is**
      entry READ (C : **out** CHARACTER);
      entry WRITE(C : **in** CHARACTER);
    end KEYBOARD_DRIVER;

Examples of specifications of single tasks: 9

```
task PRODUCER_CONSUMER is
   entry READ (V : out ITEM);
   entry WRITE(E : in  ITEM);
end;

task CONTROLLER is
   entry REQUEST(LEVEL)(D : ITEM);   --  a family of entries
end CONTROLLER;

task USER;  --  has no entries
```

Example of task specification and corresponding body: 10

```
task PROTECTED_ARRAY is
   --  INDEX and ITEM are global types
   entry READ (N : in INDEX; V : out ITEM);
   entry WRITE(N : in INDEX; E : in  ITEM);
end;

task body PROTECTED_ARRAY is
   TABLE : array(INDEX) of ITEM := (INDEX => NULL_ITEM);
begin
   loop
      select
         accept READ (N : in INDEX; V : out ITEM) do
            V := TABLE(N);
         end READ;
      or
         accept WRITE(N : in INDEX; E : in  ITEM) do
            TABLE(N) := E;
         end WRITE;
      end select;
   end loop;
end PROTECTED_ARRAY;
```

Note:

A task specification specifies the interface of tasks of the task type with other tasks of the same or   11
of different types, and also with the main program.

References: declaration 3.1, declarative part 3.9, elaboration 3.9, entry 9.5, entry declaration 9.5, exception handler   12
11.2, identifier 2.3, main program 10.1, object 3.2, object declaration 3.2.1, representation clause 13.1, reserved
word 2.9, simple name 4.1, sequence of statements 5.1, type 3.3, type declaration 3.3.1

9.2 Task Types and Task Objects

A task type is a limited type (see 7.4.4). Hence neither assignment nor the predefined comparison   1
for equality and inequality are defined for objects of task types; moreover, the mode **out** is not
allowed for a formal parameter whose type is a task type.

2   A task object is an object whose type is a task type. The value of a task object designates a task that has the entries of the corresponding task type, and whose execution is specified by the corresponding task body. If a task object is the object, or a subcomponent of the object, declared by an object declaration, then the value of the task object is defined by the elaboration of the object declaration. If a task object is the object, or a subcomponent of the object, created by the evaluation of an allocator, then the value of the task object is defined by the evaluation of the allocator. For all parameter modes, if an actual parameter designates a task, the associated formal parameter designates the same task; the same holds for a subcomponent of an actual parameter and the corresponding subcomponent of the associated formal parameter; finally, the same holds for generic parameters.

3   *Examples:*

```
CONTROL  : RESOURCE;
TELETYPE : KEYBOARD_DRIVER;
POOL     : array(1 .. 10) of KEYBOARD_DRIVER;
--  see also examples of declarations of single tasks in 9.1
```

4   *Example of access type designating task objects:*

```
type KEYBOARD is access KEYBOARD_DRIVER;

TERMINAL : KEYBOARD := new KEYBOARD_DRIVER;
```

Notes:

5   Since a task type is a limited type, it can appear as the definition of a limited private type in a private part, and as a generic actual parameter associated with a formal parameter whose type is a limited type. On the other hand, the type of a generic formal parameter of mode **in** must not be a limited type and hence cannot be a task type.

6   Task objects behave as constants (a task object always designates the same task) since their values are implicitly defined either at declaration or allocation, or by a parameter association, and since no assignment is available. However the reserved word **constant** is not allowed in the declaration of a task object since this would require an explicit initialization. A task object that is a formal parameter of mode **in** is a constant (as is any formal parameter of this mode).

7   If an application needs to store and exchange task identities, it can do so by defining an access type designating the corresponding task objects and by using access values for identification purposes (see above example). Assignment is available for such an access type as for any access type.

8   Subtype declarations are allowed for task types as for other types, but there are no constraints applicable to task types.

9   *References:* access type 3.8, actual parameter 6.4.1, allocator 4.8, assignment 5.2, component declaration 3.7, composite type 3.3, constant 3.2.1, constant declaration 3.2.1, constraint 3.3, designate 3.8 9.1, elaboration 3.9, entry 9.5, equality operator 4.5.2, formal parameter 6.2, formal parameter mode 6.2, generic actual parameter 12.3, generic association 12.3, generic formal parameter 12.1, generic formal parameter mode 12.1.1, generic unit 12, inequality operator 4.5.2, initialization 3.2.1, limited type 7.4.4, object 3.2, object declaration 3.2.1, parameter association 6.4, private part 7.2, private type 7.4, reserved word 2.9, subcomponent 3.3, subprogram 6, subtype declaration 3.3.2, task body 9.1, type 3.3

9.3 Task Execution - Task Activation

A task body defines the execution of any task that is designated by a task object of the corresponding task type. The initial part of this execution is called the *activation* of the task object, and also that of the designated task; it consists of the elaboration of the declarative part, if any, of the task body. The execution of different tasks, in particular their activation, proceeds in parallel.

If an object declaration that declares a task object occurs immediately within a declarative part, then the activation of the task object starts after the elaboration of the declarative part (that is, after passing the reserved word **begin** following the declarative part); similarly if such a declaration occurs immediately within a package specification, the activation starts after the elaboration of the declarative part of the package body. The same holds for the activation of a task object that is a subcomponent of an object declared immediately within a declarative part or package specification. The first statement following the declarative part is executed only after conclusion of the activation of these task objects.

Should an exception be raised by the activation of one of these tasks, that task becomes a completed task (see 9.4); other tasks are not directly affected. Should one of these tasks thus become completed during its activation, the exception TASKING_ERROR is raised upon conclusion of the activation of all of these tasks (whether successfully or not); the exception is raised at a place that is immediately before the first statement following the declarative part (immediately after the reserved word **begin**). Should several of these tasks thus become completed during their activation, the exception TASKING_ERROR is raised only once.

Should an exception be raised by the elaboration of a declarative part or package specification, then any task that is created (directly or indirectly) by this elaboration and that is not yet activated becomes terminated and is therefore never activated (see section 9.4 for the definition of a terminated task).

For the above rules, in any package body without statements, a null statement is assumed. For any package without a package body, an implicit package body containing a single null statement is assumed. If a package without a package body is declared immediately within some program unit or block statement, the implicit package body occurs at the end of the declarative part of the program unit or block statement; if there are several such packages, the order of the implicit package bodies is undefined.

A task object that is the object, or a subcomponent of the object, created by the evaluation of an allocator is activated by this evaluation. The activation starts after any initialization for the object created by the allocator; if several subcomponents are task objects, they are activated in parallel. The access value designating such an object is returned by the allocator only after the conclusion of these activations.

Should an exception be raised by the activation of one of these tasks, that task becomes a completed task; other tasks are not directly affected. Should one of these tasks thus become completed during its activation, the exception TASKING_ERROR is raised upon conclusion of the activation of all of these tasks (whether successfully or not); the exception is raised at the place where the allocator is evaluated. Should several of these tasks thus become completed during their activation, the exception TASKING_ERROR is raised only once.

Should an exception be raised by the initialization of the object created by an allocator (hence before the start of any activation), any task designated by a subcomponent of this object becomes terminated and is therefore never activated.

9   *Example:*

```
procedure P is
   A, B : RESOURCE;   --   elaborate the task objects A, B
   C    : RESOURCE;   --   elaborate the task object C
begin
   --   the tasks A, B, C are activated in parallel before the first statement
   ...
end;
```

Notes:

10   An entry of a task can be called before the task has been activated. If several tasks are activated in parallel, the execution of any of these tasks need not await the end of the activation of the other tasks. A task may become completed during its activation either because of an exception or because it is aborted (see 9.10).

11   *References:* allocator 4.8, completed task 9.4, declarative part 3.9, elaboration 3.9, entry 9.5, exception 11, handling an exception 11.4, package body 7.1, parallel execution 9, statement 5, subcomponent 3.3, task body 9.1, task object 9.2, task termination 9.4, task type 9.1, tasking_error exception 11.1

9.4 Task Dependence - Termination of Tasks

1   Each task *depends* on at least one master. A *master* is a construct that is either a task, a currently executing block statement or subprogram, or a library package (a package declared within another program unit is not a master). The dependence on a master is a direct dependence in the following two cases:

2   (a) The task designated by a task object that is the object, or a subcomponent of the object, created by the evaluation of an allocator depends on the master that elaborates the corresponding access type definition.

3   (b) The task designated by any other task object depends on the master whose execution creates the task object.

4   Furthermore, if a task depends on a given master that is a block statement executed by another master, then the task depends also on this other master, in an indirect manner; the same holds if the given master is a subprogram called by another master, and if the given master is a task that depends (directly or indirectly) on another master. Dependences exist for objects of a private type whose full declaration is in terms of a task type.

5   A task is said to have *completed* its execution when it has finished the execution of the sequence of statements that appears after the reserved word **begin** in the corresponding body. Similarly a block or a subprogram is said to have completed its execution when it has finished the execution of the corresponding sequence of statements. For a block statement, the execution is also said to be completed when it reaches an exit, return, or goto statement transferring control out of the block. For a procedure, the execution is also said to be completed when a corresponding return statement is reached. For a function, the execution is also said to be completed after the evaluation of the result expression of a return statement. Finally the execution of a task, block statement, or subprogram is completed if an exception is raised by the execution of its sequence of statements and there is no corresponding handler, or, if there is one, when it has finished the execution of the corresponding handler.

If a task has no dependent task, its *termination* takes place when it has completed its execution. 6
After its termination, a task is said to be *terminated*. If a task has dependent tasks, its termination
takes place when the execution of the task is completed and all dependent tasks are terminated. A
block statement or subprogram body whose execution is completed is not left until all of its dependent tasks are terminated.

Termination of a task otherwise takes place if and only if its execution has reached an open ter- 7
minate alternative in a select statement (see 9.7.1), and the following conditions are satisfied:

- The task depends on some master whose execution is completed (hence not a library 8
  package).

- Each task that depends on the master considered is either already terminated or similarly 9
  waiting on an open terminate alternative of a select statement.

When both conditions are satisfied, the task considered becomes terminated, together with all 10
tasks that depend on the master considered.

Example: 11

```
declare
   type GLOBAL is access RESOURCE;        --  see 9.1
   A, B  : RESOURCE;
   G     : GLOBAL;
begin
   --   activation of A and B
   declare
      type LOCAL is access RESOURCE;
      X  : GLOBAL  := new RESOURCE;  --  activation of X.all
      L  : LOCAL   := new RESOURCE;  --  activation of L.all
      C  : RESOURCE;
   begin
      --   activation of C
      G := X;  --   both G and X designate the same task object
      ...
   end;   --   await termination of C and L.all (but not X.all)
   ...
end;   --   await termination of A, B, and G.all
```

Notes:

The rules given for termination imply that all tasks that depend (directly or indirectly) on a given 12
master and that are not already terminated, can be terminated (collectively) if and only if each of
them is waiting on an open terminate alternative of a select statement and the execution of the
given master is completed.

The usual rules apply to the main program. Consequently, termination of the main program awaits 13
termination of any dependent task even if the corresponding task type is declared in a library
package. On the other hand, termination of the main program does not await termination of tasks
that depend on library packages; the language does not define whether such tasks are required to
terminate.

For an access type derived from another access type, the corresponding access type definition is 14
that of the parent type; the dependence is on the master that elaborates the ultimate parent access
type definition.

15   A renaming declaration defines a new name for an existing entity and hence creates no further dependence.

1C   *References:* access type 3.8, allocator 4.8, block statement 5.6, declaration 3.1, designate 3.8 9.1, exception 11, exception handler 11.2, exit statement 5.7, function 6.5, goto statement 5.9, library unit 10.1, main program 10.1, object 3.2, open alternative 9.7.1, package 7, program unit 6, renaming declaration 8.5, return statement 5.8, selective wait 9.7.1, sequence of statements 5.1, statement 5, subcomponent 3.3, subprogram body 6.3, subprogram call 6.4, task body 9.1, task object 9.2, terminate alternative 9.7.1

9.5 Entries, Entry Calls, and Accept Statements

1   Entry calls and accept statements are the primary means of synchronization of tasks, and of communicating values between tasks. An entry declaration is similar to a subprogram declaration and is only allowed in a task specification. The actions to be performed when an entry is called are specified by corresponding accept statements.

2
```
entry_declaration ::=
    entry identifier [(discrete_range)] [formal_part];

entry_call_statement ::= entry_name [actual_parameter_part];

accept_statement ::=
    accept entry_simple_name [(entry_index)] [formal_part] [do
        sequence_of_statements
    end [entry_simple_name]];

entry_index ::= expression
```

3   An entry declaration that includes a discrete range (see 3.6.1) declares a *family* of distinct entries having the same formal part (if any); that is, one such entry for each value of the discrete range. The term *single entry* is used in the definition of any rule that applies to any entry other than one of a family. The task designated by an object of a task type has (or owns) the entries declared in the specification of the task type.

4   Within the body of a task, each of its single entries or entry families can be named by the corresponding simple name. The name of an entry of a family takes the form of an indexed component, the family simple name being followed by the index in parentheses; the type of this index must be the same as that of the discrete range in the corresponding entry family declaration. Outside the body of a task an entry name has the form of a selected component, whose prefix denotes the task object, and whose selector is the simple name of one of its single entries or entry families. .

5   A single entry overloads a subprogram, an enumeration literal, or another single entry if they have the same identifier. Overloading is not defined for entry families. A single entry or an entry of an entry family can be renamed as a procedure as explained in section 8.5.

6   The parameter modes defined for parameters of the formal part of an entry declaration are the same as for a subprogram declaration and have the same meaning (see 6.2). The syntax of an entry call statement is similar to that of a procedure call statement, and the rules for parameter associations are the same as for subprogram calls (see 6.4.1 and 6.4.2).

An accept statement specifies the actions to be performed at a call of a named entry (it can be an entry of a family). The formal part of an accept statement must conform to the formal part given in the declaration of the single entry or entry family named by the accept statement (see section 6.3.1 for the conformance rules). If a simple name appears at the end of an accept statement, it must repeat that given at the start.

7

An accept statement for an entry of a given task is only allowed within the corresponding task body; excluding within the body of any program unit that is, itself, inner to the task body; and excluding within another accept statement for either the same single entry or an entry of the same family. (One consequence of this rule is that a task can execute accept statements only for its own entries.) A task body can contain more than one accept statement for the same entry.

8

For the elaboration of an entry declaration, the discrete range, if any, is evaluated and the formal part, if any, is then elaborated as for a subprogram declaration.

9

Execution of an accept statement starts with the evaluation of the entry index (in the case of an entry of a family). Execution of an entry call statement starts with the evaluation of the entry name; this is followed by any evaluations required for actual parameters in the same manner as for a subprogram call (see 6.4). Further execution of an accept statement and of a corresponding entry call statement are synchronized.

10

If a given entry is called by only one task, there are two possibilities:

11

- If the calling task issues an entry call statement before a corresponding accept statement is reached by the task owning the entry, the execution of the calling task is *suspended*.

12

- If a task reaches an accept statement prior to any call of that entry, the execution of the task is suspended until such a call is received.

13

When an entry has been called and a corresponding accept statement has been reached, the sequence of statements, if any, of the accept statement is executed by the called task (while the calling task remains suspended). This interaction is called a *rendezvous*. Thereafter, the calling task and the task owning the entry continue their execution in parallel.

14

If several tasks call the same entry before a corresponding accept statement is reached, the calls are queued; there is one queue associated with each entry. Each execution of an accept statement removes one call from the queue. The calls are processed in the order of arrival.

15

An attempt to call an entry of a task that has completed its execution raises the exception TASKING_ERROR at the point of the call, in the calling task; similarly, this exception is raised at the point of the call if the called task completes its execution before accepting the call (see also 9.10 for the case when the called task becomes abnormal). The exception CONSTRAINT_ERROR is raised if the index of an entry of a family is not within the specified discrete range.

16

Examples of entry declarations:

17

```
entry READ(V : out ITEM);
entry SEIZE;
entry REQUEST(LEVEL)(D : ITEM);   --   a family of entries
```

Examples of entry calls:

18

```
CONTROL.RELEASE;                      --   see 9.2 and 9.1
PRODUCER_CONSUMER.WRITE(E);           --   see 9.1
POOL(5).READ(NEXT_CHAR);              --   see 9.2 and 9.1
CONTROLLER.REQUEST(LOW)(SOME_ITEM);   --   see 9.1
```

19   *Examples of accept statements:*

     accept SEIZE;

     accept READ(V : **out** ITEM) **do**
       V := LOCAL_ITEM;
     end READ;

     accept REQUEST(LOW)(D : ITEM) **do**
       ...
     end REQUEST;

Notes:

20   The formal part given in an accept statement is not elaborated; it is only used to identify the corresponding entry.

21   An accept statement can call subprograms that issue entry calls. An accept statement need not have a sequence of statements even if the corresponding entry has parameters. Equally, it can have a sequence of statements even if the corresponding entry has no parameters. The sequence of statements of an accept statement can include return statements. A task can call its own entries but it will, of course, deadlock. The language permits conditional and timed entry calls (see 9.7.2 and 9.7.3). The language rules ensure that a task can only be in one entry queue at a given time.

22   If the bounds of the discrete range of an entry family are integer literals, the index (in an entry name or accept statement) must be of the predefined type INTEGER (see 3.6.1).

23   *References:* abnormal task 9.10, actual parameter part 6.4, completed task 9.4, conditional entry call 9.7.2, conformance rules 6.3.1, constraint_error exception 11.1, designate 9.1, discrete range 3.6.1, elaboration 3.1 3.9, enumeration literal 3.5.1, evaluation 4.5, expression 4.4, formal part 6.1, identifier 2.3, indexed component 4.1.1, integer type 3.5.4, name 4.1, object 3.2, overloading 6.6 8.7, parallel execution 9, prefix 4.1, procedure 6, procedure call 6.4, renaming declaration 8.5, return statement 5.8, scope 8.2, selected component 4.1.3, selector 4.1.3, sequence of statements 5.1, simple expression 4.4, simple name 4.1, subprogram 6, subprogram body 6.3, subprogram declaration 6.1, task 9, task body 9.1, task specification 9.1, tasking_error exception 11.1, timed entry call 9.7.3

9.6 Delay Statements, Duration, and Time

1   The execution of a delay statement evaluates the simple expression, and suspends further execution of the task that executes the delay statement, for at least the duration specified by the resulting value.

2   delay_statement ::= **delay** simple_expression;

3   The simple expression must be of the predefined fixed point type DURATION; its value is expressed in seconds; a delay statement with a negative value is equivalent to a delay statement with a zero value.

4   Any implementation of the type DURATION must allow representation of durations (both positive and negative) up to at least 86400 seconds (one day); the smallest representable duration, DURATION'SMALL must not be greater than twenty milliseconds (whenever possible, a value not greater than fifty microseconds should be chosen). Note that DURATION'SMALL need not correspond to the basic clock cycle, the named number SYSTEM.TICK (see 13.7).

The definition of the type TIME is provided in the predefined library package CALENDAR. The ⁵
function CLOCK returns the current value of TIME at the time it is called. The functions YEAR,
MONTH, DAY and SECONDS return the corresponding values for a given value of the type TIME;
the procedure SPLIT returns all four corresponding values. Conversely, the function TIME_OF
combines a year number, a month number, a day number, and a duration, into a value of type
TIME. The operators "+" and "-" for addition and subtraction of times and durations, and the
relational operators for times, have the conventional meaning.

The exception TIME_ERROR is raised by the function TIME_OF if the actual parameters do not form ⁶
a proper date. This exception is also raised by the operators "+" and "-" if, for the given operands,
these operators cannot return a date whose year number is in the range of the corresponding subtype, or if the operator "-" cannot return a result that is in the range of the type DURATION.

```
package CALENDAR is                                                          7
   type TIME is private;

   subtype YEAR_NUMBER   is INTEGER   range 1901 .. 2099;
   subtype MONTH_NUMBER  is INTEGER   range 1 .. 12;
   subtype DAY_NUMBER    is INTEGER   range 1 .. 31;
   subtype DAY_DURATION  is DURATION  range 0.0 .. 86_400.0;

   function CLOCK return TIME;

   function YEAR    (DATE : TIME) return YEAR_NUMBER;
   function MONTH   (DATE : TIME) return MONTH_NUMBER;
   function DAY     (DATE : TIME) return DAY_NUMBER;
   function SECONDS (DATE : TIME) return DAY_DURATION;

   procedure SPLIT ( DATE    : in   TIME;
                     YEAR    : out  YEAR_NUMBER;
                     MONTH   : out  MONTH_NUMBER;
                     DAY     : out  DAY_NUMBER;
                     SECONDS : out  DAY_DURATION);

   function TIME_OF( YEAR    : YEAR_NUMBER;
                     MONTH   : MONTH_NUMBER;
                     DAY     : DAY_NUMBER;
                     SECONDS : DAY_DURATION := 0.0) return TIME;


   function "+"   (LEFT : TIME;      RIGHT : DURATION)  return TIME;
   function "+"   (LEFT : DURATION;  RIGHT : TIME)      return TIME;
   function "-"   (LEFT : TIME;      RIGHT : DURATION)  return TIME;
   function "-"   (LEFT : TIME;      RIGHT : TIME)      return DURATION;

   function "<"   (LEFT, RIGHT : TIME) return BOOLEAN;
   function "<="  (LEFT, RIGHT : TIME) return BOOLEAN;
   function ">"   (LEFT, RIGHT : TIME) return BOOLEAN;
   function ">="  (LEFT, RIGHT : TIME) return BOOLEAN;

   TIME_ERROR : exception; --  can be raised by TIME_OF, "+", and "-"

private
   -- implementation-dependent
end;
```

8   *Examples:*

```
delay 3.0;   --   delay 3.0 seconds

declare
  use CALENDAR;
  --   INTERVAL is a global constant of type DURATION
  NEXT_TIME : TIME := CLOCK + INTERVAL;
begin
  loop
    delay NEXT_TIME - CLOCK;
    --   some actions
    NEXT_TIME := NEXT_TIME + INTERVAL;
  end loop;
end;
```

Notes:

9   The second example causes the loop to be repeated every INTERVAL seconds on average. This interval between two successive iterations is only approximate.   However, there will be no cumulative drift as long as the duration of each iteration is (sufficiently) less than INTERVAL.

10   *References:* adding operator 4.5, duration C, fixed point type 3.5.9, function call 6.4, library unit 10.1, operator 4.5, package 7, private type 7.4, relational operator 4.5, simple expression 4.4, statement 5, task 9, type 3.3

9.7   Select Statements

1   There are three forms of select statements.   One form provides a selective wait for one or more alternatives.   The other two provide conditional and timed entry calls.

2   select_statement ::= selective_wait
      | conditional_entry_call | timed_entry_call

3   *References:* selective wait 9.7.1, conditional entry call 9.7.2, timed entry call 9.7.3

9.7.1   Selective Waits

1   This form of the select statement allows a combination of waiting for, and selecting from, one or more alternatives.   The selection can depend on conditions associated with each alternative of the selective wait.

```
selective_wait  ::=
    select
      select_alternative
  { or
      select_alternative}
  [ else
      sequence_of_statements]
    end select;

select_alternative ::=
  [ when condition =>]
      selective_wait_alternative

selective_wait_alternative ::= accept_alternative
  | delay_alternative | terminate_alternative

accept_alternative  ::= accept_statement [sequence_of_statements]

delay_alternative  ::= delay_statement [sequence_of_statements]

terminate_alternative ::= terminate;
```

A selective wait must contain at least one accept alternative. In addition a selective wait can con- 3
tain either a terminate alternative (only one), or one or more delay alternatives, or an else part;
these three possibilities are mutually exclusive.

A select alternative is said to be *open* if it does not start with **when** and a condition, or if the condi- 4
tion is TRUE. It is said to be *closed* otherwise.

For the execution of a selective wait, any conditions specified after **when** are evaluated in some 5
order that is not defined by the language; open alternatives are thus determined. For an open
delay alternative, the delay expression is also evaluated. Similarly, for an open accept alternative
for an entry of a family, the entry index is also evaluated. Selection and execution of one open
alternative, or of the else part, then completes the execution of the selective wait; the rules for this
selection are described below.

Open accept alternatives are first considered. Selection of one such alternative takes place 6
immediately if a corresponding rendezvous is possible, that is, if there is a corresponding entry call
issued by another task and waiting to be accepted. If several alternatives can thus be selected,
one of them is selected arbitrarily (that is, the language does not define which one). When such an
alternative is selected, the corresponding accept statement and possible subsequent statements
are executed. If no rendezvous is immediately possible and there is no else part, the task waits
until an open selective wait alternative can be selected.

Selection of the other forms of alternative or of an else part is performed as follows: 7

● An open delay alternative will be selected if no accept alternative can be selected before the 8
specified delay has elapsed (immediately, for a negative or zero delay in the absence of
queued entry calls); any subsequent statements of the alternative are then executed. If several
delay alternatives can thus be selected (that is, if they have the same delay), one of them is
selected arbitrarily.

● The else part is selected and its statements are executed if no accept alternative can be 9
immediately selected, in particular, if all alternatives are closed.

● An open terminate alternative is selected if the conditions stated in section 9.4 are satisfied. 10
It is a consequence of other rules that a terminate alternative cannot be selected while there is
a queued entry call for any entry of the task.

　　　　　　　　　　　　　　　　　　　　　　　　Selective Waits 9.7.1

11 The exception PROGRAM_ERROR is raised if all alternatives are closed and there is no else part.

12 *Examples of a select statement:*

```
select
   accept DRIVER_AWAKE_SIGNAL;
or
   delay 30.0*SECONDS;
   STOP_THE_TRAIN;
end select;
```

13 *Example of a task body with a select statement:*

```
task body RESOURCE is
   BUSY : BOOLEAN := FALSE;
begin
   loop
      select
         when not BUSY =>
            accept SEIZE do
               BUSY := TRUE;
            end;
      or
            accept RELEASE do
               BUSY := FALSE;
            end;
      or
            terminate;
      end select;
   end loop;
end RESOURCE;
```

Notes:

14 A selective wait is allowed to have several open delay alternatives. A selective wait is allowed to have several open accept alternatives for the same entry.

15 *References:* accept statement 9.5, condition 5.3, declaration 3.1, delay expression 9.6, delay statement 9.6, duration 9.6, entry 9.5, entry call 9.5, entry index 9.5, program_error exception 11.1, queued entry call 9.5, rendezvous 9.5, select statement 9.7, sequence of statements 5.1, task 9

9.7.2 Conditional Entry Calls

1 A conditional entry call issues an entry call that is then canceled if a rendezvous is not immediately possible.

2
```
conditional_entry_call ::=
   select
      entry_call_statement
      [ sequence_of_statements]
   else
      sequence_of_statements
   end select;
```

For the execution of a conditional entry call, the entry name is first evaluated. This is followed by any evaluations required for actual parameters as in the case of a subprogram call (see 6.4).   3

The entry call is canceled if the execution of the called task has not reached a point where it is ready to accept the call (that is, either an accept statement for the corresponding entry, or a select statement with an open accept alternative for the entry), or if there are prior queued entry calls for this entry. If the called task has reached a select statement, the entry call is canceled if an accept alternative for this entry is not selected.   4

If the entry call is canceled, the statements of the else part are executed. Otherwise, the rendez-vous takes place; and the optional sequence of statements after the entry call is then executed.   5

The execution of a conditional entry call raises the exception TASKING_ERROR if the called task has already completed its execution (see also 9.10 for the case when the called task becomes abnormal).   6

Example: 7

```
procedure SPIN(R : RESOURCE) is
begin
  loop
    select
      R.SEIZE;
      return;
    else
      null;  --  busy waiting
    end select;
  end loop;
end;
```

References: abnormal task 9.10, accept statement 9.5, actual parameter part 6.4, completed task 9.4, entry call   8
statement 9.5, entry family 9.5, entry index 9.5, evaluation 4.5, expression 4.4, open alternative 9.7.1, queued entry
call 9.5, rendezvous 9.5, select statement 9.7, sequence of statements 5.1, task 9, tasking_error exception 11.1

9.7.3 Timed Entry Calls

A timed entry call issues an entry call that is canceled if a rendezvous is not started within a given delay.   1

```
timed_entry_call ::=                                    2
    select
        entry_call_statement
      [ sequence_of_statements]
    or
        delay_alternative
    end select;
```

3   For the execution of a timed entry call, the entry name is first evaluated. This is followed by any evaluations required for actual parameters as in the case of a subprogram call (see 6.4). The expression stating the delay is then evaluated, and the entry call is finally issued.

4   If a rendezvous can be started within the specified duration (or immediately, as for a conditional entry call, for a negative or zero delay), it is performed and the optional sequence of statements after the entry call is then executed. Otherwise, the entry call is canceled when the specified duration has expired, and the optional sequence of statements of the delay alternative is executed.

5   The execution of a timed entry call raises the exception TASKING_ERROR if the called task completes its execution before accepting the call (see also 9.10 for the case when the called task becomes abnormal).

6   *Example:*

```
select
   CONTROLLER.REQUEST(MEDIUM)(SOME_ITEM);
or
   delay 45.0;
   --  controller too busy, try something else
end select;
```

7   *References:* abnormal task 9.10, accept statement 9.5, actual parameter part 6.4, completed task 9.4, conditional entry call 9.7.2, delay expression 9.6, delay statement 9.6, duration 9.6, entry call statement 9.5, entry family 9.5, entry index 9.5, evaluation 4.5, expression 4.4, rendezvous 9.5, sequence of statements 5.1, task 9, tasking_error exception 11.1

9.8 Priorities

1   Each task may (but need not) have a priority, which is a value of the subtype PRIORITY (of the type INTEGER) declared in the predefined library package SYSTEM (see 13.7). A lower value indicates a lower degree of urgency; the range of priorities is implementation-defined. A priority is associated with a task if a pragma

     pragma PRIORITY (*static*_expression);

2   appears in the corresponding task specification; the priority is given by the value of the expression. A priority is associated with the main program if such a pragma appears in its outermost declarative part. At most one such pragma can appear within a given task specification or for a subprogram that is a library unit, and these are the only allowed places for this pragma. A pragma PRIORITY has no effect if it occurs in a subprogram other than the main program.

3   The specification of a priority is an indication given to assist the implementation in the allocation of processing resources to parallel tasks when there are more tasks eligible for execution than can be supported simultaneously by the available processing resources.   The effect of priorities on scheduling is defined by the following rule:

4   If two tasks with different priorities are both eligible for execution and could sensibly be executed using the same physical processors and the same other processing resources, then it cannot be the case that the task with the lower priority is executing while the task with the higher priority is not.

For tasks of the same priority, the scheduling order is not defined by the language. For tasks 5 without explicit priority, the scheduling rules are not defined, except when such tasks are engaged in a rendezvous. If the priorities of both tasks engaged in a rendezvous are defined, the rendezvous is executed with the higher of the two priorities. If only one of the two priorities is defined, the rendezvous is executed with at least that priority. If neither is defined, the priority of the rendezvous is undefined.

Notes:

The priority of a task is static and therefore fixed. However, the priority during a rendezvous is not 6 necessarily static since it also depends on the priority of the task calling the entry. Priorities should be used only to indicate relative degrees of urgency; they should not be used for task synchronization.

References: declarative part 3.9, entry call statement 9.5, integer type 3.5.4, main program 10.1, package system 7 13.7, pragma 2.8, rendezvous 9.5, static expression 4.9, subtype 3.3, task 9, task specification 9.1

9.9 Task and Entry Attributes

For a task object or value T the following attributes are defined: 1

T'CALLABLE   Yields the value FALSE when the execution of the task designated by T is 2 either completed or terminated, or when the task is abnormal. Yields the value TRUE otherwise. The value of this attribute is of the predefined type BOOLEAN.

T'TERMINATED   Yields the value TRUE if the task designated by T is terminated. Yields the 3 value FALSE otherwise. The value of this attribute is of the predefined type BOOLEAN.

In addition, the representation attributes STORAGE_SIZE, SIZE, and ADDRESS are defined for a 4 task object T or a task type T (see 13.7.2).

The attribute COUNT is defined for an entry E of a task unit T. The entry can be either a single 5 entry or an entry of a family (in either case the name of the single entry or entry family can be either a simple or an expanded name). This attribute is only allowed within the body of T, but excluding within any program unit that is, itself, inner to the body of T.

E'COUNT   Yields the number of entry calls presently queued on the entry E (if the 6 attribute is evaluated by the execution of an accept statement for the entry E, the count does not include the calling task). The value of this attribute is of the type *universal_integer*.

Note:

Algorithms interrogating the attribute E'COUNT should take precautions to allow for the increase 7 of the value of this attribute for incoming entry calls, and its decrease, for example with timed entry calls.

References: abnormal task 9.10, accept statement 9.5, attribute 4.1.4, boolean type 3.5.3, completed task 9.4, 8 designate 9.1, entry 9.5, false boolean value 3.5.3, queue of entry calls 9.5, storage unit 13.7, task 9, task object 9.2, task type 9.1, terminated task 9.4, timed entry call 9.7.3, true boolean value 3.5.3, universal_integer type 3.5.4

9.10 Abort Statements

1   An abort statement causes one or more tasks to become *abnormal*, thus preventing any further rendezvous with such tasks.

2   abort_statement ::= **abort** *task*_name {, *task*_name};

3   The determination of the type of each task name uses the fact that the type of the name is a task type.

4   For the execution of an abort statement, the given task names are evaluated in some order that is not defined by the language. Each named task then becomes abnormal unless it is already terminated; similarly, any task that depends on a named task becomes abnormal unless it is already terminated.

5   Any abnormal task whose execution is suspended at an accept statement, a select statement, or a delay statement becomes completed; any abnormal task whose execution is suspended at an entry call, and that is not yet in a corresponding rendezvous, becomes completed and is removed from the entry queue; any abnormal task that has not yet started its activation becomes completed (and hence also terminated). This completes the execution of the abort statement.

6   The completion of any other abnormal task need not happen before completion of the abort statement. It must happen no later than when the abnormal task reaches a synchronization point that is one of the following: the end of its activation; a point where it causes the activation of another task; an entry call; the start or the end of an accept statement; a select statement; a delay statement; an exception handler; or an abort statement. If a task that calls an entry becomes abnormal while in a rendezvous, its termination does not take place before the completion of the rendezvous (see 11.5).

7   The call of an entry of an abnormal task raises the exception TASKING_ERROR at the place of the call. Similarly, the exception TASKING_ERROR is raised for any task that has called an entry of an abnormal task, if the entry call is still queued or if the rendezvous is not yet finished (whether the entry call is an entry call statement, or a conditional or timed entry call); the exception is raised no later than the completion of the abnormal task. The value of the attribute CALLABLE is FALSE for any task that is abnormal (or completed).

8   If the abnormal completion of a task takes place while the task updates a variable, then the value of this variable is undefined.

9   *Example:*

    abort USER, TERMINAL.**all**, POOL(3);

Notes:

10 An abort statement should be used only in extremely severe situations requiring unconditional termination. A task is allowed to abort any task, including itself.

11 *References:* abnormal in rendezvous 11.5, accept statement 9.5, activation 9.3, attribute 4.1.4, callable (predefined attribute) 9.9, conditional entry call 9.7.2, delay statement 9.6, dependent task 9.4, entry call statement 9.5, evaluation of a name 4.1, exception handler 11.2, false boolean value 3.5.3, name 4.1, queue of entry calls 9.5, rendezvous 9.5, select statement 9.7, statement 5, task 9, tasking_error exception 11.1, terminated task 9.4, timed entry call 9.7.3

9.11 Shared Variables

The normal means of communicating values between tasks is by entry calls and accept statements. 1

If two tasks read or update a *shared* variable (that is, a variable accessible by both), then neither of them may assume anything about the order in which the other performs its operations, except at the points where they synchronize. Two tasks are synchronized at the start and at the end of their rendezvous. At the start and at the end of its activation, a task is synchronized with the task that causes this activation. A task that has completed its execution is synchronized with any other task. 2

For the actions performed by a program that uses shared variables, the following assumptions can always be made: 3

- If between two synchronization points of a task, this task reads a shared variable whose type is a scalar or access type, then the variable is not updated by any other task at any time between these two points. 4

- If between two synchronization points of a task, this task updates a shared variable whose type is a scalar or access type, then the variable is neither read nor updated by any other task at any time between these two points. 5

The execution of the program is erroneous if any of these assumptions is violated. 6

If a given task reads the value of a shared variable, the above assumptions allow an implementation to maintain local copies of the value (for example, in registers or in some other form of temporary storage); and for as long as the given task neither reaches a synchronization point nor updates the value of the shared variable, the above assumptions imply that, for the given task, reading a local copy is equivalent to reading the shared variable itself. 7

Similarly, if a given task updates the value of a shared variable, the above assumptions allow an implementation to maintain a local copy of the value, and to defer the effective store of the local copy into the shared variable until a synchronization point, provided that every further read or update of the variable by the given task is treated as a read or update of the local copy. On the other hand, an implementation is not allowed to introduce a store, unless this store would also be executed in the canonical order (see 11.6). 8

The pragma SHARED can be used to specify that every read or update of a variable is a synchronization point for that variable; that is, the above assumptions always hold for the given variable (but not necessarily for other variables). The form of this pragma is as follows: 9

    pragma SHARED(*variable*_simple_name);

This pragma is allowed only for a variable declared by an object declaration and whose type is a scalar or access type; the variable declaration and the pragma must both occur (in this order) immediately within the same declarative part or package specification; the pragma must appear before any occurrence of the name of the variable, other than in an address clause. 10

An implementation must restrict the objects for which the pragma SHARED is allowed to objects for which each of direct reading and direct updating is implemented as an indivisible operation. 11

References: accept statement 9.5, activation 9.3, assignment 5.2, canonical order 11.6, declarative part 3.9, entry 12
call statement 9.5, erroneous 1.6, global 8.1, package specification 7.1, pragma 2.8, read a value 6.2, rendezvous 9.5, simple name 3.1 4.1, task 9, type 3.3, update a value 6.2, variable 3.2.1

         Shared Variables 9.11

9.12 Example of Tasking

1   The following example defines a buffering task to smooth variations between the speed of output of a producing task and the speed of input of some consuming task. For instance, the producing task may contain the statements

2
```
loop
    -- produce the next character CHAR
    BUFFER.WRITE(CHAR);
    exit when CHAR = ASCII.EOT;
end loop;
```

3   and the consuming task may contain the statements

4
```
loop
    BUFFER.READ(CHAR);
    -- consume the character CHAR
    exit when CHAR = ASCII.EOT;
end loop;
```

5   The buffering task contains an internal pool of characters processed in a round-robin fashion. The pool has two indices, an IN_INDEX denoting the space for the next input character and an OUT_INDEX denoting the space for the next output character.

6
```
task BUFFER is
    entry READ (C : out  CHARACTER);
    entry WRITE (C : in   CHARACTER);
end;

task body BUFFER is
    POOL_SIZE : constant INTEGER := 100;
    POOL      : array(1 .. POOL_SIZE) of CHARACTER;
    COUNT     : INTEGER range 0 .. POOL_SIZE := 0;
    IN_INDEX, OUT_INDEX : INTEGER range 1 .. POOL_SIZE := 1;
begin
    loop
        select
            when COUNT < POOL_SIZE =>
                accept WRITE(C : in CHARACTER) do
                    POOL(IN_INDEX) := C;
                end;
                IN_INDEX := IN_INDEX mod POOL_SIZE + 1;
                COUNT    := COUNT + 1;
        or when COUNT > 0 =>
                accept READ(C : out CHARACTER) do
                    C := POOL(OUT_INDEX);
                end;
                OUT_INDEX := OUT_INDEX mod POOL_SIZE + 1;
                COUNT     := COUNT - 1;
        or
            terminate;
        end select;
    end loop;
end BUFFER;
```

10. Program Structure and Compilation Issues

The overall structure of programs and the facilities for separate compilation are described in this chapter. A program is a collection of one or more compilation units submitted to a compiler in one or more compilations. Each compilation unit specifies the separate compilation of a construct which can be a subprogram declaration or body, a package declaration or body, a generic declaration or body, or a generic instantiation. Alternatively this construct can be a subunit, in which case it includes the body of a subprogram, package, task unit, or generic unit declared within another compilation unit.

References: compilation 10.1, compilation unit 10.1, generic body 12.2, generic declaration 12.1, generic instantiation 12.3, package body 7.1, package declaration 7.1, subprogram body 6.3, subprogram declaration 6.1, subunit 10.2, task body 9.1, task unit 9

10.1 Compilation Units - Library Units

The text of a program can be submitted to the compiler in one or more compilations. Each compilation is a succession of compilation units.

```
compilation  ::=  {compilation_unit}

compilation_unit  ::=
    context_clause library_unit | context_clause secondary_unit

library_unit  ::=
      subprogram_declaration  |  package_declaration
    | generic_declaration     |  generic_instantiation
    | subprogram_body

secondary_unit  ::=  library_unit_body | subunit

library_unit_body  ::=  subprogram_body | package_body
```

The compilation units of a program are said to belong to a *program library*. A compilation unit defines either a library unit or a secondary unit. A secondary unit is either the separately compiled proper body of a library unit, or a subunit of another compilation unit. The designator of a separately compiled subprogram (whether a library unit or a subunit) must be an identifier. Within a program library the simple names of all library units must be distinct identifiers.

The effect of compiling a library unit is to define (or redefine) this unit as one that belongs to the program library. For the visibility rules, each library unit acts as a declaration that occurs immediately within the package STANDARD.

The effect of compiling a secondary unit is to define the body of a library unit, or in the case of a subunit, to define the proper body of a program unit that is declared within another compilation unit.

6   A subprogram body given in a compilation unit is interpreted as a secondary unit if the program library already contains a library unit that is a subprogram with the same name; it is otherwise interpreted both as a library unit and as the corresponding library unit body (that is, as a secondary unit).

7   The compilation units of a compilation are compiled in the given order. A pragma that applies to the whole of a compilation must appear before the first compilation unit of that compilation.

8   A subprogram that is a library unit can be used as a *main program* in the usual sense. Each main program acts as if called by some environment task; the means by which this execution is initiated are not prescribed by the language definition. An implementation may impose certain requirements on the parameters and on the result, if any, of a main program (these requirements must be stated in Appendix F). In any case, every implementation is required to allow, at least, main programs that are parameterless procedures, and every main program must be a subprogram that is a library unit.

Notes:

9   A simple program may consist of a single compilation unit. A compilation need not have any compilation units; for example, its text can consist of pragmas.

10   The designator of a library function cannot be an operator symbol, but a renaming declaration is allowed to rename a library function as an operator. Two library subprograms must have distinct simple names and hence cannot overload each other. However, renaming declarations are allowed to define overloaded names for such subprograms, and a locally declared subprogram is allowed to overload a library subprogram. The expanded name STANDARD.L can be used for a library unit L (unless the name STANDARD is hidden) since library units act as declarations that occur immediately within the package STANDARD.

11   *References:* allow 1.6, context clause 10.1.1, declaration 3.1, designator 6.1, environment 10.4, generic declaration 12.1, generic instantiation 12.3, hiding 8.3, identifier 2.3, library unit 10.5, local declaration 8.1, must 1.6, name 4.1, occur immediately within 8.1, operator 4.5, operator symbol 6.1, overloading 6.6 8.7, package body 7.1, package declaration 7.1, parameter of a subprogram 6.2, pragma 2.8, procedure 6.1, program unit 6, proper body 3.9, renaming declaration 8.5, simple name 4.1, standard package 8.6, subprogram 6, subprogram body 6.3, subprogram declaration 6.1, subunit 10.2, task 9, visibility 8.3

10.1.1 Context Clauses - With Clauses

1   A context clause is used to specify the library units whose names are needed within a compilation unit.

2   context_clause ::= {with_clause {use_clause}}

    with_clause ::= **with** *unit*_simple_name {, *unit*_simple_name};

3   The names that appear in a context clause must be the simple names of library units. The simple name of any library unit is allowed within a with clause. The only names allowed in a use clause of a context clause are the simple names of library packages mentioned by previous with clauses of the context clause. A simple name declared by a renaming declaration is not allowed in a context clause.

4   The with clauses and use clauses of the context clause of a library unit *apply* to this library unit and also to the secondary unit that defines the corresponding body (whether such a clause is repeated or not for this unit). Similarly, the with clauses and use clauses of the context clause of a compilation unit *apply* to this unit and also to its subunits, if any.

If a library unit is named by a with clause that applies to a compilation unit, then this library unit is   5
directly visible within the compilation unit, except where hidden; the library unit is visible as if
declared immediately within the package STANDARD (see 8.6).

Dependences among compilation units are defined by with clauses; that is, a compilation unit that   6
mentions other library units in its with clauses *depends* on those library units. These dependences
between units are taken into account for the determination of the allowed order of compilation
(and recompilation) of compilation units, as explained in section 10.3, and for the determination of
the allowed order of elaboration of compilation units, as explained in section 10.5.

Notes:

A library unit named by a with clause of a compilation unit is visible (except where hidden) within   7
the compilation unit and hence can be used as a corresponding program unit. Thus within the
compilation unit, the name of a library package can be given in use clauses and can be used to
form expanded names; a library subprogram can be called; and instances of a library generic unit
can be declared.

The rules given for with clauses are such that the same effect is obtained whether the name of a   8
library unit is mentioned once or more than once by the applicable with clauses, or even within a
given with clause.

Example 1 : A main program:

The following is an example of a main program consisting of a single compilation unit: a procedure   9
for printing the real roots of a quadratic equation. The predefined package TEXT_IO and a user-
defined package REAL_OPERATIONS (containing the definition of the type REAL and of the
packages REAL_IO and REAL_FUNCTIONS) are assumed to be already present in the program
library. Such packages may be used by other main programs.

```
with TEXT_IO, REAL_OPERATIONS; use REAL_OPERATIONS;          10
procedure QUADRATIC_EQUATION is
   A, B, C, D : REAL;
   use  REAL_IO,            -- achieves direct visibility of GET and PUT for REAL
        TEXT_IO,            -- achieves direct visibility of PUT for strings and of NEW_LINE
        REAL_FUNCTIONS;     -- achieves direct visibility of SQRT
begin
   GET(A); GET(B); GET(C);
   D := B**2 - 4.0*A*C;
   if  D < 0.0 then
      PUT("Imaginary Roots.");
   else
      PUT("Real Roots : X1 = ");
      PUT((-B - SQRT(D))/(2.0*A)); PUT(" X2 = ");
      PUT((-B + SQRT(D))/(2.0*A));
   end if;
   NEW_LINE;
end QUADRATIC_EQUATION;
```

Notes on the example:

The with clauses of a compilation unit need only mention the names of those library subprograms   11
and packages whose visibility is actually necessary within the unit. They need not (and should not)
mention other library units that are used in turn by some of the units named in the with clauses,
unless these other library units are also used directly by the current compilation unit. For example,
the body of the package REAL_OPERATIONS may need elementary operations provided by other
packages. The latter packages should not be named by the with clause of QUADRATIC_EQUATION
since these elementary operations are not directly called within its body.

Context Clauses - With Clauses 10.1.1

12   *References:* allow 1.6, compilation unit 10.1, direct visibility 8.3, elaboration 3.9, generic body 12.2, generic unit 12.1, hiding 8.3, instance 12.3, library unit 10.1, main program 10.1, must 1.6, name 4.1, package 7, package body 7.1, package declaration 7.1, procedure 6.1, program unit 6, secondary unit 10.1, simple name 4.1, standard predefined package 8.6, subprogram body 6.3, subprogram declaration 6.1, subunit 10.2, type 3.3, use clause 8.4, visibility 8.3

10.1.2 Examples of Compilation Units

1   A compilation unit can be split into a number of compilation units. For example, consider the following program.

2

```
procedure PROCESSOR is

    SMALL : constant := 20;
    TOTAL : INTEGER := 0;

    package STOCK is
        LIMIT : constant := 1000;
        TABLE : array (1 .. LIMIT) of INTEGER;
        procedure RESTART;
    end STOCK;

    package body STOCK is
        procedure RESTART is
        begin
            for N in 1 .. LIMIT loop
                TABLE(N) := N;
            end loop;
        end;
    begin
        RESTART;
    end STOCK;

    procedure UPDATE(X : INTEGER) is
        use STOCK;
    begin
        ...
        TABLE(X) := TABLE(X) + SMALL;
        ...
    end UPDATE;

begin
    ...
    STOCK.RESTART;    -- reinitializes TABLE
    ...
end PROCESSOR;
```

3   The following three compilation units define a program with an effect equivalent to the above example (the broken lines between compilation units serve to remind the reader that these units need not be contiguous texts).

Example 2 : Several compilation units: 4

```
package STOCK is
   LIMIT  : constant := 1000;
   TABLE : array (1 .. LIMIT) of INTEGER;
   procedure RESTART;
end STOCK;
```

```
package body STOCK is
   procedure RESTART is
   begin
      for N in 1 .. LIMIT loop
         TABLE(N) := N;
      end loop;
   end;
begin
   RESTART;
end STOCK;
```

```
with STOCK;
procedure PROCESSOR is

   SMALL  : constant  := 20;
   TOTAL  : INTEGER  := 0;

   procedure UPDATE(X : INTEGER) is
      use STOCK;
   begin
      ...
      TABLE(X) := TABLE(X) + SMALL;
      ...
   end UPDATE;
begin
   ...
   STOCK.RESTART;  --  reinitializes TABLE
   ...
end PROCESSOR;
```

Note that in the latter version, the package STOCK has no visibility of outer identifiers other than   8
the predefined identifiers (of the package STANDARD). In particular, STOCK does not use any
identifier declared in PROCESSOR such as SMALL or TOTAL; otherwise STOCK could not have
been extracted from PROCESSOR in the above manner. The procedure PROCESSOR, on the other
hand, depends on STOCK and mentions this package in a with clause. This permits the inner
occurrences of STOCK in the expanded name STOCK.RESTART and in the use clause.

These three compilation units can be submitted in one or more compilations. For example, it is   9
possible to submit the package specification and the package body together and in this order in a
single compilation.

References: compilation unit 10.1, declaration 3.1, identifier 2.3, package 7, package body 7.1, package specification   10
7.1, program 10, standard package 8.6, use clause 8.4, visibility 8.3, with clause 10.1.1

10.2 Subunits of Compilation Units

A subunit is used for the separate compilation of the proper body of a program unit declared within another compilation unit. This method of splitting a program permits hierarchical program development.

```
body_stub ::=
    subprogram_specification is separate;
  | package body package_simple_name is separate;
  | task body task_simple_name is separate;

subunit ::=
    separate (parent_unit_name) proper_body
```

A body stub is only allowed as the body of a program unit (a subprogram, a package, a task unit, or a generic unit) if the body stub occurs immediately within either the specification of a library package or the declarative part of another compilation unit.

If the body of a program unit is a body stub, a separately compiled subunit containing the corresponding proper body is required. In the case of a subprogram, the subprogram specifications given in the proper body and in the body stub must conform (see 6.3.1).

Each subunit mentions the name of its *parent unit*, that is, the compilation unit where the corresponding body stub is given. If the parent unit is a library unit, it is called the *ancestor* library unit. If the parent unit is itself a subunit, the parent unit name must be given in full as an expanded name, starting with the simple name of the ancestor library unit. The simple names of all subunits that have the same ancestor library unit must be distinct identifiers.

Visibility within the proper body of a subunit is the visibility that would be obtained at the place of the corresponding body stub (within the parent unit) if the with clauses and use clauses of the subunit were appended to the context clause of the parent unit. If the parent unit is itself a subunit, then the same rule is used to define the visibility within the proper body of the parent unit.

The effect of the elaboration of a body stub is to elaborate the proper body of the subunit.

Notes:

Two subunits of different library units in the same program library need not have distinct identifiers. In any case, their full expanded names are distinct, since the simple names of library units are distinct and since the simple names of all subunits that have a given library unit as ancestor unit are also distinct. By means of renaming declarations, overloaded subprogram names that rename (distinct) subunits can be introduced.

A library unit that is named by the with clause of a subunit can be hidden by a declaration (with the same identifier) given in the proper body of the subunit. Moreover, such a library unit can even be hidden by a declaration given within a parent unit since a library unit acts as if declared in STANDARD; this however does not affect the interpretation of the with clauses themselves, since only names of library units can appear in with clauses.

References: compilation unit 10.1, conform 6.3.1, context clause 10.1.1, declaration 3.1, declarative part 3.9, direct visibility 8.3, elaboration 3.9, expanded name 4.1.3, generic body 12.2, generic unit 12, hidden declaration 8.3, identifier 2.3, library unit 10.1, local declaration 8.1, name 4.1, occur immediately within 8.1, overloading 8.3, package 7, package body 7.1, package specification 7.1, program 10, program unit 6, proper body 3.9, renaming declaration 8.5, separate compilation 10.1, simple name 4.1, subprogram 6, subprogram body 6.3, subprogram specification 6.1, task 9, task body 9.1, task unit 9.1, use clause 8.4, visibility 8.3, with clause 10.1.1

10.2.1 Examples of Subunits

The procedure TOP is first written as a compilation unit without subunits.

```
with TEXT_IO;
procedure TOP is

   type REAL is digits 10;
   R, S : REAL := 1.0;

   package FACILITY is
      PI : constant := 3.14159_26536;
      function    F (X : REAL) return REAL;
      procedure   G (Y, Z : REAL);
   end FACILITY;

   package body FACILITY is
      --   some local declarations followed by

      function F(X : REAL) return REAL is
      begin
         --   sequence of statements of F
         ...
      end F;

      procedure G(Y, Z : REAL) is
         --   local procedures using TEXT_IO
         ...
      begin
         --   sequence of statements of G
         ...
      end G;
   end FACILITY;

   procedure TRANSFORM(U : in out REAL) is
      use FACILITY;
   begin
      U := F(U);
      ...
   end TRANSFORM;
begin -- TOP
   TRANSFORM(R);
   ...
   FACILITY.G(R, S);
end TOP;
```

3   The body of the package FACILITY and that of the procedure TRANSFORM can be made into separate subunits of TOP. Similarly, the body of the procedure G can be made into a subunit of FACILITY as follows.

4   *Example 3:*

5

```
procedure TOP is

    type REAL is digits 10;
    R, S : REAL := 1.0;

    package FACILITY is
        PI : constant := 3.14159_26536;
        function    F (X : REAL) return REAL;
        procedure   G (Y, Z : REAL);
    end FACILITY;

    package body FACILITY is separate;                    --  stub of FACILITY
    procedure TRANSFORM(U : in out REAL) is separate;     --  stub of TRANSFORM

begin  --  TOP
    TRANSFORM(R);
    ...
    FACILITY.G(R, S);
end TOP;
```

6

```
separate (TOP)
procedure TRANSFORM(U : in out REAL) is
    use FACILITY;
begin
    U := F(U);
    ...
end TRANSFORM;
```

7

```
separate (TOP)
package body FACILITY is
    --  some local declarations followed by

    function F(X : REAL) return REAL is
    begin
        --  sequence of statements of F
        ...
    end F;

    procedure G(Y, Z : REAL) is separate;                --  stub of G
end FACILITY;
```

```
with TEXT_IO;                                                                              8
separate (TOP.FACILITY)                          --  full name of FACILITY
procedure G(Y, Z : REAL) is
    --  local procedures using TEXT_IO
    ...
begin
    --  sequence of statements of G
    ...
end G;
```

In the above example TRANSFORM and FACILITY are subunits of TOP, and G is a subunit of   9
FACILITY. The visibility in the split version is the same as in the initial version except for one
change: since TEXT_IO is only used within G, the corresponding with clause is written for G
instead of for TOP. Apart from this change, the same identifiers are visible at corresponding
program points in the two versions. For example, all of the following are (directly) visible within
the proper body of the subunit G: the procedure TOP, the type REAL, the variables R and S, the
package FACILITY and the contained named number PI and subprograms F and G.

References: body stub 10.2, compilation unit 10.1, identifier 2.3, local declaration 8.1, named number 3.2, package   10
7, package body 7.1, procedure 6, procedure body 6.3, proper body 3.9, subprogram 6, type 3.3, variable 3.2.1,
visibility 8.3, with clause 10.1.1

10.3 Order of Compilation

The rules defining the order in which units can be compiled are direct consequences of the visibility   1
rules and, in particular, of the fact that any library unit that is mentioned by the context clause of a
compilation unit is visible in the compilation unit.

A compilation unit must be compiled after all library units named by its context clause. A secon-   2
dary unit that is a subprogram or package body must be compiled after the corresponding library
unit. Any subunit of a parent compilation unit must be compiled after the parent compilation unit.

If any error is detected while attempting to compile a compilation unit, then the attempted com-   3
pilation is rejected and it has no effect whatsoever on the program library; the same holds for
recompilations (no compilation unit can become obsolete because of such a recompilation).

The order in which the compilation units of a program are compiled must be consistent with the   4
partial ordering defined by the above rules.

Similar rules apply for recompilations. A compilation unit is potentially affected by a change in any   5
library unit named by its context clause. A secondary unit is potentially affected by a change in the
corresponding library unit. The subunits of a parent compilation unit are potentially affected by a
change of the parent compilation unit. If a compilation unit is successfully recompiled, the compilation units potentially affected by this change are obsolete and must be recompiled unless they
are no longer needed. An implementation may be able to reduce the compilation costs if it can
deduce that some of the potentially affected units are not actually affected by the change.

6 The subunits of a unit can be recompiled without affecting the unit itself. Similarly, changes in a subprogram or package body do not affect other compilation units (apart from the subunits of the body) since these compilation units only have access to the subprogram or package specification. An implementation is only allowed to deviate from this rule for inline inclusions, for certain compiler optimizations, and for certain implementations of generic program units, as described below.

7 • If a pragma INLINE is applied to a subprogram declaration given in a package specification, inline inclusion will only be achieved if the package body is compiled before units calling the subprogram. In such a case, inline inclusion creates a *dependence* of the calling unit on the package body, and the compiler must recognize this dependence when deciding on the need for recompilation. If a calling unit is compiled before the package body, the pragma may be ignored by the compiler for such calls (a warning that inline inclusion was not achieved may be issued). Similar considerations apply to a separately compiled subprogram for which an INLINE pragma is specified.

8 • For optimization purposes, an implementation may compile several units of a given compilation in a way that creates further dependences among these compilation units. The compiler must then take these dependences into account when deciding on the need for recompilations.

9 • An implementation may require that a generic declaration and the corresponding proper body be part of the same compilation, whether the generic unit is itself separately compiled or is local to another compilation unit. An implementation may also require that subunits of a generic unit be part of the same compilation.

10 *Examples of Compilation Order:*

11 (a) In example 1 (see 10.1.1): The procedure QUADRATIC_EQUATION must be compiled after the library packages TEXT_IO and REAL_OPERATIONS since they appear in its with clause.

12 (b) In example 2 (see 10.1.2): The package body STOCK must be compiled after the corresponding package specification.

13 (c) In example 2 (see 10.1.2): The specification of the package STOCK must be compiled before the procedure PROCESSOR. On the other hand, the procedure PROCESSOR can be compiled either before or after the package body STOCK.

14 (d) In example 3 (see 10.2.1): The procedure G must be compiled after the package TEXT_IO since this package is named by the with clause of G. On the other hand, TEXT_IO can be compiled either before or after TOP.

15 (e) In example 3 (see 10.2.1): The subunits TRANSFORM and FACILITY must be compiled after the main program TOP. Similarly, the subunit G must be compiled after its parent unit FACILITY.

Notes:

16 For library packages, it follows from the recompilation rules that a package body is made obsolete by the recompilation of the corresponding specification. If the new package specification is such that a package body is not required (that is, if the package specification does not contain the declaration of a program unit), then the recompilation of a body for this package is not required. In any case, the obsolete package body must not be used and can therefore be deleted from the program library.

References: compilation 10.1, compilation unit 10.1, context clause 10.1.1, elaboration 3.9, generic body 12.2,   17
generic declaration 12.1, generic unit 12, library unit 10.1, local declaration 8.1, name 4.1, package 7, package body
7.1, package specification 7.1, parent unit 10.2, pragma inline 6.3.2, procedure 6.1, procedure body 6.3, proper body
3.9, secondary unit 10.1, subprogram body 6.3, subprogram declaration 6.1, subprogram specification 6.1, subunit
10.2, type 3.3, variable 3.2.1, visibility 8.3, with clause 10.1.1

10.4 The Program Library

Compilers are required to enforce the language rules in the same manner for a program consisting   1
of several compilation units (and subunits) as for a program submitted as a single compilation.
Consequently, a library file containing information on the compilation units of the program library
must be maintained by the compiler or compiling environment. This information may include symbol tables and other information pertaining to the order of previous compilations.

A normal submission to the compiler consists of the compilation unit(s) and the library file. The   2
latter is used for checks and is updated for each compilation unit successfully compiled.

Notes:

A single program library is implied for the compilation units of a compilation. The possible   3
existence of different program libraries and the means by which they are named are not concerns
of the language definition; they are concerns of the programming environment.

There should be commands for creating the program library of a given program or of a given family   4
of programs. These commands may permit the reuse of units of other program libraries. Finally,
there should be commands for interrogating the status of the units of a program library. The form
of these commands is not specified by the language definition.

References: compilation unit 10.1, context clause 10.1.1, order of compilation 10.3, program 10.1, program library   5
10.1, subunit 10.2, use clause 8.4, with clause 10.1.1

10.5 Elaboration of Library Units

Before the execution of a main program, all library units needed by the main program are   1
elaborated, as well as the corresponding library unit bodies, if any. The library units needed by the
main program are: those named by with clauses applicable to the main program, to its body, and
to its subunits; those named by with clauses applicable to these library units themselves, to the
corresponding library unit bodies, and to their subunits; and so on, in a transitive manner.

The elaboration of these library units and of the corresponding library unit bodies is performed in   2
an order consistent with the partial ordering defined by the with clauses (see 10.3). In addition, a
library unit mentioned by the context clause of a subunit must be elaborated before the body of the
ancestor library unit of the subunit.

An order of elaboration that is consistent with this partial ordering does not always ensure that   3
each library unit body is elaborated before any other compilation unit whose elaboration neces-
sitates that the library unit body be already elaborated. If the prior elaboration of library unit
bodies is needed, this can be requested by a pragma ELABORATE. The form of this pragma is as
follows:

    pragma ELABORATE (*library_unit*_simple_name {, *library_unit*_simple_name});

                                                              Elaboration of Library Units 10.5

4 These pragmas are only allowed immediately after the context clause of a compilation unit (before the subsequent library unit or secondary unit). Each argument of such a pragma must be the simple name of a library unit mentioned by the context clause, and this library unit must have a library unit body. Such a pragma specifies that the library unit body must be elaborated before the given compilation unit. If the given compilation unit is a subunit, the library unit body must be elaborated before the body of the ancestor library unit of the subunit.

5 The program is illegal if no consistent order can be found (that is, if a circularity exists). The elaboration of the compilation units of the program is performed in some order that is otherwise not defined by the language.

6 *References:* allow 1.6, argument of a pragma 2.8, compilation unit 10.1, context clause 10.1.1, dependence between compilation units 10.3, elaboration 3.9, illegal 1.6, in some order 1.6, library unit 10.1, name 4.1, main program 10.1, pragma 2.8, secondary unit 10.1, separate compilation 10.1, simple name 4.1, subunit 10.2, with clause 10.1.1

10.6 Program Optimization

1 Optimization of the elaboration of declarations and the execution of statements may be performed by compilers. In particular, a compiler may be able to optimize a program by evaluating certain expressions, in addition to those that are static expressions. Should one of these expressions, whether static or not, be such that an exception would be raised by its evaluation, then the code in that path of the program can be replaced by code to raise the exception; the same holds for exceptions raised by the evaluation of names and simple expressions. (See also section 11.6.)

2 A compiler may find that some statements or subprograms will never be executed, for example, if their execution depends on a condition known to be FALSE. The corresponding object machine code can then be omitted. This rule permits the effect of *conditional compilation* within the language.

Note:

3 An expression whose evaluation is known to raise an exception need not represent an error if it occurs in a statement or subprogram that is never executed. The compiler may warn the programmer of a potential error.

4 *References:* condition 5.3, declaration 3.1, elaboration 3.9, evaluation 4.5, exception 11, expression 4.4, false boolean value 3.5.3, program 10, raising of exceptions 11.3, statement 5, static expression 4.9, subprogram 6

11. Exceptions

This chapter defines the facilities for dealing with errors or other exceptional situations that arise during program execution. Such a situation is called an *exception*. To *raise* an exception is to abandon normal program execution so as to draw attention to the fact that the corresponding situation has arisen. Executing some actions, in response to the arising of an exception, is called *handling* the exception.

An exception declaration declares a name for an exception. An exception can be raised by a raise statement, or it can be raised by another statement or operation that *propagates* the exception. When an exception arises, control can be transferred to a user-provided exception handler at the end of a block statement or at the end of the body of a subprogram, package, or task unit.

References: block statement 5.6, error situation 1.6, exception handler 11.2, name 4.1, package body 7.1, propagation of an exception 11.4.1 11.4.2, raise statement 11.3, subprogram body 6.3, task body 9.1

11.1 Exception Declarations

An exception declaration declares a name for an exception. The name of an exception can only be used in raise statements, exception handlers, and renaming declarations.

    exception_declaration ::= identifier_list : **exception**;

An exception declaration with several identifiers is equivalent to a sequence of single exception declarations, as explained in section 3.2. Each single exception declaration declares a name for a different exception. In particular, if a generic unit includes an exception declaration, the exception declarations implicitly generated by different instantiations of the generic unit refer to distinct exceptions (but all have the same identifier). The particular exception denoted by an exception name is determined at compilation time and is the same regardless of how many times the exception declaration is elaborated. Hence, if an exception declaration occurs in a recursive subprogram, the exception name denotes the same exception for all invocations of the recursive subprogram.

The following exceptions are predefined in the language; they are raised when the situations described are detected.

CONSTRAINT_ERROR   This exception is raised in any of the following situations: upon an attempt to violate a range constraint, an index constraint, or a discriminant constraint; upon an attempt to use a record component that does not exist for the current discriminant values; and upon an attempt to use a selected component, an indexed component, a slice, or an attribute, of an object designated by an access value, if the object does not exist because the access value is null.

6   NUMERIC_ERROR   This exception is raised by the execution of a predefined numeric operation that cannot deliver a correct result (within the declared accuracy for real types); this includes the case where an implementation uses a predefined numeric operation for the execution, evaluation, or elaboration of some construct. The rules given in section 4.5.7 define the cases in which an implementation is not required to raise this exception when such an error situation arises; see also section 11.6.

7   PROGRAM_ERROR   This exception is raised upon an attempt to call a subprogram, to activate a task, or to elaborate a generic instantiation, if the body of the corresponding unit has not yet been elaborated. This exception is also raised if the end of a function is reached (see 6.5); or during the execution of a selective wait that has no else part, if this execution determines that all alternatives are closed (see 9.7.1). Finally, depending on the implementation, this exception may be raised upon an attempt to execute an action that is erroneous, and for incorrect order dependences (see 1.6).

8   STORAGE_ERROR   This exception is raised in any of the following situations: when the dynamic storage allocated to a task is exceeded; during the evaluation of an allocator, if the space available for the collection of allocated objects is exhausted; or during the elaboration of a declarative item, or during the execution of a subprogram call, if storage is not sufficient.

9   TASKING_ERROR   This exception is raised when exceptions arise during intertask communication (see 9 and 11.5).

Note:

10   The situations described above can arise without raising the corresponding exceptions, if the pragma SUPPRESS has been used to give permission to omit the corresponding checks (see 11.7).

11   *Examples of user-defined exception declarations:*

        SINGULAR   : **exception**;
        ERROR   : **exception**;
        OVERFLOW, UNDERFLOW : **exception**;

12   *References:* access value 3.8, collection 3.8, declaration 3.1, exception 11, exception handler 11.2, generic body 12.2, generic instantiation 12.3, generic unit 12, identifier 2.3, implicit declaration 12.3, instantiation 12.3, name 4.1, object 3.2, raise statement 11.3, real type 3.5.6, record component 3.7, return statement 5.8, subprogram 6, subprogram body 6.3, task 9, task body 9.1

13   *Constraint_error exception contexts:* aggregate 4.3.1 4.3.2, allocator 4.8, assignment statement 5.2 5.2.1, constraint 3.3.2, discrete type attribute 3.5.5, discriminant constraint 3.7.2, elaboration of a generic formal parameter 12.3.1 12.3.2 12.3.4 12.3.5, entry index 9.5, exponentiating operator 4.5.6, index constraint 3.6.1, indexed component 4.1.1, logical operator 4.5.1, null access value 3.8, object declaration 3.2.1, parameter association 6.4.1, qualified expression 4.7, range constraint 3.5, selected component 4.1.3, slice 4.1.2, subtype indication 3.3.2, type conversion 4.6

14   *Numeric_error exception contexts:* discrete type attribute 3.5.5, implicit conversion 3.5.4 3.5.6 4.6, numeric operation 3.5.5 3.5.8 3.5.10, operator of a numeric type 4.5 4.5.7

15   *Program_error exception contexts:* collection 3.8, elaboration 3.9, elaboration check 3.9 7.3 9.3 12.2, erroneous 1.6, incorrect order dependence 1.6, leaving a function 6.5, selective wait 9.7.1

Storage_error exception contexts: allocator 4.8   16

Tasking error exception contexts: abort statement 9.10, entry call 9.5 9.7.2 9.7.3, exceptions during task   17
communication 11.5, task activation 9.3

11.2 Exception Handlers

The response to one or more exceptions is specified by an exception handler.   1

```
exception_handler ::=
    when exception_choice {| exception_choice} =>
        sequence_of_statements

exception_choice ::= exception_name | others
```

An exception handler occurs in a construct that is either a block statement or the body of a sub-   3
program, package, task unit, or generic unit. Such a construct will be called a *frame* in this
chapter. In each case the syntax of a frame that has exception handlers includes the following
part:

```
begin
    sequence_of_statements
exception
    exception_handler
    {exception_handler}
end
```

The exceptions denoted by the exception names given as exception choices of a frame must all be   5
distinct. The exception choice **others** is only allowed for the last exception handler of a frame and
as its only exception choice; it stands for all exceptions not listed in previous handlers of the frame,
including exceptions whose names are not visible at the place of the exception handler.

The exception handlers of a frame handle exceptions that are raised by the execution of the   6
sequence of statements of the frame. The exceptions handled by a given exception handler are
those named by the corresponding exception choices.

Example: 7

```
begin
    --    sequence of statements
exception
    when SINGULAR | NUMERIC_ERROR =>
        PUT(" MATRIX IS SINGULAR ");
    when others =>
        PUT(" FATAL ERROR ");
        raise ERROR;
end;
```

Note:

The same kinds of statement are allowed in the sequence of statements of each exception handler   8
as are allowed in the sequence of statements of the frame.   For example, a return statement is
allowed in a handler within a function body.

9   *References:* block statement 5.6, declarative part 3.9, exception 11, exception handling 11.4, function body 6.3, generic body 12.2, generic unit 12.1, name 4.1, package body 7.1, raise statement 11.3, return statement 5.8, sequence of statements 5.1, statement 5, subprogram body 6.3, task body 9.1, task unit 9 9.1, visibility 8.3

11.3 Raise Statements

1   A raise statement raises an exception.

2   raise_statement ::= **raise** [*exception*_name];

3   For the execution of a raise statement with an exception name, the named exception is raised. A raise statement without an exception name is only allowed within an exception handler (but not within the sequence of statements of a subprogram, package, task unit, or generic unit, enclosed by the handler); it raises again the exception that caused transfer to the innermost enclosing handler.

4   *Examples:*

     raise SINGULAR;
     raise NUMERIC_ERROR;   --   explicitly raising a predefined exception

     raise;   --   only within an exception handler

5   *References:* exception 11, generic unit 12, name 4.1, package 7, sequence of statements 5.1, subprogram 6, task unit 9

11.4 Exception Handling

1   When an exception is raised, normal program execution is abandoned and control is transferred to an exception handler. The selection of this handler depends on whether the exception is raised during the execution of statements or during the elaboration of declarations.

2   *References:* declaration 3.1, elaboration 3.1 3.9, exception 11, exception handler 11.2, raising of exceptions 11.3, statement 5

11.4.1 Exceptions Raised During the Execution of Statements

1   The handling of an exception raised by the execution of a sequence of statements depends on whether the innermost frame or accept statement that encloses the sequence of statements is a frame or an accept statement. The case where an accept statement is innermost is described in section 11.5. The case where a frame is innermost is presented here.

Different actions take place, depending on whether or not this frame has a handler for the exception, and on whether the exception is raised in the sequence of statements of the frame or in that of an exception handler. 2

If an exception is raised in the sequence of statements of a frame that has a handler for the exception, execution of the sequence of statements of the frame is abandoned and control is transferred to the exception handler. The execution of the sequence of statements of the handler completes the execution of the frame (or its elaboration if the frame is a package body). 3

If an exception is raised in the sequence of statements of a frame that does not have a handler for the exception, execution of this sequence of statements is abandoned. The next action depends on the nature of the frame: 4

(a) For a subprogram body, the same exception is raised again at the point of call of the subprogram, unless the subprogram is the main program itself, in which case execution of the main program is abandoned. 5

(b) For a block statement, the same exception is raised again immediately after the block statement (that is, within the innermost enclosing frame or accept statement). 6

(c) For a package body that is a declarative item, the same exception is raised again immediately after this declarative item (within the enclosing declarative part). If the package body is that of a subunit, the exception is raised again at the place of the corresponding body stub. If the package is a library unit, execution of the main program is abandoned. 7

(d) For a task body, the task becomes completed. 8

An exception that is raised again (as in the above cases (a), (b), and (c)) is said to be *propagated*, either by the execution of the subprogram, the execution of the block statement, or the elaboration of the package body. No propagation takes place in the case of a task body. If the frame is a subprogram or a block statement and if it has dependent tasks, the propagation of an exception takes place only after termination of the dependent tasks. 9

Finally, if an exception is raised in the sequence of statements of an exception handler, execution of this sequence of statements is abandoned. Subsequent actions (including propagation, if any) are as in the cases (a) to (d) above, depending on the nature of the frame. 10

Example: 11

```
function FACTORIAL (N : POSITIVE) return FLOAT is
begin
   if N = 1 then
      return 1.0;
   else
      return FLOAT(N) * FACTORIAL(N-1);
   end if;
exception
   when NUMERIC_ERROR => return FLOAT'SAFE_LARGE;
end FACTORIAL;
```

If the multiplication raises NUMERIC_ERROR, then FLOAT'SAFE_LARGE is returned by the handler. This value will cause further NUMERIC_ERROR exceptions to be raised by the evaluation of the expression in each of the remaining invocations of the function, so that for large values of N the function will ultimately return the value FLOAT'SAFE_LARGE. 12

13 *Example:*

```
procedure P is
   ERROR : exception;
   procedure R;

   procedure Q is
   begin
      R;
      ...                     --  error situation (2)
   exception
      ...
      when ERROR =>   --  handler E2
      ...
   end Q;

   procedure R is
   begin
      ...                     --  error situation (3)
   end R;

begin
   ...                        --  error situation (1)
   Q;
   ...
exception
   ...
   when ERROR =>   --  handler E1
   ...
end P;
```

14 The following situations can arise:

15 (1) If the exception ERROR is raised in the sequence of statements of the outer procedure P, the handler E1 provided within P is used to complete the execution of P.

16 (2) If the exception ERROR is raised in the sequence of statements of Q, the handler E2 provided within Q is used to complete the execution of Q. Control will be returned to the point of call of Q upon completion of the handler.

17 (3) If the exception ERROR is raised in the body of R, called by Q, the execution of R is abandoned and the same exception is raised in the body of Q. The handler E2 is then used to complete the execution of Q, as in situation (2).

18 Note that in the third situation, the exception raised in R results in (indirectly) transferring control to a handler that is part of Q and hence not enclosed by R. Note also that if a handler were provided within R for the exception choice **others**, situation (3) would cause execution of this handler, rather than direct termination of R.

19 Lastly, if ERROR had been declared in R, rather than in P, the handlers E1 and E2 could not provide an explicit handler for ERROR since this identifier would not be visible within the bodies of P and Q. In situation (3), the exception could however be handled in Q by providing a handler for the exception choice **others**.

Notes:

The language does not define what happens when the execution of the main program is abandoned after an unhandled exception.   20

The predefined exceptions are those that can be propagated by the basic operations and the predefined operators.   21

The case of a frame that is a generic unit is already covered by the rules for subprogram and package bodies, since the sequence of statements of such a frame is not executed but is the template for the corresponding sequences of statements of the subprograms or packages obtained by generic instantiation.   22

References: accept statement 9.5, basic operation 3.3.3, block statement 5.6, body stub 10.2, completion 9.4, declarative item 3.9, declarative part 3.9, dependent task 9.4, elaboration 3.1 3.9, exception 11, exception handler 11.2, frame 11.2, generic instantiation 12.3, generic unit 12, library unit 10.1, main program 10.1, numeric_error exception 11.1, package 7, package body 7.1, predefined operator 4.5, procedure 6.1, sequence of statements 5.1, statement 5, subprogram 6, subprogram body 6.3, subprogram call 6.4, subunit 10.2, task 9, task body 9.1   23

11.4.2 Exceptions Raised During the Elaboration of Declarations

If an exception is raised during the elaboration of the declarative part of a given frame, this elaboration is abandoned. The next action depends on the nature of the frame: 1

(a) For a subprogram body, the same exception is raised again at the point of call of the subprogram, unless the subprogram is the main program itself, in which case execution of the main program is abandoned.   2

(b) For a block statement, the same exception is raised again immediately after the block statement.   3

(c) For a package body that is a declarative item, the same exception is raised again immediately after this declarative item, in the enclosing declarative part. If the package body is that of a subunit, the exception is raised again at the place of the corresponding body stub. If the package is a library unit, execution of the main program is abandoned.   4

(d) For a task body, the task becomes completed, and the exception TASKING_ERROR is raised at the point of activation of the task, as explained in section 9.3.   5

Similarly, if an exception is raised during the elaboration of either a package declaration or a task declaration, this elaboration is abandoned; the next action depends on the nature of the declaration.   6

(e) For a package declaration or a task declaration, that is a declarative item, the exception is raised again immediately after the declarative item in the enclosing declarative part or package specification. For the declaration of a library package, the execution of the main program is abandoned.   7

An exception that is raised again (as in the above cases (a), (b), (c) and (e)) is said to be *propagated*, either by the execution of the subprogram or block statement, or by the elaboration of the package declaration, task declaration, or package body.   8

9   *Example of an exception in the declarative part of a block statement (case (b)):*

```
procedure P is
   ...
begin
   declare
      N : INTEGER := F;   --  the function F may raise ERROR
   begin
      ...
   exception
      when ERROR =>       --  handler E1
   end;
   ...
exception
   when ERROR =>          --  handler E2
end P;

   --  if the exception ERROR is raised in the declaration of N, it is handled by E2
```

10 *References:* activation 9.3, block statement 5.6, body stub 10.2, completed task 9.4, declarative item 3.9, declarative part 3.9, elaboration 3.1 3.9, exception 11, frame 11.2, library unit 10.1, main program 10.1, package body 7.1, package declaration 7.1, package specification 7.1, subprogram 6, subprogram body 6.3, subprogram call 6.4, subunit 10.2, task 9, task body 9.1, task declaration 9.1, tasking_error exception 11.1

11.5 Exceptions Raised During Task Communication

1   An exception can be propagated to a task communicating, or attempting to communicate, with another task. An exception can also be propagated to a calling task if the exception is raised during a rendezvous.

2   When a task calls an entry of another task, the exception TASKING_ERROR is raised in the calling task, at the place of the call, if the called task is completed before accepting the entry call or is already completed at the time of the call.

3   A rendezvous can be completed abnormally in two cases:

4   (a) When an exception is raised within an accept statement, but not handled within an inner frame. In this case, the execution of the accept statement is abandoned and the same exception is raised again immediately after the accept statement within the called task; the exception is also propagated to the calling task at the point of the entry call.

5   (b) When the task containing the accept statement is completed abnormally as the result of an abort statement. In this case, the exception TASKING_ERROR is raised in the calling task at the point of the entry call.

6   On the other hand, if a task issuing an entry call becomes abnormal (as the result of an abort statement) no exception is raised in the called task. If the rendezvous has not yet started, the entry call is cancelled. If the rendezvous is in progress, it completes normally, and the called task is unaffected.

References: abnormal task 9.10, abort statement 9.10, accept statement 9.5, completed task 9.4, entry call 9.5,   7
exception 11, frame 11.2, rendezvous 9.5, task 9, task termination 9.4, tasking_error exception 11.1

11.6 Exceptions and Optimization

The purpose of this section is to specify the conditions under which an implementation is allowed   1
to perform certain actions either earlier or later than specified by other rules of the language.

In general, when the language rules specify an order for certain actions (the *canonical order*), an   2
implementation may only use an alternative order if it can guarantee that the effect of the program
is not changed by the reordering. In particular, no exception should arise for the execution of the
reordered program if none arises for the execution of the program in the canonical order. When,
on the other hand, the order of certain actions is not defined by the language, any order can be
used by the implementation. (For example, the arguments of a predefined operator can be evaluated in any order since the rules given in section 4.5 do not require a specific order of evaluation.)

Additional freedom is left to an implementation for reordering actions involving predefined opera-   3
tions that are either predefined operators or basic operations other than assignments. This
freedom is left, as defined below, even in the case where the execution of these predefined operations may propagate a (predefined) exception:

(a) For the purpose of establishing whether the same effect is obtained by the execution of cer-   4
tain actions in the canonical and in an alternative order, it can be assumed that none of the
predefined operations invoked by these actions propagates a (predefined) exception, provided
that the two following requirements are met by the alternative order: first, an operation must
not be invoked in the alternative order if it is not invoked in the canonical order; second, for
each operation, the innermost enclosing frame or accept statement must be the same in the
alternative order as in the canonical order, and the same exception handlers must apply.

(b) Within an expression, the association of operators with operands is specified by the syntax.   5
However, for a sequence of predefined operators of the same precedence level (and in the
absence of parentheses imposing a specific association), any association of operators with
operands is allowed if it satisfies the following requirement: an integer result must be equal to
that given by the canonical left-to-right order; a real result must belong to the result model
interval defined for the canonical left-to-right order (see 4.5.7). Such a reordering is allowed
even if it may remove an exception, or introduce a further predefined exception.

Similarly, additional freedom is left to an implementation for the evaluation of numeric simple   6
expressions. For the evaluation of a predefined operation, an implementation is allowed to use the
operation of a type that has a range wider than that of the base type of the operands, provided that
this delivers the exact result (or a result within the declared accuracy, in the case of a real type),
even if some intermediate results lie outside the range of the base type. The exception
NUMERIC_ERROR need not be raised in such a case. In particular, if the numeric expression is an
operand of a predefined relational operator, the exception NUMERIC_ERROR need not be raised by
the evaluation of the relation, provided that the correct BOOLEAN result is obtained.

A predefined operation need not be invoked at all, if its only possible effect is to propagate a prede-   7
fined exception. Similarly, a predefined operation need not be invoked if the removal of subsequent
operations by the above rule renders this invocation ineffective.

Notes:

8   Rule (b) applies to predefined operators but not to the short-circuit control forms.

9   The expression SPEED < 300_000.0 can be replaced by TRUE if the value 300_000.0 lies outside the base type of SPEED, even though the implicit conversion of the numeric literal would raise the exception NUMERIC_ERROR.

10   *Example:*

```
declare
   N : INTEGER;
begin
   N := 0;                    -- (1)
   for J in 1 .. 10 loop
      N := N + J**A(K);       -- A and K are global variables
   end loop;
   PUT(N);
exception
   when others => PUT("Some error arose"); PUT(N);
end;
```

11   The evaluation of A(K) may be performed before the loop, and possibly immediately before the assignment statement (1) even if this evaluation can raise an exception. Consequently, within the exception handler, the value of N is either the undefined initial value or a value later assigned. On the other hand, the evaluation of A(K) cannot be moved before **begin** since an exception would then be handled by a different handler. For this reason, the initialization of N in the declaration itself would exclude the possibility of having an undefined initial value of N in the handler.

12   *References:* accept statement 9.5, accuracy of real operations 4.5.7, assignment 5.2, base type 3.3, basic operation 3.3.3, conversion 4.6, error situation 11, exception 11, exception handler 11.2, frame 11.2, numeric_error exception 11.1, predefined operator 4.5, predefined subprogram 8.6, propagation of an exception 11.4, real type 3.5.6, undefined value 3.2.1

11.7 Suppressing Checks

1   The presence of a SUPPRESS pragma gives permission to an implementation to omit certain run-time checks. The form of this pragma is as follows:

    pragma SUPPRESS (identifier [, [ON =>] name]);

2   The identifier is that of the check that can be omitted. The name (if present) must be either a simple name or an expanded name and it must denote either an object, a type or subtype, a task unit, or a generic unit; alternatively the name can be a subprogram name, in which case it can stand for several visible overloaded subprograms.

A pragma SUPPRESS is only allowed immediately within a declarative part or immediately within a package specification. In the latter case, the only allowed form is with a name that denotes an entity (or several overloaded subprograms) declared immediately within the package specification. The permission to omit the given check extends from the place of the pragma to the end of the declarative region associated with the innermost enclosing block statement or program unit. For a pragma given in a package specification, the permission extends to the end of the scope of the named entity.

If the pragma includes a name, the permission to omit the given check is further restricted: it is given only for operations on the named object or on all objects of the base type of a named type or subtype; for calls of a named subprogram; for activations of tasks of the named task type; or for instantiations of the given generic unit.

The following checks correspond to situations in which the exception CONSTRAINT_ERROR may be raised; for these checks, the name (if present) must denote either an object or a type.

ACCESS_CHECK   When accessing a selected component, an indexed component, a slice, or an attribute, of an object designated by an access value, check that the access value is not null.

DISCRIMINANT_CHECK   Check that a discriminant of a composite value has the value imposed by a discriminant constraint. Also, when accessing a record component, check that it exists for the current discriminant values.

INDEX_CHECK   Check that the bounds of an array value are equal to the corresponding bounds of an index constraint. Also, when accessing a component of an array object, check for each dimension that the given index value belongs to the range defined by the bounds of the array object. Also, when accessing a slice of an array object, check that the given discrete range is compatible with the range defined by the bounds of the array object.

LENGTH_CHECK   Check that there is a matching component for each component of an array, in the case of array assignments, type conversions, and logical operators for arrays of boolean components.

RANGE_CHECK   Check that a value satisfies a range constraint. Also, for the elaboration of a subtype indication, check that the constraint (if present) is compatible with the type mark. Also, for an aggregate, check that an index or discriminant value belongs to the corresponding subtype. Finally, check for any constraint checks performed by a generic instantiation.

The following checks correspond to situations in which the exception NUMERIC_ERROR is raised. The only allowed names in the corresponding pragmas are names of numeric types.

DIVISION_CHECK   Check that the second operand is not zero for the operations /, **rem** and **mod**.

OVERFLOW_CHECK   Check that the result of a numeric operation does not overflow.

The following check corresponds to situations in which the exception PROGRAM_ERROR is raised. The only allowed names in the corresponding pragmas are names denoting task units, generic units, or subprograms.

ELABORATION_CHECK   When either a subprogram is called, a task activation is accomplished, or a generic instantiation is elaborated, check that the body of the corresponding unit has already been elaborated.

16   The following check corresponds to situations in which the exception STORAGE_ERROR is raised. The only allowed names in the corresponding pragmas are names denoting access types, task units, or subprograms.

17   STORAGE_CHECK   Check that execution of an allocator does not require more space than is available for a collection. Check that the space available for a task or subprogram has not been exceeded.

18   If an error situation arises in the absence of the corresponding run-time checks, the execution of the program is erroneous (the results are not defined by the language).

19   *Examples:*

```
pragma SUPPRESS(RANGE_CHECK);
pragma SUPPRESS(INDEX_CHECK, ON => TABLE);
```

Notes:

20   For certain implementations, it may be impossible or too costly to suppress certain checks. The corresponding SUPPRESS pragma can be ignored. Hence, the occurrence of such a pragma within a given unit does not guarantee that the corresponding exception will not arise; the exceptions may also be propagated by called units.

21   *References:* access type 3.8, access value 3.8, activation 9.3, aggregate 4.3, allocator 4.8, array 3.6, attribute 4.1.4, block statement 5.6, collection 3.8, compatible 3.3.2, component of an array 3.6, component of a record 3.7, composite type 3.3, constraint 3.3, constraint_error exception 11.1, declarative part 3.9, designate 3.8, dimension 3.6, discrete range 3.6, discriminant 3.7.1, discriminant constraint 3.7.2, elaboration 3.1 3.9, erroneous 1.6, error situation 11, expanded name 4.1.3, generic body 11.1, generic instantiation 12.3, generic unit 12, identifier 2.3, index 3.6, index constraint 3.6.1, indexed component 4.1.1, null access value 3.8, numeric operation 3.5.5 3.5.8 3.5.10, numeric type 3.5, numeric_error exception 11.1, object 3.2, operation 3.3.3, package body 7.1, package specification 7.1, pragma 2.8, program_error exception 11.1, program unit 6, propagation of an exception 11.4, range constraint 3.5, record type 3.7, simple name 4.1, slice 4.1.2, subprogram 6, subprogram body 6.3, subprogram call 6.4, subtype 3.3, subunit 10.2, task 9, task body 9.1, task type 9.1, task unit 9, type 3.3, type mark 3.3.2

12. Generic Units

A generic unit is a program unit that is either a generic subprogram or a generic package. A generic unit is a *template*, which is parameterized or not, and from which corresponding (nongeneric) subprograms or packages can be obtained. The resulting program units are said to be *instances* of the original generic unit.

A generic unit is declared by a generic declaration. This form of declaration has a generic formal part declaring any generic formal parameters. An instance of a generic unit is obtained as the result of a generic instantiation with appropriate generic actual parameters for the generic formal parameters. An instance of a generic subprogram is a subprogram. An instance of a generic package is a package.

Generic units are templates. As templates they do not have the properties that are specific to their nongeneric counterparts. For example, a generic subprogram can be instantiated but it cannot be called. In contrast, the instance of a generic subprogram is a nongeneric subprogram; hence, this instance can be called but it cannot be used to produce further instances.

References: declaration 3.1, generic actual parameter 12.3, generic declaration 12.1, generic formal parameter 12.1, generic formal part 12.1, generic instantiation 12.3, generic package 12.1, generic subprogram 12.1, instance 12.3, package 7, program unit 6, subprogram 6

12.1 Generic Declarations

A generic declaration declares a generic unit, which is either a generic subprogram or a generic package. A generic declaration includes a generic formal part declaring any generic formal parameters. A generic formal parameter can be an object; alternatively (unlike a parameter of a subprogram), it can be a type or a subprogram.

```
generic_declaration ::= generic_specification;

generic_specification ::=
      generic_formal_part subprogram_specification
    | generic_formal_part package_specification

generic_formal_part ::= generic {generic_parameter_declaration}

generic_parameter_declaration ::=
      identifier_list : [in [out]] type_mark [:= expression];
    | type identifier is generic_type_definition;
    | private_type_declaration
    | with subprogram_specification [is name];
    | with subprogram_specification [is <>];

generic_type_definition ::=
      (<>) | range <> | digits <> | delta <>
    | array_type_definition | access_type_definition
```

3   The terms generic formal object (or simply, *formal object*), generic formal type (or simply, *formal type*), and generic formal subprogram (or simply, *formal subprogram*) are used to refer to corresponding generic formal parameters.

4   The only form of subtype indication allowed within a generic formal part is a type mark (that is, the subtype indication must not include an explicit constraint). The designator of a generic subprogram must be an identifier.

5   Outside the specification and body of a generic unit, the name of this program unit denotes the generic unit. In contrast, within the declarative region associated with a generic subprogram, the name of this program unit denotes the subprogram obtained by the current instantiation of the generic unit. Similarly, within the declarative region associated with a generic package, the name of this program unit denotes the package obtained by the current instantiation.

6   The elaboration of a generic declaration has no other effect.

7   *Examples of generic formal parts:*

```
generic       -- parameterless

generic
  SIZE : NATURAL; --  formal object

generic
  LENGTH  : INTEGER := 200;              -- formal object with a default expression
  AREA    : INTEGER := LENGTH*LENGTH; -- formal object with a default expression

generic
  type ITEM  is private;                    -- formal type
  type INDEX is (<>);                       -- formal type
  type ROW   is array(INDEX range <>) of ITEM; -- formal type
  with function "<"(X, Y : ITEM) return BOOLEAN;     -- formal subprogram
```

8   *Examples of generic declarations declaring generic subprograms:*

```
generic
  type ELEM is private;
procedure EXCHANGE(U, V : in out ELEM);

generic
  type ITEM is private;
  with function "*"(U, V : ITEM) return ITEM is <>;
function SQUARING(X : ITEM) return ITEM;
```

9   *Example of a generic declaration declaring a generic package:*

```
generic
  type ITEM      is private;
  type VECTOR  is array (POSITIVE range <>) of ITEM;
  with function SUM(X, Y : ITEM) return ITEM;
package ON_VECTORS is
  function SUM   (A, B  : VECTOR) return VECTOR;
  function SIGMA (A       : VECTOR) return ITEM;
  LENGTH_ERROR : exception;
end;
```

Notes:

Within a generic subprogram, the name of this program unit acts as the name of a subprogram.   10
Hence this name can be overloaded, and it can appear in a recursive call of the current instantiation. For the same reason, this name cannot appear after the reserved word **new** in a (recursive) generic instantiation.

An expression that occurs in a generic formal part is either the default expression for a generic for-   11
mal object of mode **in**, or a constituent of an entry name given as default name for a formal subprogram, or the default expression for a parameter of a formal subprogram. Default expressions for generic formal objects and default names for formal subprograms are only evaluated for generic instantiations that use such defaults. Default expressions for parameters of formal subprograms are only evaluated for calls of the formal subprograms that use such defaults. (The usual visibility rules apply to any name used in a default expression: the denoted entity must therefore be visible at the place of the expression.)

Neither generic formal parameters nor their attributes are allowed constituents of static expres-   12
sions (see 4.9).

References: access type definition 3.8, array type definition 3.6, attribute 4.1.4, constraint 3.3, declaration 3.1,   13
designator 6.1, elaboration has no other effect 3.1, entity 3.1, expression 4.4, function 6.5, generic instantiation 12.3,
identifier 2.3, identifier list 3.2, instance 12.3, name 4.1, object 3.2, overloading 6.6 8.7, package specification 7.1,
parameter of a subprogram 6.2, private type definition 7.4, procedure 6.1, reserved word 2.9, static expression 4.9,
subprogram 6, subprogram specification 6.1, subtype indication 3.3.2, type 3.3, type mark 3.3.2

12.1.1 Generic Formal Objects

The first form of generic parameter declaration declares generic formal objects. The type of a   1
generic formal object is the base type of the type denoted by the type mark given in the generic parameter declaration. A generic parameter declaration with several identifiers is equivalent to a sequence of single generic parameter declarations, as explained in section 3.2.

A generic formal object has a mode that is either **in** or **in out**. In the absence of an explicit mode   2
indication in a generic parameter declaration, the mode **in** is assumed; otherwise the mode is the one indicated. If a generic parameter declaration ends with an expression, the expression is the *default expression* of the generic formal parameter. A default expression is only allowed if the mode is **in** (whether this mode is indicated explicitly or implicitly). The type of a default expression must be that of the corresponding generic formal parameter.

A generic formal object of mode **in** is a constant whose value is a copy of the value supplied as the   3
matching generic actual parameter in a generic instantiation, as described in section 12.3. The type of a generic formal object of mode **in** must not be a limited type; the subtype of such a generic formal object is the subtype denoted by the type mark given in the generic parameter declaration.

A generic formal object of mode **in out** is a variable and denotes the object supplied as the   4
matching generic actual parameter in a generic instantiation, as described in section 12.3. The constraints that apply to the generic formal object are those of the corresponding generic actual parameter.

Note:

5 The constraints that apply to a generic formal object of mode **in out** are those of the corresponding generic actual parameter (not those implied by the type mark that appears in the generic parameter declaration). Whenever possible (to avoid confusion) it is recommended that the name of a base type be used for the declaration of such a formal object. If, however, the base type is anonymous, it is recommended that the subtype name defined by the type declaration for the base type be used.

6 *References:* anonymous type 3.3.1, assignment 5.2, base type 3.3, constant declaration 3.2, constraint 3.3, declaration 3.1, generic actual parameter 12.3, generic formal object 12.1, generic formal parameter 12.1, generic instantiation 12.3, generic parameter declaration 12.1, identifier 2.3, limited type 7.4.4, matching generic actual parameter 12.3, mode 6.1, name 4.1, object 3.2, simple name 4.1, subtype 3.3, type declaration 3.3, type mark 3.3.2, variable 3.2.1

12.1.2 Generic Formal Types

1 A generic parameter declaration that includes a generic type definition or a private type declaration declares a generic formal type. A generic formal type denotes the subtype supplied as the corresponding actual parameter in a generic instantiation, as described in 12.3(d). However, within a generic unit, a generic formal type is considered as being distinct from all other (formal or nonformal) types. The form of constraint applicable to a formal type in a subtype indication depends on the class of the type as for a nonformal type.

2 The only form of discrete range that is allowed within the declaration of a generic formal (constrained) array type is a type mark.

3 The discriminant part of a generic formal private type must not include a default expression for a discriminant. (Consequently, a variable that is declared by an object declaration must be constrained if its type is a generic formal type with discriminants.)

4 Within the declaration and body of a generic unit, the operations available for values of a generic formal type (apart from any additional operation specified by a generic formal subprogram) are determined by the generic parameter declaration for the formal type:

5 (a) For a private type declaration, the available operations are those defined in section 7.4.2 (in particular, assignment, equality, and inequality are available for a private type unless it is limited).

6 (b) For an array type definition, the available operations are those defined in section 3.6.2 (for example, they include the formation of indexed components and slices).

7 (c) For an access type definition, the available operations are those defined in section 3.8.2 (for example, allocators can be used).

8 The four forms of generic type definition in which a *box* appears (that is, the compound delimiter <>) correspond to the following major forms of scalar type:

9 (d) Discrete types: (<>)

The available operations are the operations common to enumeration and integer types; these are defined in section 3.5.5.

(e) Integer types: **range** <>   10

The available operations are the operations of integer types defined in section 3.5.5.

(f) Floating point types: **digits** <>   11

The available operations are those defined in section 3.5.8.

(g) Fixed point types: **delta** <>   12

The available operations are those defined in section 3.5.10.

In all of the above cases (a) through (f), each operation implicitly associated with a formal type   13
(that is, other than an operation specified by a formal subprogram) is implicitly declared at the
place of the declaration of the formal type. The same holds for a formal fixed point type, except for
the multiplying operators that deliver a result of the type *universal_fixed* (see 4.5.5), since these
special operators are declared in the package STANDARD.

For an instantiation of the generic unit, each of these operations is the corresponding basic opera-   14
tion or predefined operator of the matching actual type. For an operator, this rule applies even if
the operator has been redefined for the actual type or for some parent type of the actual type.

Examples of generic formal types: 15

```
type ITEM is private;
type BUFFER(LENGTH : NATURAL) is limited private;

type ENUM  is (<>);
type INT   is range <>;
type ANGLE is delta <>;
type MASS  is digits <>;

type TABLE is array (ENUM) of ITEM;
```

Example of a generic formal part declaring a formal integer type: 16

```
generic
  type RANK is range <>;
  FIRST  : RANK := RANK'FIRST;
  SECOND : RANK := FIRST + 1;  --  the operator "+" of the type RANK
```

References: access type definition 3.8, allocator 4.8, array type definition 3.6, assignment 5.2, body of a generic unit   17
12.2, class of type 3.3, constraint 3.3, declaration 3.1, declaration of a generic unit 12.1, discrete range 3.6, discrete
type 3.5, discriminant part 3.7.1, enumeration type 3.5.1, equality 4.5.2, fixed point type 3.5.9, floating point type
3.5.7, generic actual type 12.3, generic formal part 12.1, generic formal subprogram 12.1.3, generic formal type 12.1,
generic parameter declaration 12.1, generic type definition 12.1, indexed component 4.1.1, inequality 4.5.2, instantiation 12.3, integer type 3.5.4, limited private type 7.4.4, matching generic actual type 12.3.2 12.3.3 12.3.4 12.3.5,
multiplying operator 4.5 4.5.5, operation 3.3, operator 4.5, parent type 3.4, private type definition 7.4, scalar type 3.5,
slice 4.1.2, standard package 8.6 C, subtype indication 3.3.2, type mark 3.3.2, universal_fixed 3.5.9

12.1.3 Generic Formal Subprograms

1   A generic parameter declaration that includes a subprogram specification declares a generic formal subprogram.

2   Two alternative forms of defaults can be specified in the declaration of a generic formal subprogram. In these forms, the subprogram specification is followed by the reserved word **is** and either a box or the name of a subprogram or entry. The matching rules for these defaults are explained in section 12.3.6.

3   A generic formal subprogram denotes the subprogram, enumeration literal, or entry supplied as the corresponding generic actual parameter in a generic instantiation, as described in section 12.3(f).

4   *Examples of generic formal subprograms:*

```
with function INCREASE(X : INTEGER) return INTEGER;
with function SUM(X, Y : ITEM) return ITEM;

with function "+"(X, Y : ITEM) return ITEM is <>;
with function IMAGE(X : ENUM) return STRING is ENUM'IMAGE;

with procedure UPDATE is DEFAULT_UPDATE;
```

Notes:

5   The constraints that apply to a parameter of a formal subprogram are those of the corresponding parameter in the specification of the matching actual subprogram (not those implied by the corresponding type mark in the specification of the formal subprogram). A similar remark applies to the result of a function. Whenever possible (to avoid confusion), it is recommended that the name of a base type be used rather than the name of a subtype in any declaration of a formal subprogram. If, however, the base type is anonymous, it is recommended that the subtype name defined by the type declaration be used.

6   The type specified for a formal parameter of a generic formal subprogram can be any visible type, including a generic formal type of the same generic formal part.

7   *References:* anonymous type 3.3.1, base type 3.3, box delimiter 12.1.2, constraint 3.3, designator 6.1, generic actual parameter 12.3, generic formal function 12.1, generic formal subprogram 12.1, generic instantiation 12.3, generic parameter declaration 12.1, identifier 2.3, matching generic actual subprogram 12.3.6, operator symbol 6.1, parameter of a subprogram 6.2, renaming declaration 8.5, reserved word 2.9, scope 8.2, subprogram 6, subprogram specification 6.1, subtype 3.3.2, type 3.3, type mark 3.3.2

12.2 Generic Bodies

1   The body of a generic subprogram or generic package is a template for the bodies of the corresponding subprograms or packages obtained by generic instantiations. The syntax of a generic body is identical to that of a nongeneric body.

2   For each declaration of a generic subprogram, there must be a corresponding body.

The elaboration of a generic body has no other effect than to establish that the body can from then on be used as the template for obtaining the corresponding instances.   3

Example of a generic procedure body: 4

```
procedure EXCHANGE(U, V : in out ELEM) is     --  see example in 12.1
   T : ELEM;  --  the generic formal type
begin
   T := U;
   U := V;
   V := T;
end EXCHANGE;
```

Example of a generic function body: 5

```
function SQUARING(X : ITEM) return ITEM is     --  see example in 12.1
begin
   return X*X;  --  the formal operator "*"
end;
```

Example of a generic package body: 6

```
package body ON_VECTORS is   --  see example in 12.1

   function SUM(A, B : VECTOR) return VECTOR is
      RESULT  : VECTOR(A'RANGE);      --  the formal type VECTOR
      BIAS    : constant INTEGER := B'FIRST - A'FIRST;
   begin
      if A'LENGTH /= B'LENGTH then
         raise LENGTH_ERROR;
      end if;

      for N in A'RANGE loop
         RESULT(N) := SUM(A(N), B(N + BIAS));      --  the formal function SUM
      end loop;
      return RESULT;
   end;

   function SIGMA(A : VECTOR) return ITEM is
      TOTAL : ITEM := A(A'FIRST);               --  the formal type ITEM
   begin
      for N in A'FIRST + 1 .. A'LAST loop
         TOTAL := SUM(TOTAL, A(N));             --  the formal function SUM
      end loop;
      return TOTAL;
   end;
end;
```

References: body 3.9, elaboration 3.9, generic body 12.1, generic instantiation 12.3, generic package 12.1, generic   7
subprogram 12.1, instance 12.3, package body 7.1, package 7, subprogram 6, subprogram body 6.3

12.3 Generic Instantiation

1 An instance of a generic unit is declared by a generic instantiation.

2
```
generic_instantiation ::=
      package identifier is
          new generic_package_name [generic_actual_part];
    | procedure identifier is
          new generic_procedure_name [generic_actual_part];
    | function designator is
          new generic_function_name [generic_actual_part];

generic_actual_part ::=
    (generic_association {, generic_association})

generic_association ::=
    [generic_formal_parameter =>] generic_actual_parameter

generic_formal_parameter ::= parameter_simple_name | operator_symbol

generic_actual_parameter ::= expression | variable_name
    | subprogram_name | entry_name | type_mark
```

3 An explicit generic actual parameter must be supplied for each generic formal parameter, unless the corresponding generic parameter declaration specifies that a default can be used. Generic associations can be either positional or named, in the same manner as parameter associations of subprogram calls (see 6.4). If two or more formal subprograms have the same designator, then named associations are not allowed for the corresponding generic parameters.

4 Each generic actual parameter must *match* the corresponding generic formal parameter. An expression can match a formal object of mode **in**; a variable name can match a formal object of mode **in out**; a subprogram name or an entry name can match a formal subprogram; a type mark can match a formal type. The detailed rules defining the allowed matches are given in sections 12.3.1 to 12.3.6; these are the only allowed matches.

5 The instance is a copy of the generic unit, apart from the generic formal part; thus the instance of a generic package is a package, that of a generic procedure is a procedure, and that of a generic function is a function. For each occurrence, within the generic unit, of a name that denotes a given entity, the following list defines which entity is denoted by the corresponding occurrence within the instance.

6 (a) For a name that denotes the generic unit: The corresponding occurrence denotes the instance.

7 (b) For a name that denotes a generic formal object of mode **in**:   The corresponding name denotes a constant whose value is a copy of the value of the associated generic actual parameter.

8 (c) For a name that denotes a generic formal object of mode **in out**:   The corresponding name denotes the variable named by the associated generic actual parameter.

9 (d) For a name that denotes a generic formal type: The corresponding name denotes the subtype named by the associated generic actual parameter (the actual subtype).

10 (e) For a name that denotes a discriminant of a generic formal type: The corresponding name denotes the corresponding discriminant (there must be one) of the actual type associated with the generic formal type.

(f) For a name that denotes a generic formal subprogram: The corresponding name denotes the [11]
     subprogram, enumeration literal, or entry named by the associated generic actual parameter
     (the actual subprogram).

(g) For a name that denotes a formal parameter of a generic formal subprogram: The cor- [12]
     responding name denotes the corresponding formal parameter of the actual subprogram
     associated with the formal subprogram.

(h) For a name that denotes a local entity declared within the generic unit: The corresponding [13]
     name denotes the entity declared by the corresponding local declaration within the instance.

(i) For a name that denotes a global entity declared outside of the generic unit: The cor- [14]
     responding name denotes the same global entity.

Similar rules apply to operators and basic operations: in particular, formal operators follow a rule [15]
similar to rule (f), local operations follow a rule similar to rule (h), and operations for global types
follow a rule similar to rule (i). In addition, if within the generic unit a predefined operator or basic
operation of a formal type is used, then within the instance the corresponding occurrence refers to
the corresponding predefined operation of the actual type associated with the formal type.

The above rules apply also to any type mark or (default) expression given within the generic formal [16]
part of the generic unit.

For the elaboration of a generic instantiation, each expression supplied as an explicit generic actual [17]
parameter is first evaluated, as well as each expression that appears as a constituent of a variable
name or entry name supplied as an explicit generic actual parameter; these evaluations proceed in
some order that is not defined by the language. Then, for each omitted generic association (if any),
the corresponding default expression or default name is evaluated; such evaluations are performed in the order of the generic parameter declarations. Finally, the implicitly generated instance
is elaborated. The elaboration of a generic instantiation may also involve certain constraint checks
as described in later subsections.

Recursive generic instantiation is not allowed in the following sense: if a given generic unit [18]
includes an instantiation of a second generic unit, then the instance generated by this instantiation
must not include an instance of the first generic unit (whether this instance is generated directly, or
indirectly by intermediate instantiations).

Examples of generic instantiations (see 12.1): [19]

```
procedure  SWAP  is new  EXCHANGE(ELEM => INTEGER);
procedure  SWAP  is new  EXCHANGE(CHARACTER);   --  SWAP is overloaded

function  SQUARE is new  SQUARING (INTEGER);  --  "*" of INTEGER used by default
function  SQUARE is new  SQUARING (ITEM => MATRIX, "*" => MATRIX_PRODUCT);
function  SQUARE is new  SQUARING (MATRIX, MATRIX_PRODUCT); -- same as previous

package  INT_VECTORS is new  ON_VECTORS(INTEGER, TABLE, "+");
```

Examples of uses of instantiated units: [20]

```
SWAP(A, B);
A := SQUARE(A);

T  : TABLE(1 .. 5) := (10, 20, 30, 40, 50);
N  : INTEGER := INT_VECTORS.SIGMA(T);  --  150 (see 12.2 for the body of SIGMA)

use  INT_VECTORS;
M  : INTEGER := SIGMA(T);  --  150
```

Notes:

21 Omission of a generic actual parameter is only allowed if a corresponding default exists. If default expressions or default names (other than simple names) are used, they are evaluated in the order in which the corresponding generic formal parameters are declared.

22 If two overloaded subprograms declared in a generic package specification differ only by the (formal) type of their parameters and results, then there exist legal instantiations for which all calls of these subprograms from outside the instance are ambiguous. For example:

```
generic
   type A is (<>);
   type B is private;
package G is
   function NEXT(X : A) return A;
   function NEXT(X : B) return B;
end;

package P is new G(A => BOOLEAN, B => BOOLEAN);
-- calls of P.NEXT are ambiguous
```

23 *References:* declaration 3.1, designator 6.1, discriminant 3.7.1, elaboration 3.1 3.9, entity 3.1, entry name 9.5, evaluation 4.5, expression 4.4, generic formal object 12.1, generic formal parameter 12.1, generic formal subprogram 12.1, generic formal type 12.1, generic parameter declaration 12.1, global declaration 8.1, identifier 2.3, implicit declaration 3.1, local declaration 8.1, mode in 12.1.1, mode in out 12.1.1, name 4.1, operation 3.3, operator symbol 6.1, overloading 6.6 8.7, package 7, simple name 4.1, subprogram 6, subprogram call 6.4, subprogram name 6.1, subtype declaration 3.3.2, type mark 3.3.2, variable 3.2.1, visibility 8.3

12.3.1 Matching Rules for Formal Objects

1 A generic formal parameter of mode **in** of a given type is matched by an expression of the same type. If a generic unit has a generic formal object of mode **in**, a check is made that the value of the expression belongs to the subtype denoted by the type mark, as for an explicit constant declaration (see 3.2.1). The exception CONSTRAINT_ERROR is raised if this check fails.

2 A generic formal parameter of mode **in out** of a given type is matched by the name of a variable of the same type. The variable must not be a formal parameter of mode **out** or a subcomponent thereof. The name must denote a variable for which renaming is allowed (see 8.5).

Notes:

3 The type of a generic actual parameter of mode **in** must not be a limited type. The constraints that apply to a generic formal parameter of mode **in out** are those of the corresponding generic actual parameter (see 12.1.1).

4 *References:* constraint 3.3, constraint_error exception 11.1, expression 4.4, formal parameter 6.1, generic actual parameter 12.3, generic formal object 12.1.1, generic formal parameter 12.1, generic instantiation 12.3, generic unit 12.1, limited type 7.4.4, matching generic actual parameter 12.3, mode in 12.1.1, mode in out 12.1.1, mode out 6.2, name 4.1, raising of exceptions 11, satisfy 3.3, subcomponent 3.3, type 3.3, type mark 3.3.2, variable 3.2.1

12.3.2 Matching Rules for Formal Private Types

A generic formal private type is matched by any type or subtype (the actual subtype) that satisfies the following conditions:

- If the formal type is not limited, the actual type must not be a limited type. (If, on the other hand, the formal type is limited, no such condition is imposed on the corresponding actual type, which can be limited or not limited.)

- If the formal type has a discriminant part, the actual type must be a type with the same number of discriminants; the type of a discriminant that appears at a given position in the discriminant part of the actual type must be the same as the type of the discriminant that appears at the same position in the discriminant part of the formal type; and the actual subtype must be unconstrained. (If, on the other hand, the formal type has no discriminants, the actual type is allowed to have discriminants.)

Furthermore, consider any occurrence of the name of the formal type at a place where this name is used as an unconstrained subtype indication. The actual subtype must not be an unconstrained array type or an unconstrained type with discriminants, if any of these occurrences is at a place where either a constraint or default discriminants would be required for an array type or for a type with discriminants (see 3.6.1 and 3.7.2). The same restriction applies to occurrences of the name of a subtype of the formal type, and to occurrences of the name of any type or subtype derived, directly or indirectly, from the formal type.

If a generic unit has a formal private type with discriminants, the elaboration of a corresponding generic instantiation checks that the subtype of each discriminant of the actual type is the same as the subtype of the corresponding discriminant of the formal type. The exception CONSTRAINT_ERROR is raised if this check fails.

References: array type 3.6, constraint 3.3, constraint_error exception 11.1, default expression for a discriminant 3.7.1, derived type 3.4, discriminant 3.7.1, discriminant part 3.7.1, elaboration 3.9, generic actual type 12.3, generic body 12.2, generic formal type 12.1.2, generic instantiation 12.3, generic specification 12.1, limited type 7.4.4, matching generic actual parameter 12.3, name 4.1, private type 7.4, raising of exceptions 11, subtype 3.3, subtype indication 3.3.2, type 3.3, type with discriminants 3.3, unconstrained array type 3.6, unconstrained subtype 3.3

12.3.3 Matching Rules for Formal Scalar Types

A generic formal type defined by (<>) is matched by any discrete subtype (that is, any enumeration or integer subtype). A generic formal type defined by **range** <> is matched by any integer subtype. A generic formal type defined by **digits** <> is matched by any floating point subtype. A generic formal type defined by **delta** <> is matched by any fixed point subtype. No other matches are possible for these generic formal types.

References: box delimiter 12.1.2, discrete type 3.5, enumeration type 3.5.1, fixed point type 3.5.9, floating point type 3.5.7, generic actual type 12.3, generic formal type 12.1.2, generic type definition 12.1, integer type 3.5.4, matching generic actual parameter 12.3, scalar type 3.5

12.3.4 Matching Rules for Formal Array Types

1 A formal array type is matched by an actual array subtype that satisfies the following conditions:

2 ● The formal array type and the actual array type must have the same dimensionality; the formal type and the actual subtype must be either both constrained or both unconstrained.

3 ● For each index position, the index type must be the same for the actual array type as for the formal array type.

4 ● The component type must be the same for the actual array type as for the formal array type. If the component type is other than a scalar type, then the component subtypes must be either both constrained or both unconstrained.

5 If a generic unit has a formal array type, the elaboration of a corresponding instantiation checks that the constraints (if any) on the component type are the same for the actual array type as for the formal array type, and likewise that for any given index position the index subtypes or the discrete ranges have the same bounds. The exception CONSTRAINT_ERROR is raised if this check fails.

6 *Example:*

```
--  given the generic package

generic
   type ITEM      is private;
   type INDEX     is (<>);
   type VECTOR    is array (INDEX range <>) of ITEM;
   type TABLE     is array (INDEX) of ITEM;
package P is
   ...
end;

--  and the types

type MIX      is array (COLOR range <>) of BOOLEAN;
type OPTION   is array (COLOR) of BOOLEAN;

--  then  MIX  can match VECTOR and OPTION can match TABLE

package R is new P( ITEM    => BOOLEAN, INDEX => COLOR,
                    VECTOR  => MIX,     TABLE => OPTION);

--  Note that MIX cannot match TABLE and OPTION cannot match VECTOR
```

Note:

7 For the above rules, if any of the index or component types of the formal array type is itself a formal type, then within the instance its name denotes the corresponding actual subtype (see 12.3(d)).

8 *References:* array type 3.6, array type definition 3.6, component of an array 3.6, constrained array type 3.6, constraint 3.3, constraint_error exception 11.1, elaboration 3.9, formal type 12.1, generic formal type 12.1.2, generic instantiation 12.3, index 3.6, index constraint 3.6.1, matching generic actual parameter 12.3, raise statement 11.3, subtype 3.3, unconstrained array type 3.6

12.3.5 Matching Rules for Formal Access Types

A formal access type is matched by an actual access subtype if the type of the designated objects   1
is the same for the actual type as for the formal type. If the designated type is other than a scalar
type, then the designated subtypes must be either both constrained or both unconstrained.

If a generic unit has a formal access type, the elaboration of a corresponding instantiation checks   2
that any constraints on the designated objects are the same for the actual access subtype as for
the formal access type. The exception CONSTRAINT_ERROR is raised if this check fails.

Example: 3

```
--   the formal types of the generic package

generic
   type NODE  is private;
   type LINK   is access NODE;
package P is
   ...
end;

--   can be matched by the actual types

type CAR;
type CAR_NAME is access CAR;

type CAR is
   record
      PRED, SUCC : CAR_NAME;
      NUMBER     : LICENSE_NUMBER;
      OWNER      : PERSON;
   end record;


--   in the following generic instantiation

package R is new P(NODE => CAR, LINK => CAR_NAME);
```

Note:

For the above rules, if the designated type is itself a formal type, then within the instance its name   4
denotes the corresponding actual subtype (see 12.3(d)).

References: access type 3.8, access type definition 3.8, constraint 3.3, constraint_error exception 11.1, designate   5
3.8, elaboration 3.9, generic formal type 12.1.2, generic instantiation 12.3, matching generic actual parameter 12.3,
object 3.2, raise statement 11.3, value of access type 3.8

12.3.6 Matching Rules for Formal Subprograms

1   A formal subprogram is matched by an actual subprogram, enumeration literal, or entry if both have the same parameter and result type profile (see 6.6); in addition, parameter modes must be identical for formal parameters that are at the same parameter position.

2   If a generic unit has a default subprogram specified by a name, this name must denote a subprogram, an enumeration literal, or an entry, that matches the formal subprogram (in the above sense). The evaluation of the default name takes place during the elaboration of each instantiation that uses the default, as defined in section 12.3.

3   If a generic unit has a default subprogram specified by a box, the corresponding actual parameter can be omitted if a subprogram, enumeration literal, or entry matching the formal subprogram, and with the same designator as the formal subprogram, is directly visible at the place of the generic instantiation; this subprogram, enumeration literal, or entry is then used by default (there must be exactly one subprogram, enumeration literal, or entry satisfying the previous conditions).

4   *Example:*

```
--  given the generic function specification

generic
    type ITEM is private;
    with function "*" (U, V : ITEM) return ITEM is <>;
function SQUARING(X : ITEM) return ITEM;

--  and the function

function MATRIX_PRODUCT(A, B : MATRIX) return MATRIX;

--  the following instantiation is possible

function SQUARE is new SQUARING(MATRIX, MATRIX_PRODUCT);

--  the following instantiations are equivalent

function SQUARE is new SQUARING(ITEM => INTEGER, "*" => "*");
function SQUARE is new SQUARING(INTEGER, "*");
function SQUARE is new SQUARING(INTEGER);
```

Notes:

5   The matching rules for formal subprograms state requirements that are similar to those applying to subprogram renaming declarations (see 8.5). In particular, the name of a parameter of the formal subprogram need not be the same as that of the corresponding parameter of the actual subprogram; similarly, for these parameters, default expressions need not correspond.

6   A formal subprogram is matched by an attribute of a type if the attribute is a function with a matching specification. An enumeration literal of a given type matches a parameterless formal function whose result type is the given type.

7   *References:* attribute 4.1.4, box delimiter 12.1.2, designator 6.1, entry 9.5, function 6.5, generic actual type 12.3, generic formal subprogram 12.1.3, generic formal type 12.1.2, generic instantiation 12.3, matching generic actual parameter 12.3, name 4.1, parameter and result type profile 6.3, subprogram 6, subprogram specification 6.1, subtype 3.3, visibility 8.3

12.4 Example of a Generic Package

The following example provides a possible formulation of stacks by means of a generic package. [1]
The size of each stack and the type of the stack elements are provided as generic parameters.

```
generic                                                    2
   SIZE : POSITIVE;
   type ITEM is private;
package STACK is
   procedure PUSH (E : in    ITEM);
   procedure POP (E : out   ITEM);
   OVERFLOW, UNDERFLOW : exception;
end STACK;

package body STACK is

   type TABLE is array (POSITIVE range <>) of ITEM;
   SPACE  : TABLE(1 .. SIZE);
   INDEX  : NATURAL := 0;

   procedure PUSH(E : in ITEM) is
   begin
     if INDEX >= SIZE then
        raise OVERFLOW;
     end if;
     INDEX := INDEX + 1;
     SPACE(INDEX) := E;
   end PUSH;

   procedure POP(E : out ITEM) is
   begin
     if INDEX = 0 then
        raise UNDERFLOW;
     end if;
     E := SPACE(INDEX);
     INDEX := INDEX - 1;
   end POP;

end STACK;
```

Instances of this generic package can be obtained as follows: [3]

```
package STACK_INT  is new STACK(SIZE => 200, ITEM => INTEGER);
package STACK_BOOL is new STACK(100, BOOLEAN);
```

Thereafter, the procedures of the instantiated packages can be called as follows: [4]

```
STACK_INT.PUSH(N);
STACK_BOOL.PUSH(TRUE);
```

Example of a Generic Package 12.4

5 Alternatively, a generic formulation of the type STACK can be given as follows (package body omitted):

```
generic
   type ITEM is private;
package ON_STACKS is
   type STACK(SIZE : POSITIVE) is limited private;
   procedure PUSH (S : in out STACK; E : in    ITEM);
   procedure POP  (S : in out STACK; E : out   ITEM);
   OVERFLOW, UNDERFLOW : exception;
private
   type TABLE is array (POSITIVE range <>) of ITEM;
   type STACK(SIZE : POSITIVE) is
      record
         SPACE   : TABLE(1 .. SIZE);
         INDEX   : NATURAL := 0;
      end record;
end;
```

6 In order to use such a package, an instantiation must be created and thereafter stacks of the corresponding type can be declared:

```
declare
   package STACK_REAL is new ON_STACKS(REAL); use STACK_REAL;
   S : STACK(100);
begin
   ...
   PUSH(S, 2.54);
   ...
end;
```

13. Representation Clauses and Implementation-Dependent Features

This chapter describes representation clauses, certain implementation-dependent features, and other features that are used in system programming.

13.1 Representation Clauses

Representation clauses specify how the types of the language are to be mapped onto the underlying machine. They can be provided to give more efficient representation or to interface with features that are outside the domain of the language (for example, peripheral hardware).

```
representation_clause ::=
     type_representation_clause | address_clause

type_representation_clause ::= length_clause
   | enumeration_representation_clause | record_representation_clause
```

A type representation clause applies either to a type or to a *first named subtype* (that is, to a subtype declared by a type declaration, the base type being therefore anonymous). Such a representation clause applies to all objects that have this type or this first named subtype. At most one enumeration or record representation clause is allowed for a given type: an enumeration representation clause is only allowed for an enumeration type; a record representation clause, only for a record type. (On the other hand, more than one length clause can be provided for a given type; moreover, both a length clause and an enumeration or record representation clause can be provided.) A length clause is the only form of representation clause allowed for a type derived from a parent type that has (user-defined) derivable subprograms.

An address clause applies either to an object; to a subprogram, package, or task unit; or to an entry. At most one address clause is allowed for any of these entities.

A representation clause and the declaration of the entity to which the clause applies must both occur immediately within the same declarative part, package specification, or task specification; the declaration must occur before the clause. In the absence of a representation clause for a given declaration, a default representation of this declaration is determined by the implementation. Such a default determination occurs no later than the end of the immediately enclosing declarative part, package specification, or task specification. For a declaration given in a declarative part, this default determination occurs before any enclosed body.

In the case of a type, certain occurrences of its name imply that the representation of the type must already have been determined. Consequently these occurrences force the default determination of any aspect of the representation not already determined by a prior type representation clause. This default determination is also forced by similar occurrences of the name of a subtype of the type, or of the name of any type or subtype that has subcomponents of the type. A forcing occurrence is any occurrence other than in a type or subtype declaration, a subprogram specification, an entry declaration, a deferred constant declaration, a pragma, or a representation clause for the type itself. In any case, an occurrence within an expression is always forcing.

7   A representation clause for a given entity must not appear after an occurrence of the name of the entity if this occurrence forces a default determination of representation for the entity.

8   Similar restrictions exist for address clauses. For an object, any occurrence of its name (after the object declaration) is a forcing occurrence. For a subprogram, package, task unit, or entry, any occurrence of a representation attribute of such an entity is a forcing occurrence.

9   The effect of the elaboration of a representation clause is to define the corresponding aspects of the representation.

10   The interpretation of some of the expressions that appear in representation clauses is implementation-dependent, for example, expressions specifying addresses. An implementation may limit its acceptance of representation clauses to those that can be handled simply by the underlying hardware. If a representation clause is accepted by an implementation, the compiler must guarantee that the net effect of the program is not changed by the presence of the clause, except for address clauses and for parts of the program that interrogate representation attributes. If a program contains a representation clause that is not accepted, the program is illegal. For each implementation, the allowed representation clauses, and the conventions used for implementation-dependent expressions, must be documented in Appendix F of the reference manual.

11   Whereas a representation clause is used to impose certain characteristics of the mapping of an entity onto the underlying machine, pragmas can be used to provide an implementation with criteria for its selection of such a mapping. The pragma PACK specifies that storage minimization should be the main criterion when selecting the representation of a record or array type. Its form is as follows:

       pragma PACK (*type*_simple_name);

12   Packing means that gaps between the storage areas allocated to consecutive components should be minimized. It need not, however, affect the mapping of each component onto storage. This mapping can itself be influenced by a pragma (or controlled by a representation clause) for the component or component type. The position of a PACK pragma, and the restrictions on the named type, are governed by the same rules as for a representation clause; in particular, the pragma must appear before any use of a representation attribute of the packed entity.

13   The pragma PACK is the only language-defined representation pragma. Additional representation pragmas may be provided by an implementation; these must be documented in Appendix F. (In contrast to representation clauses, a pragma that is not accepted by the implementation is ignored.)

Note:

14   No representation clause is allowed for a generic formal type.

15   *References:* address clause 13.5, allow 1.6, body 3.9, component 3.3, declaration 3.1, declarative part 3.9, default expression 3.2.1, deferred constant declaration 7.4, derivable subprogram 3.4, derived type 3.4, entity 3.1, entry 9.5, enumeration representation clause 13.3, expression 4.4, generic formal type 12.1.2, illegal 1.6, length clause 13.2, must 1.6, name 4.1, object 3.2, occur immediately within 8.1, package 7, package specification 7.1, parent type 3.4, pragma 2.8, record representation clause 13.4, representation attribute 13.7.2 13.7.3, subcomponent 3.3, subprogram 6, subtype 3.3, subtype declaration 3.3.2, task specification 9.1, task unit 9, type 3.3, type declaration 3.3.1

13.2 Length Clauses

A length clause specifies an amount of storage associated with a type.

> length_clause ::= **for** attribute **use** simple_expression;

The expression must be of some numeric type and is evaluated during the elaboration of the length clause (unless it is a static expression). The prefix of the attribute must denote either a type or a first named subtype. The prefix is called T in what follows. The only allowed attribute designators in a length clause are SIZE, STORAGE_SIZE, and SMALL. The effect of the length clause depends on the attribute designator:

(a) Size specification: T'SIZE

The expression must be a static expression of some integer type. The value of the expression specifies an upper bound for the number of bits to be allocated to objects of the type or first named subtype T. The size specification must allow for enough storage space to accommodate every allowable value of these objects. A size specification for a composite type may affect the size of the gaps between the storage areas allocated to consecutive components. On the other hand, it need not affect the size of the storage area allocated to each component.

The size specification is only allowed if the constraints on T and on its subcomponents (if any) are static. In the case of an unconstrained array type, the index subtypes must also be static.

(b) Specification of collection size: T'STORAGE_SIZE

The prefix T must denote an access type. The expression must be of some integer type (but need not be static); its value specifies the number of storage units to be reserved for the collection, that is, the storage space needed to contain all objects designated by values of the access type and by values of other types derived from the access type, directly or indirectly. This form of length clause is not allowed for a type derived from an access type.

(c) Specification of storage for a task activation: T'STORAGE_SIZE

The prefix T must denote a task type. The expression must be of some integer type (but need not be static); its value specifies the number of storage units to be reserved for an activation (not the code) of a task of the type.

(d) Specification of *small* for a fixed point type: T'SMALL

The prefix T must denote the first named subtype of a fixed point type. The expression must be a static expression of some real type; its value must not be greater than the delta of the first named subtype. The effect of the length clause is to use this value of *small* for the representation of values of the fixed point base type. (The length clause thereby also affects the amount of storage for objects that have this type.)

Notes:

A size specification is allowed for an access, task, or fixed point type, whether or not another form of length clause is also given for the type.

14 What is considered to be part of the storage reserved for a collection or for an activation of a task is implementation-dependent. The control afforded by length clauses is therefore relative to the implementation conventions. For example, the language does not define whether the storage reserved for an activation of a task includes any storage needed for the collection associated with an access type declared within the task body. Neither does it define the method of allocation for objects denoted by values of an access type. For example, the space allocated could be on a stack; alternatively, a general dynamic allocation scheme or fixed storage could be used.

15 The objects allocated in a collection need not have the same size if the designated type is an unconstrained array type or an unconstrained type with discriminants. Note also that the allocator itself may require some space for internal tables and links. Hence a length clause for the collection of an access type does not always give precise control over the maximum number of allocated objects.

16 *Examples:*

```
-- assumed declarations:

type MEDIUM is range  0 .. 65000;
type SHORT  is delta  0.01  range -100.0  .. 100.0;
type DEGREE is delta  0.1   range -360.0  .. 360.0;

BYTE : constant := 8;
PAGE : constant := 2000;

-- length clauses:

for COLOR'SIZE     use 1*BYTE;  -- see 3.5.1
for MEDIUM'SIZE    use 2*BYTE;
for SHORT'SIZE     use 15;

for CAR_NAME'STORAGE_SIZE use  -- approximately 2000 cars
        2000*((CAR'SIZE/SYSTEM.STORAGE_UNIT) + 1);

for KEYBOARD_DRIVER'STORAGE_SIZE use 1*PAGE;

for DEGREE'SMALL use 360.0/2**(SYSTEM.STORAGE_UNIT - 1);
```

17 *Notes on the examples:*

In the length clause for SHORT, fifteen bits is the minimum necessary, since the type definition requires SHORT'SMALL = 2.0**(-7) and SHORT'MANTISSA = 14. The length clause for DEGREE forces the model numbers to exactly span the range of the type.

18 *References:* access type 3.8, allocator 4.8, allow 1.6, array type 3.6, attribute 4.1.4, collection 3.8, composite type 3.3, constraint 3.3, delta of a fixed point type 3.5.9, derived type 3.4, designate 3.8, elaboration 3.9, entity 3.1, evaluation 4.5, expression 4.4, first named subtype 13.1, fixed point type 3.5.9, index subtype 3.6, integer type 3.5.4, must 1.6, numeric type 3.5, object 3.2, real type 3.5.6, record type 3.7, small of a fixed point type 3.5.10, static constraint 4.9, static expression 4.9, static subtype 4.9, storage unit 13.7, subcomponent 3.3, system package 13.7, task 9, task activation 9.3, task specification 9.1, task type 9.2, type 3.3, unconstrained array type 3.6

13.3 Enumeration Representation Clauses

An enumeration representation clause specifies the internal codes for the literals of the enumeration type that is named in the clause.

    enumeration_representation_clause ::= **for** *type*_simple_name **use** aggregate;

The aggregate used to specify this mapping is written as a one-dimensional aggregate, for which the index subtype is the enumeration type and the component type is *universal_integer*.

All literals of the enumeration type must be provided with distinct integer codes, and all choices and component values given in the aggregate must be static. The integer codes specified for the enumeration type must satisfy the predefined ordering relation of the type.

Example:

    type MIX_CODE **is** (ADD, SUB, MUL, LDA, STA, STZ);

    for MIX_CODE **use**
       (ADD => 1, SUB => 2, MUL => 3, LDA => 8, STA => 24, STZ => 33);

Notes:

The attributes SUCC, PRED, and POS are defined even for enumeration types with a noncontiguous representation; their definition corresponds to the (logical) type declaration and is not affected by the enumeration representation clause. In the example, because of the need to avoid the omitted values, these functions are likely to be less efficiently implemented than they could be in the absence of a representation clause. Similar considerations apply when such types are used for indexing.

References: aggregate 4.3, array aggregate 4.3.2, array type 3.6, attribute of an enumeration type 3.5.5, choice 3.7.3, component 3.3, enumeration literal 3.5.1, enumeration type 3.5.1, function 6.5, index 3.6, index subtype 3.6, literal 4.2, ordering relation of an enumeration type 3.5.1, representation clause 13.1, simple name 4.1, static expression 4.9, type 3.3, type declaration 3.3.1, universal_integer type 3.5.4

13.4 Record Representation Clauses

A record representation clause specifies the storage representation of records, that is, the order, position, and size of record components (including discriminants, if any).

    record_representation_clause ::=
       for *type*_simple_name **use**
          record [alignment_clause]
             {component_clause}
          end record;

    alignment_clause ::= **at mod** *static*_simple_expression;

    component_clause ::=
       *component*_name **at** *static*_simple_expression **range** *static*_range;

3   The simple expression given after the reserved words **at mod** in an alignment clause, or after the reserved word **at** in a component clause, must be a static expression of some integer type. If the bounds of the range of a component clause are defined by simple expressions, then each bound of the range must be defined by a static expression of some integer type, but the two bounds need not have the same integer type.

4   An alignment clause forces each record of the given type to be allocated at a starting address that is a multiple of the value of the given expression (that is, the address modulo the expression must be zero). An implementation may place restrictions on the allowable alignments.

5   A component clause specifies the *storage place* of a component, relative to the start of the record. The integer defined by the static expression of a component clause is a relative address expressed in storage units. The range defines the bit positions of the storage place, relative to the storage unit. The first storage unit of a record is numbered zero. The first bit of a storage unit is numbered zero. The ordering of bits in a storage unit is machine-dependent and may extend to adjacent storage units. (For a specific machine, the size in bits of a storage unit is given by the configuration-dependent named number SYSTEM.STORAGE_UNIT.) Whether a component is allowed to overlap a storage boundary, and if so, how, is implementation-defined.

6   At most one component clause is allowed for each component of the record type, including for each discriminant (component clauses may be given for some, all, or none of the components). If no component clause is given for a component, then the choice of the storage place for the component is left to the compiler. If component clauses are given for all components, the record representation clause completely specifies the representation of the record type and must be obeyed exactly by the compiler.

7   Storage places within a record variant must not overlap, but overlap of the storage for distinct variants is allowed. Each component clause must allow for enough storage space to accommodate every allowable value of the component. A component clause is only allowed for a component if any constraint on this component or on any of its subcomponents is static.

8   An implementation may generate names that denote implementation-dependent components (for example, one containing the offset of another component). Such implementation-dependent names can be used in record representation clauses (these names need not be simple names; for example, they could be implementation-dependent attributes).

9   *Example:*

```
WORD : constant := 4;  --  storage unit is byte, 4 bytes per word

type STATE       is (A, M, W, P);
type MODE        is (FIX, DEC, EXP, SIGNIF);

type BYTE_MASK   is array (0 .. 7) of BOOLEAN;
type STATE_MASK  is array (STATE) of BOOLEAN;
type MODE_MASK   is array (MODE) of BOOLEAN;

type PROGRAM_STATUS_WORD is
  record
      SYSTEM_MASK      : BYTE_MASK;
      PROTECTION_KEY   : INTEGER range 0 .. 3;
      MACHINE_STATE    : STATE_MASK;
      INTERRUPT_CAUSE  : INTERRUPTION_CODE;
      ILC              : INTEGER range 0 .. 3;
      CC               : INTEGER range 0 .. 3;
      PROGRAM_MASK     : MODE_MASK;
      INST_ADDRESS     : ADDRESS;
  end record;
```

13.4 Record Representation Clauses   13-6

```
for PROGRAM_STATUS_WORD use
   record at mod 8;
      SYSTEM_MASK       at 0*WORD   range 0    .. 7;
      PROTECTION_KEY    at 0*WORD   range 10   .. 11;   --  bits 8, 9 unused
      MACHINE_STATE     at 0*WORD   range 12   .. 15;
      INTERRUPT_CAUSE   at 0*WORD   range 16   .. 31;
      ILC               at 1*WORD   range 0    .. 1;    --  second word
      CC                at 1*WORD   range 2    .. 3;
      PROGRAM_MASK      at 1*WORD   range 4    .. 7;
      INST_ADDRESS      at 1*WORD   range 8    .. 31;
   end record;

for PROGRAM_STATUS_WORD'SIZE use 8*SYSTEM.STORAGE_UNIT;
```

Note on the example:

The record representation clause defines the record layout. The length clause guarantees that exactly eight storage units are used. [10]

References: allow 1.6, attribute 4.1.4, constant 3.2.1, constraint 3.3, discriminant 3.7.1, integer type 3.5.4, must [11] 1.6, named number 3.2, range 3.5, record component 3.7, record type 3.7, simple expression 4.4, simple name 4.1, static constraint 4.9, static expression 4.9, storage unit 13.7, subcomponent 3.3, system package 13.7, variant 3.7.3

13.5 Address Clauses

An address clause specifies a required address in storage for an entity. [1]

    address_clause ::= **for** simple_name **use at** simple_expression; [2]

The expression given after the reserved word **at** must be of the type ADDRESS defined in the [3] package SYSTEM (see 13.7); this package must be named by a with clause that applies to the compilation unit in which the address clause occurs. The conventions that define the interpretation of a value of the type ADDRESS as an address, as an interrupt level, or whatever it may be, are implementation-dependent. The allowed nature of the simple name and the meaning of the corresponding address are as follows:

(a) Name of an object: the address is that required for the object (variable or constant). [4]

(b) Name of a subprogram, package, or task unit: the address is that required for the machine [5] code associated with the body of the program unit.

(c) Name of a single entry: the address specifies a hardware interrupt to which the single entry is [6] to be linked.

If the simple name is that of a single task, the address clause is understood to refer to the task unit [7] and not to the task object. In all cases, the address clause is only legal if exactly one declaration with this identifier occurs earlier, immediately within the same declarative part, package specification, or task specification. A name declared by a renaming declaration is not allowed as the simple name.

Address clauses should not be used to achieve overlays of objects or overlays of program units. [8] Nor should a given interrupt be linked to more than one entry. Any program using address clauses to achieve such effects is erroneous.

9   *Example:*

    for CONTROL **use at** 16#0020#; -- assuming that SYSTEM.ADDRESS is an integer type

Notes:

10   The above rules imply that if two subprograms overload each other and are visible at a given point, an address clause for any of them is not legal at this point. Similarly if a task specification declares entries that overload each other, they cannot be interrupt entries. The syntax does not allow an address clause for a library unit. An implementation may provide pragmas for the specification of program overlays.

11   *References:* address predefined type 13.7, apply 10.1.1, compilation unit 10.1, constant 3.2.1, entity 3.1, entry 9.5, erroneous 1.6, expression 4.4, library unit 10.1, name 4.1, object 3.2, package 7, pragma 2.8, program unit 6, reserved word 2.9, simple expression 4.4, simple name 4.1, subprogram 6, subprogram body 6.3, system package 13.7, task body 9.1, task object 9.2, task unit 9, type 3.3, variable 3.2.1, with clause 10.1.1

13.5.1 Interrupts

1   An address clause given for an entry associates the entry with some device that may cause an interrupt; such an entry is referred to in this section as an *interrupt entry*. If control information is supplied upon an interrupt, it is passed to an associated interrupt entry as one or more parameters of mode **in**; only parameters of this mode are allowed.

2   An interrupt acts as an entry call issued by a hardware task whose priority is higher than the priority of the main program, and also higher than the priority of any user-defined task (that is, any task whose type is declared by a task unit in the program). The entry call may be an ordinary entry call, a timed entry call, or a conditional entry call, depending on the kind of interrupt and on the implementation.

3   If a select statement contains both a terminate alternative and an accept alternative for an interrupt entry, then an implementation may impose further requirements for the selection of the terminate alternative in addition to those given in section 9.4.

4   *Example:*

    task INTERRUPT_HANDLER **is**
      entry DONE;
      for DONE **use at** 16#40#; -- assuming that SYSTEM.ADDRESS is an integer type
    end INTERRUPT_HANDLER;

Notes:

5   Interrupt entry calls need only have the semantics described above; they may be implemented by having the hardware directly execute the appropriate accept statements.

6   Queued interrupts correspond to ordinary entry calls. Interrupts that are lost if not immediately processed correspond to conditional entry calls. It is a consequence of the priority rules that an accept statement executed in response to an interrupt takes precedence over ordinary, user-defined tasks, and can be executed without first invoking a scheduling action.

One of the possible effects of an address clause for an interrupt entry is to specify the priority of the interrupt (directly or indirectly). Direct calls to an interrupt entry are allowed.

References: accept alternative 9.7.1, accept statement 9.5, address predefined type 13.7, allow 1.6, conditional entry call 9.7.2, entry 9.5, entry call 9.5, mode 6.1, parameter of a subprogram 6.2, priority of a task 9.8, select alternative 9.7.1, select statement 9.7, system package 13.7, task 9, terminate alternative 9.7.1, timed entry call 9.7.3

13.6 Change of Representation

At most one representation clause is allowed for a given type and a given aspect of its representation. Hence, if an alternative representation is needed, it is necessary to declare a second type, derived from the first, and to specify a different representation for the second type.

Example:

```
--  PACKED_DESCRIPTOR and DESCRIPTOR are two different types
--  with identical characteristics, apart from their representation

type DESCRIPTOR is
   record
      --  components of a descriptor
   end record;

type PACKED_DESCRIPTOR is new DESCRIPTOR;

for PACKED_DESCRIPTOR use
   record
      --  component clauses for some or for all components
   end record;
```

Change of representation can now be accomplished by assignment with explicit type conversions:

```
D  : DESCRIPTOR;
P  : PACKED_DESCRIPTOR;

P  := PACKED_DESCRIPTOR(D);   --   pack D
D  := DESCRIPTOR(P);          --   unpack P
```

References: assignment 5.2, derived type 3.4, type 3.3, type conversion 4.6, type declaration 3.1, representation clause 13.1

13.7 The Package System

For each implementation there is a predefined library package called SYSTEM which includes the definitions of certain configuration-dependent characteristics. The specification of the package SYSTEM is implementation-dependent and must be given in Appendix F. The visible part of this package must contain at least the following declarations.

2
```
package SYSTEM is
   type ADDRESS    is implementation_defined;
   type NAME       is implementation_defined_enumeration_type;

   SYSTEM_NAME     : constant NAME   := implementation_defined;

   STORAGE_UNIT    : constant := implementation_defined;
   MEMORY_SIZE     : constant := implementation_defined;

   -- System-Dependent Named Numbers:

   MIN_INT         : constant := implementation_defined;
   MAX_INT         : constant := implementation_defined;
   MAX_DIGITS      : constant := implementation_defined;
   MAX_MANTISSA    : constant := implementation_defined;
   FINE_DELTA      : constant := implementation_defined;
   TICK            : constant := implementation_defined;

   -- Other System-Dependent Declarations

   subtype PRIORITY is INTEGER range implementation_defined;

   ...
end SYSTEM;
```

3   The type ADDRESS is the type of the addresses provided in address clauses; it is also the type of the result delivered by the attribute ADDRESS. Values of the enumeration type NAME are the names of alternative machine configurations handled by the implementation; one of these is the constant SYSTEM_NAME. The named number STORAGE_UNIT is the number of bits per storage unit; the named number MEMORY_SIZE is the number of available storage units in the configuration; these named numbers are of the type *universal_integer*.

4   An alternative form of the package SYSTEM, with given values for any of SYSTEM_NAME, STORAGE_UNIT, and MEMORY_SIZE, can be obtained by means of the corresponding pragmas. These pragmas are only allowed at the start of a compilation, before the first compilation unit (if any) of the compilation.

5   **pragma** SYSTEM_NAME (enumeration_literal);

6   The effect of the above pragma is to use the enumeration literal with the specified identifier for the definition of the constant SYSTEM_NAME. This pragma is only allowed if the specified identifier corresponds to one of the literals of the type NAME.

7   **pragma** STORAGE_UNIT (numeric_literal);

8   The effect of the above pragma is to use the value of the specified numeric literal for the definition of the named number STORAGE_UNIT.

9   **pragma** MEMORY_SIZE (numeric_literal);

10 The effect of the above pragma is to use the value of the specified numeric literal for the definition of the named number MEMORY_SIZE.

The compilation of any of these pragmas causes an implicit recompilation of the package SYSTEM. Consequently any compilation unit that names SYSTEM in its context clause becomes obsolete after this implicit recompilation. An implementation may impose further limitations on the use of these pragmas. For example, an implementation may allow them only at the start of the first compilation, when creating a new program library.   11

Note:

It is a consequence of the visibility rules that a declaration given in the package SYSTEM is not visible in a compilation unit unless this package is mentioned by a with clause that applies (directly or indirectly) to the compilation unit.   12

References: address clause 13.5, apply 10.1.1, attribute 4.1.4, compilation unit 10.1, declaration 3.1, enumeration literal 3.5.1, enumeration type 3.5.1, identifier 2.3, library unit 10.1, must 1.6, named number 3.2, number declaration 3.2.2, numeric literal 2.4, package 7, package specification 7.1, pragma 2.8, program library 10.1, type 3.3, visibility 8.3, visible part 7.2, with clause 10.1.1   13

13.7.1 System-Dependent Named Numbers

Within the package SYSTEM, the following named numbers are declared. The numbers FINE_DELTA and TICK are of the type *universal_real*; the others are of the type *universal_integer*.   1

MIN_INT	The smallest (most negative) value of all predefined integer types.	2
MAX_INT	The largest (most positive) value of all predefined integer types.	3
MAX_DIGITS	The largest value allowed for the number of significant decimal digits in a floating point constraint.	4
MAX_MANTISSA	The largest possible number of binary digits in the mantissa of model numbers of a fixed point subtype.	5
FINE_DELTA	The smallest delta allowed in a fixed point constraint that has the range constraint -1.0 .. 1.0.	6
TICK	The basic clock period, in seconds.	7

References: allow 1.6, delta of a fixed point constraint 3.5.9, fixed point constraint 3.5.9, floating point constraint 3.5.7, integer type 3.5.4, model number 3.5.6, named number 3.2, package 7, range constraint 3.5, system package 13.7, type 3.3, universal_integer type 3.5.4, universal_real type 3.5.6   8

13.7.2 Representation Attributes

1 The values of certain implementation-dependent characteristics can be obtained by interrogating appropriate *representation attributes*. These attributes are described below.

2 For any object, program unit, label, or entry X:

3 X'ADDRESS   Yields the address of the first of the storage units allocated to X. For a sub-program, package, task unit or label, this value refers to the machine code associated with the corresponding body or statement. For an entry for which an address clause has been given, the value refers to the corresponding hardware interrupt. The value of this attribute is of the type ADDRESS defined in the package SYSTEM.

4 For any type or subtype X, or for any object X:

5 X'SIZE   Applied to an object, yields the number of bits allocated to hold the object. Applied to a type or subtype, yields the minimum number of bits that is needed by the implementation to hold any possible object of this type or sub-type. The value of this attribute is of the type *universal_integer*.

6 For the above two representation attributes, if the prefix is the name of a function, the attribute is understood to be an attribute of the function (not of the result of calling the function). Similarly, if the type of the prefix is an access type, the attribute is understood to be an attribute of the prefix (not of the designated object: attributes of the latter can be written with a prefix ending with the reserved word **all**).

7 For any component C of a record object R:

8 R.C'POSITION   Yields the offset, from the start of the first storage unit occupied by the record, of the first of the storage units occupied by C. This offset is measured in storage units. The value of this attribute is of the type *universal_integer*.

9 R.C'FIRST_BIT   Yields the offset, from the start of the first of the storage units occupied by C, of the first bit occupied by C. This offset is measured in bits. The value of this attribute is of the type *universal_integer*.

10 R.C'LAST_BIT   Yields the offset, from the start of the first of the storage units occupied by C, of the last bit occupied by C. This offset is measured in bits. The value of this attribute is of the type *universal_integer*.

11 For any access type or subtype T:

12 T'STORAGE_SIZE   Yields the total number of storage units reserved for the collection associated with the base type of T. The value of this attribute is of the type *universal_integer*.

13 For any task type or task object T:

14 T'STORAGE_SIZE   Yields the number of storage units reserved for each activation of a task of the type T or for the activation of the task object T. The value of this attribute is of the type *universal_integer*.

Notes:

For a task object X, the attribute X'SIZE gives the number of bits used to hold the object X, whereas X'STORAGE_SIZE gives the number of storage units allocated for the activation of the task designated by X. For a formal parameter X, if parameter passing is achieved by copy, then the attribute X'ADDRESS yields the address of the local copy; if parameter passing is by reference, then the address is that of the actual parameter. 15

References: access subtype 3.8, access type 3.8, activation 9.3, actual parameter 6.2, address clause 13.5, address predefined type 13.7, attribute 4.1.4, base type 3.3, collection 3.8, component 3.3, entry 9.5, formal parameter 6.1 6.2, label 5.1, object 3.2, package 7, package body 7.1, parameter passing 6.2, program unit 6, record object 3.7, statement 5, storage unit 13.7, subprogram 6, subprogram body 6.3, subtype 3.3, system predefined package 13.7, task 9, task body 9.1, task object 9.2, task type 9.2, task unit 9, type 3.3, universal_integer type 3.5.4 16

13.7.3 Representation Attributes of Real Types

For every real type or subtype T, the following machine-dependent attributes are defined, which are not related to the model numbers. Programs using these attributes may thereby exploit properties that go beyond the minimal properties associated with the numeric type (see section 4.5.7 for the rules defining the accuracy of operations with real operands). Precautions must therefore be taken when using these machine-dependent attributes if portability is to be ensured. 1

For both floating point and fixed point types: 2

T'MACHINE_ROUNDS   Yields the value TRUE if every predefined arithmetic operation on values of the base type of T either returns an exact result or performs rounding; yields the value FALSE otherwise. The value of this attribute is of the predefined type BOOLEAN. 3

T'MACHINE_OVERFLOWS   Yields the value TRUE if every predefined operation on values of the base type of T either provides a correct result, or raises the exception NUMERIC_ERROR in overflow situations (see 4.5.7); yields the value FALSE otherwise. The value of this attribute is of the predefined type BOOLEAN. 4

For floating point types, the following attributes provide characteristics of the underlying machine representation, in terms of the canonical form defined in section 3.5.7: 5

T'MACHINE_RADIX   Yields the value of the *radix* used by the machine representation of the base type of T. The value of this attribute is of the type *universal_integer*. 6

T'MACHINE_MANTISSA   Yields the number of digits in the *mantissa* for the machine representation of the base type of T (the digits are extended digits in the range 0 to T'MACHINE_RADIX -1). The value of this attribute is of the type *universal_integer*. 7

T'MACHINE_EMAX   Yields the largest value of *exponent* for the machine representation of the base type of T. The value of this attribute is of the type *universal_integer*. 8

T'MACHINE_EMIN   Yields the smallest (most negative) value of *exponent* for the machine representation of the base type of T. The value of this attribute is of the type *universal_integer*. 9

Note:

10 For many machines the largest machine representable number of type F is almost

   (F'MACHINE_RADIX)∗∗(F'MACHINE_EMAX),

11 and the smallest positive representable number is

   F'MACHINE_RADIX ∗∗ (F'MACHINE_EMIN - 1)

12 *References:* arithmetic operator 4.5, attribute 4.1.4, base type 3.3, boolean predefined type 3.5.3, false boolean
value 3.5.3, fixed point type 3.5.9, floating point type 3.5.7, model number 3.5.6, numeric type 3.5, numeric_error
exception 11.1, predefined operation 3.3.3, radix 3.5.7, real type 3.5.6, subtype 3.3, true boolean value 3.5.3, type
3.3, universal_integer type 3.5.4

13.8 Machine Code Insertions

1 A machine code insertion can be achieved by a call to a procedure whose sequence of statements
contains code statements.

2   code_statement ::= type_mark'*record*_aggregate;

3 A code statement is only allowed in the sequence of statements of a procedure body. If a
procedure body contains code statements, then within this procedure body the only allowed form
of statement is a code statement (labeled or not), the only allowed declarative items are use
clauses, and no exception handler is allowed (comments and pragmas are allowed as usual).

4 Each machine instruction appears as a record aggregate of a record type that defines the corresponding instruction. The base type of the type mark of a code statement must be declared
within the predefined library package called MACHINE_CODE; this package must be named by a
with clause that applies to the compilation unit in which the code statement occurs. An implementation is not required to provide such a package.

5 An implementation is allowed to impose further restrictions on the record aggregates allowed in
code statements. For example, it may require that expressions contained in such aggregates be
static expressions.

6 An implementation may provide machine-dependent pragmas specifying register conventions and
calling conventions. Such pragmas must be documented in Appendix F.

7 *Example:*

```
M  : MASK;
procedure SET_MASK; pragma INLINE(SET_MASK);

procedure SET_MASK is
   use MACHINE_CODE;
begin
   SI_FORMAT'(CODE => SSM, B => M'BASE_REG, D => M'DISP);
   --  M'BASE_REG and M'DISP are implementation-specific predefined attributes
end;
```

References: allow 1.6, apply 10.1.1, comment 2.7, compilation unit 10.1, declarative item 3.9, exception handler   8
11.2, inline pragma 6.3.2, labeled statement 5.1, library unit 10.1, package 7, pragma 2.8, procedure 6 6.1, procedure
body 6.3, record aggregate 4.3.1, record type 3.7, sequence of statements 5.1, statement 5, static expression 4.9, use
clause 8.4, with clause 10.1.1

13.9 Interface to Other Languages

A subprogram written in another language can be called from an Ada program provided that all   1
communication is achieved via parameters and function results. A pragma of the form

   pragma INTERFACE (*language*_name, *subprogram*_name);   2

must be given for each such subprogram; a subprogram name is allowed to stand for several   3
overloaded subprograms. This pragma is allowed at the place of a declarative item, and must apply
in this case to a subprogram declared by an earlier declarative item of the same declarative part or
package specification. The pragma is also allowed for a library unit; in this case the pragma must
appear after the subprogram declaration, and before any subsequent compilation unit. The
pragma specifies the other language (and thereby the calling conventions) and informs the compiler that an object module will be supplied for the corresponding subprogram. A body is not
allowed for such a subprogram (not even in the form of a body stub) since the instructions of the
subprogram are written in another language.

This capability need not be provided by all implementations.   An implementation may place   4
restrictions on the allowable forms and places of parameters and calls.

Example: 5

```
package FORT_LIB is
   function SQRT (X : FLOAT) return FLOAT;
   function EXP  (X : FLOAT) return FLOAT;
private
   pragma INTERFACE(FORTRAN, SQRT);
   pragma INTERFACE(FORTRAN, EXP);
end FORT_LIB;
```

Notes:

The conventions used by other language processors that call Ada programs are not part of the Ada   6
language definition. Such conventions must be defined by these other language processors.

The pragma INTERFACE is not defined for generic subprograms.   7

References: allow 1.6, body stub 10.2, compilation unit 10.1, declaration 3.1, declarative item 3.9, declarative part   8
3.9, function result 6.5, library unit 10.1, must 1.6, name 4.1, overloaded subprogram 6.6, package specification 7.1,
parameter of a subprogram 6.2, pragma 2.8, subprogram 6, subprogram body 6.3, subprogram call 6.4, subprogram
declaration 6.1

13.10 Unchecked Programming

1   The predefined generic library subprograms UNCHECKED_DEALLOCATION and UNCHECKED_CONVERSION are used for unchecked storage deallocation and for unchecked type conversions.

2
```
generic
    type OBJECT is limited private;
    type NAME   is access OBJECT;
procedure UNCHECKED_DEALLOCATION(X : in out NAME);
```

3
```
generic
    type SOURCE is limited private;
    type TARGET is limited private;
function UNCHECKED_CONVERSION(S : SOURCE) return TARGET;
```

4   *References:* generic subprogram 12.1, library unit 10.1, type 3.3

13.10.1 Unchecked Storage Deallocation

1   Unchecked storage deallocation of an object designated by a value of an access type is achieved by a call of a procedure that is obtained by instantiation of the generic procedure UNCHECKED_DEALLOCATION. For example:

```
procedure FREE is new UNCHECKED_DEALLOCATION (object_type_name, access_type_name);
```

2   Such a FREE procedure has the following effect:

3   (a)   after executing FREE(X), the value of X is **null**;

4   (b)   FREE(X), when X is already equal to **null**, has no effect;

5   (c)   FREE(X), when X is not equal to **null**, is an indication that the object designated by X is no longer required, and that the storage it occupies is to be reclaimed.

6   If X and Y designate the same object, then accessing this object through Y is erroneous if this access is performed (or attempted) after the call FREE(X); the effect of each such access is not defined by the language.

Notes:

7   It is a consequence of the visibility rules that the generic procedure UNCHECKED_DEALLOCATION is not visible in a compilation unit unless this generic procedure is mentioned by a with clause that applies to the compilation unit.

8   If X designates a task object, the call FREE(X) has no effect on the task designated by the value of this task object. The same holds for any subcomponent of the object designated by X, if this subcomponent is a task object.

9   *References:* access type 3.8, apply 10.1.1, compilation unit 10.1, designate 3.8 9.1, erroneous 1.6, generic instantiation 12.3, generic procedure 12.1, generic unit 12, library unit 10.1, null access value 3.8, object 3.2, procedure 6, procedure call 6.4, subcomponent 3.3, task 9, task object 9.2, visibility 8.3, with clause 10.1.1

13.10.2 Unchecked Type Conversions

An unchecked type conversion can be achieved by a call of a function that is obtained by instantiation of the generic function UNCHECKED_CONVERSION.

The effect of an unchecked conversion is to return the (uninterpreted) parameter value as a value of the target type, that is, the bit pattern defining the source value is returned unchanged as the bit pattern defining a value of the target type. An implementation may place restrictions on unchecked conversions, for example, restrictions depending on the respective sizes of objects of the source and target type. Such restrictions must be documented in appendix F.

Whenever unchecked conversions are used, it is the programmer's responsibility to ensure that these conversions maintain the properties that are guaranteed by the language for objects of the target type. Programs that violate these properties by means of unchecked conversions are erroneous.

Note:

It is a consequence of the visibility rules that the generic function UNCHECKED_CONVERSION is not visible in a compilation unit unless this generic function is mentioned by a with clause that applies to the compilation unit.

References: apply 10.1.1, compilation unit 10.1, erroneous 1.6, generic function 12.1, instantiation 12.3, parameter of a subprogram 6.2, type 3.3, with clause 10.1.1

14. Input-Output

Input-output is provided in the language by means of predefined packages. The generic packages SEQUENTIAL_IO and DIRECT_IO define input-output operations applicable to files containing elements of a given type. Additional operations for text input-output are supplied in the package TEXT_IO. The package IO_EXCEPTIONS defines the exceptions needed by the above three packages. Finally, a package LOW_LEVEL_IO is provided for direct control of peripheral devices.

References: direct_io package 14.2 14.2.4, io_exceptions package 14.5, low_level_io package 14.6, sequential_io package 14.2 14.2.2, text_io package 14.3

14.1 External Files and File Objects

Values input from the external environment of the program, or output to the environment, are considered to occupy *external files*. An external file can be anything external to the program that can produce a value to be read or receive a value to be written. An external file is identified by a string (the *name*). A second string (the *form*) gives further system-dependent characteristics that may be associated with the file, such as the physical organization or access rights. The conventions governing the interpretation of such strings must be documented in Appendix F.

Input and output operations are expressed as operations on objects of some *file type*, rather than directly in terms of the external files. In the remainder of this chapter, the term *file* is always used to refer to a file object; the term *external file* is used otherwise. The values transferred for a given file must all be of one type.

Input-output for sequential files of values of a single element type is defined by means of the generic package SEQUENTIAL_IO. The skeleton of this package is given below.

```
with IO_EXCEPTIONS;
generic
   type ELEMENT_TYPE is private;
package SEQUENTIAL_IO is
   type FILE_TYPE is limited private;

   type FILE_MODE is (IN_FILE, OUT_FILE);
   ...
   procedure OPEN (FILE : in out FILE_TYPE; ...);
   ...
   procedure READ  (FILE : in FILE_TYPE; ITEM : out ELEMENT_TYPE);
   procedure WRITE (FILE : in FILE_TYPE; ITEM : in ELEMENT_TYPE);
   ...
end SEQUENTIAL_IO;
```

In order to define sequential input-output for a given element type, an instantiation of this generic unit, with the given type as actual parameter, must be declared. The resulting package contains the declaration of a file type (called FILE_TYPE) for files of such elements, as well as the operations applicable to these files, such as the OPEN, READ, and WRITE procedures.

External Files and File Objects 14.1

5   Input-output for direct access files is likewise defined by a generic package called DIRECT_IO. Input-output in human-readable form is defined by the (nongeneric) package TEXT_IO.

6   Before input or output operations can be performed on a file, the file must first be associated with an external file. While such an association is in effect, the file is said to be *open*, and otherwise the file is said to be *closed*.

7   The language does not define what happens to external files after the completion of the main program (in particular, if corresponding files have not been closed). The effect of input-output for access types is implementation-dependent.

8   An open file has a *current mode*, which is a value of one of the enumeration types

```
type FILE_MODE is (IN_FILE, INOUT_FILE, OUT_FILE);   --  for DIRECT_IO
type FILE_MODE is (IN_FILE, OUT_FILE);               --  for SEQUENTIAL_IO and TEXT_IO
```

9   These values correspond respectively to the cases where only reading, both reading and writing, or only writing are to be performed. The mode of a file can be changed.

10   Several file management operations are common to the three input-output packages. These operations are described in section 14.2.1 for sequential and direct files. Any additional effects concerning text input-output are described in section 14.3.1.

11   The exceptions that can be raised by a call of an input-output subprogram are all defined in the package IO_EXCEPTIONS; the situations in which they can be raised are described, either following the description of the subprogram (and in section 14.4), or in Appendix F in the case of error situations that are implementation-dependent.

Notes:

12   Each instantiation of the generic packages SEQUENTIAL_IO and DIRECT_IO declares a different type FILE_TYPE; in the case of TEXT_IO, the type FILE_TYPE is unique.

13   A bidirectional device can often be modeled as two sequential files associated with the device, one of mode IN_FILE, and one of mode OUT_FILE. An implementation may restrict the number of files that may be associated with a given external file. The effect of sharing an external file in this way by several file objects is implementation-dependent.

14   *References:* create procedure 14.2.1, current index 14.2, current size 14.2, delete procedure 14.2.1, direct access 14.2, direct file procedure 14.2, direct_io package 14.1 14.2, enumeration type 3.5.1, exception 11, file mode 14.2.3, generic instantiation 12.3, index 14.2, input file 14.2.2, io_exceptions package 14.5, open file 14.1, open procedure 14.2.1, output file 14.2.2, read procedure 14.2.4, sequential access 14.2, sequential file 14.2, sequential input-output 14.2.2, sequential_io package 14.2 14.2.2, string 3.6.3, text_io package 14.3, write procedure 14.2.4

14.2   Sequential and Direct Files

1   Two kinds of access to external files are defined: *sequential access* and *direct access*. The corresponding file types and the associated operations are provided by the generic packages SEQUENTIAL_IO and DIRECT_IO. A file object to be used for sequential access is called a *sequential file*, and one to be used for direct access is called a *direct file*.

2   For sequential access, the file is viewed as a sequence of values that are transferred in the order of their appearance (as produced by the program or by the environment). When the file is opened, transfer starts from the beginning of the file.

For direct access, the file is viewed as a set of elements occupying consecutive positions in linear   3
order; a value can be transferred to or from an element of the file at any selected position. The
position of an element is specified by its *index*, which is a number, greater than zero, of the
implementation-defined integer type COUNT. The first element, if any, has index one; the index of
the last element, if any, is called the *current size*; the current size is zero if there are no elements.
The current size is a property of the external file.

An open direct file has a *current index*, which is the index that will be used by the next read or write   4
operation. When a direct file is opened, the current index is set to one. The current index of a direct
file is a property of a file object, not of an external file.

All three file modes are allowed for direct files. The only allowed modes for sequential files are the   5
modes IN_FILE and OUT_FILE.

References: count type 14.3, file mode 14.1, in_file 14.1, out_file 14.1   6

14.2.1 File Management

The procedures and functions described in this section provide for the control of external files; their   1
declarations are repeated in each of the three packages for sequential, direct, and text input-
output. For text input-output, the procedures CREATE, OPEN, and RESET have additional effects
described in section 14.3.1.

    procedure CREATE(FILE : **in out** FILE_TYPE;   2
                       MODE : **in** FILE_MODE := *default_mode*;
                       NAME : **in** STRING := "";
                       FORM : **in** STRING := "");

        Establishes a new external file, with the given name and form, and associates this   3
        external file with the given file. The given file is left open. The current mode of the
        given file is set to the given access mode. The default access mode is the mode
        OUT_FILE for sequential and text input-output; it is the mode INOUT_FILE for
        direct input-output. For direct access, the size of the created file is
        implementation-dependent. A null string for NAME specifies an external file that is
        not accessible after the completion of the main program (a temporary file). A null
        string for FORM specifies the use of the default options of the implementation for
        the external file.

        The exception STATUS_ERROR is raised if the given file is already open. The   4
        exception NAME_ERROR is raised if the string given as NAME does not allow the
        identification of an external file. The exception USE_ERROR is raised if, for the
        specified mode, the environment does not support creation of an external file with
        the given name (in the absence of NAME_ERROR) and form.

  procedure OPEN(FILE : **in out** FILE_TYPE;   5
                MODE : **in** FILE_MODE;
                NAME : **in** STRING;
                FORM : **in** STRING := "");

        Associates the given file with an existing external file having the given name and   6
        form, and sets the current mode of the given file to the given mode. The given file
        is left open.

7   The exception STATUS_ERROR is raised if the given file is already open. The exception NAME_ERROR is raised if the string given as NAME does not allow the identification of an external file; in particular, this exception is raised if no external file with the given name exists. The exception USE_ERROR is raised if, for the specified mode, the environment does not support opening for an external file with the given name (in the absence of NAME_ERROR) and form.

8   **procedure** CLOSE(FILE : **in out** FILE_TYPE);

9   Severs the association between the given file and its associated external file. The given file is left closed.

10   The exception STATUS_ERROR is raised if the given file is not open.

11   **procedure** DELETE(FILE : **in out** FILE_TYPE);

12   Deletes the external file associated with the given file. The given file is closed, and the external file ceases to exist.

13   The exception STATUS_ERROR is raised if the given file is not open. The exception USE_ERROR is raised if (as fully defined in Appendix F) deletion of the external file is not supported by the environment.

14   **procedure** RESET(FILE : **in out** FILE_TYPE; MODE : **in** FILE_MODE);
     procedure RESET(FILE : **in out** FILE_TYPE);

15   Resets the given file so that reading from or writing to its elements can be restarted from the beginning of the file; in particular, for direct access this means that the current index is set to one. If a MODE parameter is supplied, the current mode of the given file is set to the given mode.

16   The exception STATUS_ERROR is raised if the file is not open. The exception USE_ERROR is raised if the environment does not support resetting for the external file and, also, if the environment does not support resetting to the specified mode for the external file.

17   **function** MODE(FILE : **in** FILE_TYPE) **return** FILE_MODE;

18   Returns the current mode of the given file.

19   The exception STATUS_ERROR is raised if the file is not open.

20   **function** NAME(FILE : **in** FILE_TYPE) **return** STRING;

21   Returns a string which uniquely identifies the external file currently associated with the given file (and may thus be used in an OPEN operation). If an environment allows alternative specifications of the name (for example, abbreviations), the string returned by the function should correspond to a full specification of the name.

22   The exception STATUS_ERROR is raised if the given file is not open.

function FORM(FILE : **in** FILE_TYPE) **return** STRING; 23

> Returns the form string for the external file currently associated with the given file. 24
> If an environment allows alternative specifications of the form (for example,
> abbreviations using default options), the string returned by the function should cor-
> respond to a full specification (that is, it should indicate explicitly all options
> selected, including default options).

> The exception STATUS_ERROR is raised if the given file is not open. 25

function IS_OPEN(FILE : **in** FILE_TYPE) **return** BOOLEAN; 26

> Returns TRUE if the file is open (that is, if it is associated with an external file), 27
> otherwise returns FALSE.

References: current mode 14.1, current size 14.1, closed file 14.1, direct access 14.2, external file 14.1, file 14.1, 28
file_mode type 14.1, file_type type 14.1, form string 14.1, inout_file 14.2.4, mode 14.1, name string 14.1, name_er-
ror exception 14.4, open file 14.1, out_file 14.1, status_error exception 14.4, use_error exception 14.4

14.2.2 Sequential Input-Output

The operations available for sequential input and output are described in this section. The excep- 1
tion STATUS_ERROR is raised if any of these operations is attempted for a file that is not open.

procedure READ(FILE : **in** FILE_TYPE; ITEM : **out** ELEMENT_TYPE); 2

> Operates on a file of mode IN_FILE. Reads an element from the given file, and 3
> returns the value of this element in the ITEM parameter.

> The exception MODE_ERROR is raised if the mode is not IN_FILE. The exception 4
> END_ERROR is raised if no more elements can be read from the given file. The
> exception DATA_ERROR is raised if the element read cannot be interpreted as a
> value of the type ELEMENT_TYPE ; however, an implementation is allowed to omit
> this check if performing the check is too complex.

procedure WRITE(FILE : **in** FILE_TYPE; ITEM : **in** ELEMENT_TYPE); 5

> Operates on a file of mode OUT_FILE. Writes the value of ITEM to the given file. 6

> The exception MODE_ERROR is raised if the mode is not OUT_FILE. The exception 7
> USE_ERROR is raised if the capacity of the external file is exceeded.

function END_OF_FILE(FILE : **in** FILE_TYPE) **return** BOOLEAN; 8

> Operates on a file of mode IN_FILE. Returns TRUE if no more elements can be read 9
> from the given file; otherwise returns FALSE.

> The exception MODE_ERROR is raised if the mode is not IN_FILE. 10

References: data_error exception 14.4, element 14.1, element_type 14.1, end_error exception 14.4, external file 11
14.1, file 14.1, file mode 14.1, file_type 14.1, in_file 14.1, mode_error exception 14.4, out_file 14.1, status_error
exception 14.4, use_error exception 14.4

14.2.3 Specification of the Package Sequential_IO

```
with IO_EXCEPTIONS;
generic
   type ELEMENT_TYPE is private;
package SEQUENTIAL_IO is

   type FILE_TYPE  is limited private;

   type FILE_MODE is (IN_FILE, OUT_FILE);


   -- File management

   procedure CREATE (FILE    : in out FILE_TYPE;
                     MODE : in FILE_MODE := OUT_FILE;
                     NAME : in STRING := "";
                     FORM : in STRING := "");

   procedure OPEN   (FILE    : in out FILE_TYPE;
                     MODE : in FILE_MODE;
                     NAME : in STRING;
                     FORM : in STRING := "");

   procedure CLOSE  (FILE : in out FILE_TYPE);
   procedure DELETE (FILE : in out FILE_TYPE);
   procedure RESET  (FILE : in out FILE_TYPE; MODE : in FILE_MODE);
   procedure RESET  (FILE : in out FILE_TYPE);

   function MODE  (FILE : in FILE_TYPE) return FILE_MODE;
   function NAME  (FILE : in FILE_TYPE) return STRING;
   function FORM  (FILE : in FILE_TYPE) return STRING;

   function IS_OPEN (FILE : in FILE_TYPE) return BOOLEAN;

   -- Input and output operations

   procedure READ  (FILE : in FILE_TYPE; ITEM : out ELEMENT_TYPE);
   procedure WRITE (FILE : in FILE_TYPE; ITEM : in ELEMENT_TYPE);

   function END_OF_FILE(FILE : in FILE_TYPE) return BOOLEAN;

   -- Exceptions

   STATUS_ERROR : exception renames IO_EXCEPTIONS.STATUS_ERROR;
   MODE_ERROR   : exception renames IO_EXCEPTIONS.MODE_ERROR;
   NAME_ERROR   : exception renames IO_EXCEPTIONS.NAME_ERROR;
   USE_ERROR    : exception renames IO_EXCEPTIONS.USE_ERROR;
   DEVICE_ERROR : exception renames IO_EXCEPTIONS.DEVICE_ERROR;
   END_ERROR    : exception renames IO_EXCEPTIONS.END_ERROR;
   DATA_ERROR   : exception renames IO_EXCEPTIONS.DATA_ERROR;

private
   -- implementation-dependent
end SEQUENTIAL_IO;
```

References: close procedure 14.2.1, create procedure 14.2.1, data_error exception 14.4, delete procedure 14.2.1, device_error exception 14.4, end_error exception 14.4, end_of_file function 14.2.2, file_mode 14.1, file_type 14.1, form function 14.2.1, in_file 14.1, io_exceptions 14.4, is_open function 14.2.1, mode function 14.2.1, mode_error exception 14.4, name function 14.2.1, name_error exception 14.4, open procedure 14.2.1, out_file 14.1, read procedure 14.2.2, reset procedure 14.2.1, sequential_io package 14.2 14.2.2, status_error exception 14.4, use_error exception 14.4, write procedure 14.2.2, 2

14.2.4 Direct Input-Output

The operations available for direct input and output are described in this section. The exception   1
STATUS_ERROR is raised if any of these operations is attempted for a file that is not open.

procedure READ(FILE : **in** FILE_TYPE;   ITEM   : **out** ELEMENT_TYPE;   2
                                      FROM : **in**   POSITIVE_COUNT);
procedure READ(FILE : **in** FILE_TYPE;   ITEM   : **out** ELEMENT_TYPE);

> Operates on a file of mode IN_FILE or INOUT_FILE. In the case of the first form,   3
> sets the current index of the given file to the index value given by the parameter
> FROM. Then (for both forms) returns, in the parameter ITEM, the value of the
> element whose position in the given file is specified by the current index of the file;
> finally, increases the current index by one.

> The exception MODE_ERROR is raised if the mode of the given file is OUT_FILE.   4
> The exception END_ERROR is raised if the index to be used exceeds the size of the
> external file. The exception DATA_ERROR is raised if the element read cannot be
> interpreted as a value of the type ELEMENT_TYPE; however, an implementation is
> allowed to omit this check if performing the check is too complex.

procedure WRITE(FILE : **in** FILE_TYPE;   ITEM : **in** ELEMENT_TYPE;   5
                                      TO   : **in** POSITIVE_COUNT);
procedure WRITE(FILE : **in** FILE_TYPE;   ITEM : **in** ELEMENT_TYPE);

> Operates on a file of mode INOUT_FILE or OUT_FILE. In the case of the first form,   6
> sets the index of the given file to the index value given by the parameter TO. Then
> (for both forms) gives the value of the parameter ITEM to the element whose
> position in the given file is specified by the current index of the file;   finally,
> increases the current index by one.

> The exception MODE_ERROR is raised if the mode of the given file is IN_FILE. The   7
> exception USE_ERROR is raised if the capacity of the external file is exceeded.

procedure SET_INDEX(FILE : **in** FILE_TYPE; TO : **in** POSITIVE_COUNT);   8

> Operates on a file of any mode. Sets the current index of the given file to the given   9
> index value (which may exceed the current size of the file).

function INDEX(FILE : **in** FILE_TYPE) **return** POSITIVE_COUNT;   10

> Operates on a file of any mode. Returns the current index of the given file.   11

Direct Input-Output 14.2.4

12   function SIZE(FILE : **in** FILE_TYPE) **return** COUNT;

13   Operates on a file of any mode. Returns the current size of the external file that is
        associated with the given file.

14   function END_OF_FILE(FILE : **in** FILE_TYPE) **return** BOOLEAN;

15   Operates on a file of mode IN_FILE or INOUT_FILE. Returns TRUE if the current
        index exceeds the size of the external file; otherwise returns FALSE.

16   The exception MODE_ERROR is raised if the mode of the given file is OUT_FILE.

17   *References:* count type 14.2, current index 14.2, current size 14.2, data_error exception 14.4, element 14.1,
    element_type 14.1, end_error exception 14.4, external file 14.1, file 14.1, file mode 14.1, file_type 14.1, in_file 14.1,
    index 14.2, inout_file 14.1, mode_error exception 14.4, open file 14.1, positive_count 14.3, status_error exception
    14.4, use_error exception 14.4

14.2.5 Specification of the Package Direct_IO

```
with IO_EXCEPTIONS;
generic
   type ELEMENT_TYPE is private;
package DIRECT_IO is

   type FILE_TYPE   is limited private;

   type    FILE_MODE is (IN_FILE, INOUT_FILE, OUT_FILE);
   type    COUNT     is range 0 .. implementation_defined;
   subtype POSITIVE_COUNT is COUNT range 1 .. COUNT'LAST;


   -- File management

   procedure CREATE ( FILE  : in out FILE_TYPE;
                      MODE : in FILE_MODE := INOUT_FILE;
                      NAME : in STRING := "";
                      FORM : in STRING := "");

   procedure OPEN   ( FILE  : in out FILE_TYPE;
                      MODE : in FILE_MODE;
                      NAME : in STRING;
                      FORM : in STRING := "");

   procedure CLOSE  (FILE : in out FILE_TYPE);
   procedure DELETE (FILE : in out FILE_TYPE);
   procedure RESET  (FILE : in out FILE_TYPE; MODE : in FILE_MODE);
   procedure RESET  (FILE : in out FILE_TYPE);

   function MODE    (FILE : in FILE_TYPE) return FILE_MODE;
   function NAME    (FILE : in FILE_TYPE) return STRING;
   function FORM    (FILE : in FILE_TYPE) return STRING;

   function IS_OPEN (FILE : in FILE_TYPE) return BOOLEAN;
```

```
     -- Input and output operations

     procedure READ (FILE : in FILE_TYPE; ITEM : out ELEMENT_TYPE; FROM : POSITIVE_COUNT);
     procedure READ (FILE : in FILE_TYPE; ITEM : out ELEMENT_TYPE);

     procedure WRITE (FILE : in FILE_TYPE; ITEM : in  ELEMENT_TYPE; TO : POSITIVE_COUNT);
     procedure WRITE (FILE : in FILE_TYPE; ITEM : in  ELEMENT_TYPE);

     procedure SET_INDEX(FILE : in FILE_TYPE; TO : in POSITIVE_COUNT);

     function INDEX (FILE : in FILE_TYPE) return POSITIVE_COUNT;
     function SIZE  (FILE : in FILE_TYPE) return COUNT;

     function END_OF_FILE (FILE : in FILE_TYPE) return BOOLEAN;

     -- Exceptions

     STATUS_ERROR : exception renames IO_EXCEPTIONS.STATUS_ERROR;
     MODE_ERROR   : exception renames IO_EXCEPTIONS.MODE_ERROR;
     NAME_ERROR   : exception renames IO_EXCEPTIONS.NAME_ERROR;
     USE_ERROR    : exception renames IO_EXCEPTIONS.USE_ERROR;
     DEVICE_ERROR : exception renames IO_EXCEPTIONS.DEVICE_ERROR;
     END_ERROR    : exception renames IO_EXCEPTIONS.END_ERROR;
     DATA_ERROR   : exception renames IO_EXCEPTIONS.DATA_ERROR;

  private
     -- implementation-dependent
  end DIRECT_IO;
```

References close procedure 14.2.1, count type 14.2, create procedure 14.2.1, data_error exception 14.4, default_mode 14.2.5, delete procedure 14.2.1, device_error exception 14.4, element_type 14.2.4, end_error exception 14.4, end_of_file function 14.2.4, file_mode 14.2.5, file_type 14.2.4, form function 14.2.1, in_file 14.2.4, index function 14.2.4, inout_file 14.2.4 14.2.1, io_exceptions package 14.4, is_open function 14.2.1, mode function 14.2.1, mode_error exception 14.4, name function 14.2.1, name_error exception 14.4, open procedure 14.2.1, out_file 14.2.1, read procedure 14.2.4, set_index procedure 14.2.4, size function 14.2.4, status_error exception 14.4, use_error exception 14.4, write procedure 14.2.4 14.2.1   2

14.3 Text Input-Output

This section describes the package TEXT_IO, which provides facilities for input and output in   1
human-readable form. Each file is read or written sequentially, as a sequence of characters
grouped into lines, and as a sequence of lines grouped into pages. The specification of the package
is given below in section 14.3.10.

The facilities for file management given above, in sections 14.2.1 and 14.2.2, are available for text   2
input-output. In place of READ and WRITE, however, there are procedures GET and PUT that
input values of suitable types from text files, and output values to them. These values are provided
to the PUT procedures, and returned by the GET procedures, in a parameter ITEM. Several
overloaded procedures of these names exist, for different types of ITEM. These GET procedures
analyze the input sequences of characters as lexical elements (see Chapter 2) and return the corresponding values; the PUT procedures output the given values as appropriate lexical elements.
Procedures GET and PUT are also available that input and output individual characters treated as
character values rather than as lexical elements.

3   In addition to the procedures GET and PUT for numeric and enumeration types of ITEM that operate on text files, analogous procedures are provided that read from and write to a parameter of type STRING. These procedures perform the same analysis and composition of character sequences as their counterparts which have a file parameter.

4   For all GET and PUT procedures that operate on text files, and for many other subprograms, there are forms with and without a file parameter. Each such GET procedure operates on an input file, and each such PUT procedure operates on an output file. If no file is specified, a default input file or a default output file is used.

5   At the beginning of program execution the default input and output files are the so-called standard input file and standard output file. These files are open, have respectively the current modes IN_FILE and OUT_FILE, and are associated with two implementation-defined external files. Procedures are provided to change the current default input file and the current default output file.

6   From a logical point of view, a text file is a sequence of pages, a page is a sequence of lines, and a line is a sequence of characters; the end of a line is marked by a *line terminator*; the end of a page is marked by the combination of a line terminator immediately followed by a *page terminator*; and the end of a file is marked by the combination of a line terminator immediately followed by a page terminator and then a *file terminator*. Terminators are generated during output; either by calls of procedures provided expressly for that purpose; or implicitly as part of other operations, for example, when a bounded line length, a bounded page length, or both, have been specified for a file.

7   The actual nature of terminators is not defined by the language and hence depends on the implementation. Although terminators are recognized or generated by certain of the procedures that follow, they are not necessarily implemented as characters or as sequences of characters. Whether they are characters (and if so which ones) in any particular implementation need not concern a user who neither explicitly outputs nor explicitly inputs control characters. The effect of input or output of control characters (other than horizontal tabulation) is not defined by the language.

8   The characters of a line are numbered, starting from one; the number of a character is called its *column number*. For a line terminator, a column number is also defined: it is one more than the number of characters in the line. The lines of a page, and the pages of a file, are similarly numbered. The *current column number* is the column number of the next character or line terminator to be transferred. The *current line number* is the number of the current line. The *current page number* is the number of the current page. These numbers are values of the subtype POSITIVE_COUNT of the type COUNT (by convention, the value zero of the type COUNT is used to indicate special conditions).

```
type COUNT is range 0 .. implementation_defined;
subtype POSITIVE_COUNT is COUNT range 1 .. COUNT'LAST;
```

9   For an output file, a *maximum line length* can be specified and a *maximum page length* can be specified. If a value to be output cannot fit on the current line, for a specified maximum line length, then a new line is automatically started before the value is output; if, further, this new line cannot fit on the current page, for a specified maximum page length, then a new page is automatically started before the value is output. Functions are provided to determine the maximum line length and the maximum page length. When a file is opened with mode OUT_FILE, both values are zero: by convention, this means that the line lengths and page lengths are unbounded. (Consequently, output consists of a single line if the subprograms for explicit control of line and page structure are not used.) The constant UNBOUNDED is provided for this purpose.

10   *References:* count type 14.3.10, default current input file 14.3.2, default current output file 14.3.2, external file 14.1, file 14.1, get procedure 14.3.5, in_file 14.1, out_file 14.1, put procedure 14.3.5, read 14.2.2, sequential access 14.1, standard input file 14.3.2, standard output file 14.3.2

14.3.1 File Management

The only allowed file modes for text files are the modes IN_FILE and OUT_FILE. The subprograms [1]
given in section 14.2.1 for the control of external files, and the function END_OF_FILE given in
section 14.2.2 for sequential input-output, are also available for text files. There is also a version of
END_OF_FILE that refers to the current default input file. For text files, the procedures have the following additional effects:

- For the procedures CREATE and OPEN : After opening a file with mode OUT_FILE, the page [2]
  length and line length are unbounded (both have the conventional value zero). After opening a
  file with mode IN_FILE or OUT_FILE, the current column, current line, and current page
  numbers are set to one.

- For the procedure CLOSE: If the file has the current mode OUT_FILE, has the effect of calling [3]
  NEW_PAGE, unless the current page is already terminated; then outputs a file terminator.

- For the procedure RESET: If the file has the current mode OUT_FILE, has the effect of calling [4]
  NEW_PAGE, unless the current page is already terminated; then outputs a file terminator. If
  the new file mode is OUT_FILE, the page and line lengths are unbounded. For all modes, the
  current column, line, and page numbers are set to one.

The exception MODE_ERROR is raised by the procedure RESET upon an attempt to change the [5]
mode of a file that is either the current default input file, or the current default output file.

References: create procedure 14.2.1, current column number 14.3, current default input file 14.3, current line [6]
number 14.3, current page number 14.3, end_of_file 14.3, external file 14.1, file 14.1, file mode 14.1, file terminator
14.3, in_file 14.1, line length 14.3, mode_error exception 14.4, open procedure 14.2.1, out_file 14.1, page length
14.3, reset procedure 14.2.1

14.3.2 Default Input and Output Files

The following subprograms provide for the control of the particular default files that are used when [1]
a file parameter is omitted from a GET, PUT or other operation of text input-output described
below.

    procedure SET_INPUT(FILE : **in** FILE_TYPE); [2]

        Operates on a file of mode IN_FILE. Sets the current default input file to FILE. [3]

        The exception STATUS_ERROR is raised if the given file is not open. The exception [4]
        MODE_ERROR is raised if the mode of the given file is not IN_FILE.

    procedure SET_OUTPUT(FILE : **in** FILE_TYPE); [5]

        Operates on a file of mode OUT_FILE. Sets the current default output file to FILE. [6]

        The exception STATUS_ERROR is raised if the given file is not open. The exception [7]
        MODE_ERROR is raised if the mode of the given file is not OUT_FILE.

8   **function** STANDARD_INPUT **return** FILE_TYPE;

9   Returns the standard input file (see 14.3).

10   **function** STANDARD_OUTPUT **return** FILE_TYPE;

11   Returns the standard output file (see 14.3).

12   **function** CURRENT_INPUT **return** FILE_TYPE;

13   Returns the current default input file.

14   **function** CURRENT_OUTPUT **return** FILE_TYPE;

15   Returns the current default output file.

Note:

16   The standard input and the standard output files cannot be opened, closed, reset, or deleted, because the parameter FILE of the corresponding procedures has the mode **in out**.

17   *References:* current default file 14.3, default file 14.3, file_type 14.1, get procedure 14.3.5, mode_error exception 14.4, put procedure 14.3.5, status_error exception 14.4

14.3.3 Specification of Line and Page Lengths

1   The subprograms described in this section are concerned with the line and page structure of a file of mode OUT_FILE. They operate either on the file given as the first parameter, or, in the absence of such a file parameter, on the current default output file. They provide for output of text with a specified maximum line length or page length. In these cases, line and page terminators are output implicitly and automatically when needed. When line and page lengths are unbounded (that is, when they have the conventional value zero), as in the case of a newly opened file, new lines and new pages are only started when explicitly called for.

2   In all cases, the exception STATUS_ERROR is raised if the file to be used is not open; the exception MODE_ERROR is raised if the mode of the file is not OUT_FILE.

3   **procedure** SET_LINE_LENGTH(FILE   : **in** FILE_TYPE; TO : **in** COUNT);
     procedure SET_LINE_LENGTH(TO   : **in** COUNT);

4   Sets the maximum line length of the specified output file to the number of characters specified by TO. The value zero for TO specifies an unbounded line length.

5   The exception USE_ERROR is raised if the specified line length is inappropriate for the associated external file.

procedure SET_PAGE_LENGTH (FILE : **in** FILE_TYPE; TO : **in** COUNT);   6
procedure SET_PAGE_LENGTH (TO : **in** COUNT);

> Sets the maximum page length of the specified output file to the number of lines   7
> specified by TO. The value zero for TO specifies an unbounded page length.

> The exception USE_ERROR is raised if the specified page length is inappropriate for   8
> the associated external file.

function LINE_LENGTH(FILE : **in** FILE_TYPE) **return** COUNT;   9
function LINE_LENGTH **return** COUNT;

> Returns the maximum line length currently set for the specified output file, or zero   · 10
> if the line length is unbounded.

function PAGE_LENGTH(FILE : **in** FILE_TYPE) **return** COUNT;   11
function PAGE_LENGTH **return** COUNT;

> Returns the maximum page length currently set for the specified output file, or zero   12
> if the page length is unbounded.

References: count type 14.3, current default output file 14.3, external file 14.1, file 14.1, file_type 14.1, line 14.3,   13
line length 14.3, line terminator 14.3, maximum line length 14.3, maximum page length 14.3, mode_error exception
14.4, open file 14.1, out_file 14.1, page 14.3, page length 14.3, page terminator 14.3, status_error exception 14.4,
unbounded page length 14.3, use_error exception 14.4

14.3.4 Operations on Columns, Lines, and Pages

The subprograms described in this section provide for explicit control of line and page structure;   1
they operate either on the file given as the first parameter, or, in the absence of such a file
parameter, on the appropriate (input or output) current default file. The exception STATUS_ERROR
is raised by any of these subprograms if the file to be used is not open.

procedure NEW_LINE(FILE : **in** FILE_TYPE; SPACING : **in** POSITIVE_COUNT := 1);   2
procedure NEW_LINE(SPACING : **in** POSITIVE_COUNT := 1);

> Operates on a file of mode OUT_FILE.

> For a SPACING of one: Outputs a line terminator and sets the current column   3
> number to one. Then increments the current line number by one, except in the case
> that the current line number is already greater than or equal to the maximum page
> length, for a bounded page length; in that case a page terminator is output, the
> current page number is incremented by one, and the current line number is set to
> one.

> For a SPACING greater than one, the above actions are performed SPACING times.   4

> The exception MODE_ERROR is raised if the mode is not OUT_FILE.   5

6　**procedure** SKIP_LINE(FILE　　　: **in** FILE_TYPE; SPACING : **in** POSITIVE_COUNT := 1);
　　procedure SKIP_LINE(SPACING : **in** POSITIVE_COUNT := 1);

7　　　　Operates on a file of mode IN_FILE.

8　　　　For a SPACING of one: Reads and discards all characters until a line terminator
　　　　has been read, and then sets the current column number to one. If the line ter-
　　　　minator is not immediately followed by a page terminator, the current line number
　　　　is incremented by one. Otherwise, if the line terminator is immediately followed by
　　　　a page terminator, then the page terminator is skipped, the current page number is
　　　　incremented by one, and the current line number is set to one.

9　　　　For a SPACING greater than one, the above actions are performed SPACING times.

10　　　　The exception MODE_ERROR is raised if the mode is not IN_FILE. The exception
　　　　END_ERROR is raised if an attempt is made to read a file terminator.

11　**function** END_OF_LINE(FILE : **in** FILE_TYPE) **return** BOOLEAN;
　　function END_OF_LINE **return** BOOLEAN;

12　　　　Operates on a file of mode IN_FILE. Returns TRUE if a line terminator or a file
　　　　terminator is next; otherwise returns FALSE.

13　　　　The exception MODE_ERROR is raised if the mode is not IN_FILE.

14　**procedure** NEW_PAGE(FILE : **in** FILE_TYPE);
　　procedure NEW_PAGE;

15　　　　Operates on a file of mode OUT_FILE. Outputs a line terminator if the current line is
　　　　not terminated, or if the current page is empty (that is, if the current column and
　　　　line numbers are both equal to one). Then outputs a page terminator, which ter-
　　　　minates the current page. Adds one to the current page number and sets the cur-
　　　　rent column and line numbers to one.

16　　　　The exception MODE_ERROR is raised if the mode is not OUT_FILE.

17　**procedure** SKIP_PAGE(FILE : **in** FILE_TYPE);
　　procedure SKIP_PAGE;

18　　　　Operates on a file of mode IN_FILE. Reads and discards all characters and line
　　　　terminators until a page terminator has been read. Then adds one to the current
　　　　page number, and sets the current column and line numbers to one.

19　　　　The exception MODE_ERROR is raised if the mode is not IN_FILE. The exception
　　　　END_ERROR is raised if an attempt is made to read a file terminator.

```
function  END_OF_PAGE(FILE : in FILE_TYPE) return BOOLEAN;        20
function  END_OF_PAGE return BOOLEAN;
```

>   Operates on a file of mode IN_FILE. Returns TRUE if the combination of a line   21
>   terminator and a page terminator is next, or if a file terminator is next; otherwise
>   returns FALSE.
>
>   The exception MODE_ERROR is raised if the mode is not IN_FILE.   22

```
function  END_OF_FILE(FILE : in FILE_TYPE) return BOOLEAN;        23
function  END_OF_FILE return BOOLEAN;
```

>   Operates on a file of mode IN_FILE. Returns TRUE if a file terminator is next, or if   24
>   the combination of a line, a page, and a file terminator is next; otherwise returns
>   FALSE.
>
>   The exception MODE_ERROR is raised if the mode is not IN_FILE.   25

The following subprograms provide for the control of the current position of reading or writing in a   26
file. In all cases, the default file is the current output file.

```
procedure  SET_COL(FILE : in FILE_TYPE; TO : in POSITIVE_COUNT);        27
procedure  SET_COL(TO    : in POSITIVE_COUNT);
```

>   If the file mode is OUT_FILE: 28
>
>   >   If the value specified by TO is greater than the current column number,   29
>   >   outputs spaces, adding one to the current column number after each
>   >   space, until the current column number equals the specified value. If the
>   >   value specified by TO is equal to the current column number, there is no
>   >   effect. If the value specified by TO is less than the current column number,
>   >   has the effect of calling NEW_LINE (with a spacing of one), then outputs
>   >   (TO - 1) spaces, and sets the current column number to the specified value.
>   >
>   >   The exception LAYOUT_ERROR is raised if the value specified by TO   30
>   >   exceeds LINE_LENGTH when the line length is bounded (that is, when it
>   >   does not have the conventional value zero).
>
>   If the file mode is IN_FILE: 31
>
>   >   Reads (and discards) individual characters, line terminators, and page ter-   32
>   >   minators, until the next character to be read has a column number that
>   >   equals the value specified by TO; there is no effect if the current column
>   >   number already equals this value. Each transfer of a character or ter-
>   >   minator maintains the current column, line, and page numbers in the same
>   >   way as a GET procedure (see 14.3.5). (Short lines will be skipped until a
>   >   line is reached that has a character at the specified column position.)
>   >
>   >   The exception END_ERROR is raised if an attempt is made to read a file   33
>   >   terminator.

34
```
procedure SET_LINE(FILE  : in  FILE_TYPE; TO : in  POSITIVE_COUNT);
procedure SET_LINE(TO     : in  POSITIVE_COUNT);
```

35   If the file mode is OUT_FILE :

36   If the value specified by TO is greater than the current line number, has the
           effect of repeatedly calling NEW_LINE (with a spacing of one), until the
           current line number equals the specified value. If the value specified by TO
           is equal to the current line number, there is no effect. If the value specified
           by TO is less than the current line number, has the effect of calling
           NEW_PAGE followed by a call of NEW_LINE with a spacing equal to (TO -
           1).

37   The exception LAYOUT_ERROR is raised if the value specified by TO
           exceeds PAGE_LENGTH when the page length is bounded (that is, when it
           does not have the conventional value zero).

38   If the mode is IN_FILE :

39   Has the effect of repeatedly calling SKIP_LINE (with a spacing of one), until
           the current line number equals the value specified by TO ; there is no effect
           if the current line number already equals this value. (Short pages will be
           skipped until a page is reached that has a line at the specified line position.)

40   The exception END_ERROR is raised if an attempt is made to read a file
           terminator.

41
```
function COL(FILE  : in FILE_TYPE) return POSITIVE_COUNT;
function COL return POSITIVE_COUNT;
```

42   Returns the current column number.

43   The exception LAYOUT_ERROR is raised if this number exceeds COUNT'LAST .

44
```
function LINE(FILE  : in FILE_TYPE)  return POSITIVE_COUNT;
function LINE return POSITIVE_COUNT;
```

45   Returns the current line number.

46   The exception LAYOUT_ERROR is raised if this number exceeds COUNT'LAST .

47
```
function PAGE(FILE  : in FILE_TYPE) return POSITIVE_COUNT;
function PAGE return POSITIVE_COUNT;
```

48   Returns the current page number.

49   The exception LAYOUT_ERROR is raised if this number exceeds COUNT'LAST .

50   The column number, line number, or page number are allowed to exceed COUNT'LAST (as a
       consequence of the input or output of sufficiently many characters, lines, or pages). These events
       do not cause any exception to be raised. However, a call of COL, LINE, or PAGE raises the
       exception LAYOUT_ERROR if the corresponding number exceeds COUNT'LAST .

14.3.4 Operations on Columns, Lines, and Pages

Note:

A page terminator is always skipped whenever the preceding line terminator is skipped. An implementation may represent the combination of these terminators by a single character, provided that it is properly recognized at input. 51

References: current column number 14.3, current default file 14.3, current line number 14.3, current page number 52
14.3, end_error exception 14.4, file 14.1, file terminator 14.3, get procedure 14.3.5, in_file 14.1, layout_error exception 14.4, line 14.3, line number 14.3, line terminator 14.3, maximum page length 14.3, mode_error exception 14.4, open file 14.1, page 14.3, page length 14.3, page terminator 14.3, positive count 14.3, status_error exception 14.4

14.3.5 Get and Put Procedures

The procedures GET and PUT for items of the types CHARACTER, STRING, numeric types, and 1
enumeration types are described in subsequent sections. Features of these procedures that are common to most of these types are described in this section. The GET and PUT procedures for items of type CHARACTER and STRING deal with individual character values; the GET and PUT procedures for numeric and enumeration types treat the items as lexical elements.

All procedures GET and PUT have forms with a file parameter, written first. Where this parameter 2
is omitted, the appropriate (input or output) current default file is understood to be specified. Each procedure GET operates on a file of mode IN_FILE. Each procedure PUT operates on a file of mode OUT_FILE.

All procedures GET and PUT maintain the current column, line, and page numbers of the specified 3
file: the effect of each of these procedures upon these numbers is the resultant of the effects of individual transfers of characters and of individual output or skipping of terminators. Each transfer of a character adds one to the current column number. Each output of a line terminator sets the current column number to one and adds one to the current line number. Each output of a page terminator sets the current column and line numbers to one and adds one to the current page number. For input, each skipping of a line terminator sets the current column number to one and adds one to the current line number; each skipping of a page terminator sets the current column and line numbers to one and adds one to the current page number. Similar considerations apply to the procedures GET_LINE, PUT_LINE, and SET_COL.

Several GET and PUT procedures, for numeric and enumeration types, have *format* parameters 4
which specify field lengths; these parameters are of the nonnegative subtype FIELD of the type INTEGER.

Input-output of enumeration values uses the syntax of the corresponding lexical elements. Any 5
GET procedure for an enumeration type begins by skipping any leading blanks, or line or page terminators; a *blank* being defined as a space or a horizontal tabulation character. Next, characters are input only so long as the sequence input is an initial sequence of an identifier or of a character literal (in particular, input ceases when a line terminator is encountered). The character or line terminator that causes input to cease remains available for subsequent input.

For a numeric type, the GET procedures have a format parameter called WIDTH. If the value given 6
for this parameter is zero, the GET procedure proceeds in the same manner as for enumeration types, but using the syntax of numeric literals instead of that of enumeration literals. If a nonzero value is given, then exactly WIDTH characters are input, or the characters up to a line terminator, whichever comes first; any skipped leading blanks are included in the count. The syntax used for numeric literals is an extended syntax that allows a leading sign (but no intervening blanks, or line or page terminators).

Get and Put Procedures 14.3.5

7 Any PUT procedure, for an item of a numeric or an enumeration type, outputs the value of the item as a numeric literal, identifier, or character literal, as appropriate. This is preceded by leading spaces if required by the format parameters WIDTH or FORE (as described in later sections), and then a minus sign for a negative value; for an enumeration type, the spaces follow instead of leading. The format given for a PUT procedure is overridden if it is insufficiently wide.

8 Two further cases arise for PUT procedures for numeric and enumeration types, if the line length of the specified output file is bounded (that is, if it does not have the conventional value zero). If the number of characters to be output does not exceed the maximum line length, but is such that they cannot fit on the current line, starting from the current column, then (in effect) NEW_LINE is called (with a spacing of one) before output of the item. Otherwise, if the number of characters exceeds the maximum line length, then the exception LAYOUT_ERROR is raised and no characters are output.

9 The exception STATUS_ERROR is raised by any of the procedures GET, GET_LINE, PUT, and PUT_LINE if the file to be used is not open. The exception MODE_ERROR is raised by the procedures GET and GET_LINE if the mode of the file to be used is not IN_FILE; and by the procedures PUT and PUT_LINE, if the mode is not OUT_FILE.

10 The exception END_ERROR is raised by a GET procedure if an attempt is made to skip a file terminator. The exception DATA_ERROR is raised by a GET procedure if the sequence finally input is not a lexical element corresponding to the type, in particular if no characters were input; for this test, leading blanks are ignored; for an item of a numeric type, when a sign is input, this rule applies to the succeeding numeric literal. The exception LAYOUT_ERROR is raised by a PUT procedure that outputs to a parameter of type STRING, if the length of the actual string is insufficient for the output of the item.

11 *Examples:*

12 In the examples, here and in sections 14.3.7 and 14.3.8, the string quotes and the lower case letter b are not transferred: they are shown only to reveal the layout and spaces.

```
N : INTEGER;
...
GET(N);
```

-- Characters at input	Sequence input	Value of N
-- bb-12535b	-12535	-12535
-- bb12_535E1b	12_535E1	125350
-- bb12_535E;	12_535E	(none) DATA_ERROR raised

13 *Example of overridden width parameter:*

```
PUT(ITEM => -23, WIDTH => 2);  --  "-23"
```

14 *References:* blank 14.3.9, column number 14.3, current default file 14.3, data_error exception 14.4, end_error exception 14.4, file 14.1, fore 14.3.8, get procedure 14.3.6 14.3.7 14.3.8 14.3.9, in_file 14.1, layout_error exception 14.4, line number 14.1, line terminator 14.1, maximum line length 14.3, mode 14.1, mode_error exception 14.4, new_file procedure 14.3.4, out_file 14.1, page number 14.1, page terminator 14.1, put procedure 14.3.6 14.3.7 14.3.8 14.3.9, skipping 14.3.7 14.3.8 14.3.9, status_error exception 14.4, width 14.3.5 14.3.7 14.3.9

14.3.6 Input-Output of Characters and Strings

For an item of type CHARACTER the following procedures are provided: 1

> **procedure** GET(FILE : **in** FILE_TYPE; ITEM : **out** CHARACTER);   2
> **procedure** GET(ITEM : **out** CHARACTER);

>> After skipping any line terminators and any page terminators, reads the next   3
>> character from the specified input file and returns the value of this character in the
>> **out** parameter ITEM.

>> The exception END_ERROR is raised if an attempt is made to skip a file terminator.   4

> **procedure** PUT(FILE : **in** FILE_TYPE; ITEM : **in** CHARACTER);   5
> **procedure** PUT(ITEM : **in** CHARACTER);

>> If the line length of the specified output file is bounded (that is, does not have the   6
>> conventional value zero), and the current column number exceeds it, has the effect
>> of calling NEW_LINE with a spacing of one. Then, or otherwise, outputs the given
>> character to the file.

For an item of type STRING the following procedures are provided: 7

> **procedure** GET(FILE : **in** FILE_TYPE; ITEM : **out** STRING);   8
> **procedure** GET(ITEM : **out** STRING);

>> Determines the length of the given string and attempts that number of GET   9
>> operations for successive characters of the string (in particular, no operation is per-
>> formed if the string is null).

> **procedure** PUT(FILE : **in** FILE_TYPE; ITEM : **in** STRING);   10
> **procedure** PUT(ITEM : **in** STRING);

>> Determines the length of the given string and attempts that number of PUT   11
>> operations for successive characters of the string (in particular, no operation is per-
>> formed if the string is null).

> **procedure** GET_LINE(FILE : **in** FILE_TYPE; ITEM : **out** STRING; LAST : **out** NATURAL);   12
> **procedure** GET_LINE(ITEM : **out** STRING; LAST : **out** NATURAL);

>> Replaces successive characters of the specified string by successive characters   13
>> read from the specified input file. Reading stops if the end of the line is met, in
>> which case the procedure SKIP_LINE is then called (in effect) with a spacing of
>> one; reading also stops if the end of the string is met. Characters not replaced are
>> left undefined.

>> If characters are read, returns in LAST the index value such that ITEM (LAST) is the   14
>> last character replaced (the index of the first character replaced is ITEM'FIRST). If
>> no characters are read, returns in LAST an index value that is one less than
>> ITEM'FIRST.

>> The exception END_ERROR is raised if an attempt is made to skip a file terminator.   15

16 **procedure** PUT_LINE(FILE : **in** FILE_TYPE; ITEM : **in** STRING);
   procedure PUT_LINE(ITEM : **in** STRING);

17   Calls the procedure PUT for the given string, and then the procedure NEW_LINE with a spacing of one.

Notes:

18 In a literal string parameter of PUT, the enclosing string bracket characters are not output. Each doubled string bracket character in the enclosed string is output as a single string bracket character, as a consequence of the rule for string literals (see 2.6).

19 A string read by GET or written by PUT can extend over several lines.

20 *References:* current column number 14.3, end_error exception 14.4, file 14.1, file terminator 14.3, get procedure 14.3.5, line 14.3, line length 14.3, new_line procedure 14.3.4, page terminator 14.3, put procedure 14.3.4, skipping 14.3.5

14.3.7 Input-Output for Integer Types

1 The following procedures are defined in the generic package INTEGER_IO. This must be instantiated for the appropriate integer type (indicated by NUM in the specification).

2 Values are output as decimal or based literals, without underline characters or exponent, and preceded by a minus sign if negative. The format (which includes any leading spaces and minus sign) can be specified by an optional field width parameter. Values of widths of fields in output formats are of the nonnegative integer subtype FIELD. Values of bases are of the integer subtype NUMBER_BASE.

      subtype NUMBER_BASE **is** INTEGER **range** 2 .. 16;

3 The default field width and base to be used by output procedures are defined by the following variables that are declared in the generic package INTEGER_IO:

      DEFAULT_WIDTH : FIELD := NUM'WIDTH;
      DEFAULT_BASE   : NUMBER_BASE := 10;

4 The following procedures are provided:

5 **procedure** GET(FILE : **in** FILE_TYPE; ITEM : **out** NUM; WIDTH : **in** FIELD := 0);
   procedure GET(ITEM : **out** NUM; WIDTH : **in** FIELD := 0);

6   If the value of the parameter WIDTH is zero, skips any leading blanks, line terminators, or page terminators, then reads a plus or a minus sign if present, then reads according to the syntax of an integer literal (which may be a based literal). If a nonzero value of WIDTH is supplied, then exactly WIDTH characters are input, or the characters (possibly none) up to a line terminator, whichever comes first; any skipped leading blanks are included in the count.

7   Returns, in the parameter ITEM, the value of type NUM that corresponds to the sequence input.

8   The exception DATA_ERROR is raised if the sequence input does not have the required syntax or if the value obtained is not of the subtype NUM.

```
procedure PUT(FILE  : in FILE_TYPE;                                    9
              ITEM  : in NUM;
              WIDTH : in FIELD := DEFAULT_WIDTH;
              BASE  : in NUMBER_BASE := DEFAULT_BASE);

procedure PUT(ITEM  : in NUM;
              WIDTH : in FIELD := DEFAULT_WIDTH;
              BASE  : in NUMBER_BASE := DEFAULT_BASE);
```

Outputs the value of the parameter ITEM as an integer literal, with no underlines,   10
no exponent, and no leading zeros (but a single zero for the value zero), and a
preceding minus sign for a negative value.

If the resulting sequence of characters to be output has fewer than WIDTH   11
characters, then leading spaces are first output to make up the difference.

Uses the syntax for decimal literal if the parameter BASE has the value ten (either   12
explicitly or through DEFAULT_BASE); otherwise, uses the syntax for based literal,
with any letters in upper case.

```
procedure GET(FROM : in STRING; ITEM : out NUM; LAST : out POSITIVE);    13
```

Reads an integer value from the beginning of the given string, following the same   14
rules as the GET procedure that reads an integer value from a file, but treating the
end of the string as a file terminator. Returns, in the parameter ITEM , the value of
type NUM that corresponds to the sequence input. Returns in LAST the index
value such that FROM (LAST) is the last character read.

The exception DATA_ERROR is raised if the sequence input does not have the   15
required syntax or if the value obtained is not of the subtype NUM .

```
procedure PUT(TO   : out STRING;                                       16
              ITEM : in NUM;
              BASE : in NUMBER_BASE := DEFAULT_BASE);  .
```

Outputs the value of the parameter ITEM to the given string, following the same   17
rule as for output to a file, using the length of the given string as the value for
WIDTH.

Examples: 18

```
package INT_IO is new INTEGER_IO(SMALL_INT); use INT_IO;
-- default format used at instantiation, DEFAULT_WIDTH = 4, DEFAULT_BASE = 10

PUT(126);                               -- "b126"
PUT(-126, 7);                           -- "bbb-126"
PUT(126, WIDTH => 13, BASE => 2);       -- "bbb2#1111110#"
```

References: based literal 2.4.2, blank 14.3.5, data_error exception 14.4, decimal literal 2.4.1, field subtype 14.3.5,   19
file_type 14.1, get procedure 14.3.5, integer_io package 14.3.10, integer literal 2.4, layout_error exception 14.4, line
terminator 14.3, put procedure 14.3.5, skipping 14.3.5, width 14.3.5

                                      Input-Output for Integer Types 14.3.7

14.3.8 Input-Output for Real Types

1   The following procedures are defined in the generic packages FLOAT_IO and FIXED_IO, which must be instantiated for the appropriate floating point or fixed point type respectively (indicated by NUM in the specifications).

2   Values are output as decimal literals without underline characters. The format of each value output consists of a FORE field, a decimal point, an AFT field, and (if a nonzero EXP parameter is supplied) the letter E and an EXP field. The two possible formats thus correspond to:

    FORE . AFT

3   and to:

    FORE . AFT E EXP

4   without any spaces between these fields. The FORE field may include leading spaces, and a minus sign for negative values. The AFT field includes only decimal digits (possibly with trailing zeros). The EXP field includes the sign (plus or minus) and the exponent (possibly with leading zeros).

5   For floating point types, the default lengths of these fields are defined by the following variables that are declared in the generic package FLOAT_IO :

    DEFAULT_FORE : FIELD := 2;
    DEFAULT_AFT   : FIELD := NUM'DIGITS-1;
    DEFAULT_EXP   : FIELD := 3;

6   For fixed point types, the default lengths of these fields are defined by the following variables that are declared in the generic package FIXED_IO :

    DEFAULT_FORE : FIELD := NUM'FORE;
    DEFAULT_AFT   : FIELD := NUM'AFT;
    DEFAULT_EXP   : FIELD := 0;

7   The following procedures are provided:

8   procedure GET(FILE : in FILE_TYPE; ITEM : out NUM; WIDTH : in FIELD := 0);
    procedure GET(ITEM : out NUM; WIDTH : in FIELD := 0);

9   If the value of the parameter WIDTH is zero, skips any leading blanks, line terminators, or page terminators, then reads a plus or a minus sign if present, then reads according to the syntax of a real literal (which may be a based literal). If a nonzero value of WIDTH is supplied, then exactly WIDTH characters are input, or the characters (possibly none) up to a line terminator, whichever comes first; any skipped leading blanks are included in the count.

10   Returns, in the parameter ITEM, the value of type NUM that corresponds to the sequence input.

11   The exception DATA_ERROR is raised if the sequence input does not have the required syntax or if the value obtained is not of the subtype NUM.

```
procedure PUT(FILE  : in FILE_TYPE;
              ITEM  : in NUM;
              FORE  : in FIELD := DEFAULT_FORE;
              AFT   : in FIELD := DEFAULT_AFT;
              EXP   : in FIELD := DEFAULT_EXP);

procedure PUT(ITEM  : in NUM;
              FORE  : in FIELD := DEFAULT_FORE;
              AFT   : in FIELD := DEFAULT_AFT;
              EXP   : in FIELD := DEFAULT_EXP);
```

12

Outputs the value of the parameter ITEM as a decimal literal with the format defined by FORE, AFT and EXP. If the value is negative, a minus sign is included in the integer part. If EXP has the value zero, then the integer part to be output has as many digits as are needed to represent the integer part of the value of ITEM, overriding FORE if necessary, or consists of the digit zero if the value of ITEM has no integer part.

13

If EXP has a value greater than zero, then the integer part to be output has a single digit, which is nonzero except for the value 0.0 of ITEM.

14

In both cases, however, if the integer part to be output has fewer than FORE characters, including any minus sign, then leading spaces are first output to make up the difference. The number of digits of the fractional part is given by AFT, or is one if AFT equals zero. The value is rounded; a value of exactly one half in the last place may be rounded either up or down.

15

If EXP has the value zero, there is no exponent part. If EXP has a value greater than zero, then the exponent part to be output has as many digits as are needed to represent the exponent part of the value of ITEM (for which a single digit integer part is used), and includes an initial sign (plus or minus). If the exponent part to be output has fewer than EXP characters, including the sign, then leading zeros precede the digits, to make up the difference. For the value 0.0 of ITEM, the exponent has the value zero.

16

```
procedure GET(FROM : in STRING; ITEM : out NUM; LAST : out POSITIVE);
```

17

Reads a real value from the beginning of the given string, following the same rule as the GET procedure that reads a real value from a file, but treating the end of the string as a file terminator. Returns, in the parameter ITEM, the value of type NUM that corresponds to the sequence input. Returns in LAST the index value such that FROM(LAST) is the last character read.

18

The exception DATA_ERROR is raised if the sequence input does not have the required syntax, or if the value obtained is not of the subtype NUM.

19

```
procedure PUT(TO   : out STRING;
              ITEM : in NUM;
              AFT  : in FIELD   := DEFAULT_AFT;
              EXP  : in INTEGER := DEFAULT_EXP);
```

20

Outputs the value of the parameter ITEM to the given string, following the same rule as for output to a file, using a value for FORE such that the sequence of characters output exactly fills the string, including any leading spaces.

21

22   *Examples:*

package REAL_IO **is new** FLOAT_IO(REAL); **use** REAL_IO;
-- default format used at instantiation, DEFAULT_EXP = 3

X : REAL := -123.4567;   --   digits 8   (see 3.5.7)

PUT(X); -- default format   "-1.2345670E+02"
PUT(X, FORE => 5, AFT => 3, EXP => 2);   --   "bbb-1.235E+2"
PUT(X, 5, 3, 0);   --   "b-123.457"

Note:

23   For an item with a positive value, if output to a string exactly fills the string without leading spaces, then output of the corresponding negative value will raise LAYOUT_ERROR.

24   *References:* aft attribute 3.5.10, based literal 2.4.2, blank 14.3.5, data_error exception 14.3.5, decimal literal 2.4.1, field subtype 14.3.5, file_type 14.1, fixed_io package 14.3.10, floating_io package 14.3.10, fore attribute 3.5.10, get procedure 14.3.5, layout_error 14.3.5, line terminator 14.3.5, put procedure 14.3.5, real literal 2.4, skipping 14.3.5, width 14.3.5

14.3.9   Input-Output for Enumeration Types

1   The following procedures are defined in the generic package ENUMERATION_IO, which must be instantiated for the appropriate enumeration type (indicated by ENUM in the specification).

2   Values are output using either upper or lower case letters for identifiers. This is specified by the parameter SET, which is of the enumeration type TYPE_SET.

type TYPE_SET **is** (LOWER_CASE, UPPER_CASE);

3   The format (which includes any trailing spaces) can be specified by an optional field width parameter. The default field width and letter case are defined by the following variables that are declared in the generic package ENUMERATION_IO:

DEFAULT_WIDTH   : FIELD := 0;
DEFAULT_SETTING : TYPE_SET := UPPER_CASE;

4   The following procedures are provided:

5   **procedure** GET(FILE   : **in** FILE_TYPE; ITEM : **out** ENUM);
procedure GET(ITEM   : **out** ENUM);

6   After skipping any leading blanks, line terminators, or page terminators, reads an identifier according to the syntax of this lexical element (lower and upper case being considered equivalent), or a character literal according to the syntax of this lexical element (including the apostrophes). Returns, in the parameter ITEM, the value of type ENUM that corresponds to the sequence input.

7   The exception DATA_ERROR is raised if the sequence input does not have the required syntax, or if the identifier or character literal does not correspond to a value of the subtype ENUM.

```
procedure PUT(FILE    : in FILE_TYPE;                                    8
              ITEM    : in ENUM;
              WIDTH   : in FIELD := DEFAULT_WIDTH;
              SET     : in TYPE_SET := DEFAULT_SETTING);

procedure PUT(ITEM    : in ENUM;
              WIDTH   : in FIELD := DEFAULT_WIDTH;
              SET     : in TYPE_SET := DEFAULT_SETTING);
```

Outputs the value of the parameter ITEM as an enumeration literal (either an   9
identifier or a character literal). The optional parameter SET indicates whether
lower case or upper case is used for identifiers; it has no effect for character
literals. If the sequence of characters produced has fewer than WIDTH characters,
then trailing spaces are finally output to make up the difference.

```
procedure GET(FROM : in STRING; ITEM : out ENUM; LAST : out POSITIVE);    10
```

Reads an enumeration value from the beginning of the given string, following the   11
same rule as the GET procedure that reads an enumeration value from a file, but
treating the end of the string as a file terminator. Returns, in the parameter ITEM,
the value of type ENUM that corresponds to the sequence input. Returns in LAST
the index value such that FROM (LAST) is the last character read.

The exception DATA_ERROR is raised if the sequence input does not have the   12
required syntax, or if the identifier or character literal does not correspond to a
value of the subtype ENUM.

```
procedure PUT(TO   : out STRING;                                         13
              ITEM : in ENUM;
              SET  : in TYPE_SET := DEFAULT_SETTING);
```

Outputs the value of the parameter ITEM to the given string, following the same   14
rule as for output to a file, using the length of the given string as the value for
WIDTH.

Although the specification of the package ENUMERATION_IO would allow instantiation for an   15
integer type, this is not the intended purpose of this generic package, and the effect of such instantiations is not defined by the language.

Notes:

There is a difference between PUT defined for characters, and for enumeration values. Thus   16

```
    TEXT_IO.PUT('A');    --   outputs the character A

    package CHAR_IO is new TEXT_IO.ENUMERATION_IO(CHARACTER);
    CHAR_IO.PUT('A');    --   outputs the character 'A', between single quotes
```

The type BOOLEAN is an enumeration type, hence ENUMERATION_IO can be instantiated for this   17
type.

References: blank 14.3.5, data_error 14.3.5, enumeration_io package 14.3.10, field subtype 14.3.5, file_type 14.1,   18
get procedure 14.3.5, line terminator 14.3.5, put procedure 14.3.5, skipping 14.3.5, width 14.3.5

Input-Output for Enumeration Types 14.3.9

14.3.10 Specification of the Package Text_IO

```
with IO_EXCEPTIONS;
package TEXT_IO is

    type FILE_TYPE   is limited private;

    type FILE_MODE is (IN_FILE, OUT_FILE);

    type COUNT is range 0 .. implementation_defined;
    subtype POSITIVE_COUNT  is COUNT range 1 .. COUNT'LAST;
    UNBOUNDED : constant COUNT := 0; -- line and page length

    subtype FIELD            is INTEGER range 0 .. implementation_defined;
    subtype NUMBER_BASE is INTEGER range 2 .. 16;

    type TYPE_SET is (LOWER_CASE, UPPER_CASE);

    — File Management

    procedure CREATE  ( FILE  : in out FILE_TYPE;
                        MODE  : in FILE_MODE := OUT_FILE;
                        NAME  : in STRING     := "";
                        FORM  : in STRING     := "");

    procedure OPEN    ( FILE  : in out FILE_TYPE;
                        MODE  : in FILE_MODE;
                        NAME  : in STRING;
                        FORM  : in STRING := "");

    procedure  CLOSE  (FILE : in out FILE_TYPE);
    procedure  DELETE (FILE : in out FILE_TYPE);
    procedure  RESET  (FILE : in out FILE_TYPE; MODE : in FILE_MODE);
    procedure  RESET  (FILE : in out FILE_TYPE);

    function   MODE   (FILE : in FILE_TYPE) return FILE_MODE ;
    function   NAME   (FILE : in FILE_TYPE) return STRING;
    function   FORM   (FILE : in FILE_TYPE) return STRING;

    function   IS_OPEN (FILE : in FILE_TYPE) return BOOLEAN;

    -- Control of default input and output files

    procedure  SET_INPUT   (FILE : in FILE_TYPE);
    procedure  SET_OUTPUT (FILE : in FILE_TYPE);


    function   STANDARD_INPUT    return FILE_TYPE;
    function   STANDARD_OUTPUT   return FILE_TYPE;

    function   CURRENT_INPUT     return FILE_TYPE;
    function   CURRENT_OUTPUT    return FILE_TYPE;
```

-- Specification of line and page lengths

```
procedure  SET_LINE_LENGTH  (FILE : in FILE_TYPE; TO : in COUNT);
procedure  SET_LINE_LENGTH  (TO : in COUNT);

procedure  SET_PAGE_LENGTH  (FILE : in FILE_TYPE; TO : in COUNT);
procedure  SET_PAGE_LENGTH  (TO : in COUNT);

function   LINE_LENGTH (FILE : in FILE_TYPE) return COUNT;
function   LINE_LENGTH   return COUNT;

function   PAGE_LENGTH (FILE : in FILE_TYPE) return COUNT;
function   PAGE_LENGTH   return COUNT;
```

-- Column, Line, and Page Control

```
procedure  NEW_LINE    (FILE : in FILE_TYPE; SPACING : in POSITIVE_COUNT := 1);
procedure  NEW_LINE    (SPACING : in POSITIVE_COUNT := 1);

procedure  SKIP_LINE    (FILE : in FILE_TYPE; SPACING : in POSITIVE_COUNT := 1);
procedure  SKIP_LINE    (SPACING : in POSITIVE_COUNT := 1);

function   END_OF_LINE (FILE : in FILE_TYPE) return BOOLEAN;
function   END_OF_LINE   return BOOLEAN;

procedure  NEW_PAGE    (FILE : in FILE_TYPE);
procedure  NEW_PAGE;

procedure  SKIP_PAGE    (FILE : in FILE_TYPE);
procedure  SKIP_PAGE;

function   END_OF_PAGE (FILE : in FILE_TYPE) return BOOLEAN;
function   END_OF_PAGE return BOOLEAN;

function   END_OF_FILE  (FILE : in FILE_TYPE) return BOOLEAN;
function   END_OF_FILE   return BOOLEAN;


procedure  SET_COL (FILE : in FILE_TYPE; TO : in POSITIVE_COUNT);
procedure  SET_COL (TO    : in POSITIVE_COUNT);

procedure  SET_LINE (FILE : in FILE_TYPE; TO : in POSITIVE_COUNT);
procedure  SET_LINE (TO    : in POSITIVE_COUNT);


function COL   (FILE : in FILE_TYPE) return POSITIVE_COUNT;
function COL    return POSITIVE_COUNT;

function LINE  (FILE : in FILE_TYPE) return POSITIVE_COUNT;
function LINE return POSITIVE_COUNT;

function PAGE (FILE : in FILE_TYPE) return POSITIVE_COUNT;
function PAGE   return POSITIVE_COUNT;
```

Specification of the Package Text_IO 14.3.10

-- Character Input-Output

```
procedure  GET(FILE   : in   FILE_TYPE; ITEM : out CHARACTER);
procedure  GET(ITEM   : out  CHARACTER);
procedure  PUT(FILE   : in   FILE_TYPE; ITEM : in CHARACTER);
procedure  PUT(ITEM   : in   CHARACTER);
```

-- String Input-Output

```
procedure  GET(FILE   : in   FILE_TYPE; ITEM : out STRING);
procedure  GET(ITEM   : out  STRING);
procedure  PUT(FILE   : in   FILE_TYPE; ITEM : in STRING);
procedure  PUT(ITEM   : in   STRING);

procedure  GET_LINE(FILE : in    FILE_TYPE; ITEM : out STRING; LAST : out NATURAL);
procedure  GET_LINE(ITEM : out  STRING; LAST : out NATURAL);
procedure  PUT_LINE(FILE : in    FILE_TYPE; ITEM : in STRING);
procedure  PUT_LINE(ITEM : in    STRING);
```

-- Generic package for Input-Output of Integer Types

```
generic
   type NUM is range <>;
package INTEGER_IO is

   DEFAULT_WIDTH  : FIELD := NUM'WIDTH;
   DEFAULT_BASE   : NUMBER_BASE := 10;

   procedure GET(FILE   : in   FILE_TYPE; ITEM : out NUM; WIDTH : in FIELD := 0);
   procedure GET(ITEM   : out NUM; WIDTH : in FIELD := 0);

   procedure PUT(FILE     : in  FILE_TYPE;
                 ITEM     : in  NUM;
                 WIDTH    : in  FIELD := DEFAULT_WIDTH;
                 BASE     : in  NUMBER_BASE := DEFAULT_BASE);
   procedure PUT(ITEM     : in  NUM;
                 WIDTH    : in  FIELD := DEFAULT_WIDTH;
                 BASE     : in  NUMBER_BASE := DEFAULT_BASE);

   procedure GET(FROM  : in   STRING; ITEM : out NUM; LAST : out POSITIVE);
   procedure PUT(TO     : out STRING;
                 ITEM   : in  NUM;
                 BASE   : in  NUMBER_BASE := DEFAULT_BASE);

end INTEGER_IO;
```

-- Generic packages for Input-Output of Real Types

```
generic
    type NUM is digits <>;
package FLOAT_IO is

    DEFAULT_FORE   : FIELD := 2;
    DEFAULT_AFT    : FIELD := NUM'DIGITS-1;
    DEFAULT_EXP    : FIELD := 3;

    procedure GET(FILE : in FILE_TYPE; ITEM : out NUM; WIDTH : in FIELD := 0);
    procedure GET(ITEM : out NUM; WIDTH : in FIELD := 0);

    procedure PUT(FILE   : in FILE_TYPE;
                  ITEM   : in NUM;
                  FORE   : in FIELD := DEFAULT_FORE;
                  AFT    : in FIELD := DEFAULT_AFT;
                  EXP    : in FIELD := DEFAULT_EXP);
    procedure PUT(ITEM   : in NUM;
                  FORE   : in FIELD := DEFAULT_FORE;
                  AFT    : in FIELD := DEFAULT_AFT;
                  EXP    : in FIELD := DEFAULT_EXP);

    procedure GET(FROM   : in STRING; ITEM : out NUM; LAST : out POSITIVE);
    procedure PUT(TO     : out STRING;
                  ITEM   : in NUM;
                  AFT    : in FIELD := DEFAULT_AFT;
                  EXP    : in FIELD := DEFAULT_EXP);
end FLOAT_IO;

generic
    type NUM is delta <>;
package FIXED_IO is

    DEFAULT_FORE   : FIELD := NUM'FORE;
    DEFAULT_AFT    : FIELD := NUM'AFT;
    DEFAULT_EXP    : FIELD := 0;

    procedure GET(FILE   : in FILE_TYPE; ITEM : out NUM; WIDTH : in FIELD := 0);
    procedure GET(ITEM   : out NUM; WIDTH : in FIELD := 0);

    procedure PUT(FILE   : in FILE_TYPE;
                  ITEM   : in NUM;
                  FORE   : in FIELD := DEFAULT_FORE;
                  AFT    : in FIELD := DEFAULT_AFT;
                  EXP    : in FIELD := DEFAULT_EXP);
    procedure PUT(ITEM   : in NUM;
                  FORE   : in FIELD := DEFAULT_FORE;
                  AFT    : in FIELD := DEFAULT_AFT;
                  EXP    : in FIELD := DEFAULT_EXP);

    procedure GET(FROM   : in  STRING; ITEM : out NUM; LAST : out POSITIVE);
    procedure PUT(TO     : out STRING;
                  ITEM   : in NUM;
                  AFT    : in FIELD := DEFAULT_AFT;
                  EXP    : in FIELD := DEFAULT_EXP);

end FIXED_IO;
```

Specification of the Package Text_IO 14.3.10

-- Generic package for Input-Output of Enumeration Types

```
generic
   type ENUM is (<>);
package ENUMERATION_IO is

   DEFAULT_WIDTH    : FIELD := 0;
   DEFAULT_SETTING  : TYPE_SET := UPPER_CASE;

   procedure GET(FILE    : in FILE_TYPE; ITEM : out ENUM);
   procedure GET(ITEM    : out ENUM);

   procedure PUT(FILE    : in FILE_TYPE;
                 ITEM    : in ENUM;
                 WIDTH   : in FIELD      := DEFAULT_WIDTH;
                 SET     : in TYPE_SET   := DEFAULT_SETTING);
   procedure PUT(ITEM    : in ENUM;
                 WIDTH   : in FIELD      := DEFAULT_WIDTH;
                 SET     : in TYPE_SET   := DEFAULT_SETTING);

   procedure GET(FROM : in    STRING; ITEM : out ENUM; LAST : out POSITIVE);
   procedure PUT(TO   : out STRING;
                 ITEM : in ENUM;
                 SET  : in    TYPE_SET := DEFAULT_SETTING);
end ENUMERATION_IO;
```

-- Exceptions

```
STATUS_ERROR   : exception renames IO_EXCEPTIONS.STATUS_ERROR;
MODE_ERROR     : exception renames IO_EXCEPTIONS.MODE_ERROR;
NAME_ERROR     : exception renames IO_EXCEPTIONS.NAME_ERROR;
USE_ERROR      : exception renames IO_EXCEPTIONS.USE_ERROR;
DEVICE_ERROR   : exception renames IO_EXCEPTIONS.DEVICE_ERROR;
END_ERROR      : exception renames IO_EXCEPTIONS.END_ERROR;
DATA_ERROR     : exception renames IO_EXCEPTIONS.DATA_ERROR;
LAYOUT_ERROR   : exception renames IO_EXCEPTIONS.LAYOUT_ERROR;

private
   -- implementation-dependent
end TEXT_IO;
```

14.4 Exceptions in Input-Output

1   The following exceptions can be raised by input-output operations. They are declared in the package IO_EXCEPTIONS , defined in section 14.5; this package is named in the context clause for each of the three input-output packages. Only outline descriptions are given of the conditions under which NAME_ERROR , USE_ERROR , and DEVICE_ERROR are raised; for full details see Appendix F. If more than one error condition exists, the corresponding exception that appears earliest in the following list is the one that is raised.

2   The exception STATUS_ERROR is raised by an attempt to operate upon a file that is not open, and by an attempt to open a file that is already open.

The exception MODE_ERROR is raised by an attempt to read from, or test for the end of, a file whose current mode is OUT_FILE, and also by an attempt to write to a file whose current mode is IN_FILE. In the case of TEXT_IO, the exception MODE_ERROR is also raised by specifying a file whose current mode is OUT_FILE in a call of SET_INPUT, SKIP_LINE, END_OF_LINE, SKIP_PAGE, or END_OF_PAGE; and by specifying a file whose current mode is IN_FILE in a call of SET_OUTPUT, SET_LINE_LENGTH, SET_PAGE_LENGTH, LINE_LENGTH, PAGE_LENGTH, NEW_LINE, or NEW_PAGE. 3

The exception NAME_ERROR is raised by a call of CREATE or OPEN if the string given for the parameter NAME does not allow the identification of an external file. For example, this exception is raised if the string is improper, or, alternatively, if either none or more than one external file corresponds to the string. 4

The exception USE_ERROR is raised if an operation is attempted that is not possible for reasons that depend on characteristics of the external file. For example, this exception is raised by the procedure CREATE, among other circumstances, if the given mode is OUT_FILE but the form specifies an input only device, if the parameter FORM specifies invalid access rights, or if an external file with the given name already exists and overwriting is not allowed. 5

The exception DEVICE_ERROR is raised if an input-output operation cannot be completed because of a malfunction of the underlying system. 6

The exception END_ERROR is raised by an attempt to skip (read past) the end of a file. 7

The exception DATA_ERROR may be raised by the procedure READ if the element read cannot be interpreted as a value of the required type. This exception is also raised by a procedure GET (defined in the package TEXT_IO) if the input character sequence fails to satisfy the required syntax, or if the value input does not belong to the range of the required type or subtype. 8

The exception LAYOUT_ERROR is raised (in text input-output) by COL, LINE, or PAGE if the value returned exceeds COUNT'LAST. The exception LAYOUT_ERROR is also raised on output by an attempt to set column or line numbers in excess of specified maximum line or page lengths, respectively (excluding the unbounded cases). It is also raised by an attempt to PUT too many characters to a string. 9

References: col function 14.3.4, create procedure 14.2.1, end_of_line function 14.3.4, end_of_page function 14.3.4, external file 14.1, file 14.1, form string 14.1, get procedure 14.3.5, in_file 14.1, io_exceptions package 14.5, line function 14.3.4, line_length function 14.3.4, name string 14.1, new_line procedure 14.3.4, new_page procedure 14.3.4, open procedure 14.2.1, out_file 14.1, page function 14.3.4, page_length function 14.3.4, put procedure 14.3.5, read procedure 14.2.2 14.2.3, set_input procedure 14.3.2, set_line_length 14.3.3, set_page_length 14.3.3, set_output 14.3.2, skip_line procedure 14.3.4, skip_page procedure 14.3.4, text_io package 14.3 10

Exceptions in Input-Output 14.4

14.5 Specification of the Package IO_Exceptions

1   This package defines the exceptions needed by the packages SEQUENTIAL_IO, DIRECT_IO, and
    TEXT_IO.

2
```
package IO_EXCEPTIONS is

    STATUS_ERROR   : exception;
    MODE_ERROR     : exception;
    NAME_ERROR     : exception;
    USE_ERROR      : exception;
    DEVICE_ERROR   : exception;
    END_ERROR      : exception;
    DATA_ERROR     : exception;
    LAYOUT_ERROR   : exception;

end IO_EXCEPTIONS;
```

14.6 Low Level Input-Output

1   A low level input-output operation is an operation acting on a physical device. Such an operation
    is handled by using one of the (overloaded) predefined procedures SEND_CONTROL and
    RECEIVE_CONTROL.

2   A procedure SEND_CONTROL may be used to send control information to a physical device. A
    procedure RECEIVE_CONTROL may be used to monitor the execution of an input-output operation
    by requesting information from the physical device.

3   Such procedures are declared in the standard package LOW_LEVEL_IO and have two parameters
    identifying the device and the data. However, the kinds and formats of the control information will
    depend on the physical characteristics of the machine and the device. Hence, the types of the
    parameters are implementation-defined. Overloaded definitions of these procedures should be
    provided for the supported devices.

4   The visible part of the package defining these procedures is outlined as follows:

5
```
package LOW_LEVEL_IO is
    --  declarations of the possible types for DEVICE and DATA;
    --  declarations of overloaded procedures for these types:
    procedure SEND_CONTROL      (DEVICE : device_type; DATA : in out data_type);
    procedure RECEIVE_CONTROL   (DEVICE : device_type; DATA : in out data_type);
end;
```

6   The bodies of the procedures SEND_CONTROL and RECEIVE_CONTROL for various devices can be
    supplied in the body of the package LOW_LEVEL_IO. These procedure bodies may be written with
    code statements.

14.7 Example of Input-Output

The following example shows the use of some of the text input-output facilities in a dialogue with a user at a terminal. The user is prompted to type a color, and the program responds by giving the number of items of that color available in stock, according to an inventory. The default input and output files are used. For simplicity, all the requisite instantiations are given within one subprogram; in practice, a package, separate from the procedure, would be used.

```
with TEXT_IO; use TEXT_IO;
procedure DIALOGUE is
   type COLOR is (WHITE, RED, ORANGE, YELLOW, GREEN, BLUE, BROWN);
   package COLOR_IO is new ENUMERATION_IO(ENUM => COLOR);
   package NUMBER_IO is new INTEGER_IO(INTEGER);
   use COLOR_IO, NUMBER_IO;

   INVENTORY : array (COLOR) of INTEGER := (20, 17, 43, 10, 28, 173, 87);
   CHOICE : COLOR;

   procedure ENTER_COLOR (SELECTION : out COLOR) is
   begin
      loop
         begin
            PUT ("Color selected: ");      --  prompts user
            GET (SELECTION);               --  accepts color typed, or raises exception
            return;
         exception
            when DATA_ERROR =>
               PUT("Invalid color, try again.  "); --  user has typed new line
               NEW_LINE(2);
               --  completes execution of the block statement
         end;
      end loop; --  repeats the block statement until color accepted
   end;
begin --   statements of DIALOGUE;

   NUMBER_IO.DEFAULT_WIDTH := 5;

   loop

      ENTER_COLOR(CHOICE);   --  user types color and new line

      SET_COL(5);    PUT(CHOICE); PUT(" items available:");
      SET_COL(40);   PUT(INVENTORY(CHOICE));   --  default width is 5
      NEW_LINE;
   end loop;
end DIALOGUE;
```

Example of an interaction (characters typed by the user are italicized):

```
Color selected:  Black
Invalid color, try again.

Color selected:  Blue
     BLUE  items  available:            173
Color selected:  Yellow
     YELLOW  items  available:           10
```

A. Predefined Language Attributes

This annex summarizes the definitions given elsewhere of the predefined language attributes. [1]

P'ADDRESS   For a prefix P that denotes an object, a program unit, a label, or an entry: [2]

Yields the address of the first of the storage units allocated to P. For a subprogram, package, task unit, or label, this value refers to the machine code associated with the corresponding body or statement. For an entry for which an address clause has been given, the value refers to the corresponding hardware interrupt. The value of this attribute is of the type ADDRESS defined in the package SYSTEM . (See 13.7.2.)

P'AFT   For a prefix P that denotes a fixed point subtype: [3]

Yields the number of decimal digits needed after the point to accommodate the precision of the subtype P, unless the delta of the subtype P is greater than 0.1, in which case the attribute yields the value one. (P'AFT is the smallest positive integer N for which $(10**N)*P'DELTA$ is greater than or equal to one.) The value of this attribute is of the type *universal_integer*. (See 3.5.10.)

P'BASE   For a prefix P that denotes a type or subtype: [4]

This attribute denotes the base type of P. It is only allowed as the prefix of the name of another attribute: for example, P'BASE'FIRST . (See 3.3.3.)

P'CALLABLE   For a prefix P that is appropriate for a task type: [5]

Yields the value FALSE when the execution of the task P is either completed or terminated, or when the task is abnormal; yields the value TRUE otherwise. The value of this attribute is of the predefined type BOOLEAN . (See 9.9.)

P'CONSTRAINED   For a prefix P that denotes an object of a type with discriminants: [6]

Yields the value TRUE if a discriminant constraint applies to the object P, or if the object is a constant (including a formal parameter or generic formal parameter of mode **in**); yields the value FALSE otherwise. If P is a generic formal parameter of mode **in out**, or if P is a formal parameter of mode **in out** or **out** and the type mark given in the corresponding parameter specification denotes an unconstrained type with discriminants, then the value of this attribute is obtained from that of the corresponding actual parameter. The value of this attribute is of the predefined type BOOLEAN . (See 3.7.4.)

7   P'CONSTRAINED   For a prefix P that denotes a private type or subtype:

Yields the value FALSE if P denotes an unconstrained nonformal private type with discriminants; also yields the value FALSE if P denotes a generic formal private type and the associated actual subtype is either an unconstrained type with discriminants or an unconstrained array type; yields the value TRUE otherwise. The value of this attribute is of the predefined type BOOLEAN. (See 7.4.2.)

8   P'COUNT   For a prefix P that denotes an entry of a task unit:

Yields the number of entry calls presently queued on the entry (if the attribute is evaluated within an accept statement for the entry P, the count does not include the calling task). The value of this attribute is of the type *universal_integer*. (See 9.9.)

9   P'DELTA   For a prefix P that denotes a fixed point subtype:

Yields the value of the delta specified in the fixed accuracy definition for the subtype P. The value of this attribute is of the type *universal_real*. (See 3.5.10.)

10   P'DIGITS   For a prefix P that denotes a floating point subtype:

Yields the number of decimal digits in the decimal mantissa of model numbers of the subtype P. (This attribute yields the number D of section 3.5.7.) The value of this attribute is of the type *universal_integer*. (See 3.5.8.)

11   P'EMAX   For a prefix P that denotes a floating point subtype:

Yields the largest exponent value in the binary canonical form of model numbers of the subtype P. (This attribute yields the product $4*B$ of section 3.5.7.) The value of this attribute is of the type *universal_integer*. (See 3.5.8.)

12   P'EPSILON   For a prefix P that denotes a floating point subtype:

Yields the absolute value of the difference between the model number 1.0 and the next model number above, for the subtype P. The value of this attribute is of the type *universal_real*. (See 3.5.8.)

13   P'FIRST   For a prefix P that denotes a scalar type, or a subtype of a scalar type:

Yields the lower bound of P. The value of this attribute has the same type as P. (See 3.5.)

14   P'FIRST   For a prefix P that is appropriate for an array type, or that denotes a constrained array subtype:

Yields the lower bound of the first index range. The value of this attribute has the same type as this lower bound. (See 3.6.2 and 3.8.2.)

P'FIRST(N)	For a prefix P that is appropriate for an array type, or that denotes a constrained array subtype:	15

Yields the lower bound of the N-th index range. The value of this attribute has the same type as this lower bound. The argument N must be a static expression of type *universal_integer*. The value of N must be positive (nonzero) and no greater than the dimensionality of the array. (See 3.6.2 and 3.8.2.)

P'FIRST_BIT	For a prefix P that denotes a component of a record object:	16

Yields the offset, from the start of the first of the storage units occupied by the component, of the first bit occupied by the component. This offset is measured in bits. The value of this attribute is of the type *universal_integer*. (See 13.7.2.)

P'FORE	For a prefix P that denotes a fixed point subtype:	17

Yields the minimum number of characters needed for the integer part of the decimal representation of any value of the subtype P, assuming that the representation does not include an exponent, but includes a one-character prefix that is either a minus sign or a space. (This minimum number does not include superfluous zeros or underlines, and is at least two.) The value of this attribute is of the type *universal_integer*. (See 3.5.10.)

P'IMAGE	For a prefix P that denotes a discrete type or subtype:	18

This attribute is a function with a single parameter. The actual parameter X must be a value of the base type of P. The result type is the predefined type STRING. The result is the *image* of the value of X, that is, a sequence of characters representing the value in display form. The image of an integer value is the corresponding decimal literal; without underlines, leading zeros, exponent, or trailing spaces; but with a one character prefix that is either a minus sign or a space.

The image of an enumeration value is either the corresponding identifier in upper case or the corresponding character literal (including the two apostrophes); neither leading nor trailing spaces are included. The image of a character other than a graphic character is implementation-defined. (See 3.5.5.)

P'LARGE	For a prefix P that denotes a real subtype:	19

The attribute yields the largest positive model number of the subtype P. The value of this attribute is of the type *universal_real*. (See 3.5.8 and 3.5.10.)

P'LAST	For a prefix P that denotes a scalar type, or a subtype of a scalar type:	20

Yields the upper bound of P. The value of this attribute has the same type as P. (See 3.5.)

P'LAST	For a prefix P that is appropriate for an array type, or that denotes a constrained array subtype:	21

Yields the upper bound of the first index range. The value of this attribute has the same type as this upper bound. (See 3.6.2 and 3.8.2.)

22   P'LAST(N)   For a prefix P that is appropriate for an array type, or that denotes a constrained array subtype:

Yields the upper bound of the N-th index range. The value of this attribute has the same type as this upper bound. The argument N must be a static expression of type *universal_integer*. The value of N must be positive (nonzero) and no greater than the dimensionality of the array. (See 3.6.2 and 3.8.2.)

23   P'LAST_BIT   For a prefix P that denotes a component of a record object:

Yields the offset, from the start of the first of the storage units occupied by the component, of the last bit occupied by the component. This offset is measured in bits. The value of this attribute is of the type *universal_integer*. (See 13.7.2.)

24   P'LENGTH   For a prefix P that is appropriate for an array type, or that denotes a constrained array subtype:

Yields the number of values of the first index range (zero for a null range). The value of this attribute is of the type *universal_integer*. (See 3.6.2.)

25   P'LENGTH(N)   For a prefix P that is appropriate for an array type, or that denotes a constrained array subtype:

Yields the number of values of the N-th index range (zero for a null range). The value of this attribute is of the type *universal_integer*. The argument N must be a static expression of type *universal_integer*. The value of N must be positive (nonzero) and no greater than the dimensionality of the array. (See 3.6.2 and 3.8.2.)

26   P'MACHINE_EMAX   For a prefix P that denotes a floating point type or subtype:

Yields the largest value of *exponent* for the machine representation of the base type of P. The value of this attribute is of the type *universal_integer*. (See 13.7.3.)

27   P'MACHINE_EMIN   For a prefix P that denotes a floating point type or subtype:

Yields the smallest (most negative) value of *exponent* for the machine representation of the base type of P. The value of this attribute is of the type *universal_integer*. (See 13.7.3.)

28   P'MACHINE_MANTISSA   For a prefix P that denotes a floating point type or subtype:

Yields the number of digits in the *mantissa* for the machine representation of the base type of P (the digits are extended digits in the range 0 to P'MACHINE_RADIX - 1). The value of this attribute is of the type *universal_integer*. (See 13.7.3.)

P'MACHINE_OVERFLOWS	For a prefix P that denotes a real type or subtype:

Yields the value TRUE if every predefined operation on values of the base type of P either provides a correct result, or raises the exception NUMERIC_ERROR in overflow situations; yields the value FALSE otherwise. The value of this attribute is of the predefined type BOOLEAN. (See 13.7.3.)

P'MACHINE_RADIX	For a prefix P that denotes a floating point type or subtype:

Yields the value of the *radix* used by the machine representation of the base type of P. The value of this attribute is of the type *universal_integer*. (See 13.7.3.)

P'MACHINE_ROUNDS	For a prefix P that denotes a real type or subtype:

Yields the value TRUE if every predefined arithmetic operation on values of the base type of P either returns an exact result or performs rounding; yields the value FALSE otherwise. The value of this attribute is of the predefined type BOOLEAN. (See 13.7.3.)

P'MANTISSA	For a prefix P that denotes a real subtype:

Yields the number of binary digits in the binary mantissa of model numbers of the subtype P. (This attribute yields the number B of section 3.5.7 for a floating point type, or of section 3.5.9 for a fixed point type.) The value of this attribute is of the type *universal_integer*. (See 3.5.8 and 3.5.10.)

P'POS	For a prefix P that denotes a discrete type or subtype:

This attribute is a function with a single parameter. The actual parameter X must be a value of the base type of P. The result type is the type *universal_integer*. The result is the position number of the value of the actual parameter. (See 3.5.5.)

P'POSITION	For a prefix P that denotes a component of a record object:

Yields the offset, from the start of the first storage unit occupied by the record, of the first of the storage units occupied by the component. This offset is measured in storage units. The value of this attribute is of the type *universal_integer*. (See 13.7.2.)

P'PRED	For a prefix P that denotes a discrete type or subtype:

This attribute is a function with a single parameter. The actual parameter X must be a value of the base type of P. The result type is the base type of P. The result is the value whose position number is one less than that of X. The exception CONSTRAINT_ERROR is raised if X equals P'BASE'FIRST. (See 3.5.5.)

P'RANGE	For a prefix P that is appropriate for an array type, or that denotes a constrained array subtype:

Yields the first index range of P, that is, the range P'FIRST .. P'LAST. (See 3.6.2.)

29

30

31

32

33

34

35

36

37   P'RANGE(N)   For a prefix P that is appropriate for an array type, or that denotes a constrained array subtype:

Yields the N-th index range of P, that is, the range P'FIRST(N) .. P'LAST(N). (See 3.6.2.)

38   P'SAFE_EMAX   For a prefix P that denotes a floating point type or subtype:

Yields the largest exponent value in the binary canonical form of safe numbers of the base type of P. (This attribute yields the number E of section 3.5.7.) The value of this attribute is of the type *universal_integer*. (See 3.5.8.)

39   P'SAFE_LARGE   For a prefix P that denotes a real type or subtype:

Yields the largest positive safe number of the base type of P. The value of this attribute is of the type *universal_real*. (See 3.5.8 and 3.5.10.)

40   P'SAFE_SMALL   For a prefix P that denotes a real type or subtype:

Yields the smallest positive (nonzero) safe number of the base type of P. The value of this attribute is of the type *universal_real*. (See 3.5.8 and 3.5.10.)

41   P'SIZE   For a prefix P that denotes an object:

Yields the number of bits allocated to hold the object. The value of this attribute is of the type *universal_integer*. (See 13.7.2.)

42   P'SIZE   For a prefix P that denotes any type or subtype:

Yields the minimum number of bits that is needed by the implementation to hold any possible object of the type or subtype P. The value of this attribute is of the type *universal_integer*. (See 13.7.2.)

43   P'SMALL   For a prefix P that denotes a real subtype:

Yields the smallest positive (nonzero) model number of the subtype P. The value of this attribute is of the type *universal_real*. (See 3.5.8 and 3.5.10.)

44   P'STORAGE_SIZE   For a prefix P that denotes an access type or subtype:

Yields the total number of storage units reserved for the collection associated with the base type of P. The value of this attribute is of the type *universal_integer*. (See 13.7.2.)

45   P'STORAGE_SIZE   For a prefix P that denotes a task type or a task object:

Yields the number of storage units reserved for each activation of a task of the type P or for the activation of the task object P. The value of this attribute is of the type *universal_integer*. (See 13.7.2.)

P'SUCC   For a prefix P that denotes a discrete type or subtype: 46

This attribute is a function with a single parameter. The actual parameter X must be a value of the base type of P. The result type is the base type of P. The result is the value whose position number is one greater than that of X. The exception CONSTRAINT_ERROR is raised if X equals P'BASE'LAST. (See 3.5.5.)

P'TERMINATED   For a prefix P that is appropriate for a task type: 47

Yields the value TRUE if the task P is terminated; yields the value FALSE otherwise. The value of this attribute is of the predefined type BOOLEAN. (See 9.9.)

P'VAL   For a prefix P that denotes a discrete type or subtype: 48

This attribute is a special function with a single parameter X which can be of any integer type. The result type is the base type of P. The result is the value whose position number is the *universal_integer* value corresponding to X. The exception CONSTRAINT_ERROR is raised if the *universal_integer* value corresponding to X is not in the range P'POS (P'BASE'FIRST) .. P'POS (P'BASE'LAST). (See 3.5.5.)

P'VALUE   For a prefix P that denotes a discrete type or subtype: 49

This attribute is a function with a single parameter. The actual parameter X must be a value of the predefined type STRING. The result type is the base type of P. Any leading and any trailing spaces of the sequence of characters that corresponds to X are ignored.

For an enumeration type, if the sequence of characters has the syntax of an enumeration literal and if this literal exists for the base type of P, the result is the corresponding enumeration value. For an integer type, if the sequence of characters has the syntax of an integer literal, with an optional single leading character that is a plus or minus sign, and if there is a corresponding value in the base type of P, the result is this value. In any other case, the exception CONSTRAINT_ERROR is raised. (See 3.5.5.)

P'WIDTH   For a prefix P that denotes a discrete subtype: 50

Yields the maximum image length over all values of the subtype P (the *image* is the sequence of characters returned by the attribute IMAGE). The value of this attribute is of the type *universal_integer*. (See 3.5.5.)

B. Predefined Language Pragmas

This annex defines the pragmas LIST, PAGE, and OPTIMIZE, and summarizes the definitions given elsewhere of the remaining language-defined pragmas. [1]

Pragma	Meaning

CONTROLLED Takes the simple name of an access type as the single argument. This pragma [2] is only allowed immediately within the declarative part or package specification that contains the declaration of the access type; the declaration must occur before the pragma. This pragma is not allowed for a derived type. This pragma specifies that automatic storage reclamation must not be performed for objects designated by values of the access type, except upon leaving the innermost block statement, subprogram body, or task body that encloses the access type declaration, or after leaving the main program (see 4.8).

ELABORATE Takes one or more simple names denoting library units as arguments. This [3] pragma is only allowed immediately after the context clause of a compilation unit (before the subsequent library unit or secondary unit). Each argument must be the simple name of a library unit mentioned by the context clause. This pragma specifies that the corresponding library unit body must be elaborated before the given compilation unit. If the given compilation unit is a subunit, the library unit body must be elaborated before the body of the ancestor library unit of the subunit (see 10.5).

INLINE Takes one or more names as arguments; each name is either the name of a [4] subprogram or the name of a generic subprogram. This pragma is only allowed at the place of a declarative item in a declarative part or package specification, or after a library unit in a compilation, but before any subsequent compilation unit. This pragma specifies that the subprogram bodies should be expanded inline at each call whenever possible; in the case of a generic subprogram, the pragma applies to calls of its instantiations (see 6.3.2).

INTERFACE Takes a language name and a subprogram name as arguments. This pragma is [5] allowed at the place of a declarative item, and must apply in this case to a subprogram declared by an earlier declarative item of the same declarative part or package specification. This pragma is also allowed for a library unit; in this case the pragma must appear after the subprogram declaration, and before any subsequent compilation unit. This pragma specifies the other language (and thereby the calling conventions) and informs the compiler that an object module will be supplied for the corresponding subprogram (see 13.9).

LIST Takes one of the identifiers ON or OFF as the single argument. This pragma is [6] allowed anywhere a pragma is allowed. It specifies that listing of the compilation is to be continued or suspended until a LIST pragma with the opposite argument is given within the same compilation. The pragma itself is always listed if the compiler is producing a listing.

MEMORY_SIZE Takes a numeric literal as the single argument. This pragma is only allowed at [7] the start of a compilation, before the first compilation unit (If any) of the compilation. The effect of this pragma is to use the value of the specified numeric literal for the definition of the named number MEMORY_SIZE (see 13.7).

8   OPTIMIZE   Takes one of the identifiers TIME or SPACE as the single argument. This pragma is only allowed within a declarative part and it applies to the block or body enclosing the declarative part. It specifies whether time or space is the primary optimization criterion.

9   PACK   Takes the simple name of a record or array type as the single argument. The allowed positions for this pragma, and the restrictions on the named type, are governed by the same rules as for a representation clause. The pragma specifies that storage minimization should be the main criterion when selecting the representation of the given type (see 13.1).

10   PAGE   This pragma has no argument, and is allowed anywhere a pragma is allowed. It specifies that the program text which follows the pragma should start on a new page (if the compiler is currently producing a listing).

11   PRIORITY   Takes a static expression of the predefined integer subtype PRIORITY as the single argument. This pragma is only allowed within the specification of a task unit or immediately within the outermost declarative part of a main program. It specifies the priority of the task (or tasks of the task type) or the priority of the main program (see 9.8).

12   SHARED   Takes the simple name of a variable as the single argument. This pragma is allowed only for a variable declared by an object declaration and whose type is a scalar or access type; the variable declaration and the pragma must both occur (in this order) immediately within the same declarative part or package specification. This pragma specifies that every read or update of the variable is a synchronization point for that variable. An implementation must restrict the objects for which this pragma is allowed to objects for which each of direct reading and direct updating is implemented as an indivisible operation (see 9.11).

13   STORAGE_UNIT   Takes a numeric literal as the single argument. This pragma is only allowed at the start of a compilation, before the first compilation unit (if any) of the compilation. The effect of this pragma is to use the value of the specified numeric literal for the definition of the named number STORAGE_UNIT (see 13.7).

14   SUPPRESS   Takes as arguments the identifier of a check and optionally also the name of either an object, a type or subtype, a subprogram, a task unit, or a generic unit. This pragma is only allowed either immediately within a declarative part or immediately within a package specification. In the latter case, the only allowed form is with a name that denotes an entity (or several overloaded subprograms) declared immediately within the package specification. The permission to omit the given check extends from the place of the pragma to the end of the declarative region associated with the innermost enclosing block statement or program unit. For a pragma given in a package specification, the permission extends to the end of the scope of the named entity.

If the pragma includes a name, the permission to omit the given check is further restricted: it is given only for operations on the named object or on all objects of the base type of a named type or subtype; for calls of a named subprogram; for activations of tasks of the named task type; or for instantiations of the given generic unit (see 11.7).

15   SYSTEM_NAME   Takes an enumeration literal as the single argument. This pragma is only allowed at the start of a compilation, before the first compilation unit (if any) of the compilation. The effect of this pragma is to use the enumeration literal with the specified identifier for the definition of the constant SYSTEM_NAME. This pragma is only allowed if the specified identifier corresponds to one of the literals of the type NAME declared in the package SYSTEM (see 13.7).

C. Predefined Language Environment

This annex outlines the specification of the package STANDARD containing all predefined identifiers in the language. The corresponding package body is implementation-defined and is not shown.

The operators that are predefined for the types declared in the package STANDARD are given in comments since they are implicitly declared. Italics are used for pseudo-names of anonymous types (such as *universal_real*) and for undefined information (such as *implementation_defined* and *any_fixed_point_type*).

package STANDARD **is**

  type BOOLEAN **is** (FALSE, TRUE);

  -- The predefined relational operators for this type are as follows:

```
--  function  "="   (LEFT, RIGHT : BOOLEAN) return BOOLEAN;
--  function  "/="  (LEFT, RIGHT : BOOLEAN) return BOOLEAN;
--  function  "<"   (LEFT, RIGHT : BOOLEAN) return BOOLEAN;
--  function  "<="  (LEFT, RIGHT : BOOLEAN) return BOOLEAN;
--  function  ">"   (LEFT, RIGHT : BOOLEAN) return BOOLEAN;
--  function  ">="  (LEFT, RIGHT : BOOLEAN) return BOOLEAN;
```

  -- The predefined logical operators and the predefined logical negation operator are as follows:

```
--  function "and"  (LEFT, RIGHT : BOOLEAN) return BOOLEAN;
--  function "or"   (LEFT, RIGHT : BOOLEAN) return BOOLEAN;
--  function "xor"  (LEFT, RIGHT : BOOLEAN) return BOOLEAN;

--  function "not"  (RIGHT : BOOLEAN) return BOOLEAN;
```

  -- The universal type *universal_integer* is predefined.

  type INTEGER **is** *implementation_defined*;

  -- The predefined operators for this type are as follows:

```
--  function  "="   (LEFT, RIGHT : INTEGER) return BOOLEAN;
--  function  "/="  (LEFT, RIGHT : INTEGER) return BOOLEAN;
--  function  "<"   (LEFT, RIGHT : INTEGER) return BOOLEAN;
--  function  "<="  (LEFT, RIGHT : INTEGER) return BOOLEAN;
--  function  ">"   (LEFT, RIGHT : INTEGER) return BOOLEAN;
--  function  ">="  (LEFT, RIGHT : INTEGER) return BOOLEAN;
```

```
-- function  "+"    (RIGHT : INTEGER) return INTEGER;
-- function  "-"    (RIGHT : INTEGER) return INTEGER;
-- function  "abs"  (RIGHT : INTEGER) return INTEGER;


-- function  "+"    (LEFT, RIGHT : INTEGER) return INTEGER;
-- function  "-"    (LEFT, RIGHT : INTEGER) return INTEGER;
-- function  "*"    (LEFT, RIGHT : INTEGER) return INTEGER;
-- function  "/"    (LEFT, RIGHT : INTEGER) return INTEGER;
-- function  "rem"  (LEFT, RIGHT : INTEGER) return INTEGER;
-- function  "mod"  (LEFT, RIGHT : INTEGER) return INTEGER;


-- function  "**"   (LEFT : INTEGER; RIGHT : INTEGER) return INTEGER;
```

7   -- An implementation may provide additional predefined integer types. It is recommended that the
-- names of such additional types end with INTEGER as in SHORT_INTEGER or LONG_INTEGER.
-- The   specification   of each operator for the type *universal_integer*, or for any additional
-- predefined integer type, is obtained by replacing INTEGER by the name of the type in the
-- specification of the corresponding operator of the type INTEGER, except for the right operand
-- of the exponentiating operator.

8   -- The universal type *universal_real* is predefined.

9   **type** FLOAT **is** *implementation_defined*;

-- The predefined operators for this type are as follows:

```
-- function  "="    (LEFT, RIGHT : FLOAT) return BOOLEAN;
-- function  "/="   (LEFT, RIGHT : FLOAT) return BOOLEAN;
-- function  "<"    (LEFT, RIGHT : FLOAT) return BOOLEAN;
-- function  "<="   (LEFT, RIGHT : FLOAT) return BOOLEAN;
-- function  ">"    (LEFT, RIGHT : FLOAT) return BOOLEAN;
-- function  ">="   (LEFT, RIGHT : FLOAT) return BOOLEAN;


-- function  "+"    (RIGHT : FLOAT) return FLOAT;
-- function  "-"    (RIGHT : FLOAT) return FLOAT;
-- function  "abs"  (RIGHT : FLOAT) return FLOAT;


-- function  "+"    (LEFT, RIGHT : FLOAT) return FLOAT;
-- function  "-"    (LEFT, RIGHT : FLOAT) return FLOAT;
-- function  "*"    (LEFT, RIGHT : FLOAT) return FLOAT;
-- function  "/"    (LEFT, RIGHT : FLOAT) return FLOAT;


-- function  "**"   (LEFT : FLOAT; RIGHT : INTEGER) return FLOAT;
```

10   -- An implementation may provide additional predefined floating point types. It is recom-
-- mended that the names of such additional types end with FLOAT as in SHORT_FLOAT or
-- LONG_FLOAT. The specification of each operator for the type *universal_real*, or for any
-- additional predefined floating point type, is obtained by replacing FLOAT by the name of the
-- type in the specification of the corresponding operator of the type FLOAT.

-- In addition, the following operators are predefined for universal types: ¹¹

-- **function** "*" (LEFT : *universal_integer*;   RIGHT : *universal_real*)   **return** *universal_real*;
-- **function** "*" (LEFT : *universal_real*;   RIGHT : *universal_integer*) **return** *universal_real*;
-- **function** "/" (LEFT : *universal_real*;   RIGHT : *universal_integer*) **return** *universal_real*;

-- The type *universal_fixed* is predefined. The only operators declared for this type are

-- **function** "*" (LEFT : *any_fixed_point_type*; RIGHT : *any_fixed_point_type*) **return** *universal_fixed*;
-- **function** "/" (LEFT : *any_fixed_point_type*; RIGHT : *any_fixed_point_type*) **return** *universal_fixed*;

-- The following characters form the standard ASCII character set. Character literals cor- ¹²
-- responding to control characters are not identifiers; they are indicated in italics in this definition.

type CHARACTER **is** ¹³

(*nul*,	*soh*,	*stx*,	*etx*,	*eot*,	*enq*,	*ack*,	*bel*,
bs,	*ht*,	*lf*,	*vt*,	*ff*,	*cr*,	*so*,	*si*,
dle,	*dc1*,	*dc2*,	*dc3*,	*dc4*,	*nak*,	*syn*,	*etb*,
can,	*em*,	*sub*,	*esc*,	*fs*,	*gs*,	*rs*,	*us*,
' ',	'!',	'"',	'#',	'$',	'%',	'&',	''',
'(',	')',	'*',	'+',	',',	'-',	'.',	'/',
'0',	'1',	'2',	'3',	'4',	'5',	'6',	'7',
'8',	'9',	':',	';',	'<',	'=',	'>',	'?',
'@',	'A',	'B',	'C',	'D',	'E',	'F',	'G',
'H',	'I',	'J',	'K',	'L',	'M',	'N',	'O',
'P',	'Q',	'R',	'S',	'T',	'U',	'V',	'W',
'X',	'Y',	'Z',	'[',	'\',	']',	'^',	'_',
'`',	'a',	'b',	'c',	'd',	'e',	'f',	'g',
'h',	'i',	'j',	'k',	'l',	'm',	'n',	'o',
'p',	'q',	'r',	's',	't',	'u',	'v',	'w',
'x',	'y',	'z',	'{',	'|',	'}',	'~',	*del*);

for CHARACTER **use** -- 128 ASCII character set without holes
    (0, 1, 2, 3, 4, 5, ..., 125, 126, 127);

-- The predefined operators for the type CHARACTER are the same as for any enumeration type. ¹⁴

15 **package** ASCII **is**

-- Control characters:

NUL	: **constant** CHARACTER := *nul*;	SOH	: **constant** CHARACTER := *soh*;
STX	: **constant** CHARACTER := *stx*;	ETX	: **constant** CHARACTER := *etx*;
EOT	: **constant** CHARACTER := *eot*;	ENQ	: **constant** CHARACTER := *enq*;
ACK	: **constant** CHARACTER := *ack*;	BEL	: **constant** CHARACTER := *bel*;
BS	: **constant** CHARACTER := *bs*;	HT	: **constant** CHARACTER := *ht*;
LF	: **constant** CHARACTER := *lf*;	VT	: **constant** CHARACTER := *vt*;
FF	: **constant** CHARACTER := *ff*;	CR	: **constant** CHARACTER := *cr*;
SO	: **constant** CHARACTER := *so*;	SI	: **constant** CHARACTER := *si*;
DLE	: **constant** CHARACTER := *dle*;	DC1	: **constant** CHARACTER := *dc1*;
DC2	: **constant** CHARACTER := *dc2*;	DC3	: **constant** CHARACTER := *dc3*;
DC4	: **constant** CHARACTER := *dc4*;	NAK	: **constant** CHARACTER := *nak*;
SYN	: **constant** CHARACTER := *syn*;	ETB	: **constant** CHARACTER := *etb*;
CAN	: **constant** CHARACTER := *can*;	EM	: **constant** CHARACTER := *em*;
SUB	: **constant** CHARACTER := *sub*;	ESC	: **constant** CHARACTER := *esc*;
FS	: **constant** CHARACTER := *fs*;	GS	: **constant** CHARACTER := *gs*;
RS	: **constant** CHARACTER := *rs*;	US	: **constant** CHARACTER := *us*;
DEL	: **constant** CHARACTER := *del*;		

-- Other characters:

EXCLAM	: **constant** CHARACTER := '!';	QUOTATION	: **constant** CHARACTER := '"';
SHARP	: **constant** CHARACTER := '#';	DOLLAR	: **constant** CHARACTER := '$';
PERCENT	: **constant** CHARACTER := '%';	AMPERSAND	: **constant** CHARACTER := '&';
COLON	: **constant** CHARACTER := ':';	SEMICOLON	: **constant** CHARACTER := ';';
QUERY	: **constant** CHARACTER := '?';	AT_SIGN	: **constant** CHARACTER := '@';
L_BRACKET	: **constant** CHARACTER := '[';	BACK_SLASH	: **constant** CHARACTER := '\';
R_BRACKET	: **constant** CHARACTER := ']';	CIRCUMFLEX	: **constant** CHARACTER := '^';
UNDERLINE	: **constant** CHARACTER := '_';	GRAVE	: **constant** CHARACTER := '`';
L_BRACE	: **constant** CHARACTER := '{';	BAR	: **constant** CHARACTER := '	';
R_BRACE	: **constant** CHARACTER := '}';	TILDE	: **constant** CHARACTER := '~';

-- Lower case letters:

LC_A : **constant** CHARACTER := 'a';
...
LC_Z : **constant** CHARACTER := 'z';

end ASCII;

16 -- Predefined subtypes:

subtype NATURAL **is** INTEGER **range** O .. INTEGER'LAST;
subtype POSITIVE **is** INTEGER **range** 1 .. INTEGER'LAST;

-- Predefined string type: 17

type STRING **is array**(POSITIVE **range** <>) **of** CHARACTER;

pragma PACK(STRING);

-- The predefined operators for this type are as follows: 18

```
-- function "="   (LEFT, RIGHT : STRING) return BOOLEAN;
-- function "/="  (LEFT, RIGHT : STRING) return BOOLEAN;
-- function "<"   (LEFT, RIGHT : STRING) return BOOLEAN;
-- function "<="  (LEFT, RIGHT : STRING) return BOOLEAN;
-- function ">"   (LEFT, RIGHT : STRING) return BOOLEAN;
-- function ">="  (LEFT, RIGHT : STRING) return BOOLEAN;
```

```
-- function "&" (LEFT : STRING;     RIGHT : STRING)    return STRING;
-- function "&" (LEFT : CHARACTER;  RIGHT : STRING)    return STRING;
-- function "&" (LEFT : STRING;     RIGHT : CHARACTER) return STRING;
-- function "&" (LEFT : CHARACTER;  RIGHT : CHARACTER) return STRING;
```

type DURATION **is delta** *implementation_defined* **range** *implementation_defined*;   19

-- The predefined operators for the type DURATION are the same as for any fixed point type.

-- The predefined exceptions: 20

```
CONSTRAINT_ERROR  : exception;
NUMERIC_ERROR     : exception;
PROGRAM_ERROR     : exception;
STORAGE_ERROR     : exception;
TASKING_ERROR     : exception;
```

end STANDARD;

Certain aspects of the predefined entities cannot be completely described in the language itself.   21
For example, although the enumeration type BOOLEAN can be written showing the two
enumeration literals FALSE and TRUE, the short-circuit control forms cannot be expressed in the
language.

Note:

The language definition predefines the following library units: 22

-	The package CALENDAR	(see 9.6)
-	The package SYSTEM	(see 13.7)
-	The package MACHINE_CODE (if provided)	(see 13.8)
-	The generic procedure UNCHECKED_DEALLOCATION	(see 13.10.1)
-	The generic function UNCHECKED_CONVERSION	(see 13.10.2)
-	The generic package SEQUENTIAL_IO	(see 14.2.3)
-	The generic package DIRECT_IO	(see 14.2.5)
-	The package TEXT_IO	(see 14.3.10)
-	The package IO_EXCEPTIONS	(see 14.5)
-	The package LOW_LEVEL_IO	(see 14.6)

D. Glossary

This appendix is informative and is not part of the standard definition of the Ada programming language. Italicized terms in the abbreviated descriptions below either have glossary entries themselves or are described in entries for related terms.

Accept statement. See *entry*.

Access type. A value of an access type (an *access value*) is either a null value, or a value that *designates* an *object* created by an *allocator*. The designated object can be read and updated via the access value. The definition of an access type specifies the type of the objects designated by values of the access type. See also *collection*.

Actual parameter. See *parameter*.

Aggregate. The evaluation of an aggregate yields a value of a *composite type*. The value is specified by giving the value of each of the *components*. Either *positional association* or *named association* may be used to indicate which value is associated with which component.

Allocator. The evaluation of an allocator creates an *object* and returns a new *access value* which *designates* the object.

Array type. A value of an array type consists of *components* which are all of the same *subtype* (and hence, of the same type). Each component is uniquely distinguished by an *index* (for a one-dimensional array) or by a sequence of indices (for a multidimensional array). Each index must be a value of a *discrete type* and must lie in the correct index *range*.

Assignment. Assignment is the *operation* that replaces the current value of a *variable* by a new value. An *assignment statement* specifies a variable on the left, and on the right, an *expression* whose value is to be the new value of the variable.

Attribute. The evaluation of an attribute yields a predefined characteristic of a named entity; some attributes are *functions*.

Block statement. A block statement is a single statement that may contain a sequence of statements. It may also include a *declarative part*, and *exception handlers*; their effects are local to the block statement.

Body. A body defines the execution of a *subprogram*, *package*, or *task*. A *body stub* is a form of body that indicates that this execution is defined in a separately compiled *subunit*.

Collection. A collection is the entire set of *objects* created by evaluation of *allocators* for an *access type*.

Compilation unit. A compilation unit is the *declaration* or the *body* of a *program unit*, presented for compilation as an independent text. It is optionally preceded by a *context clause*, naming other compilation units upon which it depends by means of one more *with* clauses.

Component. A component is a value that is a part of a larger value, or an *object* that is part of a larger object.

Composite type. A composite type is one whose values have *components*. There are two kinds of composite type: *array types* and *record types*.

Constant. See *object*.

Constraint. A constraint determines a subset of the values of a *type*. A value in that subset *satisfies* the constraint.

Context clause. See *compilation unit*.

Declaration. A declaration associates an identifier (or some other notation) with an entity. This association is in effect within a region of text called the *scope* of the declaration. Within the scope of a declaration, there are places where it is possible to use the identifier to refer to the associated declared entity. At such places the identifier is said to be a *simple name* of the entity; the *name* is said to *denote* the associated entity.

Declarative Part. A declarative part is a sequence of *declarations*. It may also contain related information such as *subprogram bodies* and *representation clauses*.

Denote. See *declaration*.

Derived Type. A derived type is a *type* whose operations and values are replicas of those of an existing type. The existing type is called the *parent type* of the derived type.

Designate. See *access type*, *task*.

Direct visibility. See *visibility*.

Discrete Type. A discrete type is a *type* which has an ordered set of distinct values. The discrete types are the *enumeration* and *integer types*. Discrete types are used for indexing and iteration, and for choices in case statements and record *variants*.

Discriminant. A discriminant is a distinguished *component* of an *object* or value of a *record type*. The *subtypes* of other components, or even their presence or absence, may depend on the value of the discriminant.

Discriminant constraint. A discriminant constraint on a *record type* or *private type* specifies a value for each *discriminant* of the *type*.

Elaboration. The elaboration of a *declaration* is the process by which the declaration achieves its effect (such as creating an *object*); this process occurs during program execution.

Entry. An entry is used for communication between *tasks*. Externally, an entry is called just as a *subprogram* is called; its internal behavior is specified by one or more *accept statements* specifying the actions to be performed when the entry is called.

Enumeration type. An enumeration type is a *discrete type* whose values are represented by enumeration literals which are given explicitly in the *type declaration*. These enumeration literals are either *identifiers* or *character literals*.

Evaluation. The evaluation of an *expression* is the process by which the value of the expression is computed. This process occurs during program execution.

Exception. An exception is an error situation which may arise during program execution. To *raise* an exception is to abandon normal program execution so as to signal that the error has taken place. An *exception handler* is a portion of program text specifying a response to the exception. Execution of such a program text is called *handling* the exception.

Expanded name. An expanded name *denotes* an entity which is *declared* immediately within some construct. An expanded name has the form of a *selected component*: the *prefix* denotes the construct (a *program unit*; or a *block*, loop, or *accept statement*); the *selector* is the *simple name* of the entity.

Expression. An expression defines the computation of a value.

Fixed point type. See *real type*.

Floating point type. See *real type*.

Formal parameter. See *parameter*.

Function. See *subprogram*.

Generic unit. A generic unit is a template either for a set of *subprograms* or for a set of *packages*. A subprogram or package created using the template is called an *instance* of the generic unit. A *generic instantiation* is the kind of *declaration* that creates an instance.

A generic unit is written as a subprogram or package but with the specification prefixed by a *generic formal part* which may declare *generic formal parameters*. A generic formal parameter is either a *type*, a *subprogram*, or an *object*. A generic unit is one of the kinds of *program unit*.

Handler. See *exception*.

Index. See *array type*.

Index constraint. An index constraint for an *array type* specifies the lower and upper bounds for each index *range* of the array type.

Indexed component. An indexed component *denotes* a *component* in an *array*. It is a form of *name* containing *expressions* which specify the values of the *indices* of the array component. An indexed component may also denote an *entry* in a family of entries.

Instance. See *generic unit*.

Integer type. An integer type is a *discrete type* whose values represent all integer numbers within a specific *range*.

Lexical element. A lexical element is an identifier, a *literal*, a delimiter, or a comment.

Limited type. A limited type is a *type* for which neither assignment nor the predefined comparison for equality is implicitly declared. All *task* types are limited. A *private type* can be defined to be limited. An equality operator can be explicitly declared for a limited type.

Literal. A literal represents a value literally, that is, by means of letters and other characters. A literal is either a numeric literal, an enumeration literal, a character literal, or a string literal.

Mode. See *parameter*.

Model number. A model number is an exactly representable value of a *real type*. Operations of a real type are defined in terms of operations on the model numbers of the type.

The properties of the model numbers and of their operations are the minimal properties preserved by all implementations of the real type.

Name. A name is a construct that stands for an entity: it is said that the name *denotes* the entity, and that the entity is the meaning of the name. See also *declaration*, *prefix*.

Named association. A named association specifies the association of an item with one or more positions in a list, by naming the positions.

Object. An object contains a value. A program creates an object either by *elaborating* an *object declaration* or by *evaluating* an *allocator*. The declaration or allocator specifies a *type* for the object: the object can only contain values of that type.

Operation. An operation is an elementary action associated with one or more *types*. It is either implicitly declared by the *declaration* of the type, or it is a *subprogram* that has a *parameter* or *result* of the type.

Operator. An operator is an operation which has one or two operands. A unary operator is written before an operand; a binary operator is written between two operands. This notation is a special kind of *function call*. An operator can be declared as a function. Many operators are implicitly declared by the *declaration* of a *type* (for example, most type declarations imply the declaration of the equality operator for values of the type).

Overloading. An identifier can have several alternative meanings at a given point in the program text: this property is called *overloading*. For example, an overloaded enumeration literal can be an identifier that appears in the definitions of two or more *enumeration types*. The effective meaning of an overloaded identifier is determined by the context. *Subprograms*, *aggregates*, *allocators*, and string *literals* can also be overloaded.

Package. A package specifies a group of logically related entities, such as *types*, *objects* of those types, and *subprograms* with *parameters* of those types. It is written as a *package declaration* and a *package body*. The package declaration has a *visible part*, containing the *declarations* of all entities that can be explicitly used outside the package. It may also have a *private part* containing structural details that complete the specification of the visible entities, but which are irrelevant to the user of the package. The *package body* contains implementations of *subprograms* (and possibly *tasks* as other *packages*) that have been specified in the package declaration. A package is one of the kinds of *program unit*.

Parameter. A parameter is one of the named entities associated with a *subprogram*, *entry*, or *generic unit*, and used to communicate with the corresponding subprogram body, *accept statement* or generic body. A *formal parameter* is an identifier used to denote the named entity within the body. An *actual parameter* is the particular entity associated with the corresponding formal parameter by a *subprogram call*, *entry call*, or *generic instantiation*. The *mode* of a formal parameter specifies whether the associated actual parameter supplies a value for the formal parameter, or the formal supplies a value for the actual parameter, or both. The association of actual parameters with formal parameters can be specified by *named associations*, by *positional associations*, or by a combination of these.

Parent type. See *derived type*.

Positional association. A positional association specifies the association of an item with a position in a list, by using the same position in the text to specify the item.

Pragma. A pragma conveys information to the compiler.

Prefix. A prefix is used as the first part of certain kinds of name. A prefix is either a *function call* or a *name*.

Private part. See *package*.

Private type. A private type is a *type* whose structure and set of values are clearly defined, but not directly available to the user of the type. A private type is known only by its *discriminants* (if any) and by the set of *operations* defined for it. A private type and its applicable operations are defined in the *visible part* of a *package*, or in a *generic formal part*. *Assignment*, equality, and inequality are also defined for private types, unless the private type is *limited*.

Procedure. See *subprogram*.

Program. A program is composed of a number of *compilation units*, one of which is a *subprogram* called the *main program*. Execution of the program consists of execution of the main program, which may invoke subprograms declared in the other compilation units of the program.

Program unit. A program unit is any one of a *generic unit*, *package*, *subprogram*, or *task unit*.

Qualified expression. A qualified expression is an *expression* preceded by an indication of its *type* or *subtype*. Such qualification is used when, in its absence, the expression might be ambiguous (for example as a consequence of *overloading*).

Raising an exception. See *exception*.

Range. A range is a contiguous set of values of a *scalar type*. A range is specified by giving the lower and upper bounds for the values. A value in the range is said to *belong* to the range.

Range constraint. A range constraint of a *type* specifies a *range*, and thereby determines the subset of the values of the type that *belong* to the range.

Real type. A real type is a *type* whose values represent approximations to the real numbers. There are two kinds of real type: *fixed point types* are specified by absolute error bound; *floating point types* are specified by a relative error bound expressed as a number of significant decimal digits.

Record type. A value of a record type consists of *components* which are usually of different *types* or *subtypes*. For each component of a record value or record *object*, the definition of the record type specifies an identifier that uniquely determines the component within the record.

Renaming declaration. A renaming declaration declares another *name* for an entity.

Rendezvous. A rendezvous is the interaction that occurs between two parallel *tasks* when one task has called an *entry* of the other task, and a corresponding *accept statement* is being executed by the other task on behalf of the calling task.

Representation clause. A representation clause directs the compiler in the selection of the mapping of a *type*, an *object*, or a *task* onto features of the underlying machine that executes a program. In some cases, representation clauses completely specify the mapping; in other cases, they provide criteria for choosing a mapping.

Satisfy. See *constraint, subtype.*

Scalar type. An *object* or value of a scalar *type* does not have *components*. A scalar type is either a *discrete type* or a *real type*. The values of a scalar type are ordered.

Scope. See *declaration.*

Selected component. A selected component is a *name* consisting of a *prefix* and of an identifier called the *selector*. Selected components are used to denote record components, *entries*, and *objects* designated by access values; they are also used as *expanded names*.

Selector. See *selected component.*

Simple name. See *declaration, name.*

Statement. A statement specifies one or more actions to be performed during the execution of a *program*.

Subcomponent. A subcomponent is either a *component*, or a component of another subcomponent.

Subprogram. A subprogram is either a *procedure* or a *function*. A procedure specifies a sequence of actions and is invoked by a *procedure call* statement. A function specifies a sequence of actions and also returns a value called the *result*, and so a *function call* is an *expression*. A subprogram is written as a *subprogram declaration*, which specifies its *name, formal parameters*, and (for a function) its result; and a *subprogram body* which specifies the sequence of actions. The subprogram call specifies the *actual parameters* that are to be associated with the formal parameters. A subprogram is one of the kinds of *program unit*.

Subtype. A subtype of a *type* characterizes a subset of the values of the type. The subset is determined by a *constraint* on the type. Each value in the set of values of a subtype *belongs* to the subtype and *satisfies* the constraint determining the subtype.

Subunit. See *body.*

Task. A task operates in parallel with other parts of the program. It is written as a *task specification* (which specifies the *name* of the task and the names and *formal parameters* of its entries), and a *task body* which defines its execution. A *task unit* is one of the kinds of *program unit*. A *task type* is a *type* that permits the subsequent *declaration* of any number of similar tasks of the type. A value of a task type is said to *designate* a task.

Type. A type characterizes both a set of values, and a set of *operations* applicable to those values. A *type definition* is a language construct that defines a type. A particular type is either an *access type*, an *array type*, a *private type*, a *record type*, a *scalar type*, or a *task type*.

Use clause. A use clause achieves *direct visibility* of *declarations* that appear in the *visible parts* of named *packages*.

Variable. See *object*.

Variant part. A variant part of a *record* specifies alternative record *components*, depending on a *discriminant* of the record. Each value of the discriminant establishes a particular alternative of the variant part.

Visibility. At a given point in a program text, the *declaration* of an entity with a certain identifier is said to be *visible* if the entity is an acceptable meaning for an occurrence at that point of the identifier. The declaration is *visible* by *selection* at the place of the *selector* in a *selected component* or at the place of the name in a *named association*. Otherwise, the declaration is *directly visible*, that is, if the identifier alone has that meaning.

Visible part. See *package*.

With clause. See *compilation unit*.

E. Syntax Summary

2.1

```
graphic_character ::= basic_graphic_character
    | lower_case_letter | other_special_character

basic_graphic_character ::=
    upper_case_letter | digit
    | special_character | space_character

basic_character ::=
    basic_graphic_character | format_effector
```

2.3

```
identifier ::=
    letter {[underline] letter_or_digit}

letter_or_digit ::= letter | digit

letter ::= upper_case_letter | lower_case_letter
```

2.4

```
numeric_literal ::= decimal_literal | based_literal
```

2.4.1

```
decimal_literal ::= integer [.integer] [exponent]

integer ::= digit {[underline] digit}

exponent ::= E [+] integer | E - integer
```

2.4.2

```
based_literal ::=
    base # based_integer [.based_integer] # [exponent]

base ::= integer

based_integer ::=
    extended_digit {[underline] extended_digit}

extended_digit ::= digit | letter
```

2.5

```
character_literal ::= 'graphic_character'
```

2.6

```
string_literal ::= "{graphic_character}"
```

2.8

```
pragma ::=
    pragma identifier [(argument_association
                       {, argument_association})];

argument_association ::=
    [argument_identifier =>] name
    | [argument_identifier =>] expression
```

3.1

```
basic_declaration ::=
    object_declaration      | number_declaration
    | type_declaration      | subtype_declaration
    | subprogram_declaration | package_declaration
    | task_declaration      | generic_declaration
    | exception_declaration | generic_instantiation
    | renaming_declaration  | deferred_constant_declaration
```

3.2

```
object_declaration ::=
    identifier_list : [constant] subtype_indication [:= expression];
    | identifier_list : [constant] constrained_array_definition
                                              [:= expression];

number_declaration ::=
    identifier_list : constant := universal_static_expression;

identifier_list ::=   identifier {, identifier}
```

3.3.1

```
type_declaration ::=   full_type_declaration
    | incomplete_type_declaration | private_type_declaration

full_type_declaration ::=
    type identifier [discriminant_part] is type_definition;

type_definition ::=
    enumeration_type_definition | integer_type_definition
    | real_type_definition      | array_type_definition
    | record_type_definition    | access_type_definition
    | derived_type_definition
```

3.3.2

```
subtype_declaration ::=
    subtype identifier is subtype_indication;

subtype_indication ::=   type_mark [constraint]

type_mark ::= type_name | subtype_name

constraint ::=
    range_constraint      | floating_point_constraint
    | fixed_point_constraint | index_constraint
    | discriminant_constraint
```

3.4

```
derived_type_definition ::= new subtype_indication
```

3.5

```
range_constraint ::=   range range

range ::=   range_attribute
    | simple_expression .. simple_expression
```

3.5.1

```
enumeration_type_definition ::=
  (enumeration_literal_specification
   | enumeration_literal_specification|)

enumeration_literal_specification ::=   enumeration_literal

enumeration_literal ::=   identifier | character_literal
```

3.5.4

```
integer_type_definition ::=   range_constraint
```

3.5.6

```
real_type_definition ::=
  floating_point_constraint | fixed_point_constraint
```

3.5.7

```
floating_point_constraint ::=
  floating_accuracy_definition [range_constraint]

floating_accuracy_definition ::=
  digits static_simple_expression
```

3.5.9

```
fixed_point_constraint ::=
  fixed_accuracy_definition [range_constraint]

fixed_accuracy_definition ::=
  delta static_simple_expression
```

3.6

```
array_type_definition ::=
  unconstrained_array_definition | constrained_array_definition

unconstrained_array_definition ::=
  array(index_subtype_definition {, index_subtype_definition}) of
    component_subtype_indication

constrained_array_definition ::=
  array index_constraint of component_subtype_indication

index_subtype_definition ::= type_mark range <>

index_constraint ::=   (discrete_range {, discrete_range})

discrete_range ::= discrete_subtype_indication | range
```

3.7

```
record_type_definition ::=
  record
    component_list
  end record

component_list ::=
    component_declaration {component_declaration}
  | {component_declaration} variant_part
  | null;

component_declaration ::=
  identifier_list : component_subtype_definition [:= expression];

component_subtype_definition ::=   subtype_indication
```

3.7.1

```
discriminant_part ::=
  (discriminant_specification {; discriminant_specification})

discriminant_specification ::=
  identifier_list : type_mark [:= expression]
```

3.7.2

```
discriminant_constraint ::=
  (discriminant_association {, discriminant_association})

discriminant_association ::=
  |discriminant_simple_name {| discriminant_simple_name|
    expression
```

3.7.3

```
variant_part ::=
  case discriminant_simple_name is
      variant
    | variant|
  end case;

variant ::=
  when choice {| choice| =>
    component_list

choice ::= simple_expression
  | discrete_range | others | component_simple_name
```

3.8

```
access_type_definition ::= access subtype_indication
```

3.8.1

```
incomplete_type_declaration ::=
  type identifier [discriminant_part];
```

3.9

```
declarative_part ::=
  |basic_declarative_item| {later_declarative_item}

basic_declarative_item ::= basic_declaration
  | representation_clause | use_clause

later_declarative_item ::= body
  | subprogram_declaration | package_declaration
  | task_declaration      | generic_declaration
  | use_clause            | generic_instantiation

body ::= proper_body | body_stub

proper_body ::=
  subprogram_body | package_body | task_body
```

Syntax Summary

4.1

```
name ::= simple_name
    | character_literal    | operator_symbol
    | indexed_component    | slice
    | selected_component   | attribute

simple_name ::= identifier

prefix ::= name | function_call
```

4.1.1

```
indexed_component ::= prefix(expression {, expression})
```

4.1.2

```
slice ::= prefix(discrete_range)
```

4.1.3

```
selected_component ::= prefix.selector

selector ::= simple_name
    | character_literal | operator_symbol | all
```

4.1.4

```
attribute ::= prefix'attribute_designator

attribute_designator ::=
    simple_name [(universal_static_expression)]
```

4.3

```
aggregate ::=
    (component_association {, component_association})

component_association ::=
    [choice {| choice} => ] expression
```

4.4

```
expression ::=
        relation {and relation}   | relation {and then relation}
    |   relation {or relation}    | relation {or else relation}
    |   relation {xor relation}

relation ::=
        simple_expression [relational_operator simple_expression]
    |   simple_expression [not] in range
    |   simple_expression [not] in type_mark

simple_expression ::=
    [unary_adding_operator] term {binary_adding_operator term}

term ::= factor {multiplying_operator factor}

factor ::= primary [** primary] | abs primary | not primary

primary ::=
        numeric_literal | null | aggregate | string_literal
    |   name | allocator | function_call | type_conversion
    |   qualified_expression | (expression)
```

4.5

```
logical_operator    ::= and | or | xor

relational_operator ::= = | /= | < | <= | > | >=

binary_adding_operator ::= + | - | &

unary_adding_operator ::= + | -

multiplying_operator ::= * | / | mod | rem

highest_precedence_operator ::= ** | abs | not
```

4.6

```
type_conversion ::= type_mark(expression)
```

4.7

```
qualified_expression ::=
    type_mark'(expression) | type_mark'aggregate
```

4.8

```
allocator ::=
    new subtype_indication | new qualified_expression
```

5.1

```
sequence_of_statements ::= statement {statement}

statement ::=
    {label} simple_statement | {label} compound_statement

simple_statement ::= null_statement
    | assignment_statement | procedure_call_statement
    | exit_statement       | return_statement
    | goto_statement       | entry_call_statement
    | delay_statement      | abort_statement
    | raise_statement      | code_statement

compound_statement ::=
        if_statement      | case_statement
    |   loop_statement    | block_statement
    |   accept_statement  | select_statement

label ::= <<label_simple_name>>

null_statement ::= null;
```

5.2

```
assignment_statement ::=
    variable_name := expression;
```

5.3

```
if_statement ::=
    if condition then
        sequence_of_statements
    {elsif condition then
        sequence_of_statements}
    {else
        sequence_of_statements}
    end if;

condition ::= boolean_expression
```

5.4

```
case_statement ::=
    case expression is
        case_statement_alternative
        | case_statement_alternative|
    end case;

case_statement_alternative ::=
    when choice {| choice | =>
        sequence_of_statements
```

5.5

```
loop_statement ::=
    |loop_simple_name:|
        | iteration_scheme| loop
            sequence_of_statements
        end loop |loop_simple_name|;

iteration_scheme ::= while condition
    | for loop_parameter_specification

loop_parameter_specification ::=
    identifier in [reverse] discrete_range
```

5.6

```
block_statement ::=
    |block_simple_name:|
        | declare
            declarative_part|
        begin
            sequence_of_statements
        | exception
            exception_handler
            | exception_handler|]
        end |block_simple_name|;
```

5.7

```
exit_statement ::=
    exit |loop_name| [when condition];
```

5.8

```
return_statement ::= return [expression];
```

5.9

```
goto_statement ::= goto label_name;
```

6.1

```
subprogram_declaration ::= subprogram_specification;

subprogram_specification ::=
        procedure identifier [formal_part]
    | function designator [formal_part] return type_mark

designator ::= identifier | operator_symbol

operator_symbol ::= string_literal

formal_part ::=
    (parameter_specification {; parameter_specification})

parameter_specification ::=
    identifier_list : mode type_mark [:= expression]

mode ::= [in] | in out | out
```

6.3

```
subprogram_body ::=
    subprogram_specification is
        | declarative_part|
    begin
        sequence_of_statements
    | exception
        exception_handler
        : exception_handler|]
    end |designator|;
```

6.4

```
procedure_call_statement ::=
    procedure_name [actual_parameter_part];

function_call ::=
    function_name [actual_parameter_part]

actual_parameter_part ::=
    (parameter_association {, parameter_association})

parameter_association ::=
    | formal_parameter =>| actual_parameter

formal_parameter ::= parameter_simple_name

actual_parameter ::=
    expression | variable_name | type_mark(variable_name)
```

7.1

```
package_declaration ::= package_specification;

package_specification ::=
    package identifier is
        |basic_declarative_item|
    | private
        |basic_declarative_item|]
    end |package_simple_name|

package_body ::=
    package body package_simple_name is
        | declarative_part|
    | begin
        sequence_of_statements
    | exception
        exception_handler
        : exception_handler|]]
    end |package_simple_name|;
```

7.4

```
private_type_declaration ::=
    type identifier [discriminant_part] is [limited] private;

deferred_constant_declaration ::=
    identifier_list : constant type_mark;
```

8.4

```
use_clause ::= use package_name {, package_name};
```

8.5

```
renaming_declaration ::=
        identifier : type_mark       renames object_name;
    | identifier : exception       renames exception_name;
    | package identifier           renames package_name;
    | subprogram_specification     renames
                                   subprogram_or_entry_name;
```

9.1

task_declaration ::= task_specification;

task_specification ::=
  task |type| identifier |is
      entry_declaration|
    :representation_clause|
  end |task_simple_name]]

task_body ::=
    task body task_simple_name is
      | declarative_part|
    begin
        sequence_of_statements
  | exception
        exception_handler
        exception_handler|]
    end |task_simple_name];

9.5

entry_declaration ::=
  entry identifier |(discrete_range)| [formal_part];

entry_call_statement ::=
  entry_name |actual_parameter_part];

accept_statement ::=
  accept entry_simple_name |(entry_index)| [formal_part] [do
    sequence_of_statements
  end |entry_simple_name]];

entry_index ::= expression

9.6

delay_statement ::= delay simple_expression;

9.7

select_statement ::= selective_wait
  | conditional_entry_call | timed_entry_call

9.7.1

selective_wait ::=
    select
      select_alternative
  | or
      select_alternative|
  | else
      sequence_of_statements|
    end select;

select_alternative ::=
  | when condition =>|
    selective_wait_alternative

selective_wait_alternative ::= accept_alternative
  | delay_alternative | terminate_alternative

accept_alternative ::=
  accept_statement |sequence_of_statements|

delay_alternative ::=
  delay_statement |sequence_of_statements|

terminate_alternative ::= terminate;

9.7.2

conditional_entry_call ::=
  select
      entry_call_statement
    | sequence_of_statements|
  else
      sequence_of_statements
  end select;

9.7.3

timed_entry_call ::=
  select
      entry_call_statement
    | sequence_of_statements|
  or
      delay_alternative
  end select;

9.10

abort_statement ::= abort task_name |, task_name];

10.1

compilation ::= |compilation_unit|

compilation_unit ::=
      context_clause library_unit
  | context_clause secondary_unit

library_unit ::=
      subprogram_declaration | package_declaration
  | generic_declaration | generic_instantiation
  | subprogram_body

secondary_unit ::= library_unit_body | subunit

library_unit_body ::= subprogram_body | package_body

10.1.1

context_clause ::= |with_clause |use_clause||

with_clause ::=
  with unit_simple_name |, unit_simple_name];

10.2

body_stub ::=
      subprogram_specification is separate;
  | package body package_simple_name is separate;
  | task body task_simple_name is separate;

subunit ::= separate (parent_unit_name) proper_body

11.1

exception_declaration ::= identifier_list : exception;

11.2

exception_handler ::=
  when exception_choice || exception_choice| =>
    sequence_of_statements

exception_choice ::= exception_name | others

11.3

raise_statement ::= raise |exception_name];

12.1

generic_declaration ::= generic_specification;

generic_specification ::=
    generic_formal_part subprogram_specification
  | generic_formal_part package_specification

generic_formal_part ::= **generic** {generic_parameter_declaration}

generic_parameter_declaration ::=
    identifier_list : [**in** [**out**]] type_mark [:= expression];
  | **type** identifier **is** generic_type_definition;
  | private_type_declaration
  | **with** subprogram_specification [**is** name];
  | **with** subprogram_specification [**is** <>];

generic_type_definition ::=
    (<>) | **range** <> | **digits** <> | **delta** <>
  | array_type_definition | access_type_definition

12.3

generic_instantiation ::=
    package identifier **is**
        new *generic_package*_name [generic_actual_part];
  | **procedure** identifier **is**
        new *generic_procedure*_name [generic_actual_part];
  | **function** designator **is**
        new *generic_function*_name [generic_actual_part];

generic_actual_part ::=
    (generic_association {, generic_association})

generic_association ::=
    [generic_formal_parameter =>] generic_actual_parameter

generic_formal_parameter ::=
    *parameter*_simple_name | operator_symbol

generic_actual_parameter ::= expression | *variable*_name
  | *subprogram*_name | *entry*_name | type_mark

13.1

representation_clause ::=
    type_representation_clause | address_clause

type_representation_clause ::= length_clause
  | enumeration_representation_clause
  | record_representation_clause

13.2

length_clause ::= **for** attribute **use** simple_expression;

13.3

enumeration_representation_clause ::=
    for *type*_simple_name **use** aggregate;

13.4

record_representation_clause ::=
    for *type*_simple_name **use**
        record [alignment_clause]
            {component_clause}
        end record:

alignment_clause ::= **at mod** *static*_simple_expression;

component_clause ::=
    *component*_name **at** *static*_simple_expression
                        range *static*_range;

13.5

address_clause ::=
    for simple_name **use at** simple_expression;

13.8

code_statement ::= type_mark'*record*_aggregate;

Syntax Cross Reference

In the list given below each syntactic category is followed by the section number where it is defined. For example:

adding_operator   4.5

In addition, each syntactic category is followed by the names of other categories in whose definition it appears. For example, adding_operator appears in the definition of simple_expression:

adding_operator   4.5
   simple_expression   4.4

An ellipsis (...) is used when the syntactic category is not defined by a syntax rule. For example:

lower_case_letter   ...

All uses of parentheses are combined in the term "()". The italicized prefixes used with some terms have been deleted here.

abort	...	**actual_parameter**		6.4
abort_statement	9.10	parameter_association		6.4
abort_statement	9.10	**actual_parameter_part**		6.4
simple_statement	5.1	entry_call_statement		9.5
		function_call		6.4
abs	...	procedure_call_statement		6.4
factor	4.4			
highest_precedence_operator	4.5	**address_clause**		13.5
		representation_clause		13.1
accept	...			
accept_statement	9.5	**aggregate**		4.3
		code_statement		13.8
accept_alternative	9.7.1	enumeration_representation_clause		13.3
selective_wait_alternative	9.7.1	primary		4.4
		qualified_expression		4.7
accept_statement	9.5			
accept_alternative	9.7.1	**alignment_clause**		13.4
compound_statement	5.1	record_representation_clause		13.4
access	...			
access_type_definition	3.8	**all**		...
		selector		4.1.3
access_type_definition	3.8			
generic_type_definition	12.1	**allocator**		4.8
type_definition	3.3.1	primary		4.4

F. Implementation-Dependent Characteristics

The Ada language definition allows for certain machine-dependences in a controlled manner. No machine-dependent syntax or semantic extensions or restrictions are allowed. The only allowed implementation-dependences correspond to implementation-dependent pragmas and attributes, certain machine-dependent conventions as mentioned in chapter 13, and certain allowed restrictions on representation clauses.

The reference manual of each Ada implementation must include an appendix (called Appendix F) that describes all implementation-dependent characteristics. The appendix F for a given implementation must list in particular:

(1) The form, allowed places, and effect of every implementation-dependent pragma.

(2) The name and the type of every implementation-dependent attribute.

(3) The specification of the package SYSTEM (see 13.7).

(4) The list of all restrictions on representation clauses (see 13.1)

(5) The conventions used for any implementation-generated name denoting implementation-dependent components (see 13.4).

(6) The interpretation of expressions that appear in address clauses, including those for interrupts (see 13.5).

(7) Any restriction on unchecked conversions (see 13.10.2).

(8) Any implementation-dependent characteristics of the input-output packages (see 14).

Index

An entry exists in this index for each technical term or phrase that is defined in the reference manual. The term or phrase is in boldface and is followed by the section number where it is defined, also in boldface, for example:

Record aggregate 4.3.1

References to other sections that provide additional information are shown after a semicolon, for example:

Record aggregate 4.3.1;   4.3

References to other related entries in the index follow in brackets, and a line that is indented below a boldface entry gives the section numbers where particular uses of the term or phrase can be found; for example:

Record aggregate 4.3.1;   4.3
[see also: aggregate]
   as a basic operation 3.3.3;   3.7.4
   in a code statement 13.8

The index also contains entries for different parts of a phrase, entries that correct alternative terminology, and entries directing the reader to information otherwise hard to find, for example:

Check
[see: suppress pragma]

Abandon elaboration or evaluation (of declarations or statements)
[see: exception, raise statement]

Abnormal task 9.10; 9.9
[see also: abort statement]
   as recipient of an entry call 9.7.2, 9.7.3, 11.5; 9.5
   raising tasking_error in a calling task 11.5; 9.5

Abort statement 9.10
[see also: abnormal task, statement, task]
   as a simple statement 5.1

Abs unary operator 4.5.6; 4.5
[see also: highest precedence operator]
   as an operation of a fixed point type 3.5.10
   as an operation of a floating point type 3.5.8
   as an operation of an integer type 3.5.5
   in a factor 4.4

Absolute value operation 4.5.6

Accept alternative (of a selective wait) **9.7.1**
   for an interrupt entry 13.5.1

Accept statement 9.5; 9, D
[see also: entry call statement, simple name in..., statement, task]
   accepting a conditional entry call 9.7.2
   accepting a timed entry call 9.7.3
   and optimization with exceptions 11.6
   as a compound statement 5.1
   as part of a declarative region 8.1
   entity denoted by an expanded name 4.1.3

   in an abnormal task 9.10
   in a select alternative 9.7.1
   including an exit statement 5.7
   including a goto statement 5.9
   including a return statement 5.8
   raising an exception 11.5
   to communicate values 9.11

Access to external files 14.2

Access type 3.8; 3.3, D
[see also: allocator, appropriate for a type, class of type, collection, derived type of an access type, null access value, object designated by...]
   as a derived type 3.4
   as a generic formal type 12.1.2, 12.3.5
   deallocation [see: unchecked_deallocation]
   designating a limited type 7.4.4
   designating a task type determining task dependence 9.4
   formal parameter 6.2
   name in a controlled pragma 4.8
   object initialization 3.2.1
   operation 3.8.2
   prefix 4.1
   value designating an object 3.2, 4.8
   value designating an object with discriminants 5.2
   with a discriminant constraint 3.7.2
   with an index constraint 3.6.1

Access type definition 3.8; 3.3.1, 12.1.2
   as a generic type definition 12.1

Access_check
[see: constraint_error, suppress]

Accuracy
    of a numeric operation 4.5.7
    of a numeric operation of a universal type 4.10

Activation
    [see: task activation]

Actual object
    [see: generic actual object]

Actual parameter 6.4.1; D; (of an operator) **6.7**; (of a subprogram) 6.4; 6.2, 6.3
    [see also: entry call, formal parameter, function call, procedure call statement, subprogram call]
    characteristics and overload resolution 6.6
    in a generic instantiation [see: generic actual parameter]
    of an array type 3.6.1
    of a record type 3.7.2
    of a task type 9.2
    that is an array aggregate 4.3.2
    that is a loop parameter 5.5

Actual parameter part 6.4
    in a conditional entry call 9.7.2
    in an entry call statement 9.5
    in a function call 6.4
    in a procedure call statement 6.4
    in a timed entry call 9.7.3

Actual part
    [see: actual parameter part, generic actual part]

Actual subprogram
    [see: generic actual subprogram]

Actual type
    [see: generic actual type]

Adding operator
    [see: binary adding operator, unary adding operator]

Addition operation 4.5.3
    accuracy for a real type 4.5.7

ADDRESS (predefined attribute) **13.7.2**; 3.5.5, 3.5.8, 3.5.10, 3.6.2, 3.7.4, 3.8.2, 7.4.2, 9.9, 13.7, A
    [see also: address clause, system.address]

ADDRESS (predefined type)
    [see: system.address]

Address clause 13.5; 13.1, 13.7
    [see also: storage address, system.address]
    as a representation clause 13.1
    for an entry 13.5.1

AFT (predefined attribute) for a fixed point type **3.5.10**; A

Aft field of text_io output **14.3.8**, **14.3.10**

Aggregate 4.3, D
    [see also: array aggregate, overloading of..., record aggregate]
    as a basic operation 3.3.3; 3.6.2, 3.7.4
    as a primary 4.4
    in an allocator 4.8
    in a code statement 13.8
    in an enumeration representation clause 13.3
    in a qualified expression 4.7
    must not be the argument of a conversion 4.6
    of a derived type 3.4

Alignment clause (in a record representation clause) **13.4**

All in a selected component **4.1.3**

Allocation of processing resources 9.8

Allocator 4.8; 3.8, D
    [see also: access type, collection, exception raised during..., initial value, object, overloading of...]
    as a basic operation 3.3.3; 3.8.2
    as a primary 4.4
    creating an object with a discriminant 4.8; 5.2
    for an array type 3.6.1
    for a generic formal access type 12.1.2
    for a private type 7.4.1
    for a record type 3.7.2
    for a task type 9.2; 9.3
    must not be the argument of a conversion 4.6
    raising storage_error due to the size of the collection being exceeded 11.1
    setting a task value 9.2
    without storage check 11.7

Allowed 1.6

Alternative
    [see: accept alternative, case statement alternative, closed alternative, delay alternative, open alternative, select alternative, selective wait, terminate alternative]

Ambiguity
    [see: overloading]

Ampersand
    [see: catenation]
    character 2.1
    delimiter 2.2

Ancestor library unit 10.2

And operator
    [see: logical operator]

And then control form
    [see: short circuit control form]

Anonymous type 3.3.1; 3.5.4, 3.5.7, 3.5.9, 3.6, 9.1
    anonymous base type [see: first named subtype]

ANSI (american national standards institute) **2.1**

Apostrophe character 2.1
    in a character literal 2.5

Apostrophe delimiter 2.2
    in an attribute 4.1.4
    of a qualified expression 4.7

Apply 10.1.1

Appropriate for a type **4.1**
    for an array type 4.1.1, 4.1.2
    for a record type 4.1.3
    for a task type 4.1.3

Arbitrary selection of select alternatives **9.7.1**

Argument association in a pragma **2.8**

Argument identifier in a pragma **2.8**

Arithmetic operator 4.5
    [see also: binary adding operator, exponentiating operator, multiplying operator, predefined operator, unary adding operator]
    as an operation of a fixed point type 3.5.10

Basic character 2.1
|see also: basic graphic character, character|

Basic character set 2.1
is sufficient for a program text 2.10

Basic declaration 3.1
as a basic declarative item 3.9

Basic declarative item 3.9
in a package specification 7.1; 7.2

Basic graphic character 2.1
|see also: basic character, digit, graphic character, space character, special character, upper case letter|

Basic operation 3.3.3
|see also: operation, scope of..., visibility...|
accuracy for a real type 4.5.7
implicitly declared 3.1, 3.3.3
of an access type 3.8.2
of an array type 3.6.2
of a derived type 3.4
of a discrete type 3.5.5
of a fixed point type 3.5.10
of a floating point type 3.5.8
of a limited type 7.4.4
of a private type 7.4.2
of a record type 3.7.4
of a task type 9.9
propagating an exception 11.6
raising an exception 11.4.1
that is an attribute 4.1.4

Belong
to a range 3.5
to a subtype 3.3
to a subtype of an access type 3.8

Binary adding operator 4.5; 4.5.3, C
|see also: arithmetic operator, overloading of an operator|
for time predefined type 9.6
in a simple expression 4.4
overloaded 6.7

Binary operation 4.5

Bit
|see: storage bits|

Blank skipped by a text_io procedure **14.3.5**

Block name 5.6
declaration 5.1
implicitly declared 3.1

Block statement 5.6; D
|see also: completed block statement, statement|
as a compound statement 5.1
as a declarative region 8.1
entity denoted by an expanded name 4.1.3
having dependent tasks 9.4
including an exception handler 11.2; 11
including an implicit declaration 5.1
including a suppress pragma 11.7
raising an exception 11.4.1, 11.4.2

Body 3.9; D
|see also: declaration, generic body, generic package body, generic subprogram body, library unit, package body, proper body, subprogram body, task body|
as a later declarative item 3.9

Body stub 10.2; D
acting as a subprogram declaration 6.3
as a body 3.9
as a portion of a declarative region 8.1
must be in the same declarative region as the declaration 3.9, 7.1

BOOLEAN (predefined type) **3.5.3**; C
derived 3.4; 3.5.3
result of a condition 5.3
result of an explicitly declared equality operator 6.7

Boolean expression
|see: condition, expression|

Boolean operator
|see: logical operator|

Boolean type 3.5.3
|see also: derived type of a boolean type, predefined type|
operation 3.5.5; 4.5.1, 4.5.2, 4.5.6
operation comparing real operands 4.5.7

Bound
|see: error bound, first attribute, last attribute|

Bound of an array **3.6, 3.6.1**
|see also: index range, slice|
aggregate 4.3.2
ignored due to index_check suppression 11.7
initialization in an allocator constrains the allocated object 4.8
that is a formal parameter 6.2
that is the result of an operation 4.5.1, 4.5.3, 4.5.6

Bound of a range 3.5; 3.5.4
of a discrete range in a slice 4.1.2
of a discrete range is of universal_integer type 3.6.1
of a static discrete range 4.9

Bound of a scalar type **3.5**

Bound of a slice **4.1.2**

Box compound delimiter 2.2
in a generic parameter declaration 12.1, 12.1.2, 12.1.3; 12.3.3
in an index subtype definition 3.6

Bracket
|see: label bracket, left parenthesis, parenthesized expression, right parenthesis, string bracket|

CALENDAR (predefined library package) **9.6**; C

Call
|see: conditional entry call, entry call statement, function call, procedure call statement, subprogram call, timed entry call|

CALLABLE (predefined attribute)
for an abnormal task 9.10
for a task object 9.9; A

Calling conventions
|see: subprogram declaration|
of a subprogram written in another language 13.9

Cancelation of an entry call statement **9.7.2, 9.7.3**

Compiler listing
[see: list pragma, page pragma]

Compiler optimization
[see: optimization, optimize pragma]

Completed block statement 9.4

Completed subprogram 9.4

Completed task 9.4; 9.9
[see also: tasking_error, terminated task]
as recipient of an entry call 9.5, 9.7.2, 9.7.3
becoming abnormal 9.10
completion during activation 9.3
due to an exception in the task body 11.4.1, 11.4.2

Component (of a composite type) **3.3; 3.6, 3.7, D**
[see also: component association, component clause,
component list, composite type, default expression,
dependence on a discriminant, discriminant, indexed component, object, record type, selected component, subcom-
ponent]
combined by aggregate 4.3
depending on a discriminant 3.7.1; 11.1
name starting with a prefix 4.1
of an array 3.6 [see also: array type]
of a constant 3.2.1
of a derived type 3.4
of an object 3.2
of a private type 7.4.2
of a record 3.7 [see also: record type]
of a variable 3.2.1
simple name as a choice 3.7.3
subtype 3.7
subtype itself a composite type 3.6.1, 3.7.2
that is a task object 9.3
whose type is a limited type 7.4.4

Component association 4.3
in an aggregate 4.3
including an expression that is an array aggregate
4.3.2
named component association 4.3
named component association for selective visibility
8.3
positional component association 4.3

Component clause (in a record representation clause) **13.4**

Component declaration 3.7
[see also: declaration, record type definition]
as part of a basic declaration 3.1
having an extended scope 8.2
in a component list 3.7
of an array object 3.6.1
of a record object 3.7.2
visibility 8.3

Component list 3.7
in a record type definition 3.7
in a variant 3.7.3

Component subtype definition 3.7
[see also: dependence on a discriminant]
in a component declaration 3.7

Component type
catenation with an array type 4.5.3
object initialization [see: initial value]
of an expression in an array aggregate 4.3.2
of an expression in a record aggregate 4.3.1
of a generic formal array type 12.3.4
operation determining a composite type operation
4.5.1, 4.5.2

Composite type 3.3; 3.6, 3.7, D
[see also: array type, class of type, component, discriminant, record type, subcomponent]
including a limited subcomponent 7.4.4
including a task subcomponent 9.2
object initialization 3.2.1 [see also: initial value]
of an aggregate 4.3
with a private type component 7.4.2

Compound delimiter 2.2
[see also: arrow, assignment, box, delimiter, double dot,
double star, exponentiation, greater than or equal, inequality, left label bracket, less than or equal, right label bracket]
names of delimiters 2.2

Compound statement 5.1
[see also: statement]
including the destination of a goto statement 5.9

Concatenation
[see: catenation]

Condition 5.3
[see also: expression]
determining an open alternative of a selective wait
9.7.1
in an exit statement 5.7
in an if statement 5.3
in a while iteration scheme 5.5

Conditional compilation 10.6

Conditional entry call 9.7.2; 9.7
and renamed entries 8.5
subject to an address clause 13.5.1

Conforming 6.3.1
discriminant parts 6.3.1; 3.8.1, 7.4.1
formal parts 6.3.1
formal parts in entry declarations and accept statements 9.5
subprogram specifications 6.3.1; 6.3
subprogram specifications in body stub and subunit
10.2
type marks 6.3.1; 7.4.3

Conjunction
[see: logical operator]

Constant 3.2.1; D
[see also: deferred constant, loop parameter, object]
access object 3.8
formal parameter 6.2
generic formal object 12.1.1, 12.3
in a static expression 4.9
renamed 8.5
that is a slice 4.1.2

Constant declaration 3.2.1
[see also: deferred constant declaration]
as a full declaration 7.4.3
with an array type 3.6.1
with a record type 3.7.2

CONSTRAINED (predefined attribute)
for an object of a type with discriminants 3.7.4; A
for a private type 7.4.2, A

Constrained array definition 3.6
in an object declaration 3.2, 3.2.1

Constrained array type 3.6
[see also: array type, constraint]

Constrained subtype • Dead code elimination

Delay expression ● Discrete type

Discriminant 3.3, 3.7.1; 3.7, D
[see also: component clause, component, composite type, default expression, dependence on..., record type, selected component, subcomponent]
    in a record aggregate 4.3.1
    initialization in an allocator constrains the allocated object 4.8
    of a derived type 3.4
    of a formal parameter 6.2
    of a generic actual type 12.3.2
    of a generic formal type 12.3, 12.3.2
    of an implicitly initialized object 3.2.1
    of an object designated by an access value 3.7.2; 5.2
    of a private type 7.4.2; 3.3
    of a variant part must not be of a generic formal type 3.7.3
    simple name in a variant part 3.7.3
    subcomponent of an object 3.2.1
    with a default expression 3.7.1; 3.2.1

Discriminant association 3.7.2
    in a discriminant constraint 3.7.2
    named discriminant association 3.7.2
    named discriminant association for selective visibility 8.3
    positional discriminant association 3.7.2

Discriminant constraint 3.7.2; 3.3.2, D
[see also: dependence on a discriminant]
    ignored due to access_check suppression 11.7
    in an allocator 4.8
    on an access type 3.8
    violated 11.1

Discriminant part 3.7.1; 3.7
[see also: elaboration of...]
    absent from a record type declaration 3.7
    as a portion of a declarative region 8.1
    conforming to another 3.8.1, 6.3.1, 7.4.1
    in a generic formal type declaration 3.7.1; 12.1
    in an incomplete type declaration 3.8.1
    in a private type declaration 7.4, 7.4.1
    in a type declaration 3.3, 3.3.1
    must not include a pragma 2.8
    of a full type declaration is not elaborated 3.3.1

Discriminant specification 3.7.1
[see also: default expression]
    as part of a basic declaration 3.1
    declaring a component 3.7
    having an extended scope 8.2
    in a discriminant part 3.7.1
    visibility 8.3

Discriminant_check
[see: constraint_error, suppress]

Disjunction
[see: logical operator]

Divide
    character 2.1
    delimiter 2.2

Division operation 4.5.5
    accuracy for a real type 4.5.7

Division operator
[see: multiplying operator]

Division_check
[see: numeric_error, suppress]

Dot
[see: double dot]
    character 2.1 [see also: double dot, point character]
    delimiter 2.2
    delimiter of a selected component 8.3; 4.1.3

Double dot compound delimiter 2.2

Double hyphen starting a comment 2.7

Double star compound delimiter 2.2
[see also: exponentiation compound delimiter]

DURATION (predefined type) **9.6**; C
[see also: delay expression, fixed point type]
    of alternative delay statements 9.7.1

Effect
[see: elaboration has no other effect]

ELABORATE (predefined pragma) **10.5**; B

Elaborated 3.9

Elaboration 3.9; 3.1, 3.3, 10.1, D
[see also: exception raised during..., order of elaboration]
    optimized 10.6

Elaboration has no other effect 3.1

Elaboration of
    an access type definition 3.8
    an array type definition 3.6
    a body stub 10.2
    a component declaration 3.7
    a component subtype definition 3.7
    a constrained array definition 3.6
    a declaration 3.1
    a declarative item 3.9
    a declarative part 3.9
    a deferred constant declaration 7.4.3
    a derived type definition 3.4
    a discriminant constraint 3.7.2
    a discriminant part 3.7.1
    a discriminant specification 3.7.1
    an entry declaration 9.5
    an enumeration literal specification 3.5.1
    an enumeration type definition 3.5.1
    a fixed point type declaration 3.5.9
    a floating point type declaration 3.5.7
    a formal part 6.1
    a full type declaration 3.3.1
    a generic body 12.2
    a generic declaration 12.1
    a generic instantiation 12.3
    an incomplete type declaration 3.8.1
    an index constraint 3.6.1
    an integer type definition 3.5.4
    a library unit 10.5
    a loop parameter specification 5.5
    an object declaration 3.2.1
    a package body 7.3
    a package declaration 7.2
    a parameter specification 6.1
    a private type declaration 7.4.1
    a range constraint 3.5
    a real type definition 3.5.6
    a record type definition 3.7
    a renaming declaration 8.5
    a representation clause 13.1

EPSILON (predefined attribute) **3.5.8**; A

Equal
    character 2.1
    delimiter 2.2

Equality operator 4.5; 4.5.2
    [see also: limited type, relational operator]
    explicitly declared 4.5.2, 6.7; 7.4.4
    for an access type 3.8.2
    for an array type 3.6.2
    for a generic formal type 12.1.2
    for a limited type 4.5.2, 7.4.4
    for a real type 4.5.7
    for a record type 3.7.4

Erroneous execution 1.6
    [see also: program_error]
    due to an access to a deallocated object 13.10.1
    due to an unchecked conversion violating properties
    of objects of the result type 13.10.2
    due to assignment to a shared variable 9.11
    due to changing of a discriminant value 5.2, 6.2
    due to dependence on parameter-passing
    mechanism 6.2
    due to multiple address clauses for overlaid entities
    13.5
    due to suppression of an exception check 11.7
    due to use of an undefined value 3.2.1

Error bounds of a predefined operation of a real type **3.5.9,
4.5.7**; 3.5.6, 3.5.7

Error detected at
    compilation time 1.6
    run time 1.6

Error situation 1.6, 11, 11.1; 11.6

Error that may not be detected **1.6**

Evaluation (of an expression) **4.5**; D
    [see also: compile time evaluation, expression]
    at compile time 4.9, 10.6
    of an actual parameter 6.4.1
    of an aggregate 4.3; 3.3.3
    of an allocator 4.8
    of an array aggregate 4.3.2
    of a condition 5.3, 5.5, 5.7, 9.7.1
    of a default expression 3.7.2
    of a default expression for a formal parameter 6.4.2;
    6.1
    of a discrete range 3.5; 9.5
    of a discrete range used in an index constraint 3.6.1
    of an entry index 9.5
    of an expression in an assignment statement 5.2
    of an expression in a constraint 3.3.2
    of an expression in a generic actual parameter 12.3
    of an indexed component 4.1.1
    of an initial value [see: default expression]
    of a literal 4.2; 3.3.3
    of a logical operation 4.5.1
    of a name 4.1; 4.1.1, 4.1.2, 4.1.3, 4.1.4
    of a name in an abort statement 9.10
    of a name in a renaming declaration 8.5
    of a name of a variable 5.2, 6.4.1, 12.3
    of a primary 4.4
    of a qualified expression 4.7; 4.8
    of a range 3.5
    of a record aggregate 4.3.1
    of a short circuit control form 4.5.1
    of a static expression 4.9
    of a type conversion 4.6
    of a universal expression 4.10

    of the bounds of a loop parameter 5.5
    of the conditions of a selective wait 9.7.1

Evaluation order
    [see: order of evaluation]

Exception 11; 1.6, D
    [see also: constraint_error, numeric_error, predefined ..,
    program_error, raise statement, raising of .., storage_error,
    tasking_error, time_error]
    causing a loop to be exited 5.5
    causing a transfer of control 5.1
    due to an expression evaluated at compile time
    10.6
    implicitly declared in a generic instantiation 11.1
    in input-output 14.4; 14.5
    renamed 8.5
    suppress pragma 11.7

Exception choice 11.2

Exception declaration 11.1; 11
    as a basic declaration 3.1

Exception handler 11.2; D
    in an abnormal task 9.10
    in a block statement 5.6
    in a package body 7.1; 7.3
    in a subprogram body 6.3
    in a task body 9.1
    including a raise statement 11.3
    including the destination of a goto statement 5.9
    including the name of an exception 11.1
    not allowed in a code procedure body 13.8
    raising an exception 11.4.1
    selected to handle an exception 11.4.1; 11.6

Exception handling 11.4; 11.4.1, 11.4.2, 11.5

Exception propagation 11
    delayed by a dependent task 11.4.1
    from a declaration 11.4.2
    from a predefined operation 11.6
    from a statement 11.4.1
    to a communicating task 11.5

Exception raised during execution or elaboration of
    an accept statement 11.5
    an allocator of a task 9.3
    a conditional entry 9.7.2
    a declaration 11.4.2; 11.4
    a declarative part that declares tasks 9.3
    a generic instantiation 12.3.1, 12.3.2, 12.3.4,
    12.3.5
    a selective wait 9.7.1
    a statement 11.4.1; 11.4
    a subprogram call 6.3; 6.2, 6.5
    a task 11.5
    a timed entry call 9.7.3
    task activation 9.3

Exceptions and optimization 11.6

Exclamation character 2.1
    replacing vertical bar 2.10

Exclusive disjunction
    [see: logical operator]

Execution
    [see: sequence of statements, statement, task body, task]

Exit statement 5.7
    [see also: statement]

cannot be a universal_fixed operation 4.5.5
for a generic formal access type 12.3.5
for a generic formal array type 12.3.4
for a generic formal object 12.1.1
for a generic formal private type 12.3.2
for a generic formal scalar type 12.3.3
for a generic formal subprogram 12.1.3; 12.3.6
for a generic formal type 12.1.2
is not static 4.9
that is an array aggregate 4.3.2
that is a loop parameter 5.5
that is a task type 9.2

Generic actual part 12.3

Generic actual subprogram 12.1.3, 12.3.6
[see also: generic actual parameter]

Generic actual type
[see: generic actual parameter]
for a generic formal access type 12.3.5
for a generic formal array type 12.3.4
for a generic formal scalar type 12.3.3
for a generic formal type with discriminants 12.3.2
for a generic private formal type 12.3.2
that is a private type 7.4.1

Generic association 12.3
[see also: generic actual parameter, generic formal parameter]
named generic association 12.3
named generic association for selective visibility 8.3
positional generic association 12.3

Generic body 12.2; 12.1, 12.1.2, 12.3.2
[see also: body stub, elaboration of...]
in a package body 7.1
including an exception handler 11.2; 11
including an exit statement 5.7
including a goto statement 5.9
including an implicit declaration 5.1
must be in the same declarative region as the declaration 3.9, 7.1
not yet elaborated at an instantiation 3.9

Generic declaration 12.1; 12, 12.1.2, 12.2
[see also: elaboration of...]
and body as a declarative region 8.1
and proper body in the same compilation 10.3
as a basic declaration 3.1
as a later declarative item 3.9
as a library unit 10.1
in a package specification 7.1
recompiled 10.3

Generic formal object 12.1, 12.1.1; 3.2, 12.3, 12.3.1
[see also: default expression, generic formal parameter]
of an array type 3.6.1
of a record type 3.7.2

Generic formal parameter 12.1, 12.3; 12, D
[see also: generic actual parameter, generic association, generic formal object, generic formal subprogram, generic formal type, matching, object]
as a constant 3.2.1
as a variable 3.2.1
of a limited type 7.4.4
of a task type 9.2

Generic formal part 12.1; 12, D

Generic formal subprogram 12.1, 12.1.3; 12.1.2, 12.3, 12.3.6

[see also: generic formal parameter]
formal function 12.1.3
with the same name as another 12.3

Generic formal type 12.1, 12.1.2; 12.3
[see also: constraint on..., discriminant of..., generic formal parameter, subtype indication...]
as index or component type of a generic formal array type 12.3.4
formal access type 12.1.2, 12.3.5
formal array type 12.1.2, 12.3.4
formal array type (constrained) 12.1.2
formal discrete type 12.1.2
formal enumeration type 12.1.2
formal fixed point type 12.1.2
formal floating point type 12.1.2
formal integer type 12.1.2
formal limited private type 12.3.2
formal limited type 12.1.2
formal part 12.1.2
formal private type 12.1.2, 12.3.2
formal private type with discriminants 12.3.2
formal scalar type 12.1.2, 12.3.3

Generic function
[see: generic subprogram]

Generic instance 12.3; 12, 12.1, 12.2, D
[see also: generic instantiation, scope of...]
inlined in place of each call 6.3.2
of a generic package 12.3
of a generic subprogram 12.3
raising an exception 11.4.1

Generic instantiation 12.3; 12.1, 12.1.3, 12.2, D
[see also: declaration, elaboration of..., generic actual parameter]
as a basic declaration 3.1
as a later declarative item 3.9
as a library unit 10.1
before elaboration of the body 3.9, 11.1
implicitly declaring an exception 11.1
invoking an operation of a generic actual type 12.1.2
of a predefined input-output package 14.1
recompiled 10.3
with a formal access type 12.3.5
with a formal array type 12.3.4
with a formal scalar type 12.3.3
with a formal subprogram 12.3.6

Generic package 12.1; 12
for input-output 14
instantiation 12.3; 12, 12.1 [see also: generic instantiation]
specification 12.1 [see also: generic specification]

Generic package body 12.2; 12.1
[see also: package body]

Generic parameter declaration 12.1; 12.1.1, 12.1.2, 12.1.3, 12.3
[see also: generic formal parameter]
as a declarative region 8.1
having an extended scope 8.2
visibility 8.3

Generic procedure
[see: generic subprogram]

Generic specification 12.1; 12.3.2
[see also: generic package specification, generic subprogram specification]

Identifier list 3.2
    in a component declaration 3.7
    in a deferred constant declaration 7.4
    in a discriminant specification 3.7.1
    in a generic parameter declaration for generic formal objects 12.1
    in a number declaration 3.2
    in an object declaration 3.2
    in a parameter specification 6.1

Identity operation 4.5.4

If statement 5.3
    [see also: statement]
    as a compound statement 5.1

Illegal 1.6

IMAGE (predefined attribute) **3.5.5**; A

Immediate scope 8.2; **8.3**

Immediately within (a declarative region)
    [see: occur immediately within]

Implementation defined
    [see: system dependent]

Implementation defined pragma F

Implementation dependent
    [see: system dependent]

Implicit conversion 4.6
    [see also: conversion operation, explicit conversion, subtype conversion]
    of an integer literal to an integer type 3.5.4
    of a real literal to a real type 3.5.6
    of a universal expression 3.5.4, 3.5.6
    of a universal real expression 4.5.7

Implicit declaration 3.1; **4.1**
    [see also: scope of...]
    by a type declaration 4.5
    hidden by an explicit declaration 8.3
    of a basic operation 3.1, 3.3.3
    of a block name, loop name, or label 5.1; 3.1
    of a derived subprogram 3.3.3, 3.4
    of an enumeration literal 3.3.3
    of an equality operator 6.7
    of an exception due to an instantiation 11.1
    of a library unit 8.6, 10.1
    of a predefined operator 4.5
    of universal_fixed operators 4.5.5

Implicit initialization of an object
    [see: allocator, default initial value]

Implicit representation clause
    for a derived type 3.4

In membership test
    [see: membership test]

In mode
    [see: mode in]

In out mode
    [see: mode in out]

IN_FILE (input-output file mode enumeration literal) **14.1**

Inclusive disjunction
    [see: logical operator]

Incompatibility (of constraints)
    [see: compatibility]

Incomplete type 3.8.1
    corresponding full type declaration 3.3.1

Incomplete type declaration 3.8.1; 3.3.1, 7.4.1
    as a portion of a declarative region 8.1

Incorrect order dependence 1.6
    [see also: program error]
    assignment statement 5.2
    bounds of a range constraint 3.5
    component association of an array aggregate 4.3.2
    component association of a record aggregate 4.3.1
    component subtype indication 3.6
    default expression for a component 3.2.1
    default expression for a discriminant 3.2.1
    expression 4.5
    index constraint 3.6
    library unit 10.5
    parameter association 6.4
    prefix and discrete range of a slice 4.1.2

Index 3.6; D
    [see also: array, discrete type, entry index]

INDEX (input-output function)
    in an instance of direct_io 14.2.4; 14.2.5

Index constraint 3.6, 3.6.1; D
    [see also: dependence on a discriminant]
    ignored due to index_check suppression 11.7
    in an allocator 4.8
    in a constrained array definition 3.6
    in a subtype indication 3.3.2
    on an access type 3.8
    violated 11.1

Index of an element in a direct access file **14.2**; 14.2.4

Index range 3.6
    matching 4.5.2

Index subtype 3.6

Index subtype definition 3.6

Index type
    of a choice in an array aggregate 4.3.2
    of a generic formal array type 12.3.4

Index_check
    [see: constraint_error, suppress]

Indexed component 4.1.1; 3.6, D
    as a basic operation 3.3.3; 3.3, 3.6.2, 3.8.2
    as a name 4.1
    as the name of an entry 9.5
    of a value of a generic formal array type 12.1.2

Indication
    [see: subtype indication]

Inequality compound delimiter 2.2

Inequality operator 4.5; 4.5.2
    [see also: limited type, relational operator]
    cannot be explicitly declared 6.7
    for an access type 3.8.2
    for an array type 3.6.2
    for a generic formal type 12.1.2
    for a real type 4.5.7
    for a record type 3.7.4
    not available for a limited type 7.4.4

Initial value (of an object) **3.2.1**
[see also: allocator, composite type, default expression, default initial value, default initialization]
    in an allocator 4.8; 3.8, 7.4.4
    of an array object 3.6.1
    of a constant 3.2.1
    of a constant in a static expression 4.9
    of a discriminant of a formal parameter 6.2
    of a discriminant of an object 3.7.2
    of a limited private type object 7.4.4
    of an object declared in a package 7.1
    of an out mode formal parameter 6.2
    of a record object 3.7.2

Initialization
[see: assignment, default expression, default initialization, initial value]

INLINE (predefined pragma) **6.3.2**; B
    creating recompilation dependence 10.3

INOUT_FILE (input-output file_mode enumeration literal) **14.1**

Input-output **14**
[see also: direct_io, io_exceptions, low_level_io, sequential_io, text_io]
    at device level 14.6
    exceptions 14.4; 14.5
    with a direct access file 14.2.4
    with a sequential file 14.2.2
    with a text file 14.3

Instance
[see: generic instance]

Instantiation
[see: generic instantiation]

INTEGER (predefined type) **3.5.4**; C
    as base type of a loop parameter 5.5
    as default type for the bounds of a discrete range 3.6.1; 9.5

Integer literal 2.4
[see also: based integer literal, universal_integer type]
    as a bound of a discrete range 9.5
    as a universal_integer literal 3.5.4
    in based notation 2.4.2
    in decimal notation 2.4.1

Integer part
    as a base of a based literal 2.4.2
    of a decimal literal 2.4.1

Integer predefined type 3.5.4
[see also: INTEGER, LONG_INTEGER, SHORT_INTEGER]

Integer subtype
[see: priority]
    due to an integer type definition 3.5.4

Integer type 3.5.4; 3.3, 3.5, D
[see also: discrete type, numeric type, predefined type, scalar type, system.max_int, system.min_int, universal_integer type]
    as a generic formal type 12.1.2
    as a generic parameter 12.3.3
    operation 3.5.5; 4.5.3, 4.5.4, 4.5.5, 4.5.6
    result of a conversion from a numeric type 4.6
    result of an operation out of range of the type 4.5

Integer type declaration
[see: integer type definition]

Integer type definition 3.5.4; 3.3.1
[see also: elaboration of...]

Integer type expression
    in a length clause 13.2
    in a record representation clause 13.4

INTEGER_IO (text_io inner generic package) **14.3.6**; 14.3.10

INTERFACE (predefined pragma) **13.9**; B

Interface to other languages 13.9

Interrupt 13.5

Interrupt entry 13.5.1
[see also: address attribute]

Interrupt queue
[see: entry queue]

IO_EXCEPTIONS (predefined input-output package) **14.4**; 14, 14.1, 14.2.3, 14.2.5, 14.3.10, C
    specification 14.5

IS_OPEN (input-output function)
    in an instance of direct_io 14.2.1; 14.2.5
    in an instance of sequential_io 14.2.1, 14.2.3
    in text_io 14.2.1; 14.3.10

ISO (international organization for standardization) **2.1**

ISO seven bit coded character set **2.1**

Item
[see: basic declarative item, later declarative item]

Iteration scheme 5.5
[see also: discrete type]

Label 5.1
[see also: address attribute, name, statement]
    declaration 5.1
    implicitly declared 3.1
    target of a goto statement 5.9

Label bracket
    compound delimiter 2.2

Labeled statement 5.1
    in a code statement 13.8

LARGE (predefined attribute) **3.5.8, 3.5.10**; A

LAST (predefined attribute) **A**
[see also: bound]
    for an access value 3.8.2
    for an array type 3.6.2
    for a scalar type 3.5

LAST_BIT (predefined attribute) **13.7.2**; A
[see also: record representation clause]

Later declarative item 3.9

Layout recommended
[see: paragraphing recommended]

LAYOUT_ERROR (input-output exception) **14.4**; 14.3.4, 14.3.5, 14.3.7, 14.3.8, 14.3.9, 14.3.10, 14.5

Loop name 5.5
    declaration 5.1
    implicitly declared 3.1
    in an exit statement 5.7

Loop parameter 5.5
    [see also: constant, object]
    as an object 3.2

Loop parameter specification 5.5
    [see also: elaboration of...]
    as an overload resolution context 8.7
    is a declaration 3.1

Loop statement 5.5
    [see also: statement]
    as a compound statement 5.1
    as a declarative region 8.1
    denoted by an expanded name 4.1.3
    including an exit statement 5.7

LOW_LEVEL_IO (predefined input-output package) **14.6**;
14, C

Lower bound
    [see: bound, first attribute]

Lower case letter 2.1
    [see also: graphic character]
    a to f in a based literal 2.4.2
    e in a decimal literal 2.4.1
    in an identifier 2.3

Machine code insertion 13.8

Machine dependent attribute 13.7.3

Machine representation
    [see: representation]

MACHINE_CODE (predefined package) **13.8**; C

MACHINE_EMAX (predefined attribute) **13.7.3**; 3.5.8, A

MACHINE_EMIN (predefined attribute) **13.7.3**; 3.5.8, A

MACHINE_MANTISSA (predefined attribute) **13.7.3**; 3.5.8,
A

MACHINE_OVERFLOWS (predefined attribute) **13.7.3**;
3.5.8, 3.5.10, A

MACHINE_RADIX (predefined attribute) **13.7.3**; 3.5.8, A

MACHINE_ROUNDS (predefined attribute) **13.7.3**; 3.5.8,
3.5.10, A

Main program 10.1
    execution requiring elaboration of library units 10.5
    included in the predefined package standard 8.6
    including a priority pragma 9.8
    raising an exception 11.4.1, 11.4.2
    termination 9.4

MANTISSA (predefined attribute) **3.5.8, 3.5.10**; A

Mantissa
    of a fixed point number 3.5.9
    of a floating point number 3.5.7; 13.7.3

Mark
    [see: type_mark]

Master (task) **9.4**

Matching components
    of arrays 4.5.2; 4.5.1, 5.2.1
    of records 4.5.2

Matching generic formal
    and actual parameters 12.3
    access type 12.3.5
    array type 12.3.4
    default subprogram 12.3.6; 12.1.3
    object 12.3.1; 12.1.1
    private type 12.3.2
    scalar type 12.3.3
    subprogram 12.3.6; 12.1.3
    type 12.3.2, 12.3.3, 12.3.4, 12.3.5; 12.1.2

Mathematically correct result of a numeric operation **4.5**;
4.5.7

MAX_DIGITS
    [see: system.max_digits]

MAX_INT
    [see: system.max_int]

MAX_MANTISSA
    [see: system.max_mantissa]

Maximum line length 14.3

Maximum page length 14.3

Membership test 4.4, 4.5.2
    cannot be overloaded 6.7

Membership test operation 4.5
    [see also: overloading of...]
    as a basic operation 3.3.3; 3.3, 3.5.5, 3.5.8, 3.5.10,
    3.6.2, 3.7.4, 3.8.2, 7.4.2
    for a real type 4.5.7

MEMORY_SIZE (predefined named number)
    [see: system.memory_size]

MEMORY_SIZE (predefined pragma) **13.7**; B

MIN_INT
    [see: system.min_int]

Minimization of storage
    [see: pack predefined pragma]

Minus
    character [see: hyphen character]
    character in an exponent of a numeric literal 2.4.1
    delimiter 2.2
    operator [see: binary adding operator, unary adding
    operator]
    unary operation 4.5.4

Mod operator 4.5.5
    [see also: multiplying operator]

MODE (input-output function)
    in an instance of direct_io 14.2.1; 14.2.5
    in an instance of sequential_io 14.2.1; 14.2.3
    in text_io 14.2.1; 14.3.3, 14.3.4, 14.3.10

Mode (of a file) **14.1**; 14.2.1
    of a direct access file 14.2; 14.2.5
    of a sequential access file 14.2; 14.2.3
    of a text_io file 14.3.1; 14.3.4

Mode (of a formal parameter) **6.2**; 6.1, D
[see also: formal parameter, generic formal parameter]
of a formal parameter of a derived subprogram 3.4
of a formal parameter of a renamed entry or subprogram 8.5
of a generic formal object 12.1.1

Mode in for a formal parameter **6.1, 6.2**; 3.2.1
of a function 6.5
of an interrupt entry 13.5.1

Mode in for a generic formal object **12.1.1**; 3.2.1, 12.3, 12.3.1

Mode in out for a formal parameter **6.1, 6.2**; 3.2.1
of a function is not allowed 6.5
of an interrupt entry is not allowed 13.5.1

Mode in out for a generic formal object **12.1.1**; 3.2.1, 12.3, 12.3.1

Mode out for a formal parameter **6.1, 6.2**
of a function is not allowed 6.5
of an interrupt entry is not allowed 13.5.1

MODE_ERROR (input-output exception) **14.4**; 14.2.2, 14.2.3, 14.2.4, 14.2.5, 14.3.1, 14.3.2, 14.3.3, 14.3.4, 14.3.5, 14.3.10, 14.5

Model interval of a subtype **4.5.7**

Model number (of a real type) **3.5.6**; D
[see also: real type, safe number]
accuracy of a real operation 4.5.7
of a fixed point type 3.5.9; 3.5.10
of a floating point type 3.5.7; 3.5.8

Modulus operation 4.5.5

MONTH (predefined function) **9.6**

Multidimensional array 3.6

Multiple
component declaration 3.7; 3.2
deferred constant declaration 7.4; 3.2
discriminant specification 3.7.1; 3.2
generic parameter declaration 12.1; 3.2
number declaration 3.2.2; 3.2
object declaration 3.2
parameter specification 6.1; 3.2

Multiplication operation 4.5.5
accuracy for a real type 4.5.7

Multiplying operator 4.5; 4.5.5, C
[see also: arithmetic operator, overloading of an operator]
in a term 4.4
overloaded 6.7

Must (legality requirement) **1.6**

Mutually recursive types 3.8.1; 3.3.1

NAME (input-output function)
in an instance of direct_io 14.2.1
in an instance of sequential_io 14.2.1
in text_io 14.2.1

NAME (predefined type)
[see: system.name]

Name (of an entity) **4.1**; 2.3, 3.1, D
[see also: attribute, block name, denote, designator, evaluation of..., forcing occurrence, function call, identifier, indexed component, label, loop name, loop parameter, operator symbol, renaming declaration, selected component, simple name, slice, type_mark, visibility]
as a prefix 4.1
as a primary 4.4
as the argument of a pragma 2.8
as the expression in a case statement 5.4
conflicts 8.5
declared by renaming is not allowed as prefix of certain expanded names 4.1.3
declared in a generic unit 12.3
denoting an entity 4.1
denoting an object designated by an access value 4.1
generated by an implementation 13.4
starting with a prefix 4.1; 4.1.1, 4.1.2, 4.1.3, 4.1.4

Name string (of a file) **14.1**; 14.2.1, 14.2.3, 14.2.5, 14.3, 14.3.10, 14.4

NAME_ERROR (input-output exception) **14.4**; 14.2.1, 14.2.3, 14.2.5, 14.3.10, 14.5

Named association 6.4.2, D
[see also: component association, discriminant association, generic association, parameter association]

Named block statement
[see: block name]

Named loop statement
[see: loop name]

Named number 3.2; 3.2.2
as an entity 3.1
as a primary 4.4
in a static expression 4.9

NATURAL (predefined integer subtype) **C**

Negation
[see: logical negation operation]

Negation operation (numeric) **4.5.4**

Negative exponent
in a numeric literal 2.4.1
to an exponentiation operator 4.5.6

NEW_LINE (text_io procedure) **14.3.4**; 14.3.5, 14.3.6, 14.3.10
raising an exception 14.4

NEW_PAGE (text_io procedure) **14.3.4**; 14.3.10
raising an exception 14.4

No other effect
[see: elaboration has no other effect]

Not equal
compound delimiter [see: inequality compound delimiter]
operator [see: relational operator]

Not in membership test
[see: membership test]

Not unary operator
[see: highest precedence operator]
as an operation of an array type 3.6.2
as an operation of boolean type 3.5.5
in a factor 4.4

Not yet elaborated 3.9

Null access value 3.8; 3.4, 4.2, 6.2, 11.1
[see also: default initial value of an access type object]
    causing constraint_error 4.1
    not causing constraint_error 11.7

Null array 3.6.1; 3.6
    aggregate 4.3.2
    and relational operation 4.5.2
    as an operand of a catenation 4.5.3

Null component list 3.7

Null literal 3.8, 4.2
[see also: overloading of...]
    as a basic operation 3.3.3; 3.8.2
    as a primary 4.4
    must not be the argument of a conversion 4.6

Null range 3.5
    as a choice of a variant part 3.7.3
    for a loop parameter 5.5

Null record 3.7
    and relational operation 4.5.2

Null slice 4.1.2
[see also: array type]

Null statement 5.1
[see also: statement]
    as a simple statement 5.1

Null string literal 2.6

Number
[see: based literal, decimal literal]

Number declaration 3.2, 3.2.2
    as a basic declaration 3.1

NUMBER_BASE (predefined integer subtype) **14.3.7**;
14.3.10

Numeric literal 2.4, 4.2; 2.2, 2.4.1, 2.4.2
[see also: universal type expression]
    and an adjacent separator 2.2
    as a basic operation 3.3.3
    as a primary 4.4
    as the parameter of value attribute 3.5.5
    as the result of image attribute 3.5.5
    assigned 5.2
    can be written in the basic character set 2.10
    in a conforming construct 6.3.1
    in a static expression 4.9
    in pragma memory_size 13.7
    in pragma storage_unit 13.7

Numeric operation of a universal type **4.10**

Numeric type 3.5
[see also: conversion, fixed point type, floating point type,
integer type, real type, scalar type]
    operation 4.5, 4.5.2, 4.5.3, 4.5.4, 4.5.5, 4.5.6

Numeric type expression
    in a length clause 13.2

Numeric value of a named number **3.2**

NUMERIC_ERROR (predefined exception) **11.1**
[see also: suppress pragma]
    not raised due to lost overflow conditions 13.7.3

    not raised due to optimization 11.6
    raised by a numeric operator 4.5
    raised by a predefined integer operation 3.5.4
    raised by a real result out of range of the safe
    numbers 4.5.7
    raised by a universal expression 4.10
    raised by integer division remainder or modulus
    4.5.5
    raised due to a conversion out of range 3.5.4, 3.5.6

Object 3.2; 3.2.1, D
[see also: address attribute, allocator, collection, component, constant, formal parameter, generic formal
parameter, initial value, loop parameter, size attribute,
storage bits allocated, subcomponent, variable]
    as an actual parameter 6.2
    as a generic formal parameter 12.1.1
    created by an allocator 4.8
    created by elaboration of an object declaration 3.2.1
    of an access type [see: access type object]
    of a file type [see: file]
    of a task type [see: task object]
    renamed 8.5
    subject to an address clause 13.5
    subject to a representation clause 13.1
    subject to a suppress pragma 11.7

Object declaration 3.2, 3.2.1
[see also: elaboration of..., generic parameter declaration]
    as a basic declaration 3.1
    as a full declaration 7.4.3
    implied by a task declaration 9.1
    in a package specification 7.1
    of an array object 3.6.1
    of a record object 3.7.2
    with a limited type 7.4.4
    with a task type 9.2; 9.3

Object designated
    by an access value 3.2, 3.8, 4.8; 4.1.3, 5.2, 9.2,
    11.1 [see also: task object designated...]
    by an access value denoted by a name 4.1
    by an access-to-array type 3.6.1
    by an access-to-record type 3.7.2
    by a generic formal access type value 12.3.5

Object module
    for a subprogram written in another language 13.9

Obsolete compilation unit (due to recompilation) **10.3**

Occur immediately within (a declarative region) **8.1**; 8.3,
8.4, 10.2

Omitted parameter association for a subprogram call **6.4.2**

OPEN (input-output procedure)
    in an instance of direct_io 14.2.1; 14.1, 14.2.5
    in an instance of sequential_io 14.2.1; 14.1, 14.2.3
    in text_io 14.2.1; 14.1, 14.3.1, 14.3.10
    raising an exception 14.4

Open alternative 9.7.1
[see also: alternative]
    accepting a conditional entry call 9.7.2
    accepting a timed entry call 9.7.3

Open file 14.1

Operation 3.3, 3.3.3; D
[see also: basic operation, direct visibility, operator,

in an expression 4.4
resolution 6.6
resolution context 8.7
resolved by explicit qualification 4.7

Overloading of
an aggregate 3.4
an allocator 4.8
a declaration 8.3
a designator 6.6; 6.7
an entry 9.5
an enumeration literal 3.5.1; 3.4
a generic formal subprogram 12.3
a generic unit 12.1
an identifier 6.6
a library unit by a locally declared subprogram 10.1
a library unit by means of renaming 10.1
a literal 3.4
a membership test 4.5.2
an operator 4.5, 6.7; 4.4, 6.1
an operator symbol 6.6; 6.7
a subprogram 6.6; 6.7
a subprogram subject to an interface pragma 13.9
the expression in a case statement 5.4

PACK (predefined pragma) 13.1; B

Package 7, 7.1; D
[see also: deferred constant declaration, library unit, predefined package, private part, program unit, visible part]
as a generic instance 12.3; 12
including a raise statement 11.3
named in a use clause 8.4
renamed 8.5
subject to an address clause 13.5
subject to representation clause 13.1
with a separately compiled body 10.2

Package body 7.1, 7.3; D
[see also: body stub]
as a generic body 12.2
as a proper body 3.9
as a secondary unit 10.1
as a secondary unit compiled after the corresponding library unit 10.3
in another package body 7.1
including an exception handler 11.2; 11
including an exit statement 5.7
including a goto statement 5.9
including an implicit declaration 5.1
must be in the same declarative region as the declaration 3.9
raising an exception 11.4.1, 11.4.2
recompiled 10.3
subject to a suppress pragma 11.7

Package declaration 7.1, 7.2; D
and body as a declarative region 8.1
as a basic declaration 3.1
as a later declarative item 3.9
as a library unit 10.1
determining the visibility of another declaration 8.3
elaboration raising an exception 11.4.2
in a package specification 7.1
recompiled 10.3

Package identifier 7.1

Package specification 7.1, 7.2
in a generic declaration 12.1

including an inline pragma 6.3.2
including an interface pragma 13.9
including a representation clause 13.1
including a suppress pragma 11.7

Page 14.3, 14.3.4

PAGE (predefined pragma) **B**

PAGE (text_io function) **14.3.4**; 14.3.10
raising an exception 14.4

Page length 14.3, 14.3.3; 14.3.1, 14.3.4, 14.4

Page terminator 14.3; 14.3.3, 14.3.4, 14.3.5

PAGE_LENGTH (text_io function) **14.3.3**; 14.3.10
raising an exception 14.4

Paragraphing recommended for the layout of programs **1.5**

Parallel execution
[see: task]

Parameter D
[see also: actual parameter, default expression, entry, formal parameter, formal part, function, generic actual parameter, generic formal parameter, loop parameter, mode, procedure, subprogram]
of a main program 10.1

Parameter and result type profile 6.6

Parameter association 6.4, 6.4.1
for a derived subprogram 3.4
named parameter association 6.4
named parameter association for selective visibility 8.3
omitted for a subprogram call 6.4.2
positional parameter association 6.4

Parameter declaration
[see: generic parameter declaration, parameter specification]

Parameter part
[see: actual parameter part]

Parameter specification 6.1
[see also: loop parameter specification]
as part of a basic declaration 3.1
having an extended scope 8.2
in a formal part 6.1
visibility 8.3

Parameter type profile 6.6

Parent subprogram (of a derived subprogram) **3.4**

Parent subtype (of a derived subtype) **3.4**

Parent type (of a derived type) **3.4**; D
[see also: derived type]
declared in a visible part 3.4
of a generic actual type 12.1.2
of a numeric type is predefined and anonymous 3.5.4, 3.5.7, 3.5.9

Parent unit (of a body stub) **10.2**
compiled before its subunits 10.3

Parenthesis
character 2.1
delimiter 2.2

Parenthesized expression
    as a primary 4.4; 4.5
    in a static expression 4.9

Part
    [see: actual parameter part, declarative part, discriminant
    part, formal part, generic actual part, generic formal part,
    variant part]

Partial ordering of compilation **10.3**

Percent character 2.1
    [see also: string literal]
    replacing quotation character 2.10

Period character 2.1
    [see also: dot character, point character]

Physical processor 9; 9.8

Plus
    character 2.1
    delimiter 2.2
    operator [see: binary adding operator, unary adding
    operator]
    unary operation 4.5.4

Point character 2.1
    [see also: dot]
    in a based literal 2.4.2
    in a decimal literal 2.4.1
    in a numeric literal 2.4

Point delimiter 2.2

Pointer
    [see: access type]

Portability 1.1
    of programs using real types 13.7.3; 3.5.6

POS (predefined attribute) **3.5.5**; 13.3, A

POSITION (predefined attribute) **13.7.2**; A
    [see also: record representation clause]

Position number
    as parameter to val attribute 3.5.5
    of an enumeration literal 3.5.1
    of an integer value 3.5.4
    of a value of a discrete type 3.5
    returned by pos attribute 3.5.5

Position of a component within a record
    [see: record representation clause]

Position of an element in a direct access file **14.2**

Positional association 6.4; 6.4.2, D
    [see also: component association, discriminant associa-
    tion, generic association, parameter association]

POSITIVE (predefined integer subtype) **3.6.3**; 14.3.7,
14.3.8, 14.3.9, 14.3.10, C
    as the index type of the string type 3.6.3

POSITIVE_COUNT (predefined integer subtype) **14.2.5,
14.3.10**; 14.2.4, 14.3, 14.3.4

Potentially visible declaration 8.4

Pound sterling character 2.1

Power operator
    [see: exponentiating operator]

Pragma 2.8; 2, D
    [see: predefined pragma]
    applicable to the whole of a compilation 10.1
    argument that is an overloaded subprogram name
    6.3.2, 8.7, 13.9
    for the specification of a subprogram body in
    another language 13.9
    for the specification of program overlays 13.5
    in a code procedure body 13.8
    recommending the representation of an entity 13.1
    specifying implementation conventions for code
    statements 13.8

Precedence 4.5

Precision (numeric)
    [see: delta, digits]

PRED (predefined attribute) **3.5.5**; 13.3, A

Predecessor
    [see: pred attribute]

Predefined attribute
    [see: address, base, callable, constrained, count, first,
    first_bit, image, last, last_bit, pos, pred, range, size, small,
    storage_size, succ, terminated, val, value, width]

Predefined constant 8.6; C
    [see also: system.system_name]
    for CHARACTER values [see: ascii]

Predefined exception 8.6, 11.1; 11.4.1, C
    [see also: constraint_error, io_exceptions, numeric_error,
    program_error, tasking_error, time_error]

Predefined function 8.6; C
    [see also: attribute, character literal, enumeration literal,
    predefined generic library function]

Predefined generic library function 8.6; C
    [see also: unchecked_conversion]

Predefined generic library package 8.6; C
    [see also: direct_io, input-output package, sequential_io]

Predefined generic library procedure 8.6; C
    [see also: unchecked_deallocation]

Predefined generic library subprogram 8.6; C

Predefined identifier 8.6; C

Predefined library package 8.6; C
    [see also: predefined generic library package, predefined
    package, ascii, calendar, input-output package, io_excep-
    tions, low_level_io, machine_code, system, text_io]

Predefined library subprogram
    [see: predefined generic library subprogram]

Predefined named number
    [see: system.fine_delta, system.max_digits, system.max_int,
    system.max_mantissa, system.memory_size,
    system.min_int, system.storage_unit, system.tick]

Predefined operation 3.3, 3.3.3; 8.6
    [see also: operation, predefined operator]
    accuracy for a real type 4.5.7
    of a discrete type 3.5.5
    of a fixed point type 3.5.10
    of a floating point type 3.5.8
    of a universal type 4.10
    propagating an exception 11.6

Predefined operator 4.5, 8.6; C
[see also: abs, arithmetic operator, binary adding operator, catenation, equality, exponentiating operator, highest precedence operator, inequality, limited type, logical operator, multiplying operator, operator, predefined operation, relational operator, unary adding operator]
    applied to an undefined value 3.2.1
    as an operation 3.3.3
    for an access type 3.8.2
    for an array type 3.6.2
    for a record type 3.7.4
    implicitly declared 3.3.3
    in a static expression 4.9
    of a derived type 3.4
    of a fixed point type 3.5.9
    of a floating point type 3.5.7
    of an integer type 3.5.4
    raising an exception 11.4.1

Predefined package 8.6; C
[see also: ascii, library unit, predefined library package, standard]
    for input-output 14

Predefined pragma
[see: controlled, elaborate, inline, interface, list, memory_ ze, optimize, pack, page, priority, shared, storage_unit, suppress, system_name]

Predefined subprogram 8.6; C
[see also:' input-output subprogram, library unit, predefined generic library subprogram]

Predefined subtype 8.6; C
[see also: field, natural, number_base, positive, priority]

Predefined type 8.6; C
[see also: boolean, character, count, duration, float, integer, long_float, long_integer, priority, short_float, short_integer, string, system.address, system .name, time, universal_integer, universal_real]

Prefix 4.1; D
[see also: appropriate for a type, function call, name, selected component, selector]
    in an attribute 4.1.4
    in an indexed component 4.1.1
    in a selected component 4.1.3
    in a slice 4.1.2
    that is a function call 4.1
    that is a name 4.1

Primary 4.4
    in a factor 4.4
    in a static expression 4.9

PRIORITY (predefined integer subtype) **9.8**; 13.7, C
[see also: Task priority]

PRIORITY (predefined pragma) **9.8**; 13.7, B
[see also: Task priority]

Private part (of a package) **7.2**; 7.4.1, 7.4.3, D
[see also: deferred constant declaration, private type declaration]

Private type 3.3, 7.4, 7.4.1; D
[see also: class of type, derived type of a private type, limited private type, type with discriminants]
    as a generic actual type 12.3.2
    as a generic formal type 12.1.1
    as a parent type 3.4
    corresponding full type declaration 3.3.1
    formal parameter 6.2

of a deferred constant 7.4; 3.2.1
    operation 7.4.2

Private type declaration 7.4; 7.4.1, 7.4.2
[see also: private part (of a package), visible part (of a package)]
    as a generic type declaration 12.1
    as a portion of a declarative region 8.1
    including the word 'limited' 7.4.4

Procedure 6.1; 6, D
[see also: parameter and result type profile, parameter, subprogram]
    as a main program 10.1
    as a renaming of an entry 9.5
    renamed 8.5

Procedure body
[see: subprogram body]
    including code statements 13.8

Procedure call 6.4; 6, D
[see also: subprogram call]

Procedure call statement 6.4
[see also: actual parameter, statement]
    as a simple statement 5.1
    with a parameter of a derived type 3.4

Procedure specification
[see: subprogram specification]

Processor 9

Profile
[see: parameter and result type profile, parameter type profile]

Program 10; D
[see also: main program]

Program legality 1.6

Program library 10.1, 10.4; 10.5
    creation 10.4; 13.7
    manipulation and status 10.4

Program optimization 11.6; 10.6

Program text 2.2, 10.1; 2.10

Program unit 6, 7, 9, 12; D
[see also: address attribute, generic unit, library unit, package, subprogram, task unit]
    body separately compiled [see: subunit]
    including a declaration denoted by an expanded name 4.1.3
    including a suppress pragma 11.7
    subject to an address clause 13.5
    with a separately compiled body 10.2

PROGRAM_ERROR (predefined exception) **11.1**
[see also: erroneous execution, suppress pragma]
    raised by an erroneous program or incorrect order dependence 1.6; 11.1
    raised by a generic instantiation before elaboration of the body 3.9; 12.1, 12.2
    raised by a selective wait 9.7.1
    raised by a subprogram call before elaboration of the body 3.9; 7.3
    raised by a task activation before elaboration of the body 3.9
    raised by reaching the end of a function body 6.5

Propagation of an exception
[see: exception propagation]

Proper body 3.9
  as a body 3.9
  in a subunit 10.2
  of a library unit separately compiled 10.1

PUT (text_io procedure) **14.3, 14.3.5**; 14.3.2, 14.3.10
  for character and string types 14.3.6
  for enumeration types 14.3.9
  for integer types 14.3.7
  for real types 14.3.8
  raising an exception 14.4

Qualification 4.7
  as a basic operation 3.3.3; 3.3, 3.5.5, 3.5.8, 3.5.10,
  3.6.2, 3.7.4, 3.8.2, 7.4.2
  using a name of an enumeration type as qualifier
  3.5.1

Qualified expression 4.7; D
  as a primary 4.4
  in an allocator 4.8
  in a case statement 5.4
  in a static expression 4.9
  qualification of an array aggregate 4.3.2
  to resolve an overloading ambiguity 6.6

Queue of entry calls
[see: entry queue]

Queue of interrupts
[see: entry queue]

Quotation character 2.1
  in a string literal 2.6
  replacement by percent character 2.10

Radix of a floating point type **3.5.7**; 13.7.3

Raise statement 11.3; 11
[see also: exception, statement]
  as a simple statement 5.1
  including the name of an exception 11.1

Raising of an exception **11, 11.3**; D
[see also: exception]
  causing a transfer of control 5.1

Range 3.5; D
[see also: discrete range, null range]
  as a discrete range 3.6
  in a record representation clause 13.4
  in a relation 4.4
  of an index subtype 3.6
  of an integer type containing the result of an operation 4.5
  of a predefined integer type 3.5.4
  of a real type containing the result of an operation
  4.5.7
  yielded by an attribute 4.1.4

RANGE (predefined attribute) **3.6.2**; 4.1.4, A
  for an access value 3.8.2

Range constraint 3.5; D
[see also: elaboration of...]

ignored due to range_check suppression 11.7
  in a fixed point constraint 3.5.9
  in a floating point constraint 3.5.7
  in an integer type definition 3.5.4
  in a subtype indication 3.5; 3.3.2
  on a derived subtype 3.4
  violated 11.1

Range_check
[see: constraint_error, suppress]

READ (input-output procedure)
  in an instance of direct_io 14.2.4; 14.1, 14.2,
  14.2.5
  in an instance of sequential_io 14.2.2; 14.1, 14.2,
  14.2.3

Reading the value of an object **6.2, 9.11**

Real literal 2.4
[see also: universal_real type]
  in based notation 2.4.2
  in decimal notation 2.4.1
  is of type universal_real 3.5.6

Real type 3.5.6; 3.3, 3.5, D
[see also: fixed point type, floating point type, model
number, numeric type, safe number, scalar type, univer-
sal_real type]
  accuracy of an operation 4.5.7
  representation attribute 13.7.3
  result of a conversion from a numeric type 4.5.7;
  4.6
  result of an operation out of range of the type 4.5.7

Real type definition 3.5.6; 3.3.1, 3.5.7, 3.5.9
[see also: elaboration of...]

RECEIVE_CONTROL (low_level_io procedure) **14.6**

Reciprocal operation in exponentiation by a negative integer
4.5.6

Recompilation 10.3

Record aggregate 4.3.1; 4.3
[see also: aggregate]
  as a basic operation 3.3.3; 3.7.4
  in a code statement 13.8

Record component
[see: component, record type, selected component]

Record representation clause 13.4
[see also: first_bit attribute, last_bit attribute, position
attribute]
  as a representation clause 13.1

Record type 3.7; 3.3, D
[see also: component, composite type, discriminant,
matching components, subcomponent, type with discriminants, variant]
  formal parameter 6.2
  including a limited subcomponent 7.4.4
  operation 3.7.4

Record type declaration
[see: record type definition, type declaration]
  as a declarative region 8.1
  determining the visibility of another declaration 8.3

Record type definition 3.7; 3.3.1
[see also: component declaration]

Recursive
    call of a subprogram 6.1, 12.1; 6.3.2
    generic instantiation 12.1, 12.3
    types 3.8.1; 3.3.1

Reentrant subprogram 6.1

Reference (parameter passing) **6.2**

Relation (in an expression) **4.4**

Relational expression
    [see: relation, relational operator]

Relational operation 4.5.2
    of a boolean type 3.5.3
    of a discrete type 3.5.5
    of a fixed point type 3.5.10
    of a floating point type 3.5.8
    of a scalar type 3.5
    result for real operands 4.5.7

Relational operator 4.5; 4.5.2, C
    [see also: equality operator, inequality operator, ordering
relation, overloading of an operator, predefined operator]
    for an access type 3.8.2
    for an array type 3.6.2
    for a private type 7.4.2
    for a record type 3.7.4
    for time predefined type 9.6
    in a relation 4.4
    overloaded 6.7

Relative address of a component within a record
    [see: record representation clause]

Rem operator 4.5.5
    [see also: multiplying operator]

Remainder operation 4.5.5

Renaming declaration 8.5; 4.1, 12.1.3, D
    [see also: name]
    as a basic declaration 3.1
    as a declarative region 8.1
    cannot rename a universal_fixed operation 4.5.5
    for an array object 3.6.1
    for an entry 9.5
    for a record object 3.7.2
    name declared is not allowed as a prefix of certain
expanded names 4.1.3
    to overload a library unit 10.1
    to overload a subunit 10.2
    to resolve an overloading ambiguity 6.6

Rendezvous (of tasks) **9.5; 9, 9.7.1, 9.7.2, 9.7.3, D**
    during which an exception is raised 11.5
    priority 9.8
    prohibited for an abnormal task 9.10

Replacement of characters in program text **2.10**

Representation (of a type and its objects) **13.1**
    recommendation by a pragma 13.1

Representation attribute 13.7.2, 13.7.3
    as a forcing occurrence 13.1
    with a prefix that has a null value 4.1

Representation clause 13.1; 13.6, D
    [see also: address clause, elaboration of..., enumeration
representation clause, first named subtype, length clause,
record representation clause, type]
    as a basic declarative item 3.9

as a portion of a declarative region 8.1
    cannot include a forcing occurrence 13.1
    for a derived type 3.4
    for a private type 7.4.1
    implied for a derived type 3.4
    in an overload resolution context 8.7
    in a task specification 9.1

Reserved word 2.9; 2.2, 2.3

RESET (input-output procedure)
    in an instance of direct_io 14.2.1; 14.2.5
    in an instance of sequential_io 14.2.1; 14.2.3
    in text_io 14.2.1; 14.3.1, 14.3.10

Resolution of overloading
    [see: overloading]

Result subtype (of a function) **6.1**
    of a return expression 5.8

Result type profile
    [see: parameter and...]

Result type and overload resolution 6.6

Result of a function
    [see: returned value]

Return
    [see: carriage return]

Return statement 5.8
    [see also: function, statement]
    as a simple statement 5.1
    causing a loop to be exited 5.5
    causing a transfer of control 5.1
    completing block statement execution 9.4
    completing subprogram execution 9.4
    expression that is an array aggregate 4.3.2
    in a function body 6.5

Returned value
    [see: function call]
    of a function call 5.8, 6.5; 8.5
    of an instance of a generic formal function 12.1.3
    of a main program 10.1
    of an operation 3.3.3
    of a predefined operator of an integer type 3.5.4
    of a predefined operator of a real type 3.5.6, 4.5.7

Right label bracket compound delimiter **2.2**

Right parenthesis
    character 2.1
    delimiter 2.2

Rounding
    in a real-to-integer conversion 4.6
    of results of real operations 4.5.7; 13.7.3

Run time check 11.7; 11.1

Safe interval 4.5.7

Safe number (of a real type) **3.5.6; 4.5.7**
    [see also: model number, real type representation
attribute, real type]
    limit to the result of a real operation 4.5.7
    of a fixed point type 3.5.9; 3.5.10
    of a floating point type 3.5.7; 3.5.8
    result of universal expression too large 4.10

Short circuit control form 4.5, 4.5.1; 4.4
    as a basic operation 3.3.3; 3.5.5
    in an expression 4.4

SHORT_FLOAT (predefined type) **3.5.7**; C

SHORT_INTEGER (predefined type) **3.5.4**; C

Sign of a fixed point number **3.5.9**

Sign of a floating point number **3.5.7**

Significant decimal digits 3.5.7

Simple expression 4.4
    as a choice 3.7.3
    as a choice in an aggregate 4.3
    as a range bound 3.5
    for an entry index in an accept statement 9.5
    in an address clause 13.5
    in a delay statement 9.6
    in a fixed accuracy definition 3.5.9
    in a floating accuracy definition 3.5.7
    in a record representation clause 13.4
    in a relation 4.4

Simple name 4.1; 2.3, D
    [see also: block name, identifier, label, loop name, loop
    simple name, name, overloading, visibility]
    as a choice 3.7.3
    as a formal parameter 6.4
    as a label 5.1
    as a name 4.1
    before arrow compound delimiter 8.3
    in an accept statement 9.5
    in an address clause 13.5
    in an attribute designator 4.1.4
    in a conforming construct 6.3.1
    in a discriminant association 3.7.2
    in an enumeration representation clause 13.3
    in a package body 7.1
    in a package specification 7.1
    in a record representation clause 13.4
    in a selector 4.1.3
    in a suppress pragma 11.7
    in a task body 9.1
    in a variant part 3.7.3
    in a with clause 10.1.1
    versus identifier 3.1

Simple statement 5.1
    [see also: statement]

Single task 9.1

SIZE (input-output function)
    in an instance of direct_io 14.2.4; 14.2.5

SIZE (predefined attribute) **13.7.2**; A
    [see also: storage bits]
    specified by a length clause 13.2

SKIP_LINE (text_io procedure) **14.3.4**; 14.3.10
    raising an exception 14.4

SKIP_PAGE (text_io procedure) **14.3.4**; 14.3.10
    raising an exception 14.4

Slice 4.1.2
    [see also: array type]
    as a basic operation 3.3.3; 3.6.2, 3.8.2
    as a name 4.1
    as destination of an assignment 5.2.1
    of a constant 3.2.1

    of a derived type 3.4
    of an object as an object 3.2
    of a value of a generic formal array type 12.1.2
    of a variable 3.2.1
    starting with a prefix 4.1, 4.1.2

SMALL (predefined attribute) **3.5.8, 3.5.10**; A
    [see also: fixed point type]
    specified by a length clause 13.2

Small of a fixed point model number **3.5.9**

Some order not defined by the language
    [see: incorrect order dependence]

Space character 2.1
    [see also: basic graphic character]
    as a separator 2.2
    in a comment 2.7
    not allowed in an identifier 2.3
    not allowed in a numeric literal 2.4.1

Space character literal 2.5; 2.2

Special character 2.1
    [see also: basic graphic character, other special character]
    in a delimiter 2.2

Specification
    [see: declaration, discriminant specification, enumeration
    literal specification, generic specification, loop parameter
    specification, package specification, parameter specifica-
    tion, subprogram specification, task specification]

STANDARD (predefined package) **8.6**; C
    [see also: library unit]
    as a declarative region 8.1
    enclosing the library units of a program 10.1.1;
    10.1, 10.2
    including implicit declarations of fixed point cross-
    multiplication and cross-division 4.5.5

STANDARD_INPUT (text_io function) **14.3.2**; 14.3.10

STANDARD_OUTPUT (text_io function) **14.3.2**; 14.3.10

Star
    [see: double star]
    character 2.1
    delimiter 2.2

Statement 5.1; 5, D
    [see also: abort statement, accept statement, address
    attribute, assignment statement, block statement, case
    statement, code statement, compound statement, delay
    statement, entry call statement, exit statement, goto state-
    ment, if statement, label, loop statement, null statement,
    procedure call statement, raise statement, return state-
    ment, select statement, sequence of statements, target
    statement]
    allowed in an exception handler 11.2
    as an overload resolution context 8.7
    optimized 10.6
    raising an exception 11.4.1; 11.4
    that cannot be reached 10.6

Statement alternative
    [see: case statement alternative]

Static constraint 4.9
    on a subcomponent subject to a component clause
    13.4
    on a type 3.5.4, 3.5.7, 3.5.9, 13.2

Static discrete range 4.9
as a choice of an aggregate 4.3.2
as a choice of a case statement 5.4
as a choice of a variant part 3.7.3

Static expression 4.9; 8.7
as a bound in an integer type definition 3.5.4
as a choice in a case statement 5.4
as a choice of a variant part 3.7.3
for a choice in a record aggregate 4.3.2
for a discriminant in a record aggregate 4.3.1
in an attribute designator 4.1.4
in an enumeration representation clause 13.3
in a fixed accuracy definition 3.5.9
in a floating accuracy definition 3.5.7
in a generic unit 12.1
in a length clause 13.2
in a number declaration 3.2, 3.2.2
in a record representation clause 13.4
in priority pragma 9.8
whose type is a universal type 4.10

Static others choice 4.3.2

Static subtype 4.9
of a discriminant 3.7.3
of the expression in a case statement 5.4

STATUS_ERROR (input-output exception) **14.4**; 14.2.1,
14.2.2, 14.2.3, 14.2.4, 14.2.5, 14.3.2, 14.3.3, 14.3.4,
14.3.5, 14.3.10, 14.5

Storage address of a component **13.4**
[see also: address clause]

Storage bits
allocated to an object or type 13.2; 13.7.2 [see also:
size]
of a record component relative to a storage unit
13.4
size of a storage unit 13.7

Storage deallocation
[see: unchecked_deallocation]

Storage minimization
[see: pack pragma]

Storage reclamation 4.8

Storage representation of a record **13.4**

Storage unit 13.7
offset to the start of a record component 13.4
size of a storage unit in bits 13.7

Storage units allocated
[see: storage_size]
to a collection 13.2; 4.8, 11.1, 13.7.2
to a task activation 13.2; 9.9, 11.1, 13.7.2

Storage_check
[see: program_error exception, suppress]

STORAGE_ERROR (predefined exception) **11.1**
[see also: suppress pragma]
raised by an allocator exceeding the allocated
storage 4.8; 11.1
raised by an elaboration of a declarative item 11.1
raised by a task activation exceeding the allocated
storage 11.1
raised by the execution of a subprogram call 11.1

STORAGE_SIZE (predefined attribute) **13.7.2**; A
[see also: storage units allocated]
for an access type 3.8.2
for a task object or task type 9.9
specified by a length clause 13.2

STORAGE_UNIT (predefined named number)
[see: system.storage_unit]

STORAGE_UNIT (predefined pragma) **13.7**; B
[see also: system.storage_unit]

STRING (predefined type) **3.6.3**; C
[see also: predefined type]
as the parameter of value attribute 3.5.5
as the result of image attribute 3.5.5

String bracket 2.6; 2.10

String literal 2.6, 4.2; 2.2, 3.6.3
[see also: overloading of..., percent mark character, quotation character]
as a basic operation 3.3.3, 4.2; 3.6.2
as an operator symbol 6.1
as a primary 4.4
must not be the argument of a conversion 4.6
replaced by a catenation of basic characters 2.10

Stub
[see: body stub]

Subaggregate 4.3.2

Subcomponent 3.3; D
[see also: component, composite type, default expression,
discriminant, object]
depending on a discriminant 3.7.1; 5.2, 6.2 , 8.5
of a component for which a component clause is
given 13.4
renamed 8.5
that is a task object 9.2; 9.3
whose type is a limited type 7.4.4
whose type is a private type 7.4.1

Subprogram 6; D
[see also: actual parameter, completed subprogram,
derived subprogram, entry, formal parameter, function,
library unit, overloading of..., parameter and result type
profile, parameter, predefined subprogram, procedure,
program unit]
as a generic instance 12.3; 12
as a main program 10.1
as an operation 3.3.3; 7.4.2
including a raise statement 11.3
of a derived type 3.4
overloaded 6.6
renamed 8.5
subject to an address clause 13.5
subject to an inline pragma 6.3.2
subject to an interface pragma 13.9
subject to a representation clause 13.1
subject to a suppress pragma 11.7
with a separately compiled body 10.2

Subprogram body 6.3; 6, D
[see also: body stub]
as a generic body 12.2
as a library unit 10.1
as a proper body 3.9
as a secondary unit 10.1
as a secondary unit compiled after the corresponding library unit 10.3

having dependent tasks 9.4
in a package body 7.1
including an exception handler 11.2; 11
including an exit statement 5.7
including a goto statement 5.9
including an implicit declaration 5.1
including a return statement 5.8
including code statements must be a procedure
body 13.8
inlined in place of each call 6.3.2
must be in the same declarative region as the
declaration 3.9, 7.1
not allowed for a subprogram subject to an interface
pragma 13.9
not yet elaborated at a call 3.9
raising an exception 11.4.1, 11.4.2
recompiled 10.3

Subprogram call 6.4; 6, 6.3, 12.3
[see also: actual parameter, entry call statement, entry call, function call, procedure call statement, procedure call]
before elaboration of the body 3.9 , 11.1
statement replaced by an inlining of the body 6.3.2
statement with a default actual parameter 6.4.2
to a derived subprogram 3.4
to a generic instance 12

Subprogram declaration 6.1; 6, D
and body as a declarative region 8.1
as a basic declaration 3.1
as a later declarative item 3.9
as a library unit 10.1
as an overloaded declaration 8.3
implied by the body 6.3, 10.1
in a package specification 7.1
made directly visible by a use clause 8.4
of an operator 6.7
recompiled 10.3

Subprogram specification 6.1
and forcing occurrences 13.1
conforming to another 6.3.1
for a function 6.5
in a body stub 10.2
in a generic declaration 12.1; 12.1.3
in a renaming declaration 8.5
in a subprogram body 6.3
including the name of a private type 7.4.1
of a derived subprogram 3.4

Subtraction operation 4.5.3
for a real type 4.5.7

Subtype 3.3, 3.3.2; D
[see also: attribute of..., base attribute, constrained subtype, constraint, first named subtype, operation of..., result subtype, satisfy, size attribute, static subtype, type, unconstrained subtype]
declared by a numeric type declaration 3.5.4, 3.5.7, 3.5.9
in a membership test 4.5.2
name [see: name of a subtype, type_mark of a subtype]
not considered in overload resolution 8.7
of an access type 3.8
of an actual parameter 6.4.1
of an array type [see: constrained array type, index constraint]
of a component of an array 3.6
of a component of a record 3.7
of a constant in a static expression 4.9
of a discriminant of a generic formal type 12.3.2
of a formal parameter 6.4.1

of a formal parameter or result of a renamed subprogram or entry 8.5
of a generic formal type 12.1.2
of an index of a generic formal array type 12.3.4
of an object [see: elaboration of...]
of a private type 7.4, 7.4.1
of a real type 3.5.7, 3.5.9; 3.5.6, 4.5.7
of a record type [see: constrained record type, discriminant constraint]
of a scalar type 3.5
of a task type 9.2
of a variable 5.2
subject to a representation clause 13.1

Subtype conversion 4.6
[see also: conversion operation, explicit conversion, implicit conversion, type conversion]
in an array assignment 5.2.1; 5.2
to a real type 4.5.7

Subtype declaration 3.3.2; 3.1
and forcing occurrences 13.1
as a basic declaration 3.1
including the name of a private type 7.4.1

Subtype definition
[see: component subtype definition, dependence on a discriminant, index subtype definition]

Subtype indication 3.3.2
[see also: elaboration of...]
as a component subtype indication 3.7
as a discrete range 3.6
for a subtype of a generic formal type 12.1.2
in an access type definition 3.8
in an allocator 4.8
in an array type definition 3.6
in a component declaration 3.7
in a constrained array definition 3.6
in a derived type definition 3.4
in a generic formal part 12.1
in an object declaration 3.2, 3.2.1
in an unconstrained array definition 3.6
including a fixed point constraint 3.5.9
including a floating point constraint 3.5.7
with a range constraint 3.5

Subunit 10.2; D
[see also: library unit]
as a compilation unit 10.4
as a library unit 10.4
as a secondary unit 10.1
compiled after the corresponding parent unit 10.3
not allowed for a subprogram subject to an interface pragma 13.9
of a compilation unit subject to a context clause 10.1.1
raising an exception 11.4.1, 11.4.2
recompiled (does not affect other compilation units) 10.3

SUCC (predefined attribute) **3.5.5**; 13.3, A

Successor
[see: succ attribute]

SUPPRESS (predefined pragma) **11.7**; 11.1, B

Symbol
[see: graphical symbol, operator symbol]

Synchronization of tasks
[see: task synchronization]

Syntactic category ● Task type

of a fixed point type 3.5.9
of a floating point type 3.5.7
of an integer type 3.5.4
of a subtype 13.1

Type definition 3.3.1; D
[see also: access type definition, array type definition, derived type definition, elaboration of..., enumeration type definition, generic type definition, integer type definition, real type definition, record type definition]

Type mark (denoting a type or subtype) **3.3.2**
    as a generic actual parameter 12.3
    in an allocator 4.8
    in a code statement 13.8
    in a conversion 4.6
    in a deferred constant declaration 7.4
    in a discriminant specification 3.7.1
    in a generic formal part 12.1, 12.3
    in a generic parameter declaration 12.3.1
    in an index subtype definition 3.6
    in a parameter specification 6.1; 6.2
    in a qualified expression 4.7
    in a relation 4.4
    in a renaming declaration 8.5
    in a subprogram specification 6.1
    of a formal parameter of a generic formal subprogram 12.1.3
    of a generic formal array type 12.1.2
    of a static scalar subtype 4.9
    of the result of a generic formal function 12.1.3

Type with discriminants 3.3; 3.3.1, 3.3.2, 3.7, 3.7.1, 7.4, 7.4.1
[see also: private type, record type]
    as an actual to a formal private type 12.3.2
    as the component type of an array that is the operand of a conversion 4.6

Unary adding operator 4.4, 4.5, C; 4.5.4
[see also: arithmetic operator, overloading of an operator, predefined operator]
    as an operation of a discrete type 3.5.5
    in a simple expression 4.4
    overloaded 6.7

Unary operator 4.5; 3.5.5, 3.5.8, 3.5.10, 3.6.2, 4.5.4, 4.5.6, C
[see also: highest precedence operator, unary adding operator]

UNCHECKED_CONVERSION (predefined generic library function) **13.10.2**; 13.10, C

UNCHECKED_DEALLOCATION (predefined generic library procedure) **13.10.1**; 4.8, 13.10, C

Unconditional termination of a task
[see: abnormal task, abort statement]

Unconstrained array definition 3.6

Unconstrained array type 3.6; 3.2.1
    as an actual to a formal private type 12.3.2
    formal parameter 6.2
    subject to a length clause 13.2

Unconstrained subtype 3.3, 3.3.2
[see also: constrained subtype, constraint, subtype, type]
    indication in a generic unit 12.3.2

Unconstrained type 3.3; 3.2.1, 3.6, 3.6.1, 3.7, 3.7.2
    formal parameter 6.2
    with discriminants 6.4.1, 12.3.2

Unconstrained variable 3.3, 3.6, 3.7; 12.3.1
    as a subcomponent [see: subcomponent]

Undefined value
    of a scalar parameter 6.2
    of a scalar variable 3.2.1

Underline character 2.1
    in a based literal 2.4.2
    in a decimal literal 2.4.1
    in an identifier 2.3

Unhandled exception 11.4.1

Unit
[see: compilation unit, generic unit, library unit, program unit, storage unit, task unit]

Universal expression 4.10
    assigned 5.2
    in an attribute designator 4.1.4
    of a real type implicitly converted 4.5.7
    that is static 4.10

Universal type 4.10
[see also: conversion, implicit conversion]
    expression [see: expression, numeric literal]
    of a named number 3.2.2; 3.2
    result of an attribute [see: attribute]

UNIVERSAL_FIXED (predefined type) **3.5.9**
    result of fixed point multiplying operators 4.5.5

UNIVERSAL_INTEGER (predefined type) **3.5.4, 4.10**; C
[see also: integer literal]
    argument of a conversion 3.3.3, 4.6
    attribute 3.5.5, 13.7.1, 13.7.2, 13.7.3; 9.9
    bounds of a discrete range 3.6.1
    bounds of a loop parameter 5.5
    codes representing enumeration type values 13.3
    converted to an integer type 3.5.5
    of integer literals 2.4, 4.2
    result of an operation 4.10; 4.5

UNIVERSAL_REAL (predefined type) **3.5.6, 4.10**
[see also: real literal]
    argument of a conversion 3.3.3, 4.6
    attribute 13.7.1
    converted to a fixed point type 3.5.10
    converted to a floating point type 3.5.8
    of real literals 2.4, 4.2
    result of an operation 4.10; 4.5

Updating the value of an object **6.2**

Upper bound
[see: bound, last attribute]

Upper case letter 2.1
[see also: basic graphic character]
    A to F in a based literal 2.4.2
    E in a decimal literal 2.4.1
    in an identifier 2.3

Urgency of a task
[see: task priority]

Use clause (to achieve direct visibility) **8.4**; 8.3, D
[see also: context clause]

as a basic declarative item 3.9
as a later declarative item 3.9
in a code procedure body 13.8
in a context clause of a compilation unit 10.1.1
in a context clause of a subunit 10.2
inserted by the environment 10.4

USE_ERROR (input-output exception) **14.4**; 14.2.1, 14.2.3,
14.2.5, 14.3.3, 14.3.10, 14.5

VAL (predefined attribute) **3.5.5**; A

Value
[see: assignment, evaluation, expression, initial value,
returned value, subtype, task designated..., type]
    in a constant 3.2.1; 3.2
    in a task object 9.2
    in a variable 3.2.1, 5.2; 3.2
    of an access type [see: object designated, task
    object designated]
    of an array type 3.6; 3.6.1 [see also: array, slice]
    of a based literal 2.4.2
    of a boolean type 3.5.3
    of a character literal 2.5
    of a character type 3.5.2; 2.5, 2.6
    of a decimal literal 2.4.1
    of a fixed point type 3.5.9, 4.5.7
    of a floating point type 3.5.7, 4.5.7
    of a record type 3.7
    of a record type with discriminants 3.7.1
    of a string literal 2.6; 2.10
    of a task type [see: task designated]
    returned by a function call [see: returned value]

VALUE (predefined attribute) **3.5.5**; A

Variable 3.2.1; D
[see also: object, shared variable]
    as an actual parameter 6.2
    declared in a package body 7.3
    formal parameter 6.2
    in an assignment statement 5.2
    of an array type as destination of an assignment
    5.2.1
    of a private type 7.4.1
    renamed 8.5
    that is a slice 4.1.2

Variable declaration 3.2.1

Variant 3.7.3; 4.1.3
[see also: component clause, record type]
    in a variant part 3.7.3

Variant part 3.7.3; D
[see also: dependence on a discriminant]
    in a component list 3.7
    in a record aggregate 4.3.1

Vertical bar character 2.1
    replacement by exclamation character 2.10

Vertical bar delimiter 2.2

Vertical tabulation format effector 2.1

Violation of a constraint
[see: constraint_error exception]

Visibility 8.3; 8.2, D
[see also: direct visibility, hiding, identifier, name, operation, overloading]
    and renaming 8.5
    determining multiple meanings of an identifier 8.4,
    8.7; 8.5
    determining order of compilation 10.3
    due to a use clause 8.4
    of a basic operation 8.3
    of a character literal 8.3
    of a default for a generic formal subprogram 12.3.6
    of a generic formal parameter 12.3
    of a library unit due to a with clause 8.6, 10.1.1
    of a name of an exception 11.2
    of an operation declared in a package 7.4.2
    of an operator symbol 8.3
    of a renaming declaration 8.5
    of a subprogram declared in a package 6.3
    of declarations in a package body 7.3
    of declarations in a package specification 7.2
    of declarations in the package system 13.7
    within a subunit 10.2

Visibility by selection 8.3
[see also: basic operation, character literal, operation,
operator symbol, selected component]

Visible part (of a package) **7.2**; 3.2.1, 7.4, 7.4.1, 7.4.3, D
[see also: deferred constant declaration, private type
declaration]
    expanded name denoting a declaration in a visible
    part 8.2
    scope of a declaration in a visible part 4.1.3
    use clause naming the package 8.4
    visibility of a declaration in a visible part 8.3

Wait
[see: selective wait, task suspension]

While loop
[see: loop statement]

WIDTH (predefined attribute) **3.5.5**; A

With clause 10.1.1; D
[see also: context clause]
    determining order of compilation 10.3
    determining the implicit order of library units 8.6
    in a context clause of a compilation unit 10.1.1
    in a context clause of a subunit 10.2
    inserted by the environment 10.4
    leading to direct visibility 8.3

WRITE (input-output procedure)
    in an instance of direct_io 14.2.4; 14.1, 14.2, 14.2.5
    in an instance of sequential_io 14.2.2; 14.1, 14.2,
    14.2.3

Writing to an output file 14.1, 14.2.2, 14.2.4

Xor operator
[see: logical operator]

YEAR (predefined function) **9.6**

Postscript : Submission of Comments

For submission of comments on this standard Ada reference manual, we would appreciate them being sent by Arpanet to the address

Ada-Comment at ECLB

If you do not have Arpanet access, please send the comments by mail

Ada Joint Program Office
Office of the Under Secretary of Defense Research and Engineering
Washington, DC 20301
United States of America.

For mail comments, it will assist us if you are able to send them on 8-inch single-sided single-density IBM format diskette - but even if you can manage this, please also send us a paper copy, in case of problems with reading the diskette.

All comments are sorted and processed mechanically in order to simplify their analysis and to facilitate giving them proper consideration. To aid this process you are kindly requested to precede each comment with a three line header

!section ...
!version 1983
!topic ...

The section line includes the section number, the paragraph number enclosed in parentheses, your name or affiliation (or both), and the date in ISO standard form (year-month-day). The paragraph number is the one given in the margin of the paper form of this document (it is not contained in the ECLB files); paragraph numbers are optional, but very helpful. As an example, here is the section line of comment #1194 on a previous version:

!section 03.02.01(12) D . Taffs 82-04-26

The version line, for comments on the current standard, should only contain "!version 1983". Its purpose is to distinguish comments that refer to different versions.

The topic line should contain a one line summary of the comment. This line is essential, and you are kindly asked to avoid topics such as "Typo" or "Editorial comment" which will not convey any information when printed in a table of contents. As an example of an informative topic line consider:

!topic Subcomponents of constants are constants

Note also that nothing prevents the topic line from including all the information of a comment, as in the following topic line:

!topic Insert: "... are (implicitly) defined by a subtype declaration"

As a final example here is a complete comment received on a prior version of this manual:

!section 03.02.01(12) D . Taffs 82-04-26
!version 10
!topic Subcomponents of constants are constants

Change "component" to "subcomponent" in the last sentence.

Otherwise the statement is inconsistent with the defined use of subcomponent in 3.3, which says that subcomponents are excluded when the term component is used instead of subcomponent.

PART II

Guidelines for Ada compiler specification and selection

J.C.D. Nissen, GEC Software, London, England

B.A. Wichmann, National Physical Laboratory, Teddington, England

and others

Preface

The Ada language reference manual defines the language rather than indicating a list of the desirable properties of an implementation of the language. The purpose of this guide is to list the characteristics of an implementation that should be taken into account in the specification or selection of an Ada compiler.

This guide was produced by members of Ada-Europe, those contributing being Bob Brewer, Ted Dowling, Stephen Goldsack, Hans Jeanrond, John Nissen, Ron Pierce, Mario Refice, Peter Reid, George Romanski, Sven Tafvelin, Peter Wallis who also acted as secretary, Tim White and Brian Wichmann who also dealt with the word processing (with mechanical and secretarial assistance from the National Physical Laboratory). Helpful comments on drafts of this document have been received from other members of Ada-Europe.

Contents

1

Introduction

1.1 The need for guidance

There is a commonly held view that to specify a compiler one only needs to state the language to be accepted, the target on which compiled programs are to run, and the host on which the compiler is to run. This view may be reinforced by having the language well standardized, and by validation of the compiler. This guide intends to show how much more may need to be specified, for example the programming support environment. For an overview of this guide, see [8].

There are several reasons why one might specify a compiler. One may wish to procure a compiler which has been written; one may wish to have a compiler written; or may wish to choose between compilers. The specification is then of user requirements. On the other hand, as a compiler supplier perhaps, one may wish to produce a specification as a description of a compiler, for example to give to a potential purchaser. This guide is written from the point of view of someone wishing to know about an existing compiler, and it indicates what information may be needed from the supplier about the compiler. The guide offers a taxonomy of compiler features. The relative value of information about different features of the compiler is a matter of judgement and circumstance, but becomes extremely important when choosing between compilers. The guide attempts to give some help in this area.

1.2 How to use the Guide

Each main category is addressed descriptively, followed by a check list. It is the reader's responsibility to weight each factor according to his requirements. No liability of whatever kind shall be carried by the authors.

1.3 Structure of the Guide

The Ada Language Reference Manual (see Part 1) allows the compiler writer some options, and in Appendix F indicates what implementation dependent characteristics must be listed for a given implementation. The Portability Guide [2] includes further information required from implementors. The information needed is summarized in Chapter 3 below, except for information regarding performance which appears in Chapter 5. Every compiler will have some kind of user interface, at least to enable it to be started and to output listings, error messages etc. The existence or otherwise of an Ada Programming Support Environment (APSE) is important. The user will generally require debugging facilities which might be provided by the compiler or some other tool in its environment. Such a debugging tool will probably need to access symbol tables within the compiler. The user interface and debugging facilities are covered in Chapter 4, but the access by tools to the compiler is covered in Chapter 6.

Chapter 5 addresses issues of performance of the compiler; the time it takes to compile a program on the host, the space it consumes on the host and the time and space taken by the compiled code on the target. There is no exact measure of efficiency, except for the compilation of a given program on a given host or the execution of that program on a given target. However it may be important to obtain some indication of general efficiency, particularly if one wants to provide a compilation service. Note that, throughout the guide, a compiler is considered in terms of a host-target pair.

Parts of the compiler may need to be accessed by tools. Thus it may be important to have a 'granular' compiler, with simple interfaces between parts such that tools can use the parts separately. A tool may wish to invoke a part, for example as a procedure. So there are invocation and data interfaces to be considered. Further interfaces are involved in the host-target relationship and run-time system on host and target. There may be interfaces to other compilers to allow foreign code. All these interfaces are discussed in Chapter 6.

The guide considers rehosting and retargeting in Chapter 7. The purchaser of a compiler may wish to change the host on which the compiler runs or the target on which the compiled program runs. Thus the portability of the compiler and the ease with which it can be modified for a new target are involved.

In chapter 8, the contractual issues on the procurement of a compiler are considered. In chapter 9 the validation of Ada compilers is considered, an issue which is vital in many contexts.

2

Host and target

Details of the host configurations on which the compiler will
run, and the target configurations on which the compiled programs will
run, must obviously be specified. The compiler may produce code for the
host. It can also produce an intermediate language/representation which
may be interpreted. A third possibility is that the compiler produces code
for a target different from the host. In this case the target code can be
transferred to the intended target to be executed but it may also be used
by an emulator on the host and be emulated. Many of the issues raised in
the next chapters should be viewed in the context of each host-target
configuration.

The environment of the compiler on the host and of the compiled
program on the target must be specified. The environment may sometimes be
sufficiently specified by stating the machine's operating system (with its
release number); but sometimes a complete APSE should be specified for the
compiler's environment.

If the target is not the host, some means of transferring
compiler output from host to target will be required. A compiler defines a
host-target pair. Any change in either must be regarded as a separate
compiler which must therefore be considered separately.

Check list
    a) Host configurations
    b) Host operating system
    c) Target configurations
    d) Target operating system
    e) APSE, if applicable
    f) Host-Target communication, both for program loading
       and during program execution and debugging.

2. Host and target

3

Language-related issues

The Ada language reference manual explicitly permits implementations to differ, for instance, by the machine-specific characteristics such as INTEGER'LAST. Such dependencies are noted in the Portability Guide [2] but are repeated here for completeness. A particular application and the compiler required for it may use machine specific facilities which are overtly non-portable. Hence this section includes in its check list issues which go beyond the need for portability.

The language related issues are noted in the order in which they appear in the reference manual as follows:

Check list

    a) (LRM 2.1) Character set of the host.

    (LRM 2.1) Character set of the target.

    (LRM 2.2) Maximum number of characters on a line (of host and target).

    (LRM 2.3 and 2.4) Is the maximum character length of an identifier or numerical literal restricted other than by the line length?

    (LRM 2.8, Appendix F (1)) The form, allowed place, and effect of every implementation defined pragma.

    b) (LRM 3.2.1) The effect of using uninitialized variables. (Does the compiler flag or reject a program that depends upon such variables?)

    (LRM 3.5.1) The maximum number of elements in an

enumeration type.

(LRM 3.5.4) The value of:

INTEGER'FIRST   INTEGER'LAST

SHORT_INTEGER'FIRST   SHORT_INTEGER'LAST

LONG_INTEGER'FIRST   LONG_INTEGER'LAST

(Similarly for any other predefined integer types)

(LRM 3.5.8) The values of

FLOAT'DIGITS

SHORT_FLOAT'DIGITS

LONG_FLOAT'DIGITS

c) (LRM 4.10) Is there a limit on the range of universal values which exceeds the capacity of the compiler?

(LRM 4.10) Is there a limit on the accuracy of real universal expressions?

d) (LRM 9.6) The values of

DURATION'DELTA

DURATION'SMALL

DURATION'FIRST   DURATION'LAST

(LRM 9.8)

PRIORITY'FIRST   PRIORITY'LAST

(LRM 9.11) The restrictions on shared variables.

e) (LRM 10.1) Initiation, communication with, and restrictions on a main program.

(LRM 10.5) When tasks initiated in imported library units will terminate.

f) (LRM 11.1) Conditions under which NUMERIC_ERROR, PROGRAM_ERROR or STORAGE_ERROR is raised.

g) (LRM 13.1, Appendix F (4)) The list of all restrictions on representation clauses.

(LRM 13.4, Appendix F (5)) The conventions used for any system generated name denoting system dependent

3. LANGUAGE-RELATED ISSUES

components.

(LRM 13.5, Appendix F (6)) The interpretation of
expressions that appear in address clauses, including
those for interrupts.

(LRM 13.7.3) For a predefined floating point type F,
the value of
        F'MACHINE_ROUNDS
        F'MACHINE_RADIX
        F'MACHINE_MANTISSA
        F'MACHINE_EMAX
        F'MACHINE_EMIN
        F'MACHINE_OVERFLOWS

(LRM 13.7.3) The values outside the range of safe
numbers for real types.

(LRM 13.10.1) Any restriction on unchecked
deallocation.

(LRM 13.10.2, Appendix F (7)) Any restriction on
unchecked conversions.

h) (LRM, Appendix F (2)) The name and type of every
implementation-dependent attribute.

i) (LRM 13.7, Appendix F (3)) The specification of the
package SYSTEM.
This includes the values of:
        MIN_INT
        MAX_INT
        MAX_DIGITS
        MAX_MANTISSA
        FINE_DELTA
        TICK

j) (LRM 14, Appendix F (8)) Any implementation-dependent
characteristics of the input-output packages.

3. LANGUAGE-RELATED ISSUES

4

User interfacing and facilities

An effective compiling system must have a good interface to the user. The quality of this interface cannot be measured objectively since it is largely a matter of subjective judgement. The method of use of a compiler will determine the critical issues: for instance, a compiler may be acceptable in a batch mode but unacceptable for interactive use.

It is also important to have good quality user information as follows:

Check list

    a) Any points of general guidance on using the compiler.

    b) Instructions on how to run the compiler (as a whole, or for individual tools if so constructed).

    c) Description of compilation options and parameters.

    d) Additional explanation of compiler output messages (errors, warnings etc.)

4.1 Compiler invocation and listing management

The implementor should describe how the compiler is invoked. For example, a multi-pass compiler may be invoked as a series of tools; alternatively it may appear as one tool to the user. Parameters and options are normally supplied by the user, and these should be specified. User listing (content and format) must be described, and in particular error messages and their relation to the source text must be covered in some detail.

4.1.1 Invoking the compiler

How the compiler is called, and what input parameters must be supplied by the user (source files, program library, various options).

4.1.1 Invoking the compiler

Check list
- a) The number of tools that the user calls to perform a compilation.
- b) Description and format of parameters which must be supplied to the compiler (or its constituent tools) and the default if these are not supplied.
- c) Differences between batch and interactive invocation of the compiler.

4.1.2 Format and content of user listings

   In addition to error and warning messages, an Ada compiler will normally produce many other kinds of output to be read by the user. The information content and presentation of such information to be considered include the following:

Check list
- a) Identification of compiler release on the hard copy listing; compilation date.
- b) Source listing (selectable by user?).
- c) Relation of lines of source listing to the original file (especially if multiple input files are allowed).
- d) Error message presentation; error summary (separate or embedded in the listing, sorted in order of source position or in order of generation?)
- e) Object code listing (and any intermediate form) related to the original source text in assembler form. The effects of any reordering due to optimization should be indicated.
- f) Type map and data map listing.
- g) Cross-reference listing - within unit or across all units; format of such listings.
- h) Compiler statistics - e.g. processor usage, space used, percentage of table occupancy.

4.2 Compilation options

Compilation options are supplied by the user to control such things as the level of listings produced and the degree of optimization performed by the compiler.

Check list

    a) The options available to control listing output (for
       instance, suitable for printer or terminal).
    b) Options to specify how far the compiler will go if
       errors are present in the source.
    c) Options for checking only (without code generation).
    d) Optimization control options.

4.3 Other features

In addition to compiling source text and producing listings, the compilation system may have other features either in the compiler or as separate tools.

Check list

    a) Facility to enable the compilation listing (and hence
       the source program) associated with an object program
       to be uniquely identified from the object program.

4.4 Errors and warnings

Messages produced for the user during a compiler run may be roughly classified into errors and warnings. Errors report an unsuccessful compilation, while a warning simply alerts the user to some condition detected during a successful compilation. Some compilers may attempt to produce an executable object program even if certain kinds of errors are present in the source program.

4.4 Errors and warnings

Check list

    a) Will the compiler produce an executable object program
       even if errors are present, and if so, under what
       circumstances?

    b) Effect of executing a source statement which contains
       an error.

       Issues relating to error and warning messages in general are
discussed before those for each separate message type.

4.4.1 Compiler messages

General considerations of message format apply equally to errors and
warnings. It is expected that error messages will have a particular format
and method of presentation. There should also be an indication of their
severity.

Check list

    a) Overall structure of messages; - severity (fatal,
       serious, recoverable, warning), note: error number,
       message text.

    b) Levels of verbosity of text.

    c) What natural language is used for message texts? Can
       the user change this?

    d) Effect on messages of interactive use of the compiler.
       Can these be stored in a file for later study?

    e) Positional accuracy of messages relating to points
       within the source text.

    f) Textual accuracy of error/warning messages.

4.4.2 Error messages

These messages accompany an unsuccessful compilation.

Check list
a) Information given to help the user find the cause of an error.
b) Positional accuracy of error indications.
c) Ability to recover from compilation errors; information output by the compiler to identify a restart position. (What error correction methods are used, if any?)
d) Effect of undeclared identifiers.
e) Steps taken to avoid "cascading" of compilation errors.
f) Information output to aid the user in resolving ambiguous overloadings.

4.4.3 Warning messages

These do not necessarily indicate that the compilation was unsuccessful. They may be graded in severity (see 4.4.1 a).

Check list
a) Warning for a statement whose static properties guarantee that an exception will be raised.
b) Warning for an unusually expensive construct. (This might be influenced by the pragma OPTIMISE.)
c) Warning for a real expression whose accuracy is inherently low.
d) Warning for elimination of unreachable source code.
e) Warning for declared entities which are not used.
f) Warning for erroneous features.
g) Warning for uninitialized variables.
h) Warning for endless loop.
i) Ability to switch off certain warning messages.
j) Warning for ignored pragmas.
k) Warning for code motion affecting debugging. Similarly if local data is removed completely.

4.4.3 Warning messages

4.5 Other software supplied

In addition to compiling source text and producing listings, the compilation system may have other features either in the compiler or as separate tools.

Check list

    a) Facility for cross referencing of identifiers and names.

    b) Facility to provide the fully qualified name (i.e. result of the overloading resolution).

    c) Pretty-printing of Ada source text.

    d) Reformatting of Ada source text.

    e) Can user-supplied packages replace any of these?

    f) Can additional packages be provided by the user?

4.6 Compilation management

The Ada separate compilation system with its associated library raises a number of issues not relevant to existing languages.

Check list

    a) List of compilation units invalidated by the compilation of a unit.

    h) Automatic recompilation of units invalidated by the current compilation.

    c) Tool for displaying the structural relationship between the units in a library.

    d) Facility for management control of the use of low-level features.

    e) Facility for the user to control the deletion of superseded compilation units.

5

Performance and capacity

The design of a compiler involves many trade-offs. At compile-time there is a trade-off between compiler data space and compilation time: more compact data may take longer to access. There is a similar trade-off between data space and run-time for the compiled program on the target.

In another dimension there is a trade-off between the efficiency (space and/or time) of the compiler and the efficiency (space and/or time) of the compiled program: optimization takes compiler time for example.

The user may desire particular trade-offs to be made, but it is difficult to be certain of what a given compiler has achieved. Information should be requested on the design philosophy at least, and about optimization in particular. It may be possible to turn various optimizations on and off. Note that some optimizations, such as code motion, may make debugging difficult.

There are two aspects of performance. First, there is the performance of the host system when compiling. Secondly, there is the performance of the generated code on the target machine. These two are clearly related in that a compiler which generates optimized target code is likely to be slower to compile than a non-optimizing compiler.

The most desirable characteristics for a compiler will depend upon the application in hand. Even within one application, during testing, a fast compilation speed and good diagnostics are needed whereas during system building production quality code is needed.

5.1 Host performance and capacity

Precise metrics for the performance of compilers have not yet achieved widespread acceptance. The usual measure "lines of source per minute" begs the question as to how much Ada is in each source line, and what we mean ʰy "minute".

With Ada the use of separate compilation is almost certain to
lead to increased compilation times. In order to make some allowance for
separate compilation effects it seems preferable to include, in the total,
all lines in the specification parts of library units which are used in
the program. Elapsed times should, if possible, be measured when the
machine is dedicated to the compilation.

Check list

    a) For a specific host configuration, what is the typical
       compiling speed (in lines of source per minute)? The
       configuration should specify the workspace
       requirements for the compiler.

    b) Are there characteristics of the source text which
       significantly reduce compiling speed? (Constructs
       which are likely to influence compiling speeds include
       the length of a with clause, the compilation of a
       sub-unit rather than a unit, source text errors, and
       the presence of generic instantiations).

    c) For a small host configuration, are there restrictions
       on the size of program unit that can be compiled? (If
       so, indicate what these are.)

    d) Are there any specific restrictions ("brick walls") on
       the numbers of items of various kinds in the program
       (e.g. identifiers, strings, procedure nesting, etc)?

    e) When a program unit is recompiled, is any use made of
       the previous compilation to increase compiling speed?

    f) If a package specification is changed by adding a
       declaration, does the recompilation make units which
       used this package invalid? (In certain cases, the
       compiler could optimize this case by noting that
       recompilation is not necessary.)

5.2 Target code performance

The following check list contains many well-known areas where
compilers can take special action to generate improved object code, or
where object code performance may be critical. The list is not exhaustive

and the importance of the individual cases may vary considerably depending on the application or target configuration.

Check list

a) Are the following forms of minimizing the constraint checking performed?

```
I: INTEGER range -2 .. 2;
J: INTEGER range 0 .. 10;

type AT is access T;
V: AT;

I := 22 mod 3;     -- (1) No checks needed at run time.
I := J;            -- (2) Check on top limit only
V := new T(...);
if V.L = ... then  -- (3) No null access check needed.
                   -- (4) Current variant is correct
```

b) Is space allocated for variables declared but not accessed?

c) Are subprograms which are declared in a package but not used, loaded into the program?

d) Are static (sub)expressions always evaluated by the compiler (even when the LRM does not require it)?

e) Is dead code eliminated from if and case statements?

f) With the statement A(I) := A(I) + 1; is the address of A(I) evaluated once or twice? Also, is a special increment instruction generated?

g) With matrix computations:

```
    for I in 1 .. N loop
      for J in 1 .. M loop
        A(I, J) ...
      end loop;
    end loop;
```

Is the address of A(I, J) calculated each time by multiplication? Does hardware do this anyway? Or does

5.2 Target code performance

the compiler generate increments through the array
(strength reduction)? Or is another method used such
as Iliffe vectors?

h) Assuming N and M above are constants (but not literal
values), is index bound checking performed when
A'FIRST(1) = 1, A'LAST(1) = N etc?

i) Is the pragma INLINE acted upon?

j) Is a subprogram only called once reduced to a simple
subroutine call (or just planted in-line)?

k) As an example of the procedure calling overhead, what
is the size of the code space for Ackermann's function
and the instructions executed per call? (See [3,4]).

l) In a rendezvous, is the rendezvous code executed by
the owning task or can it be executed by the calling
task? (The Habermann-Nassi optimization [6].) In a
message-based system how are intermediate tasks
("agents", "messengers") compiled? In many cases such
tasks can be removed; how and under which conditions
is such optimization handled by the compiler?

m) How much space is required for a general and for a
passive task?

o) How many instructions are generated at scope entry for
exception handling? Is the exception overhead only
invoked when the exception is raised?

p) With a parameterless generic package, is the
executable machine code duplicated for each
instantiation?

q) If the only generic parameter is a subprogram, is the
executable code duplicated for each instantiation of
the generic package (subprogram)?

r) If a machine has only two (say) predefined integer
types, are just two copies made of a generic
package/subprogram with the sole parameter:

       type INT is range <>;
    (Same question as last one, but with floating point)

s) The circumstance under which parameters are passed by

reference or copy.

t) The time to access the clock in delay statements.

u) The time to create, interrupt, terminate, fail and
abort a task.

v) The circumstance for a reschedule and its duration.

w) Size of the run-time system.

x) Is any of the run-time system loaded if it is not
needed by the object program?

y) Has any fair comparison been undertaken with hand
coding?

5.2 Target code performance

6

Compiler and run-time interfacing

The information to be supplied in this chapter is concerned with
the internal structure of the compiler and run-time system. It is
important in the following cases.

(i) Where the user is interested in using parts of the compiler,
     or its outputs, in further tools.

(ii) Where the run-time organization is needed to allow the user
     to interface the Ada system to other languages or specific
     pieces of hardware.

It should be borne in mind that information on the internal structure of
the compiler or its data may be regarded as commercially confidential by
some suppliers. In such cases the information may not be generally
available, and will probably be subject to an additional charge and/or a
rigorous confidentiality agreement; see section 8.

Information on the run-time system should always be available,
although some parts of it, such as the source text of a run-time monitor,
may also be confidential. This section should therefore be regarded as a
guide to the questions that may be asked of the supplier; the user should
not necessarily regard it as unreasonable if the supplier declines to
provide some of the information. In such cases the user should be able to
negotiate with the supplier for the release of additional information.

6.1.1 Design criteria for compiler

The supplier should state the design aims, noting in particular any specific kinds of usage envisaged (e.g. teaching Ada, or plant control work) which may have influenced design decisions.

Check list

a) Is the compiler aimed at a particular class of users?
b) Are any specific applications envisaged? Are any included with the compiler?

6.1.2 Compiler phase and pass structure

The structure of the compiler should be described in terms of the major identifiable processing stages in transforming the source program into the final compiled program representation. The grouping of these phases into passes should also be described.

Check list

a) Which interfaces are regarded as significant for rehosting and retargeting?
b) Are any phases (especially optimization phases) options selected by either a compile-time switch or when configuring the compiler?
c) To what degree are the components of the compiler separately-executable tools?
d) Which parts are seen as useful in building other tools?

6.1.3 Compiler module structure

Given the overall compiler structure, the major functional modules (Ada packages if it is written in Ada) should be described. (Note that many functional modules are used by more than one phase or pass of a compiler). A module may be described in terms of the data structure(s) it is concerned with, and in terms of its abstract interface (e.g. an Ada package with interface subprograms).

6.1.3 Compiler module structure

Check list

   a) Can any of the compiler modules be used by tools other
      than the compiler itself? If so, how are they
      documented?

6.1.4 Intermediate program representations

   The compiler may produce several intermediate program
representations in the course of compilation; some of these may be of use
to tools other than the compiler. The abstract nature of the interface
(e.g. tree structure, abstract machine code) should be specified as should
its interface package specification or physical representation.

Check list

   a) What are the intermediate representations of the
      program within the compiler?
   b) Are any standard intermediate languages (such as Diana
      [7]) used?
   c) How are the intermediate representations accessed?
   d) Are any such representations able to be written to
      file store for subsequent use?
   e) Is there a human readable form of the intermediate
      representation?

6.1.5 Final program representation

   The compiler may produce an assembly language program or compile
into relocatable binary; it may also produce some kind of interpretive
output code. It is also important to know how the compiler and the linker
interact.

Check list

   a) What is the format of the final object program?
   b) What is the format of internal references from one
      compiled unit to another?
   c) Does the object program rely on the use of the host
      standard linker, or is a special Ada linker part of
      the compilation system?

6.1.6 Compiler interfaces to other tools

Any interfaces which exist to other tools in the compilation system should be described in terms of their function, data format and functional interface specification (see also section 6.1.3 above).

Check list

a) What interfaces exist to other tools, such as symbolic debuggers?

b) To what extent are these interfaces documented?

c) Can alternative tools be written conforming to these interfaces (if this is sensible?)

6.1.7 Compiler construction tools

The compiler may have been written using a compiler-compiler system, or special purpose tools may have been developed for use in building the compiler. Information on such tools is important for maintenance, rehosting and retargeting.

Check list

a) Were any identifiable tools used to construct the compiler (or parts of it), such as a parser generator? If so, are they available (perhaps subject to special terms) to help construct additional APSE tools?

b) To what extent are such tools documented?

6.1.8 Target dependent information

The Ada language requires some target dependent information to be available to the semantic analysis part of the compiler. This may be built into the compiler (although one hopes not), supplied by compiling a package STANDARD, supplied by a parameter file, or incorporated into a package which is linked into the compiler.

Check list

a) What arrangements are made to incorporate target-dependent information into the compiler?

b) Is such information readily changed for a new target?

6.1.8 Target dependent information

6.1.9 Installation

The process by which a copy of the compiler is made to run on the user's site must be described.

Check list

    a) How is the compiler supplied?

    b) What steps are necessary to install the compiler?

    c) Can the user install the compiler or does the supplier carry out installation?

    d) Is there an installation manual?

6.2 Run-time system issues

6.2.1 Storage management

This aspect of the run-time system concerns the way stack space is acquired and released on subprogram entry and exit, and for objects whose size cannot be determined at compile time. This should be described, together with the method or methods of space management in access type collections. Any explicit or implicit garbage collection system should be noted (including the circumstances in which unchecked deallocation can be used). Space management for library packages should also be described.

Check list

    a) Description of primary stack management.

    h) Description of secondary stack management (if any).

    c) Method of acquiring and releasing of space for tasks.

    d) Description of access type collection management.

    e) Description of heap management and garbage collection.

6.2.2 Subprogram call and parameter handling

The instruction sequences used by the compiler for calling subprograms and returning from them should be described, as should the way in which parameters of various sorts are passed. Particular attention should be given to the following items (especially for calling non-Ada subprograms).

6.2.2 Subprogram call and parameter handling

Check list

    a) Method of passing parameters.

    b) The mechanism for returning results from a subprogram
       especially where the result is a record or
       unconstrained array type.

6.2.3 Data representation

      The supplier should give details of how the various sorts of Ada
type are represented. It is particularly important to describe the method
of array access, how access types are stored, and how records (especially
those with discriminants and containing arrays) are laid out. The effect
of the PACK pragma should be noted in those cases where it has an effect.
The use and limitation of representation clauses must also be described.
The use of UNCHECKED_CONVERSION should be discussed. A knowledge of data
representation is especially necessary if other languages are to be used
with Ada or if special I/O routines are to be written.

Check list

    a) Mapping of scalar types and subtypes.

    b) Mapping of arrays.

    c) Mapping of non-discriminated records.

    d) Mapping of discriminated records.

    e) Effect of having arrays depending on discriminants.
       (Is the heap used for such objects under certain
       circumstances?)

    f) Mapping of access types.

    g) Effect of, and limitations on, representation clauses.

    h) Effect of PACK pragma.

6.2.4 Implementation of tasking

      This is a complex area, and several aspects must be considered.

Check list

    a) Storage management (e.g. acquisition of stack and heap
       space for a new task) in a multi-tasking program.

    b) The method of implementing the Ada rendezvous

6.2.4 Implementation of tasking

mechanism (for example, an Ada run-time kernel or
monitor may be defined, or the implementation may rely
on target operating system facilities).

c) The method of passing data parameters in a rendezvous.

d) The use of multi-processor architectures (if
appropriate to the target).

e) The accuracy of the real-time clock and the delay
statement.

f) The method for associating external interrupts with
task entries.

g) Any optimizations that are possible and the
circumstances under which they will be achieved.

6.2.5 Exception handling system

The supplier should describe the way in which exception numbers
are allocated, and the mechanism for finding the appropriate handler when
an exception is raised. The interaction of exceptions and tasking should
be discussed, as should the relationship between hardware detected errors
and the target operating system, and the Ada exception handling system.

Check list

    a) Description of the exception identification scheme.

    b) Mechanism and overhead of exception handling.

    c) Interaction of exceptions and tasking.

    d) Relationship with hardware and host operating system
       exceptions.

6.2.6 I/O Interfaces

The supplier should describe the way in which the Ada I/O system, and any additional system available on the target, are implemented.

Check list

    a) Availability of formatted I/O.

    b) Availability of binary I/O.

    c) Restrictions on types that can be instantiated for
       input-output.

6.2.7 Generics

The run-time implications of generics should be described by the supplier. Of particular importance are the following:

Check list

    a) The circumstances under which it is possible to share
       code between two different generic instantiations
       (including any user control that is available).

    b) Any additional object code or data requirements
       imposed by the use of generics (especially when code
       sharing is in use).

    c) The implementation of generic subprogram parameters.

6.2.8 Documentation

The supplier should produce a manual for each target giving information as outlined in the preceding sections, and any other relevant information about the target run-time system (such as the specification of out-of-line routines used to implement Ada features). This manual would

6.2.8 Documentation

normally be supplied as part of the standard arrangement to use the compiler. Some aspects of the run-time system may, however, be regarded as confidential.

Check list

    a) Is a run-time system description manual on the above lines available?

    b) Is any other information available, especially on how Ada may best be used on the target?

7

Retargeting and rehosting

7.1 Introduction and definitions

"Retargeting" is the process whereby an Ada compiler which currently generates object programs to run on one or more target computers is made to generate code to run on another kind of computer. "Rehosting" is the process whereby an Ada compiler itself is made to execute on a host computing system different from that on which it was originally available, or on a different APSE or operating system.

While retargeting could potentially involve rewriting large parts of a compiler, most compilers are now constructed from a machine-independent part and a machine-dependent part, the latter being often known as a "back-end". The back-end is the part which must be rewritten to generate object code for the new target. In addition, a run-time system must be constructed for the target. (If the compiler generates an interpretive code the problem of retargeting reduces to writing an interpreter to execute on the new target).

If the compiler is itself written in Ada, rehosting will often require a prior retargeting operation to generate an Ada compiler for the host machine, followed by the compilation of the compiler and its transfer to the host. This process may also be needed if the compiler is written in a language other than Ada. An alternative scenario is that an existing compiler is already available from the language to the new host computer; the retargeting step may then be omitted.

Finally, if the compiler is part of an APSE, rehosting the compiler will normally require the rehosting of all or part of the APSE, especially the KAPSE interfaces used by the compiler and some supporting tools.

7.2 Retargeting

7.2.1 Availability of back ends The supplier should state the target computers for which back ends are currently available; he may also say who wrote these back ends and how many users each back-end has.

Check list

    a) Back end availability.

    b) Number of users of each (to indicate the extent to which it has been exercised).

7.2.2 Procedure for retargeting

This can be described in terms of the compiler system architecture covered by section 6. Particularly important is the interface to the target-dependent parts of the compiler; this will usually be in the form of an intermediate language of some sort. In some compilers more than one level of intermediate language may be available for retargeting; there may also be a standard or recommended structure for back ends and tools to support this structure. An existing back-end may be used as a model. The Ada language requires some target dependent information to be available to the front end or machine-independent part, and the method by which this is achieved should be given. The kind of run-time system required is also important; a standard tasking monitor or storage allocation scheme may be presupposed, for example. The supplier may also place restrictions on who can carry out retargeting.

Check list

    a) Does the supplier allow other parties to retarget the compiler?

    b) What conditions are imposed if users or others are allowed to retarget?

    c) Is there a manual describing the procedure for retargeting, possibly with examples?

    d) Which compiler modules have to be rewritten on retargeting, and what are their interfaces?

    e) What is the nature of the intermediate language in use (e.g. tree structured intermediate language, linear intermediate language).

    f) Is there more than one level of intermediate language
       at which retargeting can be carried out?

    g) Are there tools, methods or standard components
       available for the construction of back ends?

    h) What are the assumptions made in the design of, and
       the requirements of, the run-time system?

    i) Are there any standard components available to help in
       the construction of the run-time system (e.g. a
       tasking monitor written in Ada)?

    j) How are machine-dependent parts of the language (code
       inserts, representation clauses, foreign code and
       data) handled by the compiler?

    k) Is there any method of relating the object code to the
       source program?

    l) How does the presence of other tools in the
       compilation system or APSE affect the back end?

7.2.3 Optimization and code quality

    While it is usually a (comparatively) straightforward matter to
generate correct object code, generation of high-quality code is in almost
all cases much more difficult, and the cost difference between a back end
which simply works, and one which produces good code can be substantial.
The questions in this section are concerned with how the compiler can be
made to generate high-quality code for a particular target.

Check list

    a) At what stages in the generation of object code can
       target-specific optimizations be made?

    b) Can additional optimization stages be incorporated,
       either at the outset or later if proved necessary?

    c) Are there alternative structures suggested for the
       production of low-cost, low-quality back ends and
       high-quality back ends?

    d) Are there any standard tools (such as a peephole
       optimizer generator), algorithms or components
       available for generating high-quality object code?

    e) How, if at all, does target-specific optimization

7.2.3 Optimization and code quality

interact with any global optimization performed by the
compiler?

f) Which optimizations (if any) are performed in the
   front end?

7.3 Rehosting

7.3.1 Availability of source code

In order to recompile the compiler it is necessary to have
access to the source code. As discussed elsewhere, restrictions may be
placed on the disclosure of source text, and some suppliers may not agree
to other parties performing rehosting. Remember that the rehosted compiler
will need to be validated.

Check list

a) Who is allowed to rehost the compiler?

b) Under what circumstances may the source text be made
   available for rehosting purposes?

7.3.2 Source language

The compiler may be written in Ada, or in some other language,
or even in a mixture of languages. Special tools (such as a parser
generator) may also be used in its construction.

Check list

a) What language or languages is the compiler written in?
   If Ada, does the source text conform to portability
   standards (see [2])?

b) Is the compiler written in full Ada, or does it avoid
   the use of certain language constructs (e.g. tasking,
   generics, real arithmetic)?

c) If the compiler is not written in Ada, what is the
   availability of compilers for the source language? How
   may such a compiler be retargeted if it is not
   immediately available on or for the new host?

d) If the compiler is generated wholly or in parts by

special-purpose tools ("compiler-compilers",
"translator-writing systems"), do these tools generate
a source program or translate directly to object code?
Can these tools be made available?

e) What languages are the tools written in?

f) If such tools do not generate an Ada (or other
language) program, how can they be retargeted?

g) Has the compiler successfully compiled itself?

7.3.3 <u>System dependencies</u>

The compiler may be written in such a way that it depends on
certain characteristics of the host system, i.e. the presence of a virtual
memory with a large virtual address space, or on a particular word length
or kind of arithmetic. It may also depend on characteristics of the host
operating system; alternatively, it may be designed to be used with a
particular KAPSE. All such system dependencies should be hidden by
suitable packaging.

<u>Check list</u>

a) Does the compiler operate in a particular APSE?

b) What other APSE (or MAPSE) tools does it require, if
any?

c) What KAPSE facilities does the compiler use?

d) If not part of an APSE, what characteristics of the
host operating system does the compiler rely on?

e) Are all such system dependencies concealed behind
module interfaces?

f) What is the minimum size of memory in which the
compiler will run on existing hosts? (Obviously the
size on the new host will depend on the
characteristics of the new host relative to existing
hosts.)

g) Is the compiler designed to use virtual memory?

h) Can the compiler be overlaid to reduce its memory
occupancy, and if so what requirements are placed on
the system?

i) Are there any other hardware characteristics that the

7.3.3 System dependencies

compiler relies upon?

j) Is the compiler sufficiently modular to allow the
implementation of critical parts (such as major data
structures) to be easily altered if this is necessary
for the new host?

k) Are hardware dependencies concealed by module
interfaces?

7.3.4 Procedures for rehosting

The procedure that must be carried out to rehost the compiler should be
described.

Check list

a) Is there a manual which describes the steps necessary
to rehost the compiler?

b) Are system dependencies adequately isolated and
documented?

c) Is there a kit of tools and/or components available to
help with rehosting?

8

Contractual matters

When considering the acquisition of an Ada compiler, the terms
on which the compiler is made available are important. The initial cost of
the compiler must be considered, as must the cost of retargeting or
rehosting it as necessary. Cost must be seen in the light of the
performance and capacity of the compiler, the quality of the object code
produced and the quality of the support and maintenance facilities
provided by the supplier. The cost of implementing a production-quality
Ada compiler is considerable (probably tens of man-years) and most
suppliers will therefore be very careful to ensure that the compiler is
not illicitly copied. Even more stringent controls must be expected where
the user wishes to obtain the source text of all or part of the compiler;
the supplier will have to be convinced that the user has a genuine reason
for requiring access to the source text and information about the
structure and interfaces of the compiler. (Idle curiosity will not
normally be regarded as sufficient reason). An additional charge will
almost certainly be made in such cases.

An exception to the above statements might occur where the
compiler was written by an academic institution or procured by a
government agency for general release. In such cases the compiler may be
freely available at a modest cost and details of its structure published.
However, the support and maintenance provisions in such cases should be
carefully examined.

In some situations the intention is to distribute the compiler
further on. It may, for example, be part of a product the compiler buyer
intends to market. In this case the conditions for redistribution must be
carefully considered.

Check list
a) What are the licencing arrangements for the compiler

8. Contractual matters

(e.g. at how many sites can the compiler be used, what
agreement does the user have to sign before the
compiler can be supplied)?

b) Can a licence to distribute the compiler further on be
bought or leased? Which parts of the compiler, run
time system, packages etc. can be distributed? Can
source be included?

c) Can a licence to use the compiler be bought outright
or leased?

d) What is the cost of a licence? Is the cost for one
machine or a central machine and several workstations,
etc?

e) What arrangements are in force for maintenance (i.e,
removal of defects from) the compiler? Such
arrangements can range from a postal service to
on-call maintenance staff?

f) What is the quality of the support available from the
supplier (i.e. documentation in the form of user
guides, run-time system manuals, telephone query
answering service, visits by supplier's support staff,
courses)?

g) What are the arrangements for charging for maintenance
and/or support of the compiler?

h) Are new releases of the compiler (especially those to
improve performance rather than correct faults)
available as part of the standard service or
separately charged?

i) What are the arrangements (if any) for the release of
information about the compiler's internal structure?

j) What is the quality of documentation on the compiler's
internal structure and interfaces (in the event that
such information is available)?

k) Are there any restrictions on use and/or distribution
of software produced by the compiler? It should be
noted that the software produced often contains a
run-time system delivered by the compiler supplier.

l) What is the financial status and trading position of

8.   CONTRACTUAL MATTERS

the company selling the compiler?

m) Does the company selling the compiler own all the
rights to the compiler including the tools needed for
maintenance?

n) If the compiler is purchased outside the country of
origin, are there any restrictions on its use
internationally?

8. CONTRACTUAL MATTERS

9

Validation

It will be a requirement for Ada compilers marketed in the USA
that they be validated. Major users of Ada in many other countries are
likely to require a validated compiler. The principal tool used for
validation will be a comprehensive set of test programs developed for the
US DoD [5]. The first four validation reports have been issued by the Ada
Joint Program Office and contain much useful information.

The market for unvalidated compilers, say for subsets of Ada, is
not yet clear. No specific consideration is given to such compilers.

Check list
a) Has the compiler been successfully validated?
b) The availability of the validation report.
c) What is the complete validation history for the
compiler?

10

References

[1] Ada Language Reference Manual (LRM),
ANSI/MIL-STD-1815A-1983. Part 1 of this publication.

[2] Guidelines for the portability of Ada programs. J C D
Nissen, P Wallis, B A Wichmann and others. Part 1 of
Ada Guidelines, Edited by J C D Nissen and P Wallis,
Ada Companion Series, CUP, 1984.

[3] How to call procedures or second thoughts on
Ackermann's function. B A Wichmann, Software -
Practice and Experience, Vol7 pp317-329, 1977.

[4] Latest results from the procedure calling test,
Ackermann's function. B A Wichmann, NPL Report DITC
3/82. March 1982.

[5] The Ada compiler validation capability. J B
Goodenough, ACM Sigplan Notices, Vol15, no 11, pp1-8,
1980.

[6] Efficient implementation of Ada tasks. I P Nassi and
A N Habermann. Research and Development Note, Digital
Equipment Corporation, Jan 1980.

[7] Diana Reference Manual. G Goos and W A Wulf
(Editors). University of Karslruhe, Report 1/81, March
1981.

[8] Requirements Analysis for Ada Compilers. P Wallis and
B A Wichmann, CACM Vol 27, No 1, pp37-41. 1984.

PART III

A selective bibliography for Ada

Helen Romanowsky

Rockwell International, Cedar Rapids, IOWA, USA

and others

Foreword

Selection is always a difficult process, and more so in such a dynamic
environment where contractual and personal interrelationships also often
reduce availability of documentation.

Some members of the editorial board nevertheless attacked the
comprehensive bibliography accumulated by Helen Romanowsky of Rockwell
(based on early work by Ray Young, and with additions by Pyle, Kok, and
Zalewski) with certain perspectives in mind; to select historically
important papers; to select Ada industry relevant papers; and to be up to
date as timescales allowed. Also, grading into categories causes
inevitable errors, especially in the sometime absence of the article.

Inclusion and classification is the opinion of the members of editorial
board who selected only, and does not imply approval or recommendation by
the board, or others who have contributed to this publication.

As in any development programme, things will change. If you have any
updated information on this bibliography, or wish to contribute to its
constant revision, please do write to me through the publishers.
Constant updates will be regularly published in the AdaTEC, Ada UK, and
Ada Europe news publications. Remember that an appended copy of the
relevant article would also be very useful.

Finally, as secretary to the board, it is my pleasure to recognize the
work done by Helen Romanowsky in an extremely short time scale we set in
order to give the industry a useful reference document to the Ada
Language and its many associated issues.

M. W. Rogers
Secretary, Ada Companion Series Editorial Board

Contents

Bibliography

Pascal to Ada - Upward Compatibility. (1981). South West Universities
    Regional Computing Center, Claverton Down, Bath, UK [Pascal,
    Ada, Programming Languages, Language Features]
Review of Coral 66 and RTL/2 Features Against Ada. (May 1979). UK
    Department of Industry, Bressenden Place, Westminster,
    United Kingdom. [Programming Languages, Language Constructs]

Ahl, D.H. (November 1981). Pascal, Ada, and Computer Literacy. Creative
    Computing. 116-123. [Programming Languages, Language
    Constructs]
Albrecht, P.F., et al. (November 1980). Source-to-Source Translation:
    Ada to Pascal and Pascal to Ada. SIGPLAN Notices. 183-193.
    [Translators, Program Transformations]
Barnes, J.G.P. (October 1979). The Development of Tasking Primitives
    in High Level Languages. Proceedings of the First European
    Symposium on Real-time Data Handling and Process Control.
    235-41. [Real-time Programming, Process Management, Ada
    LRM Chapter 9]
Barnes, J.G.P., et al. (March 1983). A Feasibility Study of the
    Conversion of RTL/2 to Ada, Technical Guide, Final Report.
    SPL International Center, SPL Project Number E1B633.
    [Source-to-Source Transliteration, Automatic Translation]
Boute, R.T. & Jackson M.I. (July 1981). A Joint Evaluation of the
    Programming Languages Ada and CHILL. IEE 4th International
    Conference on Software Engineering for Telecommunications
    Switching Systems. 214-20. [Data Types (Ada LRM Chapter 3),
    Data Abstractions, Concurrency, Exception Handling (Ada LRM
    Chapter 11)]
Brozovic, R.L. (December 1980). JOVIAL (J73) to Ada Translator System.
    Air Force Institute of Technology. Report Number
    AFIT/GCS/EE/80D-5.[SoftwareTools,Parsing Techniques,
    Language Translation]
Buneman, P., et al. (August 1980). A Codasyl Interface for Pascal and
    Ada. Moore School, University of Pennsylvania. Report
    AD-A093-440. [Pascal, Ada, Codasyl Interface, Codasyl
    Applications Writing, Coding Errors]
Currie, I.F. & Peeling, N.E. (1982). Modular Compilation Systems for
    High Level Programming Languages. NTIS AD-A121550. [Modular
    Compilation (Ada LRM Chapter 10), Algol 68, Ada, Language
    Implementation]

East, E.L. (December 1981). Continued Development of the JOVIAL (J73)
    to Ada Translator System. Air Force Institute of Technology,
    Wright-Patterson AFB. Report Number AD-A115 548/0. [Software
    Tools, Source Translation, J73, Ada]

Eastman, C.M. (November 1981). Lexical Characteristics of Keywords in
    High Level Languages. Proceedings of IEEE COMPSAC. 112-18.
    [Compilers, APL, Basic, Cobol, Fortran, Lisp, Pascal, PL/1,
    Snobol, Reserved Words (Ada LRM Section 2.9)]

Evans, A. Jr. (April 1981). A Comparison of Programming Languages: Ada,
    Praxis, Pascal, C. Lawrence Livermore National Laboratory.
    Report UCRL-15346. [Programming Languages, Language
    Constructs]

Gillman, R., et al. (February 1980). Translation of CMS-2 Programs to
    Ada (Working Paper). USC Information Sciences Institute.
    Report ISI/WP-19. [Ada, CMS-2, Source Translation]

Hofkin, M. & Hofkin, B. (November/December 1982). Ada, Modula-2, and
    Modern Software Engineering. Journal of Pascal and Ada.
    17-22. [Software Engineering, Modula-2, Ada, Information
    Hiding, Separate Compilation (Ada LRM Chapter 10),
    Multitasking (Ada LRM Chapter 9), Modularity, Data
    Abstraction (Ada LRM Chapter 3), Portability, Concurrency
    Control]

Knobe, B. (January/February 1981). Ada vs HAL/S. Journal for Guidance
    and Control. 35-40. [Aerospace Applications, Flight
    Software]

Krekel, D. (October 1979). The Ada Design Goals as Compared with the
    Design Goals of Different Programming Languages. Angewandte
    Informatik. 425-28. [Design Goals, Algol 68, Cobol,
    Fortran, Pascal, PL/1]

Meiling, E. & Palm, S.U. (1982). A Comparative Study of CHILL and Ada
    on the Basis of Denotational Descriptions. Dansk Datamatik
    Center. Report DDC 66/1982-12-31. [CHILL, Ada, Formal
    Definition]

Meiling, E. & Palm, S.U. (1982). A Comparative Study of CHILL and Ada
    on the Basis of Denotational Descriptions - A Survey. Dansk
    Datamatik Center. Report DDC 66/1982-12-02. [CHILL, Ada,
    Formal Definition]

Meiling, E. & Palm, S.U. (1982). A Storage and Environment Model for
    CHILL and Ada. Dansk Datamatik Center. Report
    DDC 66/1982-12-24. [CHILL, Ada, Storage Management]

Meiling, E. & Palm, S.U. (1982). An Abstract Syntax for Dynamic
    Semantic Analysis in CHILL and Ada. Dansk Datamatik Center.
    Report DDC 66/1982-12-23. [CHILL, Ada, Dynamic Semantics,
    Abstract Syntax]

Meiling, E. & Palm, S.U. (1982). An Abstract Syntax for Static Semantic
    Analysis in CHILL and Ada. Dansk Datamatik Center. Report
    DDC 66/1982-12-22. [CHILL, Ada, Static Semantics, Abstract
    Syntax]

Meiling, E. & Palm, S.U. (1982). Examples of Common Elaboration
    Functions for CHILL and Ada. Dansk Datamatik Center. Report
    DDC 66/1982-12-30. [CHILL, Ada, Data Types (Ada LRM Chapter
    3), Compilers]

Moffat, D.V. (February 1981). Enumerations in Pascal, Ada, and Beyond. SIGPLAN Notices. 77-82. [Enumerated Data Types (Ada LRM Section 3.5.1), Scope of Declaration (Ada LRM Section 8.2), Binding Rules, Programmer Definable Data Types (Ada LRM Chapter 3)]

Mueller, F.R. & Taft, S.T. (April 14, 1983). The Race Between C and Ada May Have Two Winners. Electronic Design. 131-38. [Separate Compilation Facilities (Ada LRM Chapter 10), Information Hiding, Data Types (Ada LRM Chapter 3), Real-time Control]

Neiman, M.J. (June 1982). JOVIAL (J73) to Ada Translator, Final Technical Report. NTIS AD-A120472. [Functional Description, Translator, Automatic Translation of Source Code, J73, Ada]

Pyle, I.C. & Wand, I.C. (1979). Programming Languages for Scientific and Industrial Process Control. Department of Computer Science, University of York. Report YCS-21. [Real-time Programming, Industrial Process Control Programs]

Rus, T. & Rattray, C.M.I. (September 1980). The Ada-Spirit: An Algebraic View of Ada-like Languages. [Programming Languages]

Sandmayr, H. (June 1981). A Comparison of Languages (Coral, Pascal, Pearl, Ada, and ESL). Computers in Industry. 123-32. [Real-time Applications]

Scheer, L.S. & McClimens, M.G. (May 1980). DoD's Ada Compared to Present Military Standard HOLs - A Look at New Capabilities. IEEE Proceedings of the National Aerospace Electronics Conference, NAECON 1980. 539-44. [Jovial, CMS-2, Fortran, Design Criteria, General Syntax, Data Typing (Ada LRM Chapter 3), Control, Functions, Real-time Processing, Programming Techniques]

Shaw, M., et al. (1981). A Comparison of Programming Languages for Software Engineering. Software - Practice and Experience, 11, 1-52. [Comparison of Programming Languages, Programming Languages, Software Engineering]

Tai, K. (February 1982). Comments on Parameter Passing Techniques in Programming Languages. SIGPLAN Notices. 24-7. [Parameter Passing (Ada LRM Sections 6.2, 6.4.1, 6.4.2, 6.6), Call-By-Value-Result, Call-By-Copy]

White, T.A.D. (January 1983). The Ada/APSE: A Successor to Coral 66 in the 1980's. Royal Signals and Radar Establishment, Malvern, England. [Coral 66 Features, Ada Features, Software Design Methodology, APSE, MASCOT]

Wichmann, B.A. (May 1982). A Comparison of Pascal and Ada. The Computer Journal. 248-52. [Comparison of Programming Languages, Packages (Ada LRM Chapter 7), Modularity]

Zemrowski, K.M. (December 1980). The Ada Language (A Comparative Analysis). Advanced Computer Techniques Corporation; Industry Measures. 1-27. [Software Engineering, Design Languages, Usability, Ada Language History, Fortran, Cobol, PL/1]

Zwittlinger, H. (December 5, 1981). Microprocessor Languages (Pascal, Chill, Ada, and Portal). Bull. Assoc. Suisse Electr. 1235-40. [Language Properties, Language Applications, Real-time Programming, Portal, Ada, Chill, Use of Interrupts (Ada LRM Section 13.5.1)]

Ada and other languages

ADA AND SOFTWARE ENGINEERING

Booch, G. (September 1981). Describing Software Design in Ada. SIGPLAN
        Notices. 42-7. [Object-Oriented Methodology, APSE]
Booch, G. (March/April 1982). Object-Oriented Design. Ada Letters.
        64-76. [Design Methodology, Information Hiding, Data
        Abstractions (Ada LRM Chapter 3)]
Bowles, K.L. (June 1982). The Impact of Ada on Software Engineering.
        AFIPS Conference Proceedings - 1982 National Computer
        Conference. 327-32. [Standardization, Program Portability,
        Program Modularity, Software Components Industry]
Downes, V.A. (1981). Software Construction with the Ada Programming
        Language. Proceedings of 6th ACM European Regional
        Conference, ICS '81, Systems Architecture. 375-82. [Software
        Component Libraries, Software Development]
Druffel, L.E. (July 1982). The Potential Effect of Ada on Software
        Engineering in the 1980's. SIGSOFT Software Engineering
        Notes. 5-11. [Embedded Computer Systems, Disciplined
        Software Development, Control Structures, Strong Typing
        (Ada LRM Chapter 3), Abstraction, Encapsulation (Ada LRM
        Chapter 7), Information Hiding, Separate Compilation (Ada LRM
        Chapter 10), Software Components, APSE]
Druffel, L.E. (September 1982). The Potential Effect of Ada on Software
        Engineering in the 1980's. Conference Record of EASCON '82,
        15th Annual Electronics and Aerospace Systems Conference,
        Washington, D. C. 161-66. [Disciplined Software
        Development, Software Components, APSE]
Eventoff, W., et al. (April 1981). Ada: A Significant Software Engineering
        Tool. Mini-Micro Systems. 208-31. [Software Engineering
        Principles, Strong Typing (Ada LRM Chapter 3), Packages (Ada
        LRM Chapter 7), Generic Types (Ada LRM Chapter 12), Tasks
        (Ada LRM Chapter 9), Separate Compilation (Ada LRM Chapter 10)]
Freeman, P. & Wasserman, A.I. (November 1982). Software Development
        Methodologies and Ada. University of California, Irvine.
        DTIC AD-A123449. [Software Development Methodologies, APSE,
        Programming Support Environment, Embedded Computer Systems]
Ghezzi, C. (October/December 1981). Programming in the Large With
        Ada: An Evaluation. Rivista di Informatica. 383-91.
        [Abstractions, Information Hiding Principles, Modularity,
        Software Design]

Ichbiah, J.D. (September 1979). Ada and the Development of Software
    Components. Speech during Proceedings of 4th International
    Conference on Software Engineering. [Software Engineering,
    Modularity, Software Components]
Klos, L.C. (1979). Software Engineering System Requirements. IEEE and
    AIAA 3rd Digital Avionics Systems Conference. 274-80.
    [Avionics Systems, Software Tools, Embedded Computer Software
    Engineering, Aerospace Test Facilities]
LeBlanc, R.J. & Goda, J.J. (April 1981). The Impact of Ada on Software
    Development. Proceedings of IEEE SOUTHEASTCON '81. 215-19.
    [Data Abstraction, Modular Program Development, Transportable
    Software]
Meijer, R.W. (October 1983). European Community Support to Software
    Engineering Development Through Ada Activities and ESPRIT.
    ESA/ESTEC Software Engineering Seminar, Nordwijk, Holland.
    Report ESA-SP-199. [Software Technology, ESPRIT, Ada,
    Ada-Europe, DDC]

ADA APPLICATIONS

Large Scale Software System Design of the AN/TYC-39 Store and Forward
          Message Switch Using the Ada Programming Language, Volumes 1,
          2, 3, & 4. (November 1982). General Dynamics, Data Systems
          Division, Fort Worth, Texas. NTIS AD-A123304, AD-A123305,
          AD-A123306, AD-A123307. [Military Software, Design
          Methodology, Requirements Specification, System
          Implementation]
Large Scale Software System Design of the Missile Minder AN/TSQ-73 Using
          the Ada Programming Language, Final Report. (November 1982).
          Control Data Corporation, Government Systems Division,
          Shrewsbury, New Jersey. NTIS AD-A123308. [Program Design
          Language, Design Methods, System Design Issues]

Basili, V., et al. (July/August 1982). Monitoring an Ada Software
          Development Project. Ada Letters. 58-61. [Techniques for
          Training and Education, Designing and Programming in Ada,
          Metrics]
Debest, X. (January/February 1983). A User-Friendly I/O System for Ada.
          Ada Letters. 101-12. [Chapter 14 of Ada LRM, Logical I/O
          Interfaces, Machine Independence, Text I/O, Sequential I/O,
          Relative I/O, Indexed I/O, External File Management, Process
          I/O]
Duncan, A.G. & Hutchison, J.S. (November 1980). Using Ada for Industrial
          Embedded Microprocessor Applications. SIGPLAN Notices.
          26-35. [Compiler Optimizations, Microprocessor Control
          Program, Modular Design, Specification Language]
Duncan, A.G. & Hutchison, J.S. (October 1982). Using Ada for Industrial
          Embedded Microprocessor Applications, II. Proceedings of the
          AdaTEC Conference on Ada. 152-61. [Exception Handling
          Facility (Ada LRM Chapter 11), Control Applications,
          Compiler Optimization]
Faasch, H., et al. (January/February 1983). Ada on a Minicomputer Network
          for Image Sequence Analysis: An Investigative Implementation.
          Ada Letters. 92-6. [Digitized TV-Image Sequences, Image
          Analysis Systems, DIANA, Ada-0 Compiler]
Falis, E. (October 1982). Design and Implementation in Ada of a Runtime
          Task Supervisor. Proceedings of the AdaTEC Conference on Ada.
          1-9. [Adam Compiler, Tasking Dynamic Semantics, Tasking
          Implementation Model]

Fernandez, J.D., et al. (March/April 1983). Experiences with Matrix
    Multiplication Using Ada Tasks. Ada Letters. 76-84. [NYU
    Ada/Ed, Tasking Facilities (Ada LRM Chapter 9), Generic
    Packages (Ada LRM Chapter 12)]
Gardner, M.R. (October 1981). Miscellaneous Discoveries Regarding
    TeleSoft Ada. Intellimac, Inc. Report IN/ATN 81-2.
    [Logical Operators, Strings]
Gardner, M.R. (December 1981). Ada Utilities. Intellimac, Inc.
    Report IN/ATN 81-3. [Commercial Applications for Ada]
Gardner, M.R. (March/April 1983). Using Ada for Commercial Software.
    Ada Letters. 56-9. [Packages (Ada LRM Chapter 7), Strong
    Typing (Ada LRM Chapter 3), Enumeration Types (Ada LRM
    Section 3.5.1, Attributes (Section 4.1.4, Appendix A),
    Exceptions (Ada LRM Chapter 11), Programmer Productivity,
    Large-Scale Commercial Applications]
Habermann, A.N., et al. (June 1979). Report on the Use of Ada for the
    Design and Implementation of Part of Gandalf. Department of
    Computer Science, Carnegie-Mellon University. CMU-CS-79-135.
    [Programming Support Environment]
Holschbach, J.M. & Kamrad, J.M. (May 1980). Radar Detection System: A
    Real-time Application Using Ada. IEEE Proceedings of the
    National Aerospace Electronics Conference, NAECON 1980.
    534-38. [Real-time Control Systems, Real-time Embedded
    Computer Applications]
Koutsotolis, A. (June 1982). Investigation of the Ada Language
    Implementation of the Hellenic Command Control and Information
    System. Naval Postgraduate School, Monterey, California.
    Report AD-A122 435/1. [Program Development, Automatic Data
    Processing Support, Software Engineering, Management, Ada
    Language Features]
Madsen, J. (January 1983). An Ada Implementation of TEXT_IO. Christian
    Rovsing A/S, Ballerup, Denmark. Report ADA/EWP/0006.
    [Portable Ada Programming System, SEQUENTIAL_IO (Ada LRM
    Chapter 14)]
Notkin, D.S. (November 1980). An Experience with Parallelism in Ada.
    SIGPLAN Notices. 9-15. [Tasking Structure, Gandalf Software
    Development Environment]
Persch, G., et al. (July/August 1983). Early Experience with the
    Programming Language Ada. Ada Letters. 63-70. [Program
    Modularization, Separate Compilation (Ada LRM Chapter 10),
    Strong Typing (Ada LRM Chapter 3), Ada-0 Compiler]
Rossi, G.F. & Zicari, R. (June 1983). Programming a Distributed
    Application with Ada. 22nd International Symposium on Mini
    and Micro Computers, ISMM, Lugano, Switzerland. [Distributed
    Programming]
Setian, J. (February 10, 1983). Ada Program Designs Linear-Phase Filter.
    Electronics. 164-65. [Ada Applications Program, Interactive
    Programs, Linear-Phase Bandpass Filter]
Winterstein, G., et al. (September 1981). Ada Documentation and
    Programming Guidelines. Institut fur Informatik II,
    University of Karlsruhe. Report 20/81.
Zalewski, J. (October 1982). Example of CAMAC Programming in Ada.
    SOCOCO '82, 3rd IFAC/IFIP Symposium on Software for Computer
    Control, Madrid, Spain. [Control Systems Programming]

ADA AS A DESIGN LANGUAGE

Alstad, J.P. (May/June 1983). Problems with Ada as a Program Design
    Language: A Position Paper. Ada Letters. 51-2. [Software
    Design, Assertions, Data Flows, Processing Requirements,
    Implementation Language, Semantics of Packages]
Beale, N.C.L. & Peyton Jones, S.L. (November 1981). An Ada Compatible
    Specification Language. Proceedings of ACM '81. 139-43.
    [Formal Specification of Software Packages, Specification
    Language, Real-time Software]
Evanczuk, S. (May 19, 1983). Ada Software Development Tools Up.
    Electronics. 157. [Byron, Program Analyzer, Document
    Generator]
Gabber, E. (January/February 1983). The Middle Way Approach for Ada
    Based PDL Syntax. Ada Letters. 64-7. [Simpler Syntax
    Design Languages, Full Syntax Design Languages, Design
    Writing, Design Constructs]
Gordon, M. (January/February 1983). The Byron(tm) Program Design
    Language. Ada Letters. 76-83. [Design Documentation,
    Successive Refinement Approach to Program Design,
    Abstractions]
Grau, J.K., et al. (1982). Ada Process Description Language Guide.
    Harris Corporation, Melbourne, Florida. [Program Design
    Language]
Hart, H. (October 1981). Ada for Design: An Approach for Transitioning
    Industry Software Developers. Proceedings of National
    Conference on Technology and Management, Alexandria, Virginia.
    [Retraining, Productivity Gains, Software Engineering, PDL,
    Training Issues]
Kerner, J.S. (September/October 1982). Should PDL/Ada Be Compilable?
    Ada Letters. 49-50. [Design Methodology, Ada-Based Design
    Languages]
Krieg-Bruckner, B. & Luckham, D.C. (November 1980). Anna: Towards a
    Language for Annotating Ada Programs. SIGPLAN Notices.
    128-38. [Formal Specifications of Programs, Formal Comment
    Facility]
Lindley, L.M. (January/February 1983). Ada Program Design Language
    Survey Update. Ada Letters. 61-3. [Automated PDL,
    Stepwise Refinement, Program Design, Automated Tools,
    Documentation]

Masters, M.W. & Kuchinski, M.J. (January/February 1983). Software
Design Prototyping Using Ada. Ada Letters. 68-75.
[Software Development Life Cycle, Program Design
Specification, Design Prototyping Methodology, Incremental
Design and Development, Verification]

Privitera, J.P. (October 1982). Ada Design Language for the Structured
Design Methodology. Proceedings of the AdaTEC Conference on
Ada. 76-90. [System Design Language, Structured Analysis
and Design Methodology]

Sammet, J.E., et al. (November 1981). PDL/Ada--A Design Language Based
on Ada. ACM '81 Conference Proceedings, Los Angeles,
California. 217-29. [Program Design Languages, Design
Methodology]

Waugh, D.W. (October 1980). Ada as a Design Language. IBM Software
Engineering Exchange. 8-12. [Program Design Language,
Rationale for PDL, PDL/Ada, Design Notation, Stepwise
Refinement Design Methodology]

ADA COMPILER VALIDATION

Ada Compiler Validation Implementer's Guide. (October 1980). Softech,
    Inc. NTIS AD-A091 760/9. [Ada Compiler Validation
    Capability, Language Standardization, Implementation
    Implications, Validation Tests]
The Ada Validation Policies and Procedures Manual. NTIS Report
    FB83 110601. [Ada Validation Organization, Implementation
    Options, Organizational Structure, Standardization]

Goodenough, J.B. (October 1980). Ada Compiler Validation Implementer's
    Guide. DTIC AD-A091760. [Ada Compiler Validation Capability,
    Language Standardization, Implementation Implications,
    Validation Tests, Ada Language Constructs]
Goodenough, J.B. (November 1980). The Ada Compiler Validation Capability.
    SIGPLAN Notices. 1-8. [Ada Compiler Validation Implementor's
    Guide, Validation Tests, Standardization, Compiler Validation
    System]
Goodenough, J.B. (June 1981). The Ada Compiler Validation Capability.
    Computer. 57-64. [ACVC Tests, Tools, Procedures and
    Documentation, Conformance to Ada Standard]
Probert, T.H. (June 1982). Ada Validation Organization: Policies and
    Procedures. MITRE Corporation, McLean, Virginia. [Ada
    Validation Organization, Implementation Options,
    Organizational Structure, Standardization]
Probert, T.H. (June 1982). Ada Validation Policies and Procedures.
    Report PB83-110601. [Ada Validation Organization,
    Implementation Options, Organizational Structures,
    Standardization]
Probert, T.H. (September/October 1982). Validation Issues #1. Ada
    Letters. 97-8. [Ada Validation Organization, Ada Compiler
    Validation Capability, Validation Test Suite]

ADA COMPILERS

432 Gets Ada Cross Compiler. (August 11, 1982). Electronics. 154-6.
[iAPX-432, Cross Development System, Compiler, Linker,
Debugging Capability]

Belmont, P.A. (March 1982). Ada TOPS-20 Prototype Compiler Documentation.
Intermetrics, Inc. Report AD-A114 131/6. [Compilers, Ada
Design Decisions]
Bjorner, D. & Oest, O.N. (1980). The DDC Ada Compiler Project; Development
Plan, Part 0: Development Methodology. Technical University
of Denmark, Lyngby, Denmark. Report DDC 80/2 (E2).
[Programming Languages, Compilers]
Bjorner, D. & Oest, O.N. (1980). The DDC Ada Compiler Project; Development
Plan, Part 1: Virtual Project Plan. Technical University of
Denmark, Lyngby, Denmark. [Programming Languages, Compilers]
Bjorner, D. & Oest, O.N. (1980). The DDC Ada Compiler Project; Development
Plan, Part 3: Document Production Plan and Deliverables.
Technical University of Denmark, Lyngby, Denmark. [Programming
Languages, Compilers]
Briggs, J.S., et al. (January 1982). Ada Workbench Compiler Project
1981. University of York, Department of Computer Science.
Report YCS.48(1982). [Compiler Development, Ada Intermediate
Representation, Parser, Code Generator, Tasking (Ada LRM
Chapter 9), Separate Compilation (Ada LRM Chapter 10),
Testing]
Bruun, H., et al. (1982). Portable Ada Programming System, Ada Static
Semantics, Well-Formedness Criteria. Dansk Datamatik Center,
Report DDC 02/1982-03-15. [Programming Languages, Compilers,
Semantics]
Clemmensen, G.B. (1982). Portable Ada Programming System, Description
of Target Environments. Dansk Datamatik Center. Report
DDC 02/1982-04-06. [Compilers, Programming Languages]
Clemmensen, G.B. & Oest, O.N. (August 1983). Formal Specification and
Development of an Ada Compiler - A VDM Case Study. Dansk
Datamatik Center. [Formal Program Specification, Formal
Program Development, Formal Definition of Programming
Languages, Compiler Development, Compiling Algorithm, Code
Generation, Software Management, Quality Assurance]

Clemmensen, G.B. & Pedersen, J.S. (1983). Portable Ada Programming
    System – DDC Ada Compiler, Back-End Compiler, Specification of
    Abstract A-Code. Dansk Datamatik Center. DDC 02/RPT/38,
    issue 1. [Compilers, Design, Programming Languages, A-Code,
    Code Generation, Abstract Syntax]
Dausmann, M., et al. (November 1979). Ada-0 Compiler Operating
    Instructions. Institut fur Informatik II, University of
    Karlsruhe. Report 22/79. [Programming Languages, Compilers,
    Command Language]
Dausmann, M., et al. (November 1979). Ada-0 Compiler: User-Manual.
    Institut fur Informatik II, University of Karlsruhe,
    Report 21/79. [Programming Languages, Compilers, User
    Interface]
Dausmann, M., et al. (November 1979). Ada-0 Reference Manual. Institut
    fur Informatik II, University of Karlsruhe, Report 20/79.
    [Programming Languages, Compilers, Ada-0 Language]
Dommergard, O. (1980). The Design of a Virtual Machine for Ada. In
    Towards a Formal Description of Ada, eds. D. Bjorner & O.N.
    Oest. New York: Springer-Verlag. [Virtual Machine,
    Instruction Set, Semantic Analysis, A-Code, Compilers]
Fishman, H. (November/December 1982). Janus – A New Ada Compiler for
    Z80 Systems. Microsystems. 70–81. [Microcomputer System,
    Compilers]
Garlington, A.R. (March 1981). Preliminary Design and Implementation of
    an Ada Pseudo-Machine. School of Engineering, Air Force
    Institute of Technology, Wright-Patterson AFB. DTIC
    AD-A100 796/2. [Compilers, Parser, Pseudo-Code, Interpreter,
    Portable Compiler, Pseudo-Machine Architecture]
Goos, G. & Winterstein, G. (November 1980). Towards a Compiler Front-End
    for Ada. SIGPLAN Notices. 36–46. [Intermediate Language,
    AIDA, Attributed Structure Tree, System Programming Language,
    Semantic Analysis, Formal Definition of Ada, Separate
    Compilation (Ada LRM Chapter 10)]
Groves, L.J. & Roger, W.J. (November 1980). The Design of a Virtual
    Machine for Ada. SIGPLAN Notices. 223–34. [Compiler
    Portability, Basic Virtual Machine Structure, Data Storage and
    Manipulation, Task Handling (Ada LRM Chapter 9)]
Hansson, H. & Rasmussen, T.B. (1982). Portable Ada Programming System,
    Supporting Packages, Global Design. Dansk Datamatik Center.
    Report DDC 02/1982-04-13. [Programming Languages, Compilers,
    Compiler Design]
Johnson, C.W., et al. (January 1981). Ada Workbench Compiler Project 1980.
    Department of Computer Science, University of York. Report
    YCS-39. [Programming Languages, Compilers]
Jones, K. (November 1982). Ada Compiler is Aimed at DEC VAX. Mini-Micro
    Systems. 138. [Compiler Implementation, University of York]
Jorgensen, J. (1982). Portable Ada Programming System, Ada Static
    Semantics, AS1 to AS2 Transformation. Dansk Datamatik
    Center. Report DDC 02/1982-02-09. [Programming Languages,
    Compilers, Semantics]
Jorgensen, J. (1982). Portable Ada Programming System, Test Front End
    Compiler, Global Design. Dansk Datamatik Center. Report
    DDC 02/1982-08-20. [Programming Languages, Compilers,
    Semantics]

Ada compilers

Lamb, D.A., et al. (October 1980). The Charrette Ada Compiler.
    Department of Computer Science, Carnegie-Mellon University,
    Report CMU-CS-80-148. [Preliminary Ada, Compiler,
    Translation, Intermediate Language]
Langer, J. (1983). The Ada BreadBoard Compiler: The Ada Linker. Bell
    Laboratories, Murray Hill, New Jersey. [Linker, Separate
    Compilation, Dependency Checking, Dependence Graph,
    Compilation Order]
Lettvin, J.D. (1983). The Ada BreadBoard Compiler: The Library and
    Dictionary. Bell Laboratories, Murray Hill, New Jersey.
    [Program Library, UNIX, Chapter 10 of Ada LRM, Dictionary
    File]
Mann, S. (April 1983). Janus/Ada, Version 3 for CP/M-based Micros.
    Infoworld. 59. [Compilers, Ada Features, Compiler
    Performance]
Meiling, E. & Pedersen, J.S. (1983). Portable Ada Programming System -
    DDC Ada Compiler, Back End Compiler, Global Design. Dansk
    Datamatik Center. DDC 02/RPT/22, issue 1. [Compilers, Back
    End Compilers, Programming Languages, Optimization, Design
    Considerations]
Murdie, J.A. (October 1982). Functional Specification of the York Ada
    Workbench Compiler. University of York, Department of
    Computer Science. Report YCS.54(1982). [Functional
    Specification, Host and Target, Language-Related Issues,
    User Interfacing and Facilities, Performance, Compiler
    Organization, Run-time System Organization]
Nissen, J.C.D., et al. (October 1982). Ada-Europe Guidelines for Ada
    Compiler Specification and Selection. National Physical
    Laboratory. NPL Report DITC 10/82. [Language-Related Issues,
    User Interfaces, Performance and Capacity, Compiler and Run-
    time Interfacing, Retargeting, Rehosting, Validation]
Nissen, J.C.D., et al. (July/August 1983). Ada-Europe Guidelines for
    Ada Compiler Specification and Selection. Ada Letters.
    37-50. [Language-Related Issues, User Interfaces, Performance
    and Capacity, Compiler and Run-time Interfacing, Retargeting,
    Rehosting, Validation]
Nowitz, D.A. (1983). The Ada BreadBoard Compiler: Code Generation. Bell
    Laboratories, Murray Hill, New Jersey. [Object Code
    Generator, DIANA, Run-time Environment]
Pedersen, J.S. (1982). Portable Ada Programming System, Dynamic Semantics,
    Description of Sequential Ada. Dansk Datamatik Center.
    Report DDC 02/1982-03-18. [Programming Languages, Compilers,
    Semantics]
Persch, G., et al. (March 1981). (Revised) Ada-0 Reference Manual.
    Institut fur Informatik II, University of Karlsruhe. Report
    R-ADA-0. [Compilers, Programming Languages, Ada-0]
Persch, G., et al. (April 1981). Ada-0 Input-Output, User Manual.
    Institut fur Informatik II, University of Karlsruhe. Report
    IO.UM. [Compilers, Input/Output Features (Ada LRM Chapter
    14), Ada-0, Programming Languages]
Quinn, M.E. (1983). The Ada BreadBoard Compiler: The DIANA Package. Bell
    Laboratories, Murray Hill, New Jersey. [DIANA, Intermediate
    Language, DIANA Reference Manual, Storage Management for
    DIANA, Node Identifiers]

Ada compilers

Quinn, M.E. (1983). The Ada BreadBoard Compiler: Semantic Analysis. Bell
    Laboratories, Murray Hill, New Jersey. [Static Semantic
    Rules, Static Checking Algorithms, Formal Definition of Ada
    Programming Language, Symbol Table]
Quinn, M.E. & Wetherell, C.S. (1983). The Ada BreadBoard Compiler: The
    Pre-Semantics Pass. Bell Laboratories, Murray Hill, New
    Jersey. [Abstract Parse Tree, Abstract Syntax Tree, Context
    Dependent Syntax Rules, LR(1) Grammar]
Rasmussen, T.B. (1982). Portable Ada Programming System – DDC Ada
    Compiler, Separate Compilation Handler, Global Design. Dansk
    Datamatik Center. Report DDC 02/1982-10-18/a. [Compilers,
    Programming Languages, Separate Compilation (Ada LRM Chapter
    10)]
Rogers, M.A. & Myers, L.M. (December 1980). An Adaptation of the Ada
    Language for Machine Generated Compilers. Naval Postgraduate
    School. NTIS AD-A097 292/7. [Compilers, YACC, LEX, Scanner
    Parser]
Rosenberg, J., et al. (November 1980). The Charrette Ada Compiler.
    SIGPLAN Notices. 72-81. [Preliminary Ada (1979),
    Intermediate Languages, TCOL-Ada, Source Program Translation,
    Run-time Support]
Rubine, D.H. (1983). A Hybrid Ada Interpreter. Bell Laboratories, Murray
    Hill, New Jersey. [Interpreter, Run-time Organization,
    Separate Compilation (Ada LRM Chapter 10), Source Level
    Debugging]
Sherman, M., et al. (November 1980). An Ada Code Generator for VAX 11/780
    with Unix. SIGPLAN Notices. 91-100. [Compilers, Subprogram
    Calls (Ada LRM Section 6.4), Parameter Passing (Ada LRM
    Sections 6.2, 6.4.1, 6.4.2, 6.6), Function Return Values
    (Ada LRM Chapter 6), Exception Handling (Ada LRM Chapter 11),
    Code Generator]
Simpson, R.T. (October 1982). The ALS Ada Compiler Front End Architecture.
    Proceedings of the AdaTEC Conference on Ada. 98-106. [Army
    Ada Language System, Intermediate Language, DIANA, Compilers,
    Ada'82]
Wetherell, C.S. (1983). The Ada BreadBoard Compiler: An Overview. Bell
    Laboratories, Murray Hill, New Jersey. [Compilers, Compiler
    Organization]
Wetherell, C.S. (1983). The Ada BreadBoard Compiler: Lexical and Syntactic
    Analysis. Bell Laboratories, Murray Hill, New Jersey.
    [Lexical Analyzer, LR(1) Parser, Tree Synthesizer, DIANA]
Wilcox, B. (July 1981). Presentation, Intermetrics ADA/TOPS-20 Compiler
    Project. Intermetrics, Inc. [Compilers, Programming
    Languages]
Winterstein, G., et al. (August 1980). The Development of a Compiler
    Front-End for Preliminary Ada: Overview. Institut fur
    Informatik II, University of Karlsruhe. Report 23/80.
    [Preliminary Ada, Compilers, Programming Languages]

ADA EDUCATION

Ada Software Design Methods Formulation. (October 1982). Softech, Inc.,
        Waltham, Massachusetts. NTIS AD-A124 998/6. [Ada Training,
        Training Curriculum]
Ada Software Design Methods Formulation, Appendices to Final Report.
        (October 1982). Softech, Inc., Waltham, Massachusetts.
        NTIS AD-A124 997/8. [Software Design Methods]
Ada Software Design Methods Formulation, Case Studies Report.
        (October 1982). Softech, Inc., Waltham, Massachusetts.
        NTIS AD-A124 996/0. [Design Problems, Embedded Computer
        Systems, Ada Usage, Ada Style, Training]

Abbott, R.J. (December 1980). Report on Teaching Ada. Science
        Applications, Inc. Report SAI-81-313-WR. [Ada Training]
Bossi, A., et al. (May/June 1983). Modular Decomposition of Ada into
        a Hierarchy of Sublanguages. Ada Letters. 53-8. [Teaching
        Methodology, Language Modularization, Stepwise Learning]
Braun, C.L. (March/April 1983). Ada Training Considerations. Ada
        Letters. 42-55. [Ada Training Curriculum, Development
        Methodologies, Ada Programming Support Environment, APSE]
Druffel, L.E. (September 1979). Ada - How Will It Affect College
        Offerings? Interface. 58-61. [Steelman, Important Ada
        Features, Programming Environment, Education]
Mathis, R.F. (June 1982). Introducing Ada into an Existing Environment.
        National Computer Conference, Houston, Texas. Paper W2-2/3.
        [Ada Education]
Romanowsky, H.E. (July 1983). The Introduction of the Ada Programming
        Language into a Commercial Environment. Department of
        Computer Science, Iowa State University, Ames, Iowa.
        [Training Issues, Training Approaches, Ada Model Course]
Rudolph, R. (May/June 1983). CSC Internal Ada Course. Ada Letters.
        78-86. [Ada Course Outline, Orientation Course for Ada]
Texel, P.P. (February 1982) Ada Education - Design Concepts and Ada
        Constructs. SIGSCE Bulletin. 201-4. [Use of Ada
        Language, Ada Education]
Waugh, D.W. (March/April 1983). An Ada Language Programming Course.
        Ada Letters. 34-41. [Ada Course Description, Writing Ada
        Programs]

Wegner, P. (October 1981). Self-Assessment Procedure VIII: A Self-
        Assessment Procedure Dealing with the Programming Language
        Ada. Communications of the ACM. 647-77. [Modular
        Programming, Subprograms (Ada LRM Chapter 6), Types (Ada LRM
        Chapter 3), Packages (Ada LRM Chapter 7), Basic Language
        Features]
Wegner, P. (September/October 1982). Ada Education and Technology
        Transfer Activities. Ada Letters. 51-60. [Programming
        Support Environments, Potential Ada Users, Design Languages,
        Software Standards, Teaching Issues, Computer-Based Education]

ADA ENVIRONMENTS

Ada Integrated Environment (AIE) Design Rationale: Technical Report
      (Interim). (March 1981). Intermetrics, Inc. & Massachusetts
      Computer Associates, Inc. Report IR-684. [Software Tools,
      Embedded Computer Software Development, APSE, MAPSE, KAPSE,
      Run-time Support System]
Ada Language System Command Language Processor B5 Specification (draft).
      (August 1981). Softech, Inc. Report 1075-30. [Command
      Language, Functional Requirements, Tools]
Ada Language System Compiler Machine-Independent Section B5 Specification
      (draft). (May 1981). Softech, Inc. Report 1075-17.1.
      [Compiler, Functional Requirements, Lexical Analysis, Parsing,
      Overloading]
Ada Language System KAPSE B5 Specification (draft). (August 1981).
      Softech, Inc. Report 1075-29. [KAPSE Functional Definition,
      KAPSE Requirements, Database]
Ada Language System Specification, Volume I (draft). (June 1981).
      Softech, Inc. Report 1075-4.2. [ALS, System Requirements,
      System Implementation Dependencies, Programming Support
      Environment, Assemblers, Compilers]
Ada Language System Specification, Volume II (draft). (June 1981).
      Softech, Inc. Report 1075-4.2. [Linkers, Exporting Programs,
      Loaders, Database, Command Language, Toolset]
Design Evaluation Report for the Ada Integrated Environment. (May 1981).
      Computer Sciences Corporation and Software Engineering
      Associates, Inc. [Software Tools, APSE]
Draft Specification of the Common APSE Interface Set (CAIS), Version 1.1.
      (September 1983). KIT/KITIA CAIS Working Group for the Ada
      Joint Program Office. NTIS AD-A134825 [APSE Interface
      Standards, Tools, Databases]
Requirements for the Programming Environment for the Common High Order
      Language: PEBBLEMAN Revised. (January 1979). [Programming
      Support Environment Requirements Statement]
System Specification for Ada Integrated Environment, Type A.
      (November 1982). Intermetrics, Inc. Report IR-676-2.
      [Functional Specification, AIE]

Adelsberger, H.H. (December 1982). ASSE - Ada Simulation Support
      Environment. 1982 Winter Simulation Conference, San Diego,
      California. 89-101. [Continuous Modelling Techniques,
      Discrete Modelling Techniques, Interactive Model Design]

Babich, W., et al. (September 1982). Design Considerations in Language
        Processing Tools for Ada. Proceedings - 6th International
        Conference on Software Engineering, Tokyo, Japan. 40-7.
        [Programming Environment, Compilers, Configuration Control]
Bever, M., et al. (October 1982). The Integration of Existing
        Database Systems in an Ada Environment. Proceedings of the
        AdaTEC Conference on Ada. 162-71. [Programming
        Environments, Database Management, Program Translation,
        Integration of Database Systems in Programming Languages]
Brender, R.F. (October 1980). The Case Against Ada as an APSE Command
        Language. SIGPLAN Notices. 27-34. [Ada Programming
        Support Environment, Stoneman, Job Control Languages]
Burns, G., et al. (February 1981). The Ada Programming System for the
        Intel 432. Proceedings of IEEE COMPCON '81. [Programming
        Support Environment, iAPX-432]
Buxton, J.N. (1980). An Informal Bibliography on Programming Support
        Environments. SIGPLAN Notices. 17-30. [Programming Support
        Environments]
Buxton, J.N. & Stenning, V. (February 1980). Requirements for Ada
        Programming Support Environments: STONEMAN. [Programming
        Support Environment, APSE Design Goals, Database, Toolset,
        User Interface, System Interface, MAPSE, KAPSE]
Buxton, J.N., et al. (July/August 1981). Recollections on the History
        of Ada Environments. Ada Letters. 16-21. [Sandman,
        Pebbleman, Compiler Validation Capability, Stoneman]
Buxton, J.N. & Druffel, L.E. (October 1980). Requirements for an Ada
        Programming Support Environment: Rationale for Stoneman.
        IEEE COMPSAC 1980. 66-72. [Stoneman, Programming Support
        Environment, Embedded Computer Systems, General Requirements,
        APSE, MAPSE, KAPSE, Database, Tools]
Devine, T.E., et al. (April 1982). JOVIAL/Ada Microprocessor Study.
        NTIS AD-A116352. [Microprocessors, J73, Ada, Compilers, AIE
        for Microprocessors, Development Systems]
Druffel, L.E. (July 1982). The Need for a Programming Discipline to
        Support the APSE: Where Does the APSE Path Lead? SIGSOFT
        Software Engineering Notes. 12-3. [Software Development
        Process, Standard Programming Support Environment]
Ferguson, S.E. (December 1982). Syntax-Directed Programming
        Environment for the Ada Programming Language. Air Force
        Institute of Technology, Wright-Patterson AFB, Ohio, School
        of Engineering. Report AD-A124 843/4. [Programming Support
        Environment, Syntax-Directed Editors, Program Tree Structure,
        Tools, Compilers]
Fisher, D.A. (October 1980). Design Issues for Ada Program Support
        Environments: A Catalogue of Issues. Science Applications,
        Inc. Report SAI-81-289-WA. [Design of an APSE, Database,
        Host System Facilities, Target Machine Facilities, Embedded
        Computer Systems]
Fisher, D.A. & Standish, T.A. (January 1979). Initial Thoughts on the
        Pebbleman Process. Institute for Defense Analyses. DTIC
        AD-A072248. [Ada, Common Language, Software Design, Software
        Maintenance, Software Environment, Software Quality, Software
        Life Cycle, Program Development Tools, Language Standards,
        Language Support and Culture, Software Tools]

Ada environments

Glass, R.L. (October 1982). Recommended: A Minimum Standard Software
    Toolset. SIGSOFT Software Engineering Notes. 3-13.
    [Program Support Environment, Software Tools]
Houghton, R.C., Jr. (February 1983). Taxonomy of Tool Features for the
    Ada Programming Support Environment (APSE), Final Report.
    National Bureau of Standards, Washington, D. C. Institute
    for Computer Sciences and Technology. Report PB83-179002.
    [Software Development Tools, APSE Features, ALS, AIE]
Hunke, H. (ed). (June 1980). Software Engineering Environments,
    Proceedings of the Symposium held in Lahnstein, Federal
    Republic of Germany. New York: North-Holland Publishing
    Company. [Program Support Environments, Arcturus,
    Concurrent Programs, Distributed Systems, Software
    Engineering, Software Development]
Kranc, M.E. (October 1982). A Command Language for the Ada Environment.
    Proceedings of the AdaTEC Conference on Ada. 181-86.
    [Minimal Ada Programming Support Environment, MAPSE, MAPSE
    Command Language]
Levy, A.J. (March/April 1982). Motivation Behind the Design of the Ada
    Atom System Environment. Ada Letters. 62-3. [Stoneman,
    Development and Maintenance of Ada Systems]
Lyons, T. (April 1982). UK Design Study for an Ada Programming Support
    Environment. EWICS 1982 Spring Meeting, Imperial College,
    London, UK. [Programming Support Environment]
McDermid, J. & Ripken, K. (July/August 1983). Life Cycle Support in the
    Ada Environment. Ada Letters. 57-62. [Large Scale Software
    Systems, APSE, Project Management, Software Development,
    Software Maintenance, Configuration Control, Software Life
    Cycle, Software Integration]
Notkin, D.S. & Habermann, A.N. (November 1979). Software Development
    Environment Issues as Related to Ada. Ada Environment
    Workshop, DoD HOLWG. [Programming Support Environment,
    Software Development]
Oberndorf, P.A. (April 1982). Kernel Ada Programming Support Environment
    (KAPSE) Interface Team, Volume I, Public Report. Naval Ocean
    Systems Center, San Diego, California. Report AD-A115 590/2.
    [Tools, Databases, Interoperability, Transportability, KAPSE,
    Interface Standards, Programming Support Environment]
Oberndorf, P.A. (October 1982). Kernel Ada Programming Support Environment
    (KAPSE) Interface Team: Public Report, Volume II. Naval Ocean
    Systems Center, San Diego, California. Report AD-A123 136/4.
    [Tools, Databases, KAPSE, Interoperability, Transportability,
    Interface Standards, Programming Support Environment]
Pyle, I.C. (March 1979). Response to Initial Thoughts on the Pebbleman
    Process. Department of Computer Science, University of York.
    [Programming Support Environment, APSE, Pebbleman]
Ryer, M. (September 1982). Developing an Ada Programming Support
    Environment. Mini-Micro Systems. 223-26. [Ada Integrated
    Environment, AIE, UNIX, Database, Command Processor]
Shenker, A. (January/February 1983). A MAPSE Command Language. Journal
    of Pascal and Ada. 35-9. [Minimal Ada Programming Support
    Environment, Ada Integrated Environment, Stoneman, Tools,
    MAPSE Command Processor]

Standish, T.A. (June 1978). Proceedings of the Irvine Workshop on
      Alternatives for the Environment, Certification, and
      Control of the DOD Common High Order Language. Department
      of Information and Computer Science, University of
      California, Irvine. NTIS AD-A089 090/5. [Validation,
      Programming Support Environment]
Standish, T.A. (June 1982). The Importance of Ada Programming Support
      Environments. 1982 National Computer Conference, AFIPS
      Conference Proceedings. 333-9. [APSE, Programming
      Productivity, Software Reliability, MAPSE, Stoneman, Software
      Project Management, Interactive Programming]
Standish, T.A. (July/August 1983). Interactive Ada in the Arcturus
      Environment. Ada Letters. 23-35. [Template-Driven Editing,
      Performance Measurement, Program Design Language, Automated
      Stepwise Refinement]
Stenning, V., et al. (June 1981). The Ada Environment: A Perspective.
      Computer. 26-36. [Ada Environment Objectives, Ada
      Environment Design, Portable Software, Program Reliability]
Thall, R.M. (October 1982). The KAPSE for the Ada Language System.
      Proceedings of the AdaTEC Conference on Ada. 31-47. [Kernel
      Ada Programming Support Environment, KAPSE, Army Ada Language
      System, ALS, Portability, Configuration Management, Software
      Tools]
Wegner, P. (April 1983). The Ada Language and Environment. Measurements
      and Control. 134-188. [Ada Language Features, Ada
      Programming Support Environment]
Woolley, B. (July 12, 1982). The Advancement of Ada [Programming
      Language]. Datalink. 11. [Programming Support
      Environment, Portability, Maintenance]

ADA TASKING FACILITIES

Baker, F.T. (October 1980). A Concurrent Module in Ada. IBM Software
    Engineering Exchange. 18-20. [Modularity, Design
    Methodology, Concurrent Programming]
Barringer, H. & Mearns, I. (March 1982). Axioms and Proof Rules for Ada
    Tasks. Proceedings of the IEE - Part E. 38-48. [Absence of
    Deadlock, Task Termination (Ada LRM Chapter 9), Exception
    Handling (Ada LRM Chapter 11), Ada Tasks (Ada LRM Chapter 9),
    Partial Correctness, Real-time Programming]
Bauner, J. & Svensson, G. (April 1980). An Implementation and Evaluation
    of the Real-time Primitives in the Programming Language Ada,
    Technical Report. Department of Telecommunication and
    Computer Systems, The Royal Institute of Technology,
    Stockholm, Sweden. TRITA-CS-8001. [Real-time Kernel,
    Real-time Synchronization Primitives, Runtime Efficiency,
    Tasking Facilities (Ada LRM Chapter 9)]
Clemmensen, G.B. & Lovengreen, H.H. (November 1981). Description of Ada
    Tasking. Dansk Datamatik Center, Lyngby, Denmark. Report
    DDC 02/1981-11-18. [Tasking Facilities (Ada LRM Chapter 9)]
Clemmensen, G.B. (October 1982). A Formal Model of Distributed Ada
    Tasking. Proceedings of the AdaTEC Conference on Ada. 224-37.
    [Formal Model, Ada Tasking (Ada LRM Chapter 9), Distributed
    Systems]
Cohen, N.H. (September/October 1982). Parallel Quicksort: An Exploration
    of Concurrent Programming in Ada. Ada Letters. 61-8.
    [Tasking (Ada LRM Chapter 9), Quicksort Algorithm]
De Bondeli, P. (August 17, 1983). Models for the Control of Concurrency
    in Ada Based on Predicate-Transition Nets. Ada-Europe:
    Parallelism and Ada. Ada-Europe Document No: WGS/Ada/WG,
    Issue 1. 15-67. [Petri-Nets, Concurrent Programs, Tasking
    (Ada LRM Chapter 9)]
Eventoff, W., et al. (November 1980). The Rendezvous and Monitor Concepts:
    Is There an Efficiency Difference? SIGPLAN Notices. 156-65.
    [Concurrent Programming Languages, Rendezvous (Ada LRM Section
    9.5), Monitors, Interprocess Communication]
German, S.M. (October 1982). Monitoring for Deadlocks in Ada Tasking.
    Proceedings of the AdaTEC Conference on Ada. 10-25. [Source
    Program Transformations, Concurrent Algorithms for Deadlock
    Monitoring, Tasking (Ada LRM Chapter 9)]
Ghezzi, C., et al. (1982). A Critical Analysis of the Ada Task System with
    Respect to Real Time Programming. CNET Report n.36. [Ada
    Tasking Facilities (Ada LRM Chapter 9)]

Ghezzi, C., et al. (1982). An Assessment of Ada as a Concurrent and
    Real-time Language. Dipartimento di Elettronica, Politecnico
    di Milano. [Ada Tasking Facilities (Ada LRM Chapter 9)]
Habermann, A.N. & Nassi, I.R. (January 1980). Efficient Implementation
    of Ada Tasks. Department of Computer Science, Carnegie-Mellon
    University. Report CMU-CS-80-103. [Ada Tasking Facilities
    (Ada LRM Chapter 9)]
Haridi, S., et al. (August 1980). An Implementation and Empirical
    Evaluation of the Tasking Facilities in Ada. Department of
    Telecommunications and Computer Systems. The Royal Institute
    of Technology, Stockholm, Sweden. Report TRITA-CS-8002.
    [Kernel Size, Kernel Performance, Tasking Implementation
    Techniques]
Haridi, S., et al. (February 1981). An Implementation and Empirical
    Evaluation of the Tasking Facilities in Ada - Summary.
    SIGPLAN Notices. 35-47. [Kernel Size, Kernel Performance,
    Tasking Implementation Techniques]
Hilfinger, P.N. (October 1982). Implementation Strategies for Ada Tasking
    Idioms. Proceedings of the AdaTEC Conference on Ada. 26-30.
    [Ada Tasking (Ada LRM Chapter 9), Tasking Idioms, Monitor
    Clusters, Agent Task]
Istravrinos, P. (September 1981). Mapping of the Ada Rendezvous Concept
    onto a Multiprocessor System. 7th Symposium on Microprocessing
    and Microprogramming, EUROMICRO '81. [Ada Tasking (Ada LRM
    Chapter 9), Multiprocessors]
Jones, A. & Ardo, A. (October 1982). Comparative Efficiency of Different
    Implementations of the Ada Rendezvous. Proceedings of the
    AdaTEC Conference on Ada. 212-23. [Ada Task Synchronization
    (Ada LRM Chapter 9), Implementation of Rendezvous Semantics,
    Server Model]
Krieg-Bruckner, B. (October 1981). Ada and the German Pay Phone: An
    Illustrative Example of Parallel Processing. Trends in
    Information Processing Systems. 3rd Conference of the European
    Cooperation in Informatics, Munich, Germany. 122-34.
    [Parallel Processing, Synchronization, Real-time Control]
Lomuto, N. (March/April 1983). Self-Reproducing Ada Tasks: The Problem
    of Termination. Ada Letters. 62-75. [Tasking Facilities
    (Ada LRM Chapter 9), Parallel Tree Search]
Lovengreen, H.H. (November 1980). On a Formal Model of the Tasking
    Concept in Ada. SIGPLAN Notices. 213-22. [Formal Task
    Modelling, Compilers, Tasking Concepts (Ada LRM Chapter 9),
    Semantics, Vienna Development Method]
Lovengreen, H.H. (1980). Parallelism in Ada. In Towards a Formal
    Description of Ada, eds. D. Bjorner & O. N. Oest.
    New York: Springer-Verlag. [Ada Tasking Semantics Modelling]
McDermid, J.A. (March 1982). Ada on Multiple Processors. Royal Signals
    and Radar Establishment, Malvern, England. DTIC AD-A114604.
    [Implementing Ada Rendezvous (Ada LRM Section 9.5), Message
    Based Communication, Two Phase Protocol, One Phase Protocol]
Nassi, I.P. & Habermann, A. (January 1980). Efficient Implementation of
    Ada Tasks. R&D Note, Digital Equipment Corporation. [Tasking
    Implementation, Compilers]

Pettus, R.O., et al. (April 1982). Ada Multi-Tasking Support for
        Microprocessor Systems. Conference Proceedings of IEEE
        SOUTHEASTCON '82, Destin, Florida. 239-42. [Tasking (Ada
        LRM Chapter 9), Microprocessors, Ada Implementations]
Pneuli, A. & DeRoever, W.P. (October 1982). Rendezvous with Ada - A Proof
        Theoretical View. Proceedings of the AdaTEC Conference on
        Ada. 129-37. [Communication and Synchronization, Ada
        Tasking (Ada LRM Chapter 9), Concurrency Modelling]
Shoja, G.C., et al. (August 1982). A Control Kernel to Support Ada
        Intertask Communication on a Distributed Multiprocessor
        Computer System. Software and Microsystems. 128-34.
        [Intertask Communication Primitives, Run-time Support
        Environment, Data Structures, Kernel Software]

ADA TEXTBOOKS

Barnes, J.G.P. (1982). Programming in Ada. Reading, Massachusetts:
        Addison-Wesley Publishing Company. (ISBN 0-201-13792-5).
        [Development of Ada, Principles of Ada Language]
Booch, G. (1983). Software Engineering With Ada. Menlo Park,
        California: Benjamin-Cummings Publishing Company. (ISBN
        0-8053-0600). [Design and Programming Style, Object-Oriented
        Design Methodology, APSE, Ada Syntax]
Downes, V.A. & Goldsack, S.J. (1982). Programming Embedded Systems With
        Ada. Englewood Cliffs, New Jersey: Prentice-Hall
        International. (ISBN 0-13-730010-7). [Philosophy of Ada
        Language, Use in Embedded Systems, Ada Language Features]
Freedman, R.S. (1982). Programming Concepts With the Ada Language.
        Princeton, New Jersey: Petrocelli Books, Inc. (ISBN
        089433-190-6). [Programming Concepts, Programming Design
        Methodologies, Ada Language Features]
Gehani, N. (1983). Ada: An Advanced Introduction. Englewood Cliffs,
        New Jersey: Prentice-Hall. (ISBN 0-13-003962-4). [Ada
        Syntax, Data Encapsulation (Ada LRM Chapter 7), Concurrency,
        Exception Handling (Ada LRM Chapter 11), Generics (Ada LRM
        Chapter 12), Program Structure, Representation Clauses (Ada
        LRM Chapter 13)]
Habermann, A.N. & Perry, D.E. (1983). Ada for Experienced Programmers.
        Reading, Massachusetts: Addison-Wesley. (ISBN 0-201-11481-X).
        [Pascal, Ada Language Features, Software Engineering]
Hibbard, P., et al. (1983). Studies in Ada Style (second edition). New
        York: Springer-Verlag. (ISBN 0-387-90816-1). [Programming
        Languages, Program Design].
Hilfinger, P.N. (1983). Abstraction Mechanisms and Language Design.
        Cambridge, Massachusetts: MIT Press. (ISBN 08134-2).
        [Programming Language Design, Abstraction Mechanisms,
        Language Complexity, Ada Language Design]
Ledgard, H. (1983). Ada: An Introduction (second edition). New York:
        Springer-Verlag. (ISBN 0-387-90814-5). [Key Ada Language
        Features]
Mayoh, B. (1982). Problem Solving With Ada. New York: John Wiley &
        Sons. (ISBN 0-471-10025-0). [Structured Programming,
        Advanced Problem Solving]
McDermid, J.A. & Ripken, K. (1983). Life Cycle Support in the Ada
        Environment. Cambridge, England: Cambridge University Press.
        (ISBN 0-521-26042-6). [Software Life Cycle, Toolsets,
        Programming Support Environments, Project Management]

McGettrick, A.D. (1982). Program Verification Using Ada. Cambridge,
        England: Cambridge University Press. (ISBN 0-521-28531-3).
        [Program Verification]
Nissen, J.C.D. & Wallis, P. (1984). Potability and Style in Ada.
        Cambridge, England: Cambridge University Press.
Saib, S. & Fritz. (1983). The Ada Programming Language: A Tutorial.
        IEEE Computer Society Press.
Stratford-Collins, M.J. (1982). Ada: A Programmer's Conversion Course.
        New York: John Wiley & Sons. [Introduction to Ada, Basic
        Control Structures, Program Units, Data Abstraction and
        Representation]
Uhl, J., et al. (1982). An Attribute Grammar for the Semantic Analysis
        of Ada. New York: Springer-Verlag. (ISBN 3-540-11571-4).
        [Static Semantics, Attribute Grammar]
Wiener, R. & Sincovec, R. (1983). Programming in Ada. New York: John
        Wiley & Sons. [Basic Control and Data Structures, Advanced
        Features, Large-Scale Program Development]
Young, S. (1983). An Introduction to Ada. New York: John Wiley & Sons.
        (ISBN 0-470-27551-0). [Structure of an Ada Program, Discrete
        Data Types (Ada LRM Chapter 3), Access Types (Ada LRM Section
        3.8), Generic Program Units (Ada LRM Chapter 12), Low Level
        Programming]

Ada textbooks

ALTERNATIVE LANGUAGE DESIGNS

Informal Language Specification (Red). Intermetrics, Inc. [Programming
        Languages, Language Design]
Language Specification (Blue). (February 15, 1978). Softech, Inc.
        [Programming Languages, Language Design]
Preliminary Design Phase Report (Blue). (February 15, 1978). Softech,
        Inc. [Programming Languages, Language Design]

Dijkstra, E.W. (October 1978). On the BLUE Language Submitted to the
        DoD. SIGPLAN Notices. 10-5. [Type Identity, Programming
        Languages]
Dijkstra, E.W. (October 1978). On the RED Language Submitted to the
        DoD. SIGPLAN Notices. 27-32. [Programming Languages,
        Language Design]
Dijkstra, E.W. (October 1978). On the YELLOW Language Submitted to the
        DoD. SIGPLAN Notices. 22-6. [Programming Languages,
        Language Design]
Nestor, J. & Van Deusen, M. (March 8, 1979). Red Language Reference
        Manual. Intermetrics, Inc. Report IR.310.2. [Programming
        Languages, Language Design]

ARCHITECTURES FOR ADA

NOKIA MPS 10 System Technical Overview, Version 1.2 (in MNS 10
    Documentation Series, Volume 1). (August 1982). Oy Softplan
    Ab, Tampere, Finland. [Ada Compilers, Stack Machine]

Arnold, R.D. (May/June 1981). The Nebula Architecture: Ada Issues.
    Ada Letters. 11-7. [Procedure Call Mechanism, Parameter
    Addressing Modes, Memory Management Strategies, Range
    Checking, Tasking (Ada LRM Chapter 9), Architectural Support
    for Ada Features]

Lahtinen, P. (September/October 1982). A Machine Architecture for Ada.
    Ada Letters. 28-33. [NOKIA MPS 10 Computer System, Stack
    Machine, Virtual Memory, Ada Tasking (Ada LRM Chapter 9),
    Ada Compiler, Exceptions (Ada LRM Chapter 11)]

Pollack, F.J., et al. (March 1982). Supporting Ada Memory Management
    in the iAPX-432. Computer Architecture News. 117-31.
    [Memory Management, Ada Visibility Rules (Ada LRM Section
    8.3), Heap-Space Management, Multi-Tasking, Compiler
    Implementation]

Rattner, J. & Lattin, W.W. (February 24, 1981). Ada Determines
    Architecture of 32-Bit Microprocessor. Electronics. 119-26.
    [iAPX-432, iMAX, Ada Compiler, Multi-user Applications,
    Operating System, Distributed Data Processing]

DEBATE ON USABILITY

Chantler, A. (October 1, 1981). Ada Too Complex? Nonsense! Computer
        Weekly. 15. [Reliability, Well-Disciplined Design and
        Implementation]
Frank, W.L. (October 5, 1981). Is Ada the Programming Language for the
        80´s? Computerworld. 37,40.
Grosch, H.R.J. (March 1, 1982). Ada, By Any Other Name is Still
        Repellent. Software News. 29. [Compilers, Language
        Complexity, Design Motivations]
Hoare, C.A.R. (February 1981). The Emperor´s Old Clothes. Communications
        of the ACM. 75-83. [Programming Languages, History of
        Programming Languages, Lessons for the Future]
Riley, J. (May 5, 1983). Euro MP Slams Useless Ada. Computer Weekly.
        2. [New Programming Languages, Fifth Generation Computer
        Languages]
van der Linden, P. (September 1981). Alternatives to COBOL: Ada.
        Computerworld Extra! 96,98-100.
Wegner, P. (January 1982). Emperors, Generals, and Programmers:
        Reflections on the Ada Controversy. Communications of the
        ACM. 80-1. [Embedded Computer Applications, Programming
        Support Environment, Programming Methodology, Ada Language
        Features]

EVOLUTION OF THE ADA LANGUAGE

Ada Programming Language. (December 10, 1980). United States Department
     of Defense. MIL-STD-1815. [Ada Language Definition, Ada
     Language Reference Manual]
DoD Common High Order Language. Phase I. Reports and Analyses. (June
     1978). NTIS AD-8950 587/6.
DoD Common High Order Language: Ada Design - Phase II Reports and
     Analyses. (January 1980). Defense Advanced Research Projects
     Agency. Report ADA-80-1-M.
Proceedings of the Ada Debut. (September 1980). Defense Advanced
     Research Projects Agency. Washington,D. C. NTIS AD-A095
     569/0. [Ada Language Features, Program Structure, Tasking
     (Ada LRM Chapter 9), Algorithmic Features]
Rationale for the Design of the Green Programming Language. (February
     1978). Honeywell, Inc. and Cii Honeywell Bull. [Language
     Constructs, Language Features]
Rationale for the Design of the Green Programming Language. (March 1979).
     Honeywell, Inc. and Cii Honeywell Bull. NTIS AD-A073 662/9.
     [Language Constructs, Numeric Types (Ada LRM Section 3.5),
     Access Types (Ada LRM Section 3.8), Language Features]
Reference Manual for the Green Programming Language. (February 1978).
     Honeywell, Inc. and Cii Honeywell Bull. [Language Features]
Reference Manual for the Green Programming Language. (March 1979).
     Honeywell, Inc. and Cii Honeywell Bull. NTIS AD-A073 661/1.
     [Language Features]
Requirements for High Order Computer Programming Languages: IRONMAN.
     (January 1977). [Programming Language Design Specification]
Requirements for High Order Computer Programming Languages: Revised
     IRONMAN. (July 1977). [Programming Language Design
     Specification]
Requirements for High Order Computer Programming Languages: STEELMAN.
     (June 1978). [Programming Language Definition]
Requirements for High Order Computer Programming Languages: TINMAN.
     (June 1976). [Programming Language Requirements, Pascal,
     PL/1, Algol 68]
Strawman. (July 1975). Department of Defense, HOLWG. [Preliminary
     Programming Language Requirements]
The Green Language - An Informal Introduction, draft. (April 1979).
     Honeywell, Inc. and Cii Honeywell Bull.
The Green Language: A Formal Definition (Preliminary Draft). (April
     1979). Honeywell, Inc. and Cii Honeywell Bull. NTIS
     AD-A073714. [Formal Language Definition, Semantics]
U. S. Department of Defense. (1983). Military Standard: Ada Programming
     Language, ANSI/MIL-STD-1815A.

Badault, et al. (July 22, 1976). LTPL-E Comments to "Tinman" (first
    version). LTPL-E/350. [Real-time Programming]
Barnes, J.G.P. (October 19, 1976). Some Comments to "Tinman."
    LTPL-E/3506C. [Real-time Programming]
Brosgol, B. (March/April 1982). Summary of Ada Language Changes. Ada
    Letters. 34-43. [Generics (Ada LRM Chapter 12), Tasks (Ada
    LRM Chapter 9), Scope and Visibility (Ada LRM Chapter 8),
    Overloading, Evaluation and Elaboration, Static Expressions,
    Universal Types, Optimizations, Exceptions (Ada LRM Chapter
    11), Input-Output (Ada LRM Chapter 14)]
Dijkstra, E.W. (October 1978). On the Green Language Submitted to the
    DoD. SIGPLAN Notices. 16-21. [Programming Languages,
    Pascal, Language Design Goals]
Estell, R.G. (March 1978). A Chapter in the History of DOD-1. SIGPLAN
    Notices. 90-2. [Historical Aspects of Ada]
Fisher, D.A. (August 1975). "Woodenman" Set of Criteria and Needed
    Characteristics for a Common DOD High Order Programming
    Language. Institute for Defense Analyses. [Programming
    Language Characteristics Description]
Fisher, D.A. (March 1978). DoD's Common Programming Language Effort.
    Computer. 24-33. [Embedded Computer Applications, Common
    Language Requirements]
Freeman, W. (editor). (1979). Proceedings of the 1978 Ironman Languages
    Seminar. Department of Computer Science, University of York.
    Report YCS-22.
Galkowski, J.T. (June 1980). A Critique of the DOD Common Language
    Effort. SIGPLAN Notices. 15-8. [Procedure Oriented
    Languages, Common Languages, Steelman, Ada]
Ichbiah, J.D., et al. (June 1979). Rationale for the Design of the Ada
    Programming Language. SIGPLAN Notices, Part B. [Ada Language
    Background and Development, Programming Languages]
Ichbiah, J.D., et al. (July 1980). Reference Manual for the Ada
    Programming Language: Proposed Standard Document.
    Government Printing Office Document Number 008-000-00354-8.
Wichmann, B.A. (April 1979). A Definition of the Semantics of Real
    Types in the Green Programming Language. National Physical
    Laboratory, Teddington, UK. Report CSU xx.
Winkler, J.F.H. (November 1981). Differences Between Preliminary and
    Final Ada. SIGPLAN Notices. 35-48. [Preliminary Ada,
    Final Ada, Language Comparison]
Wirth, N. (March 31, 1979). Comment on the Two Proposals for the
    Programming Language Ada Submitted to the Department of
    Defense.

FORMAL DEFINITION OF ADA

Formal Definition of Ada; Interim Draft. (October 1979). Honeywell, Inc. and Cii Honeywell Bull.

Formal Definition of the Ada Programming Language (Preliminary Version). (November 1980). Honeywell, Inc., Cii Honeywell Bull, and Inria. [Denotational Semantics, Static Semantics, Dynamic Semantics, Formal Semantics, Abstract Syntax]

Belz, F.C., et al. (November 1980). A Multi-Processing Implementation-Oriented Formal Definition of Ada in SEMANOL. SIGPLAN Notices. 202-12. [Preliminary Ada, Syntax, Semantics, Ada Tasking (Ada LRM Chapter 9), Exceptions (Ada LRM Chapter 11), SEMANOL System]

Berning, P.T. (September 1980). Formal SEMANOL Specification of Ada. Rome Air Development Center. RADC-TR-80-293. [Semantics, Formal Definition]

Bundgaard, J. & Schultz, L. (1980). A Denotational (Static) Semantics Method for Defining Ada Context Conditions. In Towards a Formal Description of Ada, eds. D. Bjorner & O. N. Oest. New York: Springer-Verlag. [Denotational Semantics, Representational Abstraction, Operational Abstraction]

Donzeau-Gouge, V., et al. (January/March 1980). On the Formal Definition of Ada. Rivista di Informatica. 5-14. [Procedure Oriented Languages, Formal Definition]

Drossopoulou, S., et al. (June 1982). An Attribute Grammar for Ada. SIGPLAN Notices. 334-39. [Formal Specification, Static Semantics, Attribute Grammar, Semantic Analysis, Declaration Elaboration, Overloading Resolution]

Kini, V., et al. (October 1982). Testing the INRIA Ada Formal Definition: The USC-ISI Formal Semantics Project. Proceedings of the AdaTEC Conference on Ada. 120-28. [Denotational Formal Semantic Definition (FSD), Validation of FSD, Semantics, Software Tools]

Lovengreen, H.H. (February 1980). Formal Definition of Ada: The Storage Model. Department of Computer Science, Technical University of Denmark.

Storbank Pedersen, J. (1980). A Formal Semantics Definition of Sequential Ada. In Towards a Formal Description of Ada, eds. D. Bjorner & O.N. Oest. New York: Springer-Verlag. [Denotational Dynamic Semantics, State-to-State Transformations]

INTERMEDIATE LANGUAGES

Ambler, A. & Trawick, R. (February 1983). Chartin's Graph Coloring
          Algorithm as a Method for Assigning Positions to Diana
          Attributes. SIGPLAN Notices, 37-8. [Intermediate
          Representation, Data Structure to Represent DIANA]
Appelbe, B. & Dismukes, G. (October 1982). An Operational Definition of
          Intermediate Code for Implementing a Portable Ada Compiler.
          Proceedings of the AdaTEC Conference on Ada. 266-74.
          [Intermediate Language, Compilers, I-Code, Tasking (Ada LRM
          Chapter 9), Exception Handling (Ada LRM Chapter 11), Memory
          Management]
Evans, A. & Butler, K. (eds.) (February 1983). Diana Reference Manual,
          Revision 3. Tartan Laboratories, Inc. DTIC AD-A128232.
          [Design Principles, Rationale, Abstract Syntax Tree]
Goos, G. & Wulf, W.A. (1983). Diana Reference Manual. No. 161,
          Springer-Verlag Lecture Notes in Computer Science. [Design
          Principles, Rationale, Abstract Syntax Tree]
Nestor, J.R., et al. (August 1981). IDL - Interface Description
          Language. Department of Computer Science, Carnegie-Mellon
          University. Report CMU-CS-81-139. [Intermediate Program
          Representations, Formal Model of IDL]
Roubine, O. (October 1982). LOLITA - A Low Level Intermediate Language
          for Ada. Proceedings of the AdaTEC Conference on Ada.
          251-60. [Intermediate Language, Compiler, Code Generator,
          European Ada Compiler]
Taft, S.T. (October 1982). Diana as an Internal Representation in an
          Ada-In-Ada Compiler. Proceedings of the AdaTEC Conference
          on Ada. 261-65. [Compiler, Intermediate Language, DIANA,
          Separate Compilation (Ada LRM Chapter 10), Software Virtual
          Memory Technique]

NUMERICAL ASPECTS OF ADA

A Proposed Standard for Binary Floating-Point Arithmetic. (March 1981). Computer. 51-87.

Blum, E.K. (August 1982). Programming Parallel Numerical Algorithms in Ada. In The Relationship Between Numerical Computation and Programming Languages, Proceedings of the IFIP TC 2 Working Conference, Boulder, Colorado, ed. J. K. Reid, pp. 297-304. New York: Elsevier North-Holland, Inc. [Rendezvous Concept (Ada LRM Section 9.5), Concurrent Programming, Algorithms, Programming Languages]

Cody, W.J. (1982). Floating-Point Parameters, Models and Standards. In The Relationship Between Numerical Computation and Programming Languages, ed. J. K. Reid. New York: North-Holland Publishing Company.

Cox, M.G. & Hammarling, S.J. (July 1980). Evaluation of the Language Ada for Use in Numerical Computations. Division of Numerical Analysis and Computer Science. National Physical Laboratory, Great Britain. Report DNACS 30/80. [Algorithms Libraries, Least Squares, Numerical Analysis, Programming Languages]

du Croz, J.J. (1982). Programming Languages for Numerical Subroutine Libraries. In The Relationship Between Numerical Computation and Programming Languages, ed. J. K. Reid. New York: North-Holland Publishing Company.

Feldman, S. (1982). Language Support for Floating Point. In The Relationship Between Numerical Computation and Programming Languages, ed. J. K. Reid. New York: North-Holland Publishing Company.

Firth, R. (March 1982). Preliminary Draft Specification of a Basic Mathematical Library for the High Order Programming Language Ada, Royal Military Mathematics College of Science, Wiltshire, England. [Support Packages, Libraries, Mathematical Library]

Fisher, D.A. & Wetherall, P.R. (January 1978). Rationale for Fixed-Point and Floating-Point Computation Requirements for a Common Programming Language. Institute for Defense Analyses. Report IDA-P-1035.

Ford, B. (1978). Parameterization of the Environment for Transportable Numerical Software. ACM Transactions on Mathematical Software, 4, No. 2, 100-3.

Hammarling, S.J. & Wichmann, B.A. (1982). Numerical Packages in Ada. In The Relationship Between Numerical Computation and Programming Languages, ed. J. K. Reid. New York: North-Holland Publishing Company.

Morris, A.H. (December 1981). Can Ada Replace Fortran for Numerical
        Computations? SIGPLAN Notices. 10-3. [General Numeric
        Scientific Computations, Arrays, Fortran, Ada]
Nassimi, D. & Sahni, S. (July 1982). Parallel Permutation and Sorting
        Algorithms. Journal of the ACM. 642-67.
Reid, J.K. (editor). (1982). The Relationship Between Numerical
        Computation and Programming Languages, Proceedings of the
        IFIP TC2 Working Conference, Boulder, Colorado. New York:
        North-Holland Publishing Company.
Rice, J.R. (September 1981). Survey of Programming Language Facilities
        for Numerical Mathematics. SIGNUM Newsletter, 16, No. 3.
Roubine, O. (1982). Tasking Features in Programming Languages. In The
        Relationship Between Numerical Computation and Programming
        Languages, ed. J.K. Reid. New York: North-Holland Publishing
        Company.
Symm, G.T., et al. (1983). Guidelines for the Design of Large Modular
        Scientific Libraries in Ada. Second Interim Report. NPL
        Report DITC 28/83 and MC Report NN 31/83.
Wallis, P.J.L. (March 1982). Ada Model Arithmetic: Costs and Benefits.
        Proceedings of the IEE - Part E. 75-9. [Ada Arithmetic
        Capabilities, Machine Independence, Numerical Software,
        Portability]
Whitaker, W.A. & Eicholtz, T.C. (1982). An Ada Implementation of the
        Cody-Waite Software Manual for the Elementary Functions.
        U. S. Air Force.
Wichmann, B.A. (1977). How to Call Procedures or Second Thoughts on
        Ackermann's Function. Software - Practice and Experience,
        17, 317-29.
Wichmann, B.A. (November 1980). Tutorial Material on the Real Data-Types
        in Ada, Final Technical Report. DTIC AD-A103482. [Real
        Arithmetic, Floating Point (Ada LRM Section 3.5.7), Fixed
        Point (Ada LRM Section 3.5.9), Arithmetic Types, Numeric
        Types, Approximate Computation, Blue's Algorithm]
Wichmann, B.A. (September/October/November/December 1981; January/
        February 1982). Tutorial Material on the Real Data-Types in
        Ada. Ada Letters. 15-33. [Fixed Point (Ada LRM Section
        3.5.9), Floating Point (Ada LRM Section 3.5.7), Predefined
        Operations (Ada LRM Sections 4.5, 8.6), Numeric Literals (Ada
        LRM Sections 2.4, 4.2), Portability Issues]
Wichmann, B.A. (March 1982). Latest Results From the Procedure Calling
        Test. National Physical Laboratory, Teddington, UK. NPL
        Report DITC 3/82.
Wichmann, B.A. & Hill, I.D. (June 1982). A Pseudo-Random Number Generator.
        National Physical Laboratory, Teddington, UK. NPL Report
        DITC 6/82.

OVERLOADING IN ADA

Baker, T.P. (April 1981). A One Pass Algorithm for Overloading Resolution in Ada. Department of Mathematics and Computer Science, Florida State University. [Directed Acyclic Graphs, Compilers, Parsing]

Cormack, G.V. (February 1981). An Algorithm for the Selection of Overloaded Functions in Ada. SIGPLAN Notices. 48-52. [Parsing, Recursion, Compilers]

Ganzinger, H. & Ripken, K. (February 1980). Operator Identification in Ada: Formal Specification, Complexity, and Concrete Implementation. SIGPLAN Notices. 30-42. [Operator Identification Algorithms, Translator, Overloading Rules, Expression Tree, Program Interpreters]

Janas, J.M. (September 1980). A Comment on "Operator Identification in Ada" by Ganzinger and Ripken. SIGPLAN Notices. 39-43. [Operator Identification Algorithm]

Pennello, T. & DeRemer, F. (1980). A Simplification of 'A Comment on Operator Identification in Ada' by Ganzinger and Ripken. SIGPLAN Notices, 16, No. 2, 2. [Operator Identification Algorithm, Recursion]

Pennello, T., et al. (July/August 1980). A Simplified Operator Identification Scheme for Ada. SIGPLAN Notices. 82-7. [Procedure Oriented Languages, Trees, Operator Identification Scheme, Expression Tree]

Persch, G., et al. (July 1981). Comments on "Algorithm for the Selection of Overloaded Functions in Ada." SIGPLAN Notices. 5. [Compilers, Overloading Resolution]

Runciman, C. (October/January/February 1981). Resolving Overloaded Expressions in Ada. Ada Implementor's Newsletter. [Overload Resolution Requirements, Overloading Resolution Solutions]

Schonberg, E. & Fisher, G.A. (October 1982). An Efficient Method for Handling Operator Overloading in Ada. Proceedings of the AdaTEC Conference on Ada. 107-11. [Compilers, Operator Visibility, Type Visibility, Name Resolution, Overload Resolution, User-Defined Operators]

Wallis, P.J.L. & Silverman, B.W. (April 19, 1980). Efficient Implementation of the Ada Overloading Rules. Information Processing Letters. 120-23. [Compiling, Overloading, Compilers and Generators]

UNCLASSIFIED

Ada Language Reference Card. (March 1981). Intermetrics, Inc. [Ada
        Syntax, Ada Language Features]
Ada Market to Approach $750 Million by 1986. (December 1982). Defense
        Electronics. 38-40. [Application Software Market, Support
        Software Market]
Ada Support System Study: An Initial Discussion Document. (January 31,
        1979). Systems Designers Limited.
Ada Support System Study: Phase 1 Report - Requirements and Functions
        Specification. (March 8, 1979). Systems Designers Limited
        and Software Sciences Limited.
Ada Support System Study: Phase 2 Report - Foundation Support System.
        (June 15, 1979). Systems Designers Limited and Software
        Sciences Limited.
Ada Support System Study: Phase 3 Report - Support System Interfaces.
        (November 1, 1979). Systems Designers Limited and Software
        Sciences Limited.
Ada Support System Study: Phase 4 Report - The Initial Host. (June 1,
        1980). Systems Designers Limited and Software Sciences
        Limited.
An Evaluation of the Needs and Requirements for the Establishment of an
        Ada Liaison Organization. DTIC AD-A122286.
Jean Ichbiah Assesses Ada and the Future of Microcomputers. (September
        1981). Defense Electronics. 126-27.
Implementation of Ada/MPS, Version 1.1 (in MNS 10 Documentation Series,
        Volume 2). (September 1982). Oy Softplan Ab, Tampere,
        Finland. [Ada Language Subset, System Programming Language,
        Language Features]
Nucleus/Virtual Executive, Functional Description, Version 2.0 (in MNS 10
        Documentation Series, Volume 2). (October 1982). Oy Softplan
        Ab, Tampere, Finland.
Proceedings of the ACM-SIGPLAN Symposium on the Ada Programming Language.
        (November 1980). SIGPLAN Notices. [Compilers, Ada Style,
        Ada Applications, Tasking, Execution Modes, Architectures]
Strategies for a Software Initiative. DTIC Report Number
        AD-A121737.
Strategies for a Software Initiative, Appendices. DTIC Report Number
        AD-A121738.

Andre, E. & Bogo, G. (October 1980). Ada, Abstract Data Types, and
        Distributed Databases Transactions. IEEE COMPSAC 1980.
        73-9. [Database Management Systems, Information Systems,
        Transactional Systems]

Arnborg, S. (November 1979). Ada - Latin for the Engineer? Elteknik med
    Aktuell Elektronik. 48-51. [Programming Languages, Technical
    Applications, Problem Oriented Languages]
Barnes, J.G.P. (1980). An Overview of Ada. Software - Practice and
    Experience, 10, 851-87. [Programming Languages, Ada
    Features]
Booch, G. (January 1981). Ada Promotes Software Reliability with
    Pascal-like Simplicity. EDN. 171-80. [Data Types (Ada LRM
    Chapter 3), Packages (Ada LRM Chapter 7), Tasking (Ada LRM
    Chapter 9), Exceptions (Ada LRM Chapter 11), Reliability]
Booch, G. (February 18, 1981). ACM Symposium on Ada Affirms Nonmilitary
    Interest. EDN. 59. [Compilers, History]
Booch, G. (June 23, 1982). Solve Process-Control Problems with Ada's
    Special Capabilities. EDN. 143-52. [Real-time System,
    Tasking (Ada LRM Chapter 9), Exception Handling (Ada LRM
    Chapter 11), Process Control]
Bowles, K.L. (July 22, 1982). Linked Ada Modules Shape Software Systems.
    Electronic Design. 117-26. [Modular Program Design]
Brown, M. (April 29, 1982). Language: Complex Ada Can Make the Atlantic
    Crossing. Computing. 26-7. [Ada Language Features]
Bruno, G. (October 1982). An Ada Package for Discrete Event Simulation.
    Proceedings of the AdaTEC Conference on Ada. 172-80.
    [Discrete Event Simulation Primitives, Multiprocessing
    Features, Process View of Simulation]
Bryant, R.M. (October 1982). Discrete System Simulation in Ada.
    Simulation. 111-21. [Tasks (Ada LRM Chapter 9), Packages
    Ada LRM Chapter 7), Embedded Computer Systems]
Bulman, D. (November/December 1982). Is Ada the Answer? Journal of
    Pascal and Ada. 11-6. [Reliability, Maintainability and
    Modifiability, Understandability, Generality, General Ada
    Language Background]
Bulman, D. (March/April 1983). Ada Interface. Journal of Pascal and
    Ada. 22-4. [Data Types (Ada LRM Chapter 3), COBOL, Ada]
Charles, P. & Fisher, G. (September/October 1982). A LALR(1) Grammar
    for '82 Ada. Ada Letters. 34-45. [Appendix E of Ada LRM,
    LALR Parser Generator]
Clapp, J.A., et al. (September 1977). A Cost/Benefit Analysis of High
    Order Language Standardization. MITRE. Report P 78-206.
Cornhill, D. & Gordon, M.E. (September 1980). Ada - The Latest Words
    in Process Control I. Electronic Design. 111-16. [Process
    Control, Major Ada Features]
Dausmann, M., et al. (November 1980). Efficient Recompilation Checks for
    Ada. Institut fur Informatik II, University of Karlsruhe.
    Report 30/80.
Dausmann, M., et al. (November 1980). On Reusing Units of Other Program
    Libraries. Institut fur Informatik II, University of
    Karlsruhe. Report 31/80.
Dausmann, M., et al. (November1980). SEPAREE A Separate Compilation
    System for Ada. Institut fur Informatik II, University of
    Karlsruhe. Report 32/80.
DeRemer, F. & Pennello, T. (November 1980). Syntax Chart of Ada
    Compilation.
Downes, V.A. & Goldsack, S.J. (1980). The Use of the Ada Language for
    Programming a Distributed System. In Real Time
    Programming, ed. V.H. Hasse. Oxford, England: Pergamon Press.

Downes, V.A. & Goldsack, S.J. (1980). The Use of the Ada Language for
Real-time Programming of a Distributed System. Department of
Computing and Control, Imperial College of Science and
Technology.

Emery, D.E. (January/February 1983). The Department of Defense Software
Initiative, A Summary. Ada Letters. 84-7. [Productivity,
Personnel Resources, Tools, Systems Reliability, Systems
Adaptability, Metrics, Project Management, Support Systems]

Fawcette, J. (July 1982). Ada Goes to Work. Defense Electronics.
61-81. [General Background Information on Ada Language]

Fawcette, J. (February 1983). Ada Tackles Software Bottleneck. High
Technology. 49-54. [History of Ada Language, Ada Language
Features, Compilers, Marketplace for Ada]

Filipski, G.L., et al. (November 1980). Ada as a Software Transition
Tool. SIGPLAN Notices. 176-82. [Translator, Application
Program Rehost, Language Characteristics, Language Selection
Tradeoffs, Methods of Software Transition]

Firth, R. (May 1980). Universal Ada Language Issue Report Construction
Kit. SIGPLAN Notices. 35-6.

Fox, J.M. (March 1978). Benefit Model for High Order Languages.
Decisions and Designs, Inc. Report TR-78-2-72.

Gini, G. & Gini, M. (December 1982). Ada: A Language for Robot
Programming. Computers in Industry. 253-59. [Robot
Programming Languages, Ada Features]

Glass, R.L. (July 1979). From Pascal to Pebbleman ... and Beyond.
Datamation. 146-50. [Ada Language Background]

Goldsack, S.J. (March 1981). Engineering Automation Systems with Ada.
Automation. 19-21,40. [Programming Industrial Automation,
Programming Support Environment, Modularity, Low Level
Facilities in Ada (Ada LRM Section 14.6)]

Goldsack, S.J. & Moreton, T. (March 1982). Ada Package Specifications:
Path Expressions and Monitors. Proceedings of the IEE - Part
E. 49-54. [Synchronization, Ada Package Specification (Ada
LRM Chapter 7), Ada Tasks (Ada LRM Chapter 9), Codes, Path
Expressions]

Goldsack, S.J. (December 1982). Specification and Verification in Ada;
Colloquium on 'A Review of Verification Methods for Software
and Digital Systems - Or How to Show that a Program Will
Actually Do What You Want it to Do', London, England. 5/1-5.
[Ada Features, Fully Verified Software, Program Design,
Program Construction]

Goodenough, J.B. (October 1980). Ada Syntax Cross Reference Listing.
SIGPLAN Notices. 48-56. [Ada Productions]

Goos, G. (February 1982). Ada: Purpose, Development, and Future of a
Programming Language. Angewandte Informatik. 80-9. [Ada
Language Constructs, Ada Implementation]

Hall, P.A.V. (January/February 1983). Adding Database Management to
Ada. Ada Letters. 88-91. [Database Management Capability,
Database Implementation Requirements]

Hibbard, P., et al. (October 1980). Programming in Ada: Examples.
Department of Computer Science, Carnegie-Mellon University.
CMU-CS-80-149. [Ada Programming Techniques, Efficient
Programming, Ada Language Features]

Holland, J., et al. (November 1981). An Ada Relational Database
    Interface Using Abstract Data Types. Proceedings of IEEE
    COMPSAC. 163-70. [Database Management System, Programming
    Languages]
Ichbiah, J.D. (September 1981). Ada and the Industry Form Software
    Components. 7th EUROMICRO Symposium on Microprocessing and
    Microprogramming, Paris, France. [Ada Language Features,
    Packages (Ada LRM Chapter 7), Generic Program Units (Ada LRM
    Chapter 12), Visibility Rules (Ada LRM Section 8.3), Software
    Components]
Johnson, R.C. (December 18, 1980). Ada's Modularity Sparks Interest for
    Civilian Users. Electronics. 39-40. [Packages (Ada LRM
    Chapter 7), Non-military Applications]
Johnson, R.C. (February 10, 1981). Special Report: Ada, The Ultimate
    Language? Electronics. 127-32. [Ada Language History,
    General Ada Language Features]
Johnson, R.C. (May 5, 1981). Ada and 68000 Getting Together.
    Electronics. 44,46. [Microprocessors, Compilers]
Jones, K. (June 29, 1983). DoD's 'Ada' Language Nears Commercial Mart.
    Management Information Systems Week. 14. [Compilers,
    Commercial Applications, General Background Information on
    Ada Language]
Jones, K. (February 1983). French Company Paces International
    Development. Mini-Micro Systems. 72-7. [Alsys, Compilers,
    Microprocessors, APSE Tools]
Jones, K. (March 1983). Perq Hosts Tool Development for FORTRAN-to-Ada
    Conversion. Mini-Micro Systems. 69. [Program Translation
    Tools]
Jones, K. (June 1983). Europeans Set the Pace for Several Ada
    Developments. Mini-Micro Systems. 81-82, 87-88. [Ada
    Programming Support Environment, Ada-Europe, European
    Commission]
Karp, T. (October 1981). Babbage - The Language of the Future.
    Datamation. 242,245,247.
Karten, H.A. (July 14, 1980). Ada Seen as the Language of the Future.
    Computer Careers News. 3. [General Ada Language Background
    Information]
Knight, J.C., et al. (August 1982). The Implementation and Use of Ada
    on Distributed Systems with High Reliability Requirements.
    University of Virginia, Charlottesville, Virginia. NTIS
    N82-30965. [Distributed Systems, Formal Semantic Definition
    of Ada, Tasking (Ada LRM Chapter 9)]
Ledgard, H.F. & Singer, A. (February 1982). Scaling Down Ada (Or
    Towards A Standard Ada Subset. Communications of the ACM.
    121-25. [Programming Languages, Human Factors,
    Standardization]
Legg, G. (April 28, 1983). Ada Compilers Reduce Effort and Costs of
    Real-time Applications Programming. EDN. 45-56. [Embedded
    Computer Systems, Standardization, Validation, Compilers]
Li, W. (October 1982). An Operational Semantics of Multitasking and
    Exception Handling in Ada. Proceedings of the AdaTEC
    Conference on Ada. 138-51. [Operational Semantics,
    Multitasking (Ada LRM Chapter 9), Exception Handling (Ada LRM
    Chapter 11)]

Litvintchouk, S.D. & Matsumoto, A.S. (July/August 1983). An Algebraic
        Approach to Reusable Ada Components. Ada Letters. 51-4.
        [Software Components, Design Methodology, Structured
        Specifications]
Luckham, D.C. & Polak, W. (November 1980). A Practical Method of
        Documenting and Verifying Ada Programs with Packages.
        SIGPLAN Notices. 113-22. [Formal Specification of Ada
        Programs, Documentation of Packages, Proof Rules for Package
        Constructs]
Luckham, L., et al. (July 1981). ADAM - An Ada Based Language for
        Multi-Processing. Department of Computer Science, Stanford
        University. Report STAN-CS-81-867.
MacLaren, L. (November 1980). Evolving Toward Ada in Real Time Systems.
        SIGPLAN Notices. 146-55. [Multitasking (Ada LRM Chapter 9),
        Concurrency, Asynchronous Tasks]
Maddock, R.F. & Marks, B.L. (December 1977). Towards A PL/1-Based
        "Ironman" Language. IBM. Report TR.12.168.
Marhold, G. (February 1982). Advent and Alms of Ada. Elektro-Anzeiger.
        23-5. [Process Control, Ada's Application to
        Microprocessors]
Mayoh, B.H. (1980). Parallelism in Ada Program Design and Meaning.
        In Proceedings of the Fourth "Colloque International sur
        la Programmation," ed. B. Robinet, pp. 256-68. New York:
        Springer-Verlag. [Programming, Parallel Processing]
McGettrick, A.D. (March 1982). Program Verification and Ada.
        Proceedings of the IEE - Part E. 55-62. [Reliable Programs,
        Program Verification]
Menabrea, L.F. (1843). Sketch of the Analytical Engine; Translation and
        Notes by Ada, Countess Lovelace, Richard and John E. Taylor.
Molich, R. (1982). Dansk Datamatik Center, Programming Style Guidelines.
        Dansk Datamatik Center. Report DDC 00/1982-03-19. [Ada,
        Programming Languages, Programming Style]
Nissen, J.C.D., et al. (November 1981). Ada-Europe Guidelines for the
        Portability of Ada Programs. National Physical Laboratory,
        Teddington, UK. Report DNACS 52/81. [Portability Issues,
        Reliability Issues, Packages (Ada LRM Chapter 7), Tasks (Ada
        LRM Chapter 9), Program Structure, Compilation Issues,
        Exceptions (Ada LRM Chapter 11), Generic Program Units (Ada
        LRM Chapter 12), Visibility Rules (Ada LRM Section 8.3),
        Input/Output Routines (Ada LRM Chapter 14)]
Nissen, J.C.D., et al. (March/April 1982). Ada-Europe Guidelines for
        the Portability of Ada Programs. Ada Letters. 44-61.
        [Portability Issues, Reliability Issues, Packages (Ada LRM
        Chapter 7)]
Nissen, J.C.D., et al. (1983). Ada-Europe Guidelines for the Portability
        of Ada Programs. National Physical Laboratory, Teddington,
        UK.
Oest, O. & Pedersen, J.S. (1980). Systematic Derivation of an A-Code
        Compiling Algorithm from a Denotational Semantics Definition
        of Ada. Danish Datamatics Center. Report DDC 80/14.
Olsen, E.W. & Whitehill, S.B. (March/April 1982). Ada Technology
        Development at Irvine Computer Sciences Corporation. Ada
        Letters. 77-85. [Ada Compiler, Ada Training Systems, Ada
        Environment]

Organick, E.I., et al. (November 1982). Transformation of Ada Programs
    into Silicon. Utah University, Salt Lake City, Department of
    Computer Science. Report UTEC-82-103. [VLSI Systems,
    Embedded System Applications]
Reynolds, P.F., et al. (March 1983). The Implementation and Use of Ada
    on Distributed Systems with Reliability Requirements, Final
    Report. NTIS N83-21077. [Run-time Support System, Processor
    Failures, Distributed Systems, Hardware Failures, Tasking (Ada
    LRM Chapter 9)]
Robinson, W.B. & Gordon, M.E. (October 1980). An Introduction to the Ada
    Programming Language. Advances in Instrumentation,
    Proceedings of the ISA Conference and Exposition. 251-62.
    [Process Control, Ada Background Information]
Romanovsky, I.V. (1981). Analysis of the Notion "Service." Kibernetika,
    4, 66-72.
Rossi, G.F. & Zicari, R. (1983). How to Program Distributed Applications
    in Ada. Dipartimento di Elettronica, Politecnico di Milano.
    [Distributed Programming]
Rudall, B.H. (1981). Contemporary Cybernetics: Ada Developments.
    Kybernetes, 10, No. 4, 227-28.
Russell, D.M. (May 1983). Ada Compiler Designers Now Shooting at a
    Fixed Target. Defense Electronics. 96,100-101. [ANSI
    Standardization, Compiler Validation, Transportable Programs,
    NYU Ada/Ed]
Savoysky, S. (1982). The Use of Ada for the Specification of Automata
    in Civil Engineering. In Proceedings of IFAC/IFIP
    Workshop, Kyoto, Japan, ed. T. Hasagewa, pp. 129-38. Oxford,
    England: Pergamon Press. [Specification Language, System
    Modelling, Reliability, System Development, System
    Maintenance]
Schindler, M. (August 19, 1982). Vax Minicomputers Gain Multiple-User
    Ada Capability. Electronic Design. 38-9. [Compilers,
    Run-time System, Pascal]
Schmitt, U. (November 5, 1982). Ada - A Programming Language for
    Real-time Applications. Elektronik. 105-10. [Intertask
    Communication, Task Synchronization (Ada LRM Chapter 9),
    Real-time Applications, Pascal, Algol 68, Ada Language
    Features]
Schrier, P.G. (September 29, 1982). A Golden Opportunity to
    Standardize. EDN. 25. [Standardization, Portability,
    Compiler Validation]
Schwartz, R.L. & Melliar-Smith, P.M. (July 1980). On the Suitability
    of Ada for Artificial Intelligence Applications. SRI
    International. NTIS AD-A090 790/7.
Sherman, M., et al. (October 1982). A Methodology for Programming
    Abstract Data Types in Ada. Proceedings of the AdaTEC
    Conference on Ada. 66-75. [Data Abstractions, Compiler
    Implementation, Data Abstraction Methodology, Transportable
    and Interchangeable Abstract Data Types (Ada LRM Chapter 3)]
Shinn, R. (May 1983). Ada Standard Launches New Wave of Activity.
    Systems and Software. 22,24,26. [ANSI Standard, Validation
    Suite, Compilers]
Skelly, P.G. (February 1982). The ACM Position on Standardization of
    the Ada Language. Communications of the ACM. 118-20.
    [Standardization, American National Standard Institute, ANSI]

Subrahmanyam, P. (1982). Transformation of Ada Programs into Silicon.
        Department of Computer Science, University of Utah, Salt Lake
        City, Utah. Report UTEC 82-20.
Symm, G. (March 1982). Guidelines for the Design of Large Scientific
        Libraries in Ada. Ada-Europe/EWICS paper.
Tichy, W.F. (October 1982). Adabase: A Data Base for Ada Programs.
        Proceedings of the AdaTEC Conference on Ada. 57-65.
        [Program Families, Configuration Management, Attributed
        Directed Graphs, IDL]
van der Linden, P. (March 1982). Ambiguity and Orthogonality in Ada.
        SIGPLAN Notices. 93-4. [Programming Languages, Semantics,
        Orthogonality]
van der Linden, P. (October 1982). Ada with a Microprocessor Bent or
        ´Small Surprises Come in Big Parcels.´ Colloquium on
        ´Languages for Programming Microprocessors,´ London, England,
        8/1-3. [Software Technology, Microprocessor Applications]
Wand, I.C. & Holden, J. (December 1979). Towards a Run-Time System for
        Ada. Department of Computer Science, University of York.
        Report YCS-29.
Wasserman, T. (June 1981). Ada - An Independent Review. State of the
        Art Tutorial. Infotech International Ltd., London, UK.
Wegner, P. (December 1979). Programming with Ada: An Introduction by
        Means of Graduated Examples. SIGPLAN Notices. 1-46.
        [Steelman, Ada Programming Language, System Programming,
        Embedded Computer Applications]
Whitaker, W.A. (February 1981). Summary of the Ada Implementer´s
        Meeting, December 1980. SIGPLAN Notices. 104-12. [Ada
        Language Implementations, Compilers, Validation, Ada
        Applications]
Wichmann, B.A. (November 6, 1980). How Ada Will Cut Cost of Producing
        Large-Scale Systems. Computer Weekly. 6-7. [Programming in
        the Large]
Wichmann, B.A., et al. (May 11, 1981). Guidelines for the Portability
        of Ada Programs. Portability/6/Issue 3, Ada Europe.
Winterstein, G., et al. Ada Documentation and Programming Guidelines.
        Institut fur Informatik II, University of Karlsruhe, Report
        NR 20/81.
Wirth, N. (July 12, 1979). Software and Programme Language.
        Schweizerische Technische Zeitschrift. 904-6. [Compilers,
        Information Hiding, Use of Ada Language, Programming]
Yehudai, A. (September/October 1982). Data Abstraction: Types vs.
        Objects. Ada Letters. 46-8. [Abstract Data Types (Ada
        LRM Chapter 3), Abstract Data Objects, Software Design,
        Object-Oriented Design, Packages (Ada LRM Chapter 7)]
Zalewski, J. (November/December 1981). Ada - A New Programming
        Language, Part I. Informatyka. 10-3. [Ada Language
        Features, Ada Language History]

VALIDATED COMPILERS

Data General to Offer Rolm Ada. (May 9, 1983). Electronic News. 43.
     [Ada Language Products, Ada Work Center]
DG and Rolm Take Ada Lead. (June 1983). Data Base Monthly. 1-2. [Ada
     Development Tools, Development Environment, Compilers]
First Full-Scale Ada Compiler Previewed. (November 1982). Defense
     Electronics. 93. [Compilers, Ada Work Center, Software
     Tools]
NYU Ada/Ed Users' Guide, Version 1.1 for VAX/VMS Systems. (April 1983).
     Ada Project, Courant Institute, New York University.
     NTIS AD-A128708. [ANSI Ada, Operational Semantic Definition
     of Ada, Ada Training]

Babcock, D., et al. (January 1983). Work Center Integrates Ada Equipment
     Needs. Military Electronics/Countermeasures. 22,24,26.
     [Software Development, Software Maintenance, Tools,
     Programming Support Environment]
Carlson, W.E. & Fisher, D.A. (September 1982). First Complete Ada
     Compiler Runs on a Micro. Mini-Micro Systems. 207-19.
     [Ada Features, Ada Validation, Western Digital Compiler]
Elliott, J.K. (January/February 1983). The ROLM Ada Work Center.
     Ada Letters. 97-100A. [Applications Development,
     Applications Maintenance, Ada Compiler, APSE, Programming
     Support Environment]
Johnson, R.C. (May 9, 1983). NYU's Ada Compiler Validated by DoD.
     Electronic Engineering Times. 89. [Compiler Validation,
     Test Suite]
Johnson, R.C. (June 20, 1983). Rolm Ada Compiler First to be Validated.
     Electronic Engineering Times. 1,14. [Commercial-Quality
     Compiler, Ada Development Environment]
Paul, L. (April 25, 1983). NYU Ada/Ed Compiler Gets DoD OK.
     Computerworld. 55,58. [Validation Tests, Interpreter,
     Translator, Compilers]
Paul, L. (May 9, 1983). Ada Development Systems Combine Rolm Compiler
     with DG Superminis. Computerworld. 5. [Ada Work Center,
     Software Development Environment]
Williams, J. (January 1983). Compiler and Tool Set for Ada Design and
     Implementation. Defense Electronics. 90-4. [Development
     Environment, General Ada Language Background Information]

READER'S NOTES AND ADDITIONAL REFERENCES